The Enneagram Development Guide

Ginger Lapid-Bogda, Ph.D.

The Enneagram In Business Press
Santa Monica, California

The Enneagram Development Guide

ISBN-13: 978-0-615-34250-4
ISBN-10: 0-615-34250-7
2nd edition; first published in 2007

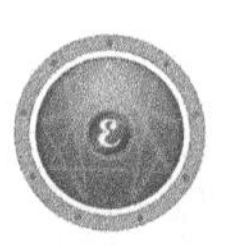

The Enneagram In Business Press
Santa Monica, California
310.829.3309

www.TheEnneagramInBusiness.com

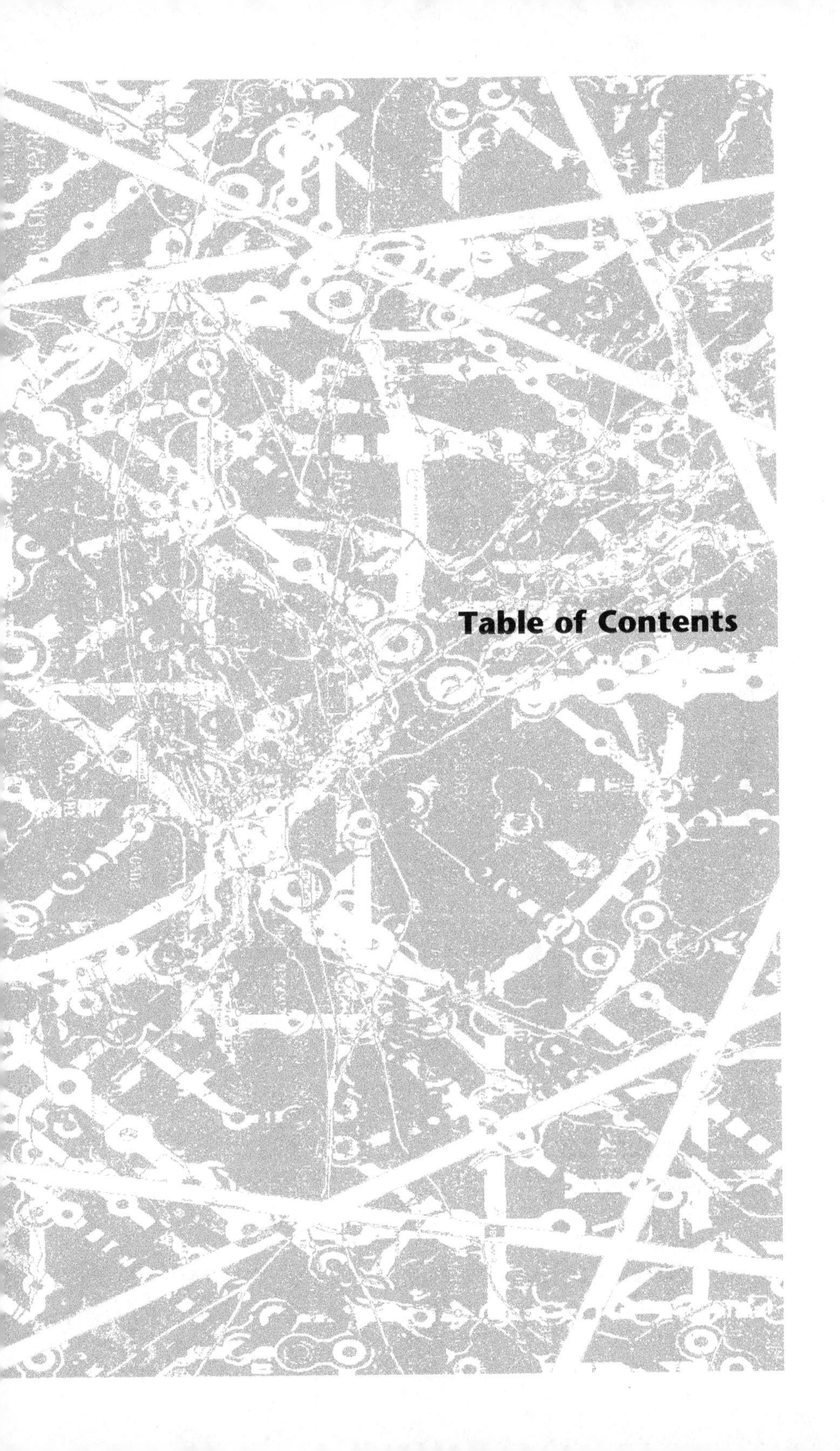

Table of Contents

Table of Contents

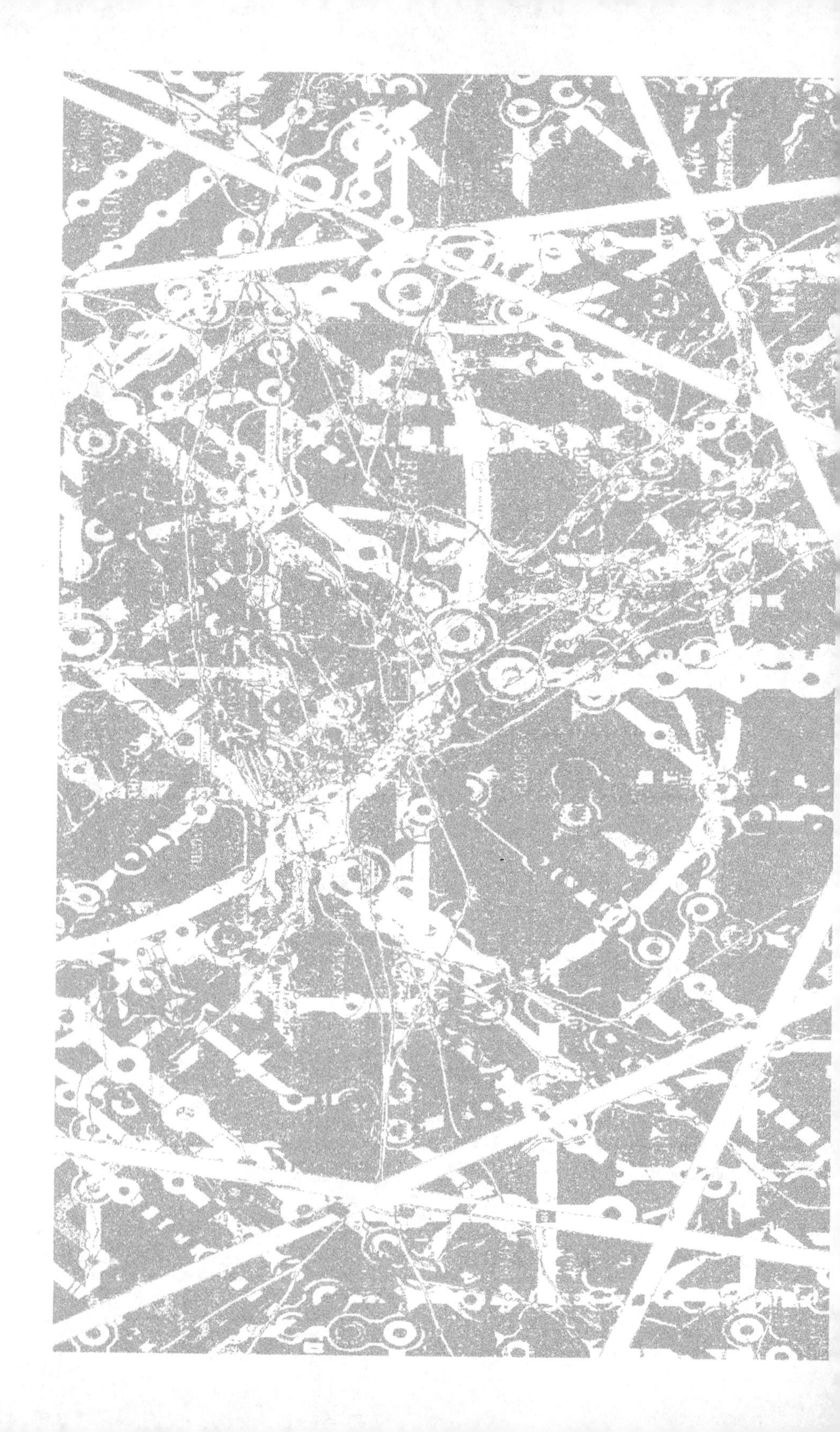

INTRODUCTION

The Enneagram Development Guide is designed for individuals who have chosen to take the path of extreme growth.

Anyone can take the route of no growth. When people make this decision — and making no decision *is* a decision — they soon find that their organization and many of their peers have moved beyond them.

Those who take the path of moderate growth, making themselves comfortable and going at their own pace, will be fine for a while, but then the organization, their peers, and their followers — if they are leaders — will begin to outpace them.

Those who follow the path of extreme growth will be amazed at their capacity and at the vitality that a commitment to growth brings. The rate of their personal development and the growth rate of the organization are aligned and synchronized. There is no greater experience.

This development guide is divided into ten sections — one for each of the nine Enneagram styles, with development activities tailored to that style, and a tenth section that includes additional developmental activities that are designed for everyone. The activities in each section cover the following topics:

- Self-Mastery
- Communication
- Feedback
- Conflict
- Teams
- Leadership
- Results Orientation
- Strategy
- Decision Making
- Organizational Change
- Transformation

Enjoy the journey.

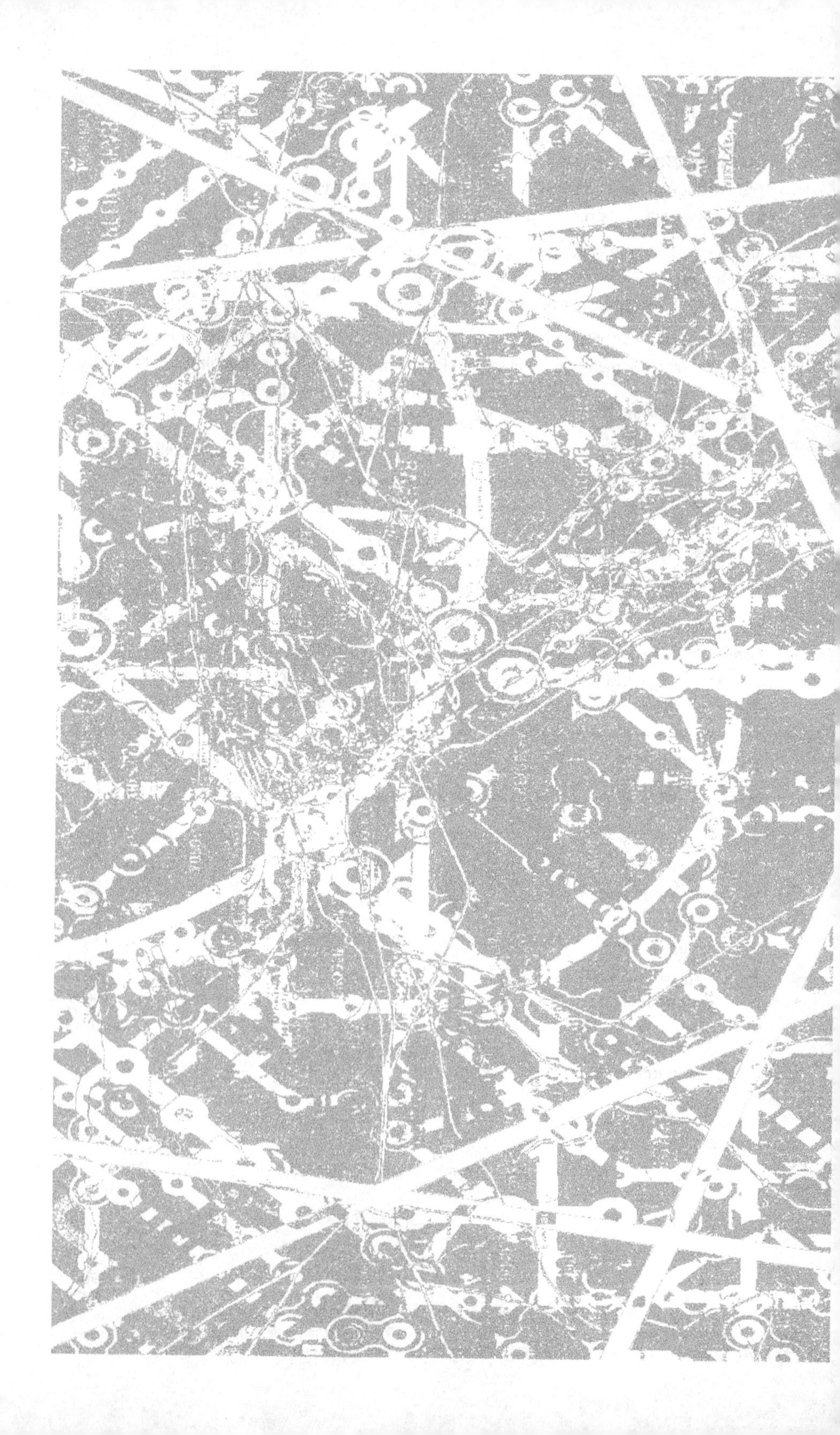

ENNEAGRAM STYLE ONE

ENNEAGRAM ONES

The search for perfection and the avoidance of mistakes

Discerning and judging, quality-focused and responsible, organized and resentful, Enneagram Ones structure their worlds and exert self-control in order to ensure that they, others around them, and their environments align as closely as possible to their refined and precise ideals and standards of excellence. Ones don't really believe that true perfection is possible, but they do believe what matters most is that people are constantly working on improvement toward these ideals.

All Ones have an internalized set of high standards, a long series of expectations about how they and others should behave, as well as how activities should be structured and executed. All Ones, however, do not necessarily share the same exact standards. In addition, some Ones worry in advance about meeting their standards and getting everything right; some Ones perceive themselves as closer to perfect than the rest of us and view themselves as role models of excellence; and some Ones direct their standards of perfection to others by constantly trying to improve them!

The One's interpersonal style is normally clear, precise, direct, and exacting, using carefully chosen words and phrases expressed in a seemingly polite manner. They are both self-controlled and spontaneously reactive, amused and skeptical, playful yet decidedly serious, and gracious, yet prone to flares of irritation or outbursts of anger.

While we can all be perfectionists at times, with high standards and a tendency to criticize both ourselves and others, for Ones, the search for perfection and the avoidance of mistakes is their primary, persistent, and driving motivation.

DEVELOPMENT STRETCHES FOR ONES

INDIVIDUALS WHO SEEK A PERFECT WORLD AND WORK DILIGENTLY TO IMPROVE BOTH THEMSELVES AND EVERYONE AND EVERYTHING AROUND THEM

CONTENTS

SELF-MASTERY DEVELOPMENT STRETCHES

Self-Mastery — the ability to understand, accept, and transform your thoughts, feelings, and behavior, with the understanding that each day will bring new challenges that are opportunities for growth — is the foundation of all personal and professional development. Self-mastery begins with self-awareness, then expands to include the elements shown in the following graphic:

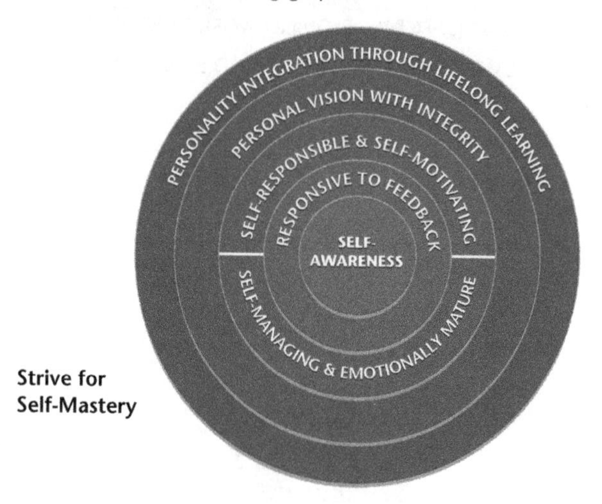

Strive for Self-Mastery

In this section on self-mastery, you will find the following:

- Three common issues for Ones related to self-mastery
- Three development stretches for working with the core issues of your Enneagram style, including one basic activity and one deeper activity for each stretch
- Three development stretches for working with your wings and arrow (stress-security) styles

Common Issues for Ones Related to Self-Mastery

Becoming accepting, calm, and serene rather than trying to make everything perfect	Letting go of being overly attentive to details and needing to have everything under control	Becoming more flexible and relaxed and less judgmental and reactive

For more insights and information about self-mastery, please refer to the following: Chapter 7, "Transforming Yourself," in *Bringing Out the Best in Yourself at Work* (McGraw-Hill, 2004) and Chapter 3, "Strive for Self-Mastery," in *What Type of Leader Are You?* (McGraw-Hill, 2007).

Development Stretches for Working with the Core Issues of Your Enneagram Style

Pay attention to your patterns of your right/wrong thinking.

Basic Activity

Without trying to change yourself, write down all the ways in which you judge, evaluate, and critique events, objects, people, and yourself. Include your language patterns (thoughts, words you have written or spoken) and nonverbal behavior, and identify what triggers these responses in you. Paradoxically, the more you become aware of this behavior without trying to change it, the more you will gradually begin to shift your responses.

Deeper Activity

Keep a daily journal and note the times you engage in judgments, opinions, criticisms, or any other behavior that reflects right/wrong thinking on your part. At the end of each week, review your journal and note the patterns related to this thinking — for example, the frequency of the behavior per day and per week; what you actually thought or said, along with your accompanying feelings, physical sensations, and body language at the time; and the external or internal events that triggered your reaction. After four weeks of keeping and reviewing this journal, note the overall patterns you discover. Ask yourself these questions: *Is your behavior consistent throughout the day and week, or are you more prone to right/wrong thinking late in the day or at other times when you are fatigued? Do you tend to exhibit this behavior toward those you know best or least well? Do you tighten all your muscles or primarily those in your face and jaw? Do you tend to react more strongly when you feel criticized, when you feel someone is responding too slowly, or under some other condition?*

Once you become aware of your patterns related to right/wrong thinking, locate a point early in the process when you could actually intercept your typical reaction — for instance, an early physical sensation (such as a jerking back of your head) or a particular line of thought (such as the thought that another person is too slow or that an idea won't work). This interception point can be thought of as a *choice point.* Once you are aware of your choice point, you can actually begin to choose to react in a different way. At that moment, you can say to yourself, *I'm about to go into my typical reactive pattern. Do I want to do that?* If your answer is no, then substitute another behavior, such as deep breathing combined with a refocusing of your thoughts on something else, particularly something positive. The new thoughts can be something positive about the other person, the event at hand, or something you like — for example, your favorite hobby or food. Every time your choice point arises, substitute an alternative behavior. You may need to experiment with alternative behaviors until you find the ones that work best for you.

For more insights and information about self-mastery, please refer to the following: Chapter 7, "Transforming Yourself," in *Bringing Out the Best in Yourself at Work* (McGraw-Hill, 2004) and Chapter 3, "Strive for Self-Mastery," in *What Type of Leader Are You?* (McGraw-Hill, 2007).

Use your feelings of resentment as a clue to deeper-seated anger.

Basic Activity

Whenever you feel irritation or resentment, ask yourself these questions: *Am I really angry about something else that has little to do with this person or situation? Is there some core value that I hold that I believe has been violated? Is there something in how I see myself or how I want to see myself that has been threatened?*

Deeper Activity

Ones are usually more familiar with resentment — a mild form of anger — than they are with deeper forms of anger, such as fury and rage. However, a deeper, suppressed anger often underlies the One's feelings of resentment. These angry feelings lie below the surface, where they accumulate and simmer. When something occurs that upsets or distresses Ones, their resentment can become fueled by these unexpressed or unresolved latent feelings. If Ones want to use their feelings of resentment as a clue to more deeply felt anger, they must first recognize their feelings of resentment as these occur.

To do this, keep a pad of paper with you and make a note of each time you feel resentful or experience less intense variations of resentment such as displeasure, irritation, or distress. Pay special attention to your body's cues, your thought processes, and your emotional reactions, and make notes of these responses.

After two weeks, review what you have written and identify the patterns of your responses. This will help you to recognize that you are actually feeling resentful at times when you otherwise might not even notice your reaction. It is common for us to not recognize feelings and reactions that we experience regularly because we are so accustomed to them. After doing this exercise, however, you will be more likely to notice when you feel resentful.

Now that you are able to identify the feeling of resentment, each time it occurs, ask yourself: *Am I only upset about what just happened, or is there more behind this?* Write down all the things that may be bothering you that are related to or may be contributing to your feelings of resentment. Make this list as long as possible by going as far back and as deeply as you can. For example, someone at work may have annoyed you by taking full credit for work to which you made a significant contribution. Write down everything else that this person has done that has bothered you, and why. Next, write down more examples of times when others have taken credit for your work or when you have failed to receive the acknowledgment you deserved. Finally, list the values you hold dear, then itemize the times when you feel others have violated these values. Continue the above process until the underlying causes of your deeper anger become apparent to you. Because these feelings may be deeply buried, do not be discouraged if the process takes several months.

For more insights and information about self-mastery, please refer to the following: Chapter 7, "Transforming Yourself," in *Bringing Out the Best in Yourself at Work* (McGraw-Hill, 2004) and Chapter 3, "Strive for Self-Mastery," in *What Type of Leader Are You?* (McGraw-Hill, 2007).

Learn to appreciate what is positive in everything — events, inanimate objects, and the behavior of other people.

Basic Activity

Whenever you have negative reactions, add an equal number of positive ones. If you try to erase or submerge your negative feelings or thoughts, they are likely to become stronger or else go underground temporarily, only to reappear more strongly at a later date. However, if you also add positive reactions, you will begin to neutralize some of the negativity and build up your ability to see the positive.

Deeper Activity

On the first day of this activity, go on an hourly treasure hunt for all that is right in the world; do this activity for two or three minutes every hour. You may still notice things that contain errors or behavior that does not reflect your standards, but try to focus instead on the elegance, beauty, or positive aspects of what you observe. For example, when you read an e-mail or letter and notice a typographical error on it, pay more attention to and acknowledge the quality of the ideas and/or the excellence in the choice of words. Similarly, when you attend a meeting that may not be running efficiently, notice and appreciate something positive about the meeting — for example, the effort that the meeting chair puts into gaining everyone's participation.

Practice this exercise every day for the next three weeks or longer, particularly at times when you find yourself overfocusing on the negative. When you feel focusing on the positive has become a more natural part of your thought process, continue doing the exercise for five minutes every day before you go to work. You can also use this exercise if you notice yourself suddenly reverting to a pattern of fault-finding only, rather than appreciating the positive as well. At these times, five minutes of a positive treasure hunt will help you to regain your balance.

For more insights and information about self-mastery, please refer to the following: Chapter 7, "Transforming Yourself," in *Bringing Out the Best in Yourself at Work* (McGraw-Hill, 2004) and Chapter 3, "Strive for Self-Mastery," in *What Type of Leader Are You?* (McGraw-Hill, 2007).

Development Stretches for Working with Your Wings and Arrow (Stress-Security) Styles

Wings are the Enneagram styles on either side of your core Enneagram style; arrow, or stress-security, styles are Enneagram styles shown with arrows pointing away or toward your core Enneagram style. Your wings and arrow styles don't change your core Enneagram style, but instead offer qualities that can broaden and enrich your patterns of thinking and feeling as well as enhance your behaviors. Your wings and arrow styles make you more complex and versatile because they provide more dimensions to your personality and serve as vehicles for self-development.

Integrate Your Nine Wing

Embrace multiple points of view.

Nines usually perceive multiple points of view, whereas Ones tend more to focus on their own opinions and perceptions. When you become strident while expressing a point of view, ask yourself: *What are the other points of view on this that are equally valid and need to be heard?* Think through the alternative perspectives without judging any of them. Nines also tend to mediate and facilitate during controversial interactions, while Ones generally take strong and firm positions during these times. When a controversy arises and you begin to take a strong position on the subject, start asking other people what they think and why.

Exercise tolerance.

Nines tend to accept their circumstances and other people without evaluation; in contrast, Ones lean toward discernment and judgment. When you feel that you want to change something or someone, move toward the Nine orientation of acceptance without judgment. When this becomes difficult, two techniques sometimes help. You can ask yourself: *How would a Nine respond in this situation?* Let the answer guide your behavior. The second technique is to appreciate how perfectly imperfect we human beings can be. This approach can lead Ones to acceptance and integration of the wrong with the right as part of the human condition.

Learn to relax.

When the going gets rough, Nines often take time for themselves, relaxing into pleasurable pastimes; during similar situations, Ones tend to push themselves harder and often engage in self-reflection and self-recrimination. When you are under a great deal of pressure, take 15 minutes to a half hour to do something pleasurable and relaxing. This will be easier to do when you set a time limit on this activity; during that time period, let yourself enjoy every minute.

For more insights and information about integrating your wings and/or arrow styles (stress-security points), please refer to the following: Chapter 1, "What Type Are You?" and the conclusion, "Stretch Your Leadership Paradigms," in *What Type of Leader Are You?* (McGraw-Hill, 2007).

Integrate Your Two Wing

Focus on people.

Twos usually focus first on other people, while Ones tend to focus on the tasks that need to be accomplished. When you begin a new task that involves other people, switch gears and experiment with focusing on the people first and the task second. Rather than jumping directly into the task, spend some time engaging people in a social conversation. Instead of offering a way to organize the work, first ask others for their ideas.

Motivate others.

Twos tend to motivate others to accomplish tasks; Ones tend to do the work themselves and then become overextended. Examine the work for which you're responsible and ask yourself this: *Who else could do some of this work, and what can I do to encourage them to take this on with enthusiasm?*

Come from your heart.

Twos can be empathic and compassionate, whereas Ones may tend to be judgmental or analytical. When you realize that you are judging or analyzing someone, shift your focus and imagine what he or she may be feeling at that moment. Pay special attention to body language clues. Think about what this person may need from you and, if possible, do or say something to address this person's needs.

Integrate Arrow Style Four (Stress Point)

Express yourself creatively.

Many Ones are creative, and they often create using their analytical skills. For example, Ones may write or draw, and they tend to analyze their creations at regular intervals. Fours, on the other hand, create using emotional spontaneity; their review of the quality often comes after they have fully expressed what they want to say or show. This delayed critique often enables the creator to have more freedom and expansiveness in his or her expression. Ones can free themselves creatively by withholding their judgment until the end of the creative act.

In addition, Fours tend to express their emotions through the creative process, which provides them with an outlet for their complex emotions. Ones can also use their emotions as the basis for their creative endeavors. Writing, movement, and the visual arts can help Ones examine and release some of the feelings that may lie below their more controlled exterior. Take an art class or explore a creative mode in which you already have talent, and choose an emotion that you are currently feeling deeply. Through your art, try to express the complex nuances of that feeling as well as its intensity and subtlety. Make self-expression your first priority.

Develop deep connections with others.

While Ones can establish deep connections with others, their tendency to judge can interfere with the development of relationships; others tend to keep some distance when they sense they are being judged. Fours, however, usually create deep interpersonal connections easily. The establishment of deep connections requires the ability to focus on the other person while at the same time staying connected to oneself. Ones can practice this when they are interacting with someone by paying attention to both feelings and thoughts — their own as well as the other person's — and focusing on themselves and the other person simultaneously. To do this, breathe into your diaphragm during conversations and ask yourself at three-minute intervals: *What am I feeling right now?* Make sure that your answer is a feeling, not a thought. Immediately after you have answered this question about yourself, ask yourself: *What do I think the other person is feeling right now?* Pay particular attention to his or her body language and tone of voice, along with the words chosen.

Become more fluid in your working style.

Ones tend to organize their lives both at work and at home in a logical, linear, and organized fashion, whereas Fours often prefer a more organic and fluid structure to their days. One of the ways Fours do this is to ask themselves at regular intervals the following questions: *What do I feel like doing right now? What is my deeper personal experience, and how am I responding to that? What is it that would give me meaning?* When Ones begin to ask themselves these same questions, it can help free them from what they ought to do or should do and help move them into a less structured, more spontaneous way of organizing their lives.

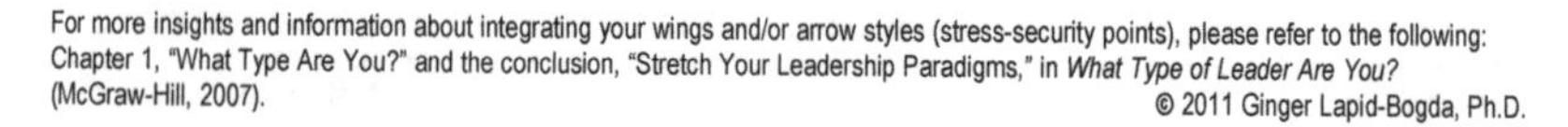
For more insights and information about integrating your wings and/or arrow styles (stress-security points), please refer to the following: Chapter 1, "What Type Are You?" and the conclusion, "Stretch Your Leadership Paradigms," in *What Type of Leader Are You?* (McGraw-Hill, 2007).

Integrate Arrow Style Seven (Security Point)

Become more spontaneous.

Sevens tend to be spontaneous and to follow their impulses, while Ones tend to be restrained and self-controlled. Sevens do what excites them and express their thoughts almost as quickly as they think them. Ones, on the other hand, act from a sense of responsibility and evaluate their words before they say them. To practice being more spontaneous, Ones can experiment with doing one activity each day that is totally unplanned. You can do this in one of two ways. First, you can ask yourself: *What do I feel like doing right now?* and then do it immediately. Leave whatever you are working on and simply engage in this spontaneous activity. The other option would be to say yes to someone who initiates a spur-of-the-moment invitation — for example, taking a walk or going to lunch. A final suggestion for increasing your spontaneity is to be less verbally censored. Spend five minutes each day saying anything that comes to your mind. Once you can do this easily, increase your time of verbal spontaneity to ten minutes. This latter practice, of course, should be done in the presence of someone who understands and supports this experiment.

Integrate work and fun.

Most Ones certainly know how to have fun, but they tend to separate work from fun. When they work, they work, and when they are not working or following through on their other responsibilities, they allow themselves time for enjoyment. Most Sevens, on the other hand, try to have fun with everything they do, including work. Ones can learn to have more fun at work by consciously integrating enjoyment with the work they do — for example, bringing food to a staff meeting, putting on a favorite CD while doing work, or putting a favorite picture within view. In addition, Ones can have fun with others at work by finding something interesting and fascinating about each individual. Ones can also learn how to place a higher priority on pleasure in their everyday lives, not just when they are on vacation or away from their normal environment.

To practice pleasure, make a list of twenty things that give you pleasure to do. Each week, do at least one activity from this list. If you start to feel guilty for taking time just to enjoy yourself, you can reassure yourself with the following thought: When you spend some time enjoying yourself every day, it will very likely improve your work and will definitely improve your health.

Explore possibilities.

Sevens tend to be flexible and optimistic, while Ones tend to be more structured and realistic. When you begin to think that there is only one best way to organize work and/or you start to discount ideas or alternatives because they seem too impractical, challenge yourself to do the following: think of at least three very different ways to organize the same work, and articulate the value of what may appear on the surface to be an impractical idea. To take this even further, ask others how they think the work could be organized, and try to elicit from others as many ideas as possible.

For more insights and information about integrating your wings and/or arrow styles (stress-security points), please refer to the following: Chapter 1, "What Type Are You?" and the conclusion, "Stretch Your Leadership Paradigms," in *What Type of Leader Are You?* (McGraw-Hill, 2007).

COMMUNICATION DEVELOPMENT STRETCHES

When you communicate with someone, three kinds of unintentional distortions may be present: speaking style, body language, and blind spots. *Speaking style* refers to your overall pattern of speaking. *Body language* includes posture, facial expressions, hand gestures, body movements, energy levels, and hundreds of other nonverbal messages. *Blind spots* are elements of your communication containing information about you that is not apparent to you but is highly visible to other people. We all unknowingly convey information through an amalgam of our speaking style, body language, and other inferential data.

The receivers of the messages you send also distort what they hear through their *distorting filters*. These are unconscious concerns or assumptions, often based on the listener's Enneagram style, that alter how someone hears what others say.

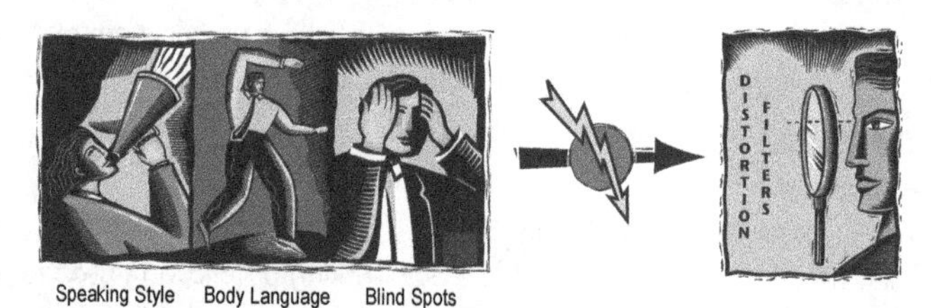

Speaking Style Body Language Blind Spots

Change one communication style behavior at a time.

It is most effective to work on changing one behavior at a time, preferably in the following sequence: speaking style, body language, blind spots, and listening distorting filters. It is easiest to change the behaviors of which we are most aware, and this sequence represents the most common order of awareness, from most to least aware.

Ones: Speaking style

- ➢ Precise, direct, exacting, concise, and detailed
- ➢ Share task-related thoughts
- ➢ Use words such as *should, ought, must, correct, excellent, good, wrong,* and *right*
- ➢ React quickly to ideas
- ➢ Defensive if criticized

Ones: Body language

- ➢ Erect posture
- ➢ Taut muscles
- ➢ Eyes focused
- ➢ Body language may reveal a negative reaction
- ➢ Clothing well coordinated and pressed

For more insights and information about communication, please refer to the following: Chapter 2, "Communicating Effectively," in *Bringing Out the Best in Yourself at Work* (McGraw-Hill, 2004) and Chapter 5, "Become an Excellent Communicator," in *What Type of Leader Are You?* (McGraw-Hill, 2007).

Ones: Blind spots

- Appear critical, impatient, or angry
- Tenacious regarding your own opinions

Ones: Distorting filters when listening to someone else

- Feeling criticized by the other person
- Preoccupation with your own ideas
- Whether, in your view, the other person is behaving correctly and responsibly

Note: Some of the above characteristics may be positive, some negative, and some neutral or mixed. They are intended as an overview to allow you to select from among them.

Use e-mails to expand and adjust your language patterns.

- Review your e-mails before you send them for language and tone.
- Delete, then change language that implies *should, ought, right, and wrong* before you send the e-mail.
- Use words that suggest flexibility and receptivity rather than categorical or emphatic thinking.
- Experiment with language that acknowledges and encourages multiple points of view as well as input or reactions.

For more insights and information about communication, please refer to the following: Chapter 2, "Communicating Effectively," in *Bringing Out the Best in Yourself at Work* (McGraw-Hill, 2004) and Chapter 5, "Become an Excellent Communicator," in *What Type of Leader Are You?* (McGraw-Hill, 2007).

FEEDBACK DEVELOPMENT STRETCHES

Honest, positive, and constructive *feedback* — direct, objective, simple, and respectful observations that one person makes about another's behavior — improves both relationships and on-the-job performance. When you offer feedback, the Feedback Formula, combined with the insights of the Enneagram, helps you tailor your delivery. When someone gives you feedback, the more receptive you are to hearing what is being said, the more likely it is that you will be able to discern what is useful and utilize what has been suggested.

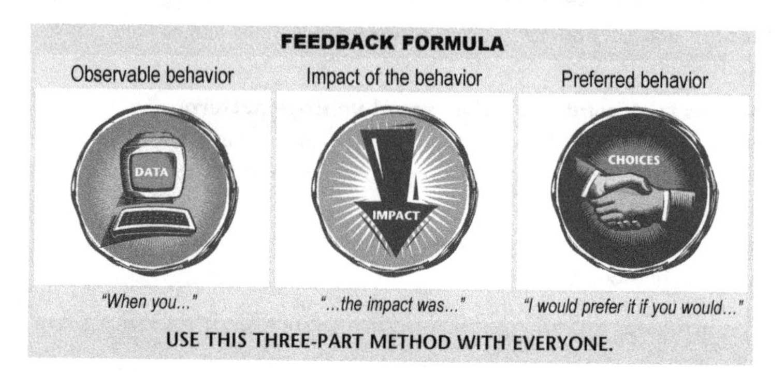

How Ones Can Enhance Their Ability to Deliver Feedback Effectively

When you offer feedback to someone, you want to be prepared and also to encourage the feedback recipient to be as receptive as possible. Remember that how and when you deliver feedback is just as important as what you actually say.

Use the three components of the **Feedback Formula** together with the following suggestions to plan and deliver the feedback.

- Utilize your skill at being very specific, but avoid being too detailed or selecting too many small items.
- Keep your capacity to generate ways someone else can improve, but work very hard to control your use of explicitly or implicitly judgmental language.
- Maintain your truthfulness, but resolve any residual anger or resentment prior to having the feedback conversation so your feelings do not show through your body language.
- Offer positive feedback as much as negative feedback; good work, even if it is not stellar, also deserves recognition.
- Remember that as hard as you work to make your own behavior impeccable, the feedback recipient may not want your help in becoming perfect.

For more insights and information about feedback, please refer to the following: Chapter 3, "Giving Constructive Feedback," in *Bringing Out the Best in Yourself at Work* (McGraw-Hill, 2004) and Chapter 5, "Become an Excellent Communicator," in *What Type of Leader Are You?* (McGraw-Hill, 2007).

How Ones Can Be More Receptive When They Receive Feedback

- When someone gives you negative feedback, it may ignite your tendency toward self-criticism. Tell yourself: *I can determine later what I agree with; let me listen now with an open mind.*
- Keep your body as relaxed as possible when you receive positive or negative feedback to help you be as open as possible to what is said. Breathing deeply can be helpful.
- Even if you don't respect or admire someone, be open to the positive or negative feedback offered. There is likely some useful information to learn.

For more insights and information about feedback, please refer to the following: Chapter 3, "Giving Constructive Feedback," in *Bringing Out the Best in Yourself at Work* (McGraw-Hill, 2004) and Chapter 5, "Become an Excellent Communicator," in *What Type of Leader Are You?* (McGraw-Hill, 2007).

CONFLICT DEVELOPMENT STRETCHES

Relationships both at work and at home often involve some degree of conflict, which may be caused by a variety of factors and usually follows the pinch-crunch cycle below:

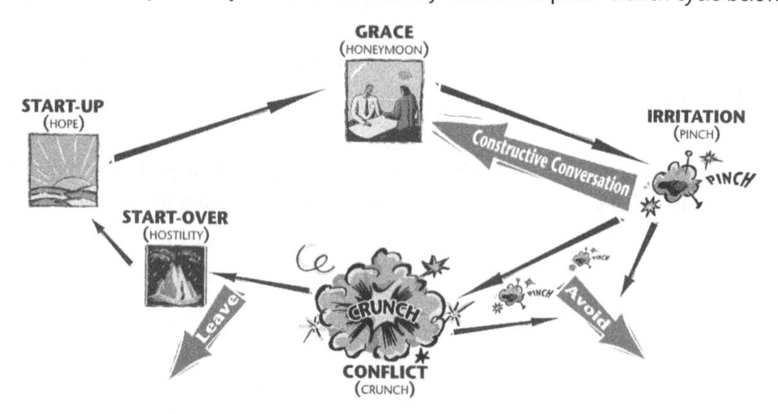

Whatever the root cause of the conflict, the Enneagram styles of the key parties involved will always be a factor in the conflict dynamics and resolution. The Enneagram enables each individual involved to make conflict resolution a constructive rather than destructive experience. The more people know themselves, understand their own responsibilities in the conflict interaction, engage in constructive self-management, and know how best to approach others through knowledge of the Enneagram, the greater the chances of a swift and effective outcome.

There are specific pinches (anger triggers) for each Enneagram style — that is, certain situations that will invariably ignite anger in a person of one style, yet may not affect someone of a different style. For Ones, these pinches include:

Being criticized · Another's lack of follow-through · Another's noncollaborative changes to a plan · Feeling deceived · Another's lack of timeliness

Development Stretches for Transforming Anger into an Opportunity for Growth

Share your likely pinches (anger triggers) with others at the beginning of your working relationship.

Give details and specific examples of these pinches so that other people know exactly what you mean. For example, "another's lack of follow-through" can mean many different things, such as not meeting long-term deadlines, not doing tasks immediately, or not returning a phone call within 24 hours.

For more insights and information about conflict, please refer to the following: Chapter 4, "Managing Conflict," in *Bringing Out the Best in Yourself at Work* (McGraw-Hill, 2004) and Chapter 5, "Become an Excellent Communicator," in *What Type of Leader Are You?* (McGraw-Hill, 2007).

Say something as soon as you are aware of feeling pinched or upset.
Ones may not be aware of feeling pinched yet may exhibit pinched behaviors, such as making curt statements, making accusations related to other issues, or feeling angry but saying nothing. When you do any of these things, ask yourself: *What is truly upsetting me?*

Additionally, because Ones tend to display their critical reactions through nonverbal behavior, try to keep your body language neutral when sharing your pinches with the other person so that he or she will react more to your words than to your non-verbal cues.

When you start to behave in ways that indicate you are feeling pinched or distressed, do something physical if you can, such as working out or taking a walk.
For Ones, this is particularly important, because it tends to put them back in touch with physical sensations and feelings. Because of this, Ones may more easily recognize the deeper causes of their anger, some of which may have very little to do directly with the pinch they have just experienced.

When you have a negative reaction and feel a pinch, ask yourself: *What does my reaction to this situation or to the other person's behavior say about me as a One and about the areas in which I can develop? How can working on my pinches and crunches help me to bring out the best in myself?*
The exploration of their behavior can lead many Ones to become self-critical; consequently, the questioning is best done through an open-ended inquiry. Examine multiple ways of considering the situation that has caused you duress, using different perspectives. For example, you can ask yourself the following sequence of questions: *As I think about three different people I know and respect who are all very different from one another, how do I think each of them would perceive this situation? What can I learn from each of them?*

Because Ones tend to suppress their anger, it often becomes bottled up and can lead to an explosive reaction over a less significant event. Pay special attention to this aspect of your anger and ask yourself this question: *What am I truly angry about?* In addition, the One's anger may be connected to deeper issues, such as feeling "not perfect enough" to be valued, or perceiving that others are not working as hard or as well but are getting away with this. Other areas of deeper issues to consider involve the One's desire to keep circumstances under control, or the One's tendency to compete with others — for example, by having the right answer, demonstrating the best behavior, or needing to be the most intelligent or most perfect. An underlying sense of losing to the competition is sometimes a deep source of anger for many Ones; understanding this often takes a profound level of self-reflection.

For more insights and information about conflict, please refer to the following: Chapter 4, "Managing Conflict," in *Bringing Out the Best in Yourself at Work* (McGraw-Hill, 2004) and Chapter 5, "Become an Excellent Communicator," in *What Type of Leader Are You?* (McGraw-Hill, 2007).

TEAM DEVELOPMENT STRETCHES

There is a difference between a group and a team. A *group* is a collection of individuals who have something in common; a *team* is a specific type of group, one composed of members who share one or more *goals* that can be reached only when there is an optimal level of *interdependence* between and among team members.

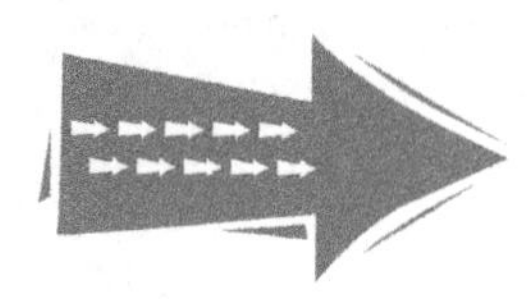

Team members also have *roles* — predictable patterns of behavior — within the team that are often related to their Enneagram styles. *Task roles* involve behaviors directed toward the work itself; *relationship roles* involve behaviors focused on feelings, relationships, and team processes, such as decision making and conflict resolution.

In addition, teams have unique yet predictable dynamics as they go through the four sequential stages of team development: *forming, storming, norming,* and *performing.* At each stage, there are questions the team must resolve before moving to the next stage.

TEAM STAGE	QUESTIONS
FORMING	*Who are we, where are we going, and are we all going there together?*
STORMING	*Can we disagree with one another in a constructive and productive way?*
NORMING	*How should we best organize ourselves and work together?*
PERFORMING	*How can we keep performing at a high level and not burn out?*

Ones: Development Stretches for Team Members and Team Leaders

Team Goals

Although you may prefer team goals that are extremely *clear, purposeful, realistic,* and *practical*, other team members may need goals that are lofty, broad, visionary, and developed by consensus. Allow yourself to be expansive and inclusive, and also to support the involvement of other people in developing and confirming the team's goals.

Team Interdependence

Although you may like to work in *low to moderately interdependent teams* with

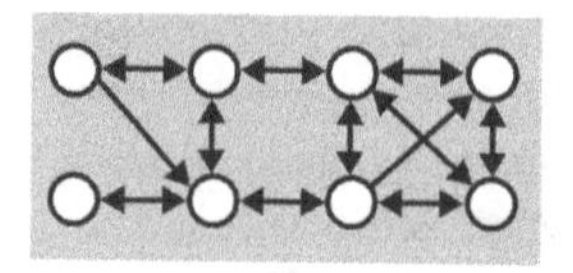

unambiguous team roles and highly competent and responsible team members, remind yourself that some teams need to work at a high level of interdependence to be effective. Too much role clarity can hinder creativity and innovation, and not every team member can realistically meet your standards of excellence at all times. Work to support the level of interdependence the team needs, as well as to develop a more accepting and flexible attitude toward all team members.

For more insights and information about teams, please refer to the following: Chapter 5, "Creating High-Performing Teams," in *Bringing Out the Best in Yourself at Work* (McGraw-Hill, 2004) and Chapter 6, "Lead High-Performing Teams," in *What Type of Leader Are You?* (McGraw-Hill, 2007).

Team Roles

Your typical task-related team role is likely to involve *structuring tasks* for the team by making suggestions about how to organize the work; your likely relationship-related team role may be *suggesting team norms* by offering ideas about how the team can operate more effectively. Stretch yourself to go beyond these typical roles and adopt the following additional team task and relationship roles:

Task Roles

New task role

Soliciting information from other team members, seeking ideas related to task topics

Relationship Roles

New relationship role

Facilitating the positive resolution of conflict by drawing out other members' feelings and perspectives and facilitating the resolution of the issues

Team Dynamics

During the four stages of team development — *forming, storming, norming,* and *performing* — experiment with expanding your repertoire of behavior in the following ways:

FORMING	STORMING	NORMING	PERFORMING
Add a strong relationship focus to your current task focus by suggesting that team members introduce themselves and get to know one another.	Garner more patience during times of team conflict, encouraging yourself and other team members to express feelings in a constructive manner.	Maintain your strength in suggesting new working agreements, make sure you seek consensus for your ideas, and encourage others to make suggestions as well.	Take care of yourself — make sure you don't work so hard that you become overextended and begin to burn out.

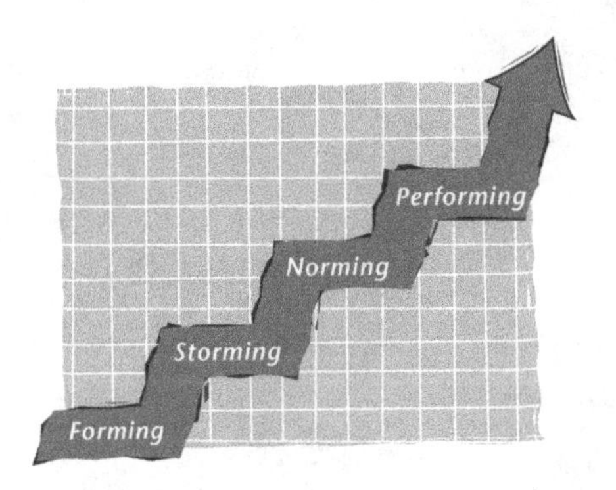

For more insights and information about teams, please refer to the following: Chapter 5, "Creating High-Performing Teams," in *Bringing Out the Best in Yourself at Work* (McGraw-Hill, 2004) and Chapter 6, "Lead High-Performing Teams," in *What Type of Leader Are You?* (McGraw-Hill, 2007).

Additional Team Development Stretches for One Team Leaders

Let go of nontactical work.

Make a list of all your team-related tasks. Next to each item, write either T for tactical work or S for strategic work. Unless you are a "working supervisor" — that is, one who is expected to do some of the hands-on work — you need to relinquish as much tactical work as possible to members of your team. Strategic work is always the team leader's responsibility. For all tactical work that can be delegated, write down the names of the team members you believe are capable of performing specific tasks, then assign the work to them.

Take time to relax and enjoy yourself.

Ones can become curt, on edge, and resentful when they have too much to do for too long a period of time. They are often able to relax while on vacation, but they have a hard time doing so otherwise. Every day, give yourself permission to spend 15 minutes just relaxing. Listen to music you like, read a magazine unrelated to work, or go for a walk by yourself and enjoy the experience of feeling unburdened.

Pay attention to the unintended consequences of your behavior on your team.

Remind yourself that each individual relationship you have with a team member —whether more positive or more negative in nature — can have unintended consequences on other members or on the team as a whole. For example, when you tolerate the difficult interpersonal behavior of a talented team member, others may perceive this as your condoning the behavior and feel disempowered in terms of dealing with this individual.

For more insights and information about teams, please refer to the following: Chapter 5, "Creating High-Performing Teams," in *Bringing Out the Best in Yourself at Work* (McGraw-Hill, 2004) and Chapter 6, "Lead High-Performing Teams," in *What Type of Leader Are You?* (McGraw-Hill, 2007).

LEADERSHIP DEVELOPMENT STRETCHES

The intense challenges of leadership are complex, demanding, unpredictable, exciting, and rewarding, and they require the ability to manage oneself and to interact effectively with hundreds of others in both stressful and exhilarating circumstances. For these reasons, leaders must spend time in honest self-reflection. Individuals who become extraordinary leaders grow in both evolutionary and revolutionary ways as they push themselves to meet challenges even they cannot predict in advance.

Excellent leadership comes in many forms, and no Enneagram style has a monopoly on greatness. However, your Enneagram style shows both your strengths as a leader and the areas that would most likely create obstacles to your success.

Enneagram Style One leaders usually display this special gift: *the pursuit of excellence.* However, their greatest strength can also become their greatest weakness: in their diligent striving for the highest quality and perfection, One leaders exhaust themselves to the point of illness and cause others to feel inadequate, criticized, or micromanaged.

Development Stretches to Enhance Your Leadership

Replace being right with being effective.

Every time you feel deeply critical of someone else, have a strongly held opinion, or believe in the rightness of a specific course of action, challenge yourself with this question: *Would I rather be right or effective?*

Delegate more.

Delegate work to other people and remember the following: delegate the "whole task," rather than only part of a project; initiate a discussion of the goals, time frames, deliverables, and process; check in periodically; and give plenty of positive reinforcement.

Have more fun at work.

Make your work less serious and more fun. Have a cartoon on your desk. Bring in your favorite tea for everyone at work to try. Show your sense of humor at work so others can enjoy your lighter side. Pass around an amusing article.

For more insights and information about leadership, please refer to the following: Chapter 6, "Leveraging Your Leadership," in *Bringing Out the Best in Yourself at Work* (McGraw-Hill, 2004) and the book, *What Type of Leader Are You?* (McGraw-Hill, 2007).

RESULTS ORIENTATION DEVELOPMENT STRETCHES

It is important to build credibility with customers by delivering sustained, high-quality results, continually driving for results, and reaching your potential. When you do this, you make gains in productivity, push the envelope of new product development, and support the organization as a leader in its field.

Work from a compelling vision.
If you are a team leader, create a vision for each project you lead, and be certain that all team members are aligned with it before you develop the project planning tasks and timelines. If you are a team member, make sure that you understand the team's vision and that your work is fully aligned with it.

If the team does not currently have a compelling vision, ask the question: *Why is what we are doing important?* Let your thinking go beyond the tasks and work products.

Although there are different ways to create compelling visions, the following process is a practical way to get started. At a team meeting (for the purpose of creating a vision), each team member lists his or her three most important goals and/or values for the project. Next, all items are written on a chart pad, and each member is given four removable red dots. Each member places a red dot next to the four items on the list that he or she believes are the most important to the success of the project. After this task is complete, the team selects the five items from the list with the most dots and, taking each item in turn, brainstorms answers to the following question: *If this value or goal were to become part of our daily way of working, how would we work on this project?*

Pay attention to people.
Pay as much attention to people's feelings and motivation as you do to all project-related tasks, particularly at the beginning of a project, at key milestones, and at times when potential obstacles to the project's success arise. Ask others about their well-being, and see what you can do to help them. Try to enjoy the people as much as you do the task.

Focus more on successes than on mistakes.
Pay particular attention to your use of right/wrong thinking, critical language, and a focus on mistakes when you're interacting with people connected to your project. The idea is to force yourself to think first about what is positive rather than what is missing the mark. In addition, when you send an e-mail to someone about anything other than a direct compliment, reread it several times and even have someone else (of a different Enneagram style) review it for tone and content before you send it.

For more insights and information about results orientation, please refer to the following: Chapter 2, "Drive for Results," in *What Type of Leader Are You?* (McGraw-Hill, 2007).

STRATEGY DEVELOPMENT STRETCHES

Leaders and individual contributors must understand the actual business of their organizations and be able to think and act strategically in both big and small ways if their teams and organizations are to reach the highest levels of performance, effectiveness, and efficiency.

"Knowing the business" and "thinking and acting strategically" go hand in hand. Unless you know the business, you have no context for thinking and acting strategically. When you have this information, you need to be able to use it in a strategic way, working from a compelling and common vision, a customer-focused mission, a smart strategy, and effective goals and tactics aligned with that strategy.

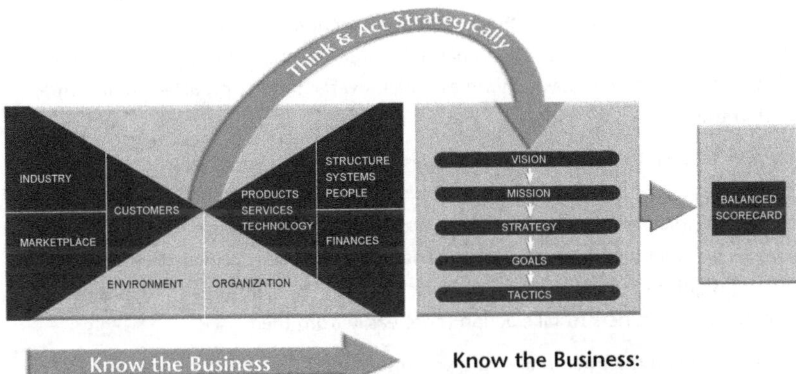

Know the Business: Think & Act Strategically

Keep the big picture in the forefront.
Whether you are a team member or a team leader, you need to take the broadest view and focus on the forest rather than the trees. If you are a leader, you need to learn to let go and leave the detail work to those who work for you. With every project for which you are responsible, ask yourself these questions on a regular basis: *Is the work I am personally doing at the strategic level — i.e., vision, mission, and strategy — and not the tactical level? Have I delegated the tactical work, or am I still involved in the more detailed level of execution?*

If you are a team member, ask yourself these questions for every task you do: *How does this work align with our team's strategy? Is it the best use of my time with regard to our vision, mission, and strategy, or is there something else that is more important for me to do?*

For more insights and information about strategy, please refer to the following: Chapter 4, "Know the Business: Think and Act Strategically," in *What Type of Leader Are You?* (McGraw-Hill, 2007).

Link all your work to the vision.
Ask yourself these questions: *What is the greater purpose of the work in front of me as well as in front of the team? What are we trying to accomplish (not in terms of goals but rather of the biggest dream or desire) in the next three to five years? What are the values underpinning these efforts that are essential to this vision?*

If you are a leader, be sure to gather input from those you work with, and make sure that the final vision is shared with everyone in your work area. When you communicate the vision, have a two-way dialogue and then make adjustments as needed.

Work strategically from the highest level of strategy.
If you are a leader, ask yourself whether the strategies you have developed are truly strategic or whether they are actually goals and tactics. Sometimes, very important goals and tactics can be strategic in nature — that is, essential to success — but they still may not be strategies, which are essential, overarching approaches to accomplishing the mission and vision.

You may be able to back into the strategies by examining your well-chosen tactics and asking yourself these questions: *As I examine the key tactics, do I find that these activities fall into similar groupings? In analyzing these similar groupings of tactics, what elements do I find they have in common?* The answer to the latter question will give you an insight into what is known as "tacit strategy." Making tacit strategies explicit enables you and others to take action more easily from them.

If you are a team member, make sure you understand your team's strategies, and be sure that you can link every task or project you do with one of these strategic areas. When you make a decision within your area of authority and are deciding among several options, ask yourself this question: *Which of these alternatives most closely aligns with our strategy?* If none of them match the strategy, consider other alternatives that do.

For more insights and information about strategy, please refer to the following: Chapter 4, "Know the Business: Think and Act Strategically," in *What Type of Leader Are You?* (McGraw-Hill, 2007).

DECISION-MAKING DEVELOPMENT STRETCHES

We all make decisions on a daily basis, but we rarely think about the process by which we make them. The wisest decisions are made utilizing our heads (rational analysis and planning), our hearts (to examine values, feelings, and impact on people), and our guts (for taking action), with all three used in an integrated way. In addition, when you are making decisions at work, you need to consider three other factors: the organizational culture, the decision-making authority structure within the organization, and the context of the decision itself.

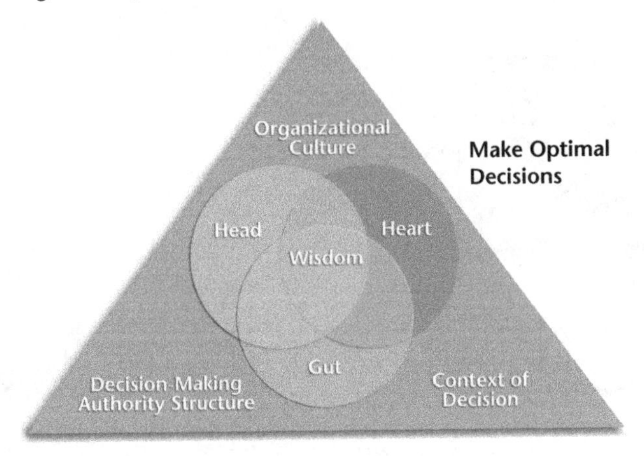

The following chart shows you how to develop each of your Centers of Intelligence (Head, Heart, and Gut) to assist you in making wise decisions.

Centers of Intelligence			
	Head Center	**Heart Center**	**Body (Gut) Center**
Activities for Ones That Develop Each Center	**Objective analysis** Be careful not to let your positive or negative opinions about another person over-shadow the objective data; don't overthink your decisions. **Astute insight** Go beyond the facts to the patterns implicit in the facts; understand the themes derived from these patterns. **Productive planning** Make sure you don't overplan a decision or overorganize its execution; allow room for new information and activities to emerge.	**Empathy** Consider both your own and other people's feelings in depth. **Authentic relating** Be willing to share deeply held feelings when discussing issues. **Compassion** Make certain you don't become too emotionally involved when making hard decisions, but don't be too cerebral either.	**Taking effective action** Turn decision making into an art form; use just enough action to get the results you want. **Steadfastness** Hold firm in your decisions, but not to the point of rigidity. **Gut-knowing** Learn to honor your gut reactions by asking yourself what it is that you know very deeply to be true; watch out for reacting too quickly.

For more insights and information about decision making, please refer to the following: Chapter 7, "Make Optimal Decisions," in *What Type of Leader Are You?* (McGraw-Hill, 2007).

ORGANIZATIONAL CHANGE DEVELOPMENT STRETCHES

In contemporary organizations, change has become a way of life. Companies exist in increasingly complex environments, with more competition, fewer resources, less time to market, higher customer expectations, increased regulation, more technology, and greater uncertainty. Organizations need to be flexible, innovative, cost-conscious, and responsive if they want to succeed. As a result, employees at all levels need to be able to embrace change and to function flexibly and effectively within their teams when an unforeseen direction must be taken.

Take Charge of Change

Ask for help and work collaboratively.
Although you may enjoy doing most of the work yourself, this is a near impossibility with the amount of work that change efforts involve. If you are a leader, delegate 50 percent more than you do normally. If you are a team member, learn to rely on other team members. Embracing taking charge of change means collaborating with others, not taking care of every detail yourself.

Notice how your reactions can be read as resistance.
Because you have strong opinions, believe you are correct most of the time, and react quickly to other people's comments, you may be seen as resisting change even when you are simply asking a question or disagreeing with a detail. When you listen fully and make an effort to integrate other points of view into your own, you are more likely to be perceived as an effective problem solver than as a resistor.

Link all aspects of the change to the vision.
If you are a leader, spend time developing the vision for the change, and link all aspects of the change to the vision — for example, the assessment, transition plan and process, and specific details related to the results of the change. If you are a team member, make sure you fully understand the vision and strategy for the change, not just the fundamentals. When you do these things, you will help keep yourself and others focused and committed.

For more insights and information about organizational change, please refer to the following: Chapter 8, "Take Charge of Change," in *What Type of Leader Are You?* (McGraw-Hill, 2007).

TRANSFORMATION DEVELOPMENT STRETCHES

In order to move from *constantly seeking a perfect world and working diligently to improve both themselves and everyone and everything around them* to the understanding that *there is an intrinsic perfection in all things,* Ones can work toward these transformations:

Mental Transformation

Transform the mental pattern of **resentment** (paying attention to flaws so that nothing ever seems good enough) *into the higher belief of* **perfection** (the insight that everything is as it should be, and that even imperfection is perfect).

Mental Activity

When you become aware that you are continuously thinking about flaws and errors, think about one or more times when you were able to accept the perfection of all things as they are in their natural state, imperfections and all. Remember those moments, and relive what was occurring within you at those times. Sustain your memory of these times until you feel completely calm and accepting.

Emotional Transformation

Transform the emotional habit of **anger** (the feeling of chronic dissatisfaction with how things are) *into the higher awareness of* **serenity** (an open-hearted acceptance of all that occurs).

Emotional Activity

When you become angry about how someone is acting or something that's taking place, remember one or more times in your life where you initially felt angry but were able to find peace and tranquility by accepting the situation as it was, not as you wanted it to be. If you can't recall such a situation, then imagine how you might feel if you could simply feel serene about life's events without trying to change them. Hold this feeling as long as possible, or until you feel relaxed and appreciative.

For more insights and information about personal transformation, please refer to the following: Chapter 7, "Transforming Yourself," in *Bringing Out the Best in Yourself at Work* (McGraw-Hill, 2004).

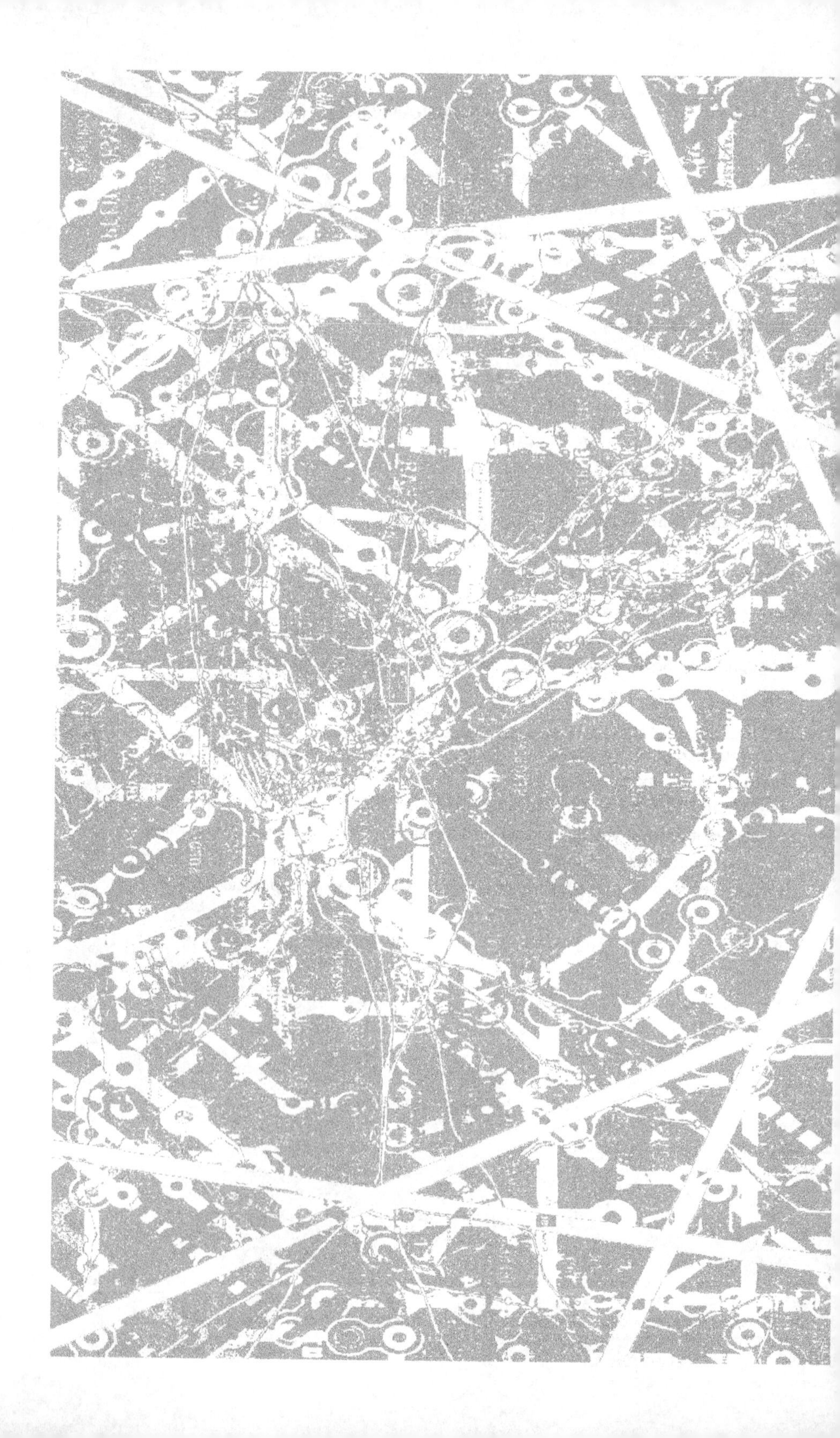

ENNEAGRAM STYLE TWO

ENNEAGRAM TWOS

The search for appreciation and the avoidance of feeling unworthy

Optimistic, generous, and emphatic, Enneagram Twos focus on the needs and behavior of others far more than on their own needs and desires; they develop an intuitive ability to know how to best support others in achieving their dreams or in minimizing their suffering. It can be misleading to think that all Twos want everyone with whom they come in contact to like them. A more accurate understanding is that Twos want, and even expect, the people they want to like them to respond favorably, but care far less — if at all — whether people they dislike find them appealing. What is true of almost all Twos is that they can become extremely distressed when someone whose opinion or affection they care about perceives them in a negative way.

Most Twos appear warm, are good listeners, and offer advice that they hope and expect others will take. Some Twos appear vulnerable, even childlike as if needing protection; other Twos exhibit more assertiveness, focusing their efforts to help or move groups or institutions in a forward direction; and other Twos derive their sense of value and importance by being desirable and indispensible to special individuals in their lives.

Twos tend to engage with others in a consistently warm way, usually asking questions of others more often than talking about themselves. While most Twos have well-developed interpersonal skills, they can also become self-effacing and uncomfortable when the focus is primarily on them.

While we can all be thoughtful and want others to value us, for Twos, the search for appreciation and the avoidance of feeling unworthy is their primary, persistent, and driving motivation.

DEVELOPMENT STRETCHES FOR TWOS

INDIVIDUALS WHO WANT TO BE LIKED, TRY TO MEET THE NEEDS OF OTHERS, AND ATTEMPT TO ORCHESTRATE THE PEOPLE AND EVENTS IN THEIR LIVES

CONTENTS

SELF-MASTERY DEVELOPMENT STRETCHES

Self-Mastery — the ability to understand, accept, and transform your thoughts, feelings, and behavior, with the understanding that each day will bring new challenges that are opportunities for growth — is the foundation of all personal and professional development. Self-mastery begins with self-awareness, then expands to include the elements shown in the following graphic:

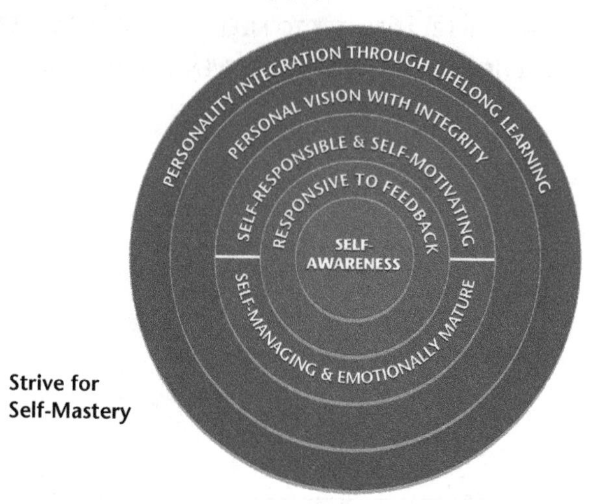

Strive for Self-Mastery

In this section on self-mastery, you will find the following:

- Three common issues for Twos related to self-mastery
- Three development stretches for working with the core issues of your Enneagram style, including one basic activity and one deeper activity for each stretch
- Three development stretches for working with your wings and arrow (stress-security) styles

Common Issues for Twos Related to Self-Mastery

Acknowledging that you have needs and desires, and focusing more on taking care of yourself and less on catering to the needs of others	Finding an internal basis for self-esteem rather than making your self-worth dependent on the reactions of others	Integrating dependence and autonomy in both your personal and professional relationships

For more insights and information about self-mastery, please refer to the following: Chapter 7, "Transforming Yourself," in *Bringing Out the Best in Yourself at Work* (McGraw-Hill, 2004) and Chapter 3, "Strive for Self-Mastery," in *What Type of Leader Are You?* (McGraw-Hill, 2007).

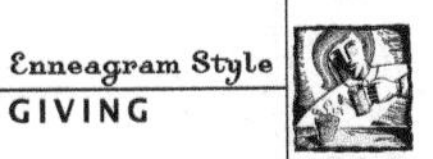

Development Stretches for Working with the Core Issues of Your Enneagram Style

Spend time alone.

Basic Activity

Engage in solo activities that allow you either to reflect or to do nice things for yourself (self-nurturing). When alone, Twos have a tendency to maintain contact with others through e-mails, phone calls, or even just thinking about someone else. Time spent truly alone will give you the chance to pay more attention to your inner experience instead of continually diverting your focus to others.

Deeper Activity

As you spend time alone, you will most likely begin to understand the degree of dependency you have on others. This can be especially enlightening for Twos, who often believe that other people are dependent on them. However, it goes both ways. When Twos give continuously, this giving often creates a dependency in the other person; at the same time, the Two becomes dependent on the need to be needed, the ability to influence others behind the scenes, and the need for personal affirmation.

Spending time alone allows Twos to understand who they really are, without the influences of other people's reactions and perceptions. This new sense of independence can be liberating for Twos.

As you practice spending time by yourself, keep in mind that for the purposes here, being alone means no phone calls, no e-mails, no letter writing, and no extended conversations with anyone. Spend one full hour each day completely alone, having no interaction with others during that time. On the weekend, carve out two to three hours solely for yourself to do exactly what you want to do, but make sure your choice of activity focuses only on you. For example, if you choose to engage in physical activity, choose an individual activity such as jogging, walking, or gardening by yourself. If you want to go to a museum, do so, but go alone and do not engage in conversation with others while there. During this time, make sure you turn off your cell phone.

Ask yourself: *What do I really need?*

Basic Activity

Becoming more aware of your feelings can lead to greater clarity about your true needs. Ask yourself what you need repeatedly until your answers become deeper. Or, ask yourself the simple question, *What am I feeling right now?* and explore your answer in depth. This latter question is important because Twos tend to repress their feelings — that is, when they have a feeling, they may either not acknowledge it or they may underestimate its depth and intensity.

For more insights and information about self-mastery, please refer to the following: Chapter 7, "Transforming Yourself," in *Bringing Out the Best in Yourself at Work* (McGraw-Hill, 2004) and Chapter 3, "Strive for Self-Mastery," in *What Type of Leader Are You?* (McGraw-Hill, 2007).

Deeper Activity

Twos usually have their emotional antenna extended to pick up cues about other people's needs; however, a continual focus on the needs of others usually results in Twos having less awareness of their own real needs. Eventually, most Twos feel short-changed in relationships. They expend so much effort on behalf of other people that they end up feeling, *But what about me?*

Twos do have needs, but because these are often unconscious or unexpressed, it becomes difficult for most Twos to get their needs met directly. Consequently, they often use indirect methods, and through this indirect behavior the Two may unconsciously attempt to control or manipulate other people. As Twos become more fully aware of their own needs, they usually become more direct in expressing them and get more of them satisfied. For example, they may take better care of themselves by not working every night until nine o'clock or by asking someone to help them on a large project.

When you return home from work each day, do the following activity. Take a sheet of paper and divide the paper into four columns, with these headings:

1. Today's needs
2. Needs met? (yes/no/partially)
3. If yes, how did I let my needs be known?
4. If no or partially met, what other options could I have used?

Next, write down the answers to the following questions under the appropriate headings: *What needs did I have today* (column 1)? *Did I get each of these needs met* (column 2)? For each yes answer, detail exactly what you did to get this need met (column 3). For each no answer, write down one explicit way in which you could get this need met (column 4).

After you have completed your lists, analyze what you have written. Did you have very few needs (three or fewer) or many needs (more than 15)? Are there themes that arise as you review the types of needs listed — for example, a need for more time for yourself or more support from others? Are most of your needs being met? Are most of your needs ones that you yourself can meet, or are they dependent on other people? Are you being mostly direct or mostly indirect in expressing your needs to others?

Do the above activity for two weeks, dating each day's work. At the end of that time, review your lists in sequence. You will probably notice some interesting patterns to your needs, which will help you to develop greater self-insight. Did your needs (both quantity and type) change over time? For instance, did you become better at getting your needs met? Did you become more direct about getting your needs met? Congratulate yourself on your accomplishments, and make a commitment to work on any areas you find troublesome, such as needing to be more direct or becoming better at meeting your needs yourself. Continue the entire activity for two more weeks, and you will begin to see marked improvement.

For more insights and information about self-mastery, please refer to the following: Chapter 7, "Transforming Yourself," in *Bringing Out the Best in Yourself at Work* (McGraw-Hill, 2004) and Chapter 3, "Strive for Self-Mastery," in *What Type of Leader Are You?* (McGraw-Hill, 2007).

Examine the ways that you give in order to get something in return.

Basic Activity

Make a list of everything you have done for other people in the last week, whether it was bringing someone home from the hospital or listening to someone for a longer time than you may have desired. Next to each item, write down what you wanted in return. Continue this list for several weeks. You may find that your behavior changes simply as a result of your becoming more aware of giving to get. If not, then reflect on the price you pay for continuing this behavior.

Deeper Activity

Twos usually give a great deal to others, but beneath their generosity is a tacit expectation that they will receive something in return. The most common expectation or hope is that the Two will be needed by others, become important to others' lives, and be perceived as a worthy human being.

Although the giving behavior of Twos may be greatly appreciated, it can also create problems. For example, Twos may give or offer things that other people don't truly want. In these cases, the other person can become angry, and/or the Two may feel unappreciated and distressed. At other times, the other person may appreciate something that the Two has done but not have known that there was an expectation for anything in return; the other person can feel hurt or angry, believing that the giving was done with no strings attached. And yet on other occasions, the other person may end up involuntarily dependent on the Two. This can be an unhealthy situation, fraught with potential conflict on both sides.

The following questions constitute an exercise that can be very helpful to you in changing the behavior of giving with the expectation of getting something back. Each time you offer, or even think about offering, to do something for someone else, ask yourself: *What am I really wanting in return for doing this? Am I doing this so that others will need me* (the creation of dependency)*? Am I doing this so that I will later feel proud that I can take care of things better than others* (the passion of pride)*? Am I doing this so that I will feel like a worthy person* (the need for personal affirmation)*?* At the end of each day, make a list of every single thing you either did do or thought of doing for someone else and what inside you really motivated you to want to help this person. After you have honestly answered this question, reconsider whether in each case your giving behavior was really in the other person's best interests, and whether it was really in your best interests. If you do this activity daily for two weeks, you will be in for some startling discoveries.

For more insights and information about self-mastery, please refer to the following: Chapter 7, "Transforming Yourself," in *Bringing Out the Best in Yourself at Work* (McGraw-Hill, 2004) and Chapter 3, "Strive for Self-Mastery," in *What Type of Leader Are You?* (McGraw-Hill, 2007).

Development Stretches for Working with Your Wings and Arrow (Stress-Security) Styles

Wings are the Enneagram styles on either side of your core Enneagram style; arrow, or stress-security, styles are Enneagram styles shown with arrows pointing away or toward your core Enneagram style. Your wings and arrow styles don't change your core Enneagram style, but instead offer qualities that can broaden and enrich your patterns of thinking and feeling as well as enhance your behaviors. Your wings and arrow styles make you more complex and versatile because they provide more dimensions to your personality and serve as vehicles for self-development.

Integrate Your One Wing

Learn to discern.

Ones tend to be discerning and can differentiate easily between excellent and sub-par work, whereas Twos tend to focus more on people's feelings about and reactions to work. When you struggle to make a tough decision, one you know is correct but may adversely affect someone you care about, ask yourself: *For the greater good of the organization and our work, what is the best thing to do?*

Add realism to your optimism.

Ones are often realistic, practical, and systematic, whereas Twos tend to be idealistic. Put every idea, yours as well as the ideas of others, through a filter that checks for realism, practicality, and systematic organization by asking the following questions: *Do we have the time and money to do this? What specific steps would be needed to implement this? Are we applying the rules systematically and uniformly?*

Assert yourself.

Ones tend to be direct and assertive in their opinions, while Twos, who may feel uncomfortable being straightforward, tend to express themselves in less forceful or clear terms — for example, by being tentative when asking questions or raising ideas. Make sure the number of times you give opinions is equal to the number of times you solicit the ideas of others. Before you ask someone a question, ask yourself whether your question is really a statement phrased as a question. When this is the case, restate your question as a statement. When you do make statements, pay attention to your tone of voice. If the tone is soft, increase its loudness for emphasis. In addition, notice whether your voice tends to get higher at the end of your statements. The voice going up at the end suggests to the listener that the statement is tentative, more like a question. In this case, work to make your voice go down at the end of a statement. You may need to tape-record your voice to hear the inflections at the end of your sentences, or you can ask a colleague or friend for feedback about it.

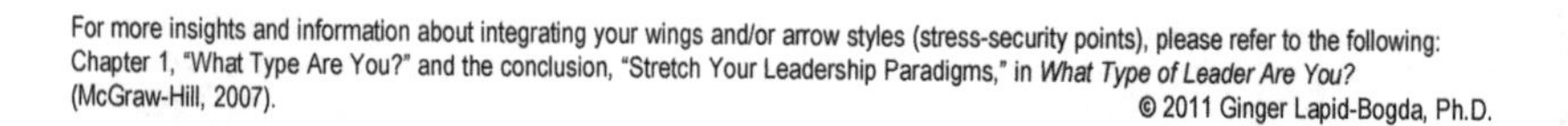
For more insights and information about integrating your wings and/or arrow styles (stress-security points), please refer to the following: Chapter 1, "What Type Are You?" and the conclusion, "Stretch Your Leadership Paradigms," in *What Type of Leader Are You?* (McGraw-Hill, 2007).

Integrate Your Three Wing

Step into the limelight.

Threes usually like being recognized directly for what they accomplish, and many Threes enjoy the spotlight. Twos, on the other hand, usually prefer helping others become successful; they like being the power behind the throne rather than being the king or queen themselves. Experiment with stepping into the limelight — for example, volunteering to give a speech or presentation rather than referring the opportunity to someone else. Initiate your own project or business and step into the leadership role rather than giving your ideas and support to other people.

Seek respect.

Threes seek respect, whereas Twos want to be liked. As Twos mature, they often change course and substitute the gaining of respect from others for being liked. This shift of focus can be helpful, but Twos need to seek self-respect more than they seek the respect of others. Like Threes, Twos need to discover that they can be respected for who they are and what they do and that true respect comes from within, regardless of the perceptions of other people. The questions to ask are these: *Do I really respect myself? What must I do to achieve self-respect that is entirely independent of what others think of me?*

Maintain your work focus.

Most Threes appear remarkably confident and work-focused even when they are distressed. Twos under duress tend to focus on people rather than work, and their general optimism becomes replaced by visible worry, anxiety, and negativity. When you feel distressed at work, focus on work and goals instead of dwelling on emotions. Whenever your optimism wanes, think about someone you respect who appears confident and does not let his or her feelings cloud the ability to function effectively. Imagine you are that person, then go about your work.

For more insights and information about integrating your wings and/or arrow styles (stress-security points), please refer to the following: Chapter 1, "What Type Are You?" and the conclusion, "Stretch Your Leadership Paradigms," in *What Type of Leader Are You?* (McGraw-Hill, 2007).

Integrate Arrow Style Eight (Stress Point)

Develop your personal power.

Twos can be quite powerful, but their power often comes more from their proximity to and association with powerful people than from a feeling of personal power. Personal power is not dependent on someone else; it is a quality that arises from how you feel about yourself, what you know, and how you communicate, among other factors. Personal power is palpable through one's physical presence and bearing. Eights often command attention, even when they say nothing. Twos can do this by being more assertive, with neither apology nor regret. This requires Twos to say what they mean and to do so forthrightly, looking directly at others when making bold statements as opposed to looking at them with soft and gentle eyes. In addition, when in the presence of other people, Twos need to focus as much attention on themselves as they do on others.

Express your anger in a direct and timely way.

Eights usually have direct access to their anger and typically express it in a clear and forceful manner. Twos can express their anger directly, but they usually do so only when they feel highly frustrated. This may mean that they have endured a situation for too long and finally explode, or the Two may have decided to write someone off and then pointedly ignored him or her. Most of the time, however, Twos do not express anger directly and rarely express it immediately.

The following activity can help Twos practice the timely and direct expression of anger. Each night, stand in front on the mirror and ask yourself: *With whom did I feel angry today, even if my anger was only frustration, impatience, or dismay?* As you look in the mirror, imagine you are expressing your anger directly to each person or group in turn; say something to each of them as you look in the mirror. Observe your face and pay attention to your words and tone of voice. If you do not sound forceful and direct, repeat the words until you feel the full force of your anger. The more you practice this, the more you will increase your ability to express anger effectively in your daily life.

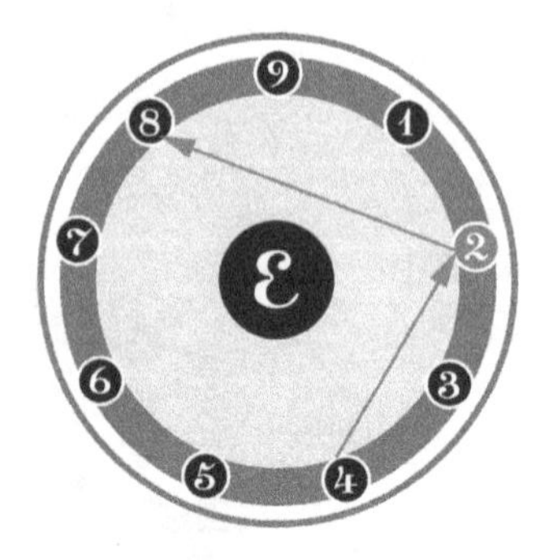

For more insights and information about integrating your wings and/or arrow styles (stress-security points), please refer to the following: Chapter 1, "What Type Are You?" and the conclusion, "Stretch Your Leadership Paradigms," in *What Type of Leader Are You?* (McGraw-Hill, 2007).

Care less about how others react to you.

It's not that Eights don't care about what others think of them; it's simply that this is not paramount in their minds when they choose whether to do or not do something. As a result, Eights have more freedom than Twos in thinking, feeling, and acting because they are not attuned to an invisible "audience" every time they react to something or contemplate taking action. Twos almost always consider the reactions of others; this is so habitual that many Twos are unaware that they do so. Whenever you contemplate an action and begin to think about the reactions of others, or whenever you feel guilty about something you've done, thought, or felt, gently confront yourself with these questions: *What do I really want? What do I really think is the best thing to do or to have done? What are my real feelings about this?*

Integrate Arrow Style Four (Security Point)

Go deep inside yourself.

When you ask a Two what he or she needs, the most common response is "I don't know" or "Needs? What needs?" If you don't know your own needs, it is difficult to identify your deeper feelings. Your needs give you clues to your feelings, and vice versa.

Fours, on the other hand, spend a great deal of time exploring the nuances of their own needs and feelings. Some of the ways in which Fours do this may be useful to Twos. Fours automatically ask themselves at fairly regular intervals: *How do I feel about this? Am I getting what I need, or is something missing here?* Twos can ask themselves these same questions every 15 minutes. Taking stock of yourself in this way gives you an ongoing report and trend analysis of your feelings and needs.

Fours also talk frequently about their feelings to others. While Twos do this too, their focus is on the other person's feelings rather than on their own. When Twos discuss their own feelings more frequently — not only as a means of venting, but also as a way to solicit the other person's perceptions about the Two's experience — they are more readily able to identify their own feelings and needs. You can practice this by talking once daily to someone else about how you feel. Make an attempt to speak with a variety of people, as you will not only be providing yourself greater opportunities for practice, but you will also be inviting a greater variety of perspectives about emotional reactions.

For more insights and information about integrating your wings and/or arrow styles (stress-security points), please refer to the following: Chapter 1, "What Type Are You?" and the conclusion, "Stretch Your Leadership Paradigms," in *What Type of Leader Are You?* (McGraw-Hill, 2007).

Dramatically increase your creativity.
Many Twos are creative, but when they adopt the Four's aesthetic sensibilities, their artistry can become more original and more dramatic, and it can make a stronger impact. Fours often draw their artistic inspiration from the depths of their emotional experiences. Twos can do this as well by asking themselves: *What are my deepest sensitivities, ones that I could express through drawing, sculpture, writing, photography, or music? What are the various ways in which I could do this?* Twos then need to take the risk of experimenting with new ways of self-expression. At first, the results may not be exactly what you want, but try to focus on the satisfaction you derive from the act of creation.

Fours also use metaphorical and symbolic thinking, common techniques in the creative process. To expand this ability, Twos can select a moving experience and compare it to something else. For example, if you observe or imagine a beautiful horse galloping, you can ask yourself: *What is my experience of this horse galloping similar to?* Your answer might be: *The horse moves with the grace of a thousand angels suspended in space.* The completion of a challenging project could be metaphorically restated in this way: *No obstacle on the course presented a barrier we could not hurdle!*

Follow your dreams.
Twos usually help others find their passion and follow their dreams, but like the cobbler's children who have no shoes, Twos are often at a loss to articulate and follow their own dreams. By contrast, Fours usually have many dreams that they follow with great gusto. Twos need to ask themselves this series of questions to determine what is truly their heart's passion: *What do I love doing? What do I long for? What would give me the greatest sense of reward and satisfaction? What have I been wanting to do for a long time, but never seem to have time for? What would happen if I put my desires first?*

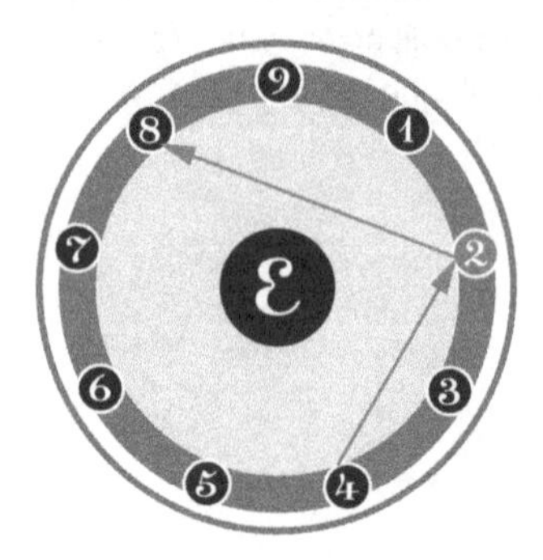

For more insights and information about integrating your wings and/or arrow styles (stress-security points), please refer to the following: Chapter 1, "What Type Are You?" and the conclusion, "Stretch Your Leadership Paradigms," in *What Type of Leader Are You?* (McGraw-Hill, 2007).

COMMUNICATION DEVELOPMENT STRETCHES

When you communicate with someone, three kinds of unintentional distortions may be present: speaking style, body language, and blind spots. *Speaking style* refers to your overall pattern of speaking. *Body language* includes posture, facial expressions, hand gestures, body movements, energy levels, and hundreds of other nonverbal messages. *Blind spots* are elements of your communication containing information about you that is not apparent to you but is highly visible to other people. We all unknowingly convey information through an amalgam of our speaking style, body language, and other inferential data.

The receivers of the messages you send also distort what they hear through their *distorting filters*. These are unconscious concerns or assumptions, often based on the listener's Enneagram style, that alter how someone hears what others say.

Speaking Style Body Language Blind Spots

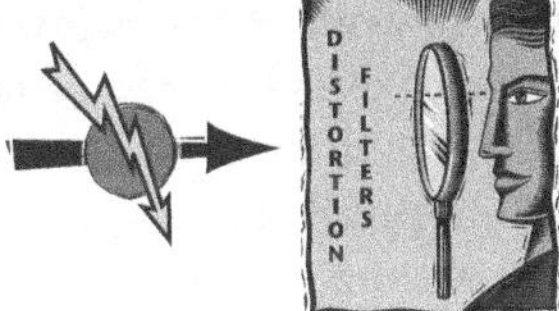

Change one communication style behavior at a time.

It is most effective to work on changing one behavior at a time, preferably in the following sequence: speaking style, body language, blind spots, and listening distorting filters. It is easiest to change the behaviors of which we are most aware, and this sequence represents the most common order of awareness, from most to least aware.

Twos: Speaking style

- Ask questions
- Give compliments
- Focus on the content of other person
- Few references to self
- Soft voice
- Angry or complaining when Twos dislike what others say

Twos: Body language

- Smiling and comfortable
- Relaxed facial expressions
- Open, graceful body movement
- When agitated, furrowed brow and facial tension

For more insights and information about communication, please refer to the following: Chapter 2, "Communicating Effectively," in *Bringing Out the Best in Yourself at Work* (McGraw-Hill, 2004) and Chapter 5, "Become an Excellent Communicator," in *What Type of Leader Are You?* (McGraw-Hill, 2007).

Twos: Blind spots

- A secondary or hidden intention may lie beneath the Two's generosity, helpfulness, and attention giving
- If disinterested in the other person, disengage precipitously

Twos: Distorting filters when listening to someone else

- Whether the other person likes you
- Whether you like the other person
- Whether you want to help the other person
- The degree of influence the other person has
- If you feel the other person plans to harm someone you wish to protect

Note: Some of the above characteristics may be positive, some negative, and some neutral or mixed. They are intended as an overview to allow you to select from among them.

Use e-mails to expand and adjust your language patterns.

- Review your e-mails before you send them for language and tone.
- Focus as much of the content on yourself as on the recipient.
- Use fewer superlatives (e.g., *great* and *terrific*).
- Avoid capitalizing complete words or phrases.
- Eliminate flattering comments.
- Use simple and direct expressions of both positive and negative feelings.
- Refrain from using strident and pointed words to express concerns.
- Encourage a respectful response from the recipient.

For more insights and information about communication, please refer to the following: Chapter 2, "Communicating Effectively," in *Bringing Out the Best in Yourself at Work* (McGraw-Hill, 2004) and Chapter 5, "Become an Excellent Communicator," in *What Type of Leader Are You?* (McGraw-Hill, 2007).

FEEDBACK DEVELOPMENT STRETCHES

Honest, positive, and constructive *feedback* — direct, objective, simple, and respectful observations that one person makes about another's behavior — improves both relationships and on-the-job performance. When you offer feedback, the Feedback Formula, combined with the insights of the Enneagram, helps you tailor your delivery. When someone gives you feedback, the more receptive you are to hearing what is being said, the more likely it is that you will be able to discern what is useful and utilize what has been suggested.

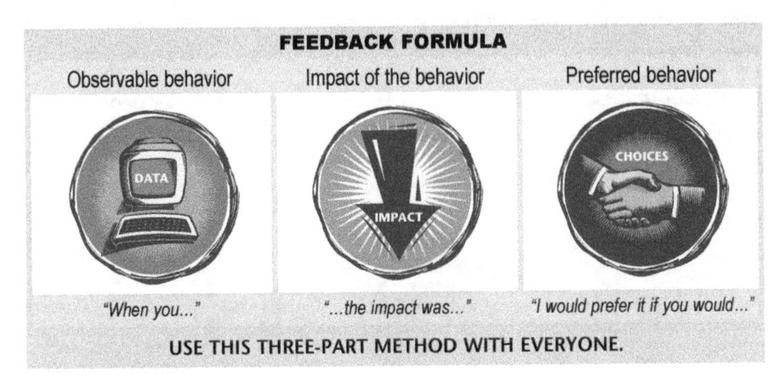

How Twos Can Enhance Their Ability to Deliver Feedback Effectively

When you offer feedback to someone, you want to be prepared and also to encourage the feedback recipient to be as receptive as possible. Remember that how and when you deliver feedback is just as important as what you actually say.

Use the three components of the Feedback Formula together with the following suggestions to plan and deliver the feedback.

- Maintain your positive regard for the other person, but not at the expense of avoiding the sharing of negative information.
- Consider the other person's feelings, but do not "fog over" the issues to keep the feedback recipient from feeling bad.
- Pay attention to the recipient's reaction, but take neither a positive nor a negative response personally.
- Maintain your perceptiveness, but remind yourself that your insights may not be accurate, especially when you are angry.
- Keep in mind that as much as you want to give to others and share your insights, the feedback recipient may not want your help and may already know the best course of action to take.

For more insights and information about feedback, please refer to the following: Chapter 3, "Giving Constructive Feedback," in *Bringing Out the Best in Yourself at Work* (McGraw-Hill, 2004) and Chapter 5, "Become an Excellent Communicator," in *What Type of Leader Are You?* (McGraw-Hill, 2007).

How Twos Can Be More Receptive When They Receive Feedback

- When someone gives you negative feedback, it may elicit in you a concern that the person doesn't like you or that you suddenly have no value. Remind yourself that one piece of negative feedback does not mean a person either likes or dislikes you, nor does negative feedback mean you are unworthy.
- You may have a belief that because you work so hard to be a good person and to treat others well, that somehow your behavior is beyond reproach. If you think about this in a thoughtful way, you will realize that no one is ever beyond reproach and even if the feedback is incorrect or a misinterpretation, it is still worth listening to.
- Remember that even though you may be very perceptive, other people can be equally or differently perceptive. Listen with a sense of open curiosity.

For more insights and information about feedback, please refer to the following: Chapter 3, "Giving Constructive Feedback," in *Bringing Out the Best in Yourself at Work* (McGraw-Hill, 2004) and Chapter 5, "Become an Excellent Communicator," in *What Type of Leader Are You?* (McGraw-Hill, 2007).

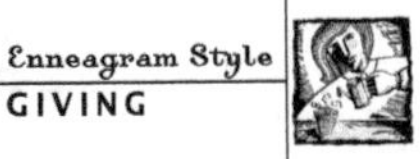

CONFLICT DEVELOPMENT STRETCHES

Relationships both at work and at home often involve some degree of conflict, which may be caused by a variety of factors and usually follows the pinch-crunch cycle below:

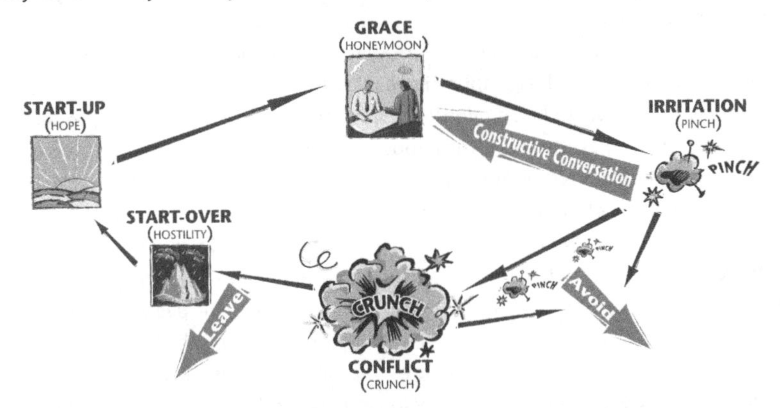

Whatever the root cause of the conflict, the Enneagram styles of the key parties involved will always be a factor in the conflict dynamics and resolution. The Enneagram enables each individual involved to make conflict resolution a constructive rather than destructive experience. The more people know themselves, understand their own responsibilities in the conflict interaction, engage in constructive self-management, and know how best to approach others through knowledge of the Enneagram, the greater the chances of a swift and effective outcome.

There are specific pinches (anger triggers) for each Enneagram style — that is, certain situations that will invariably ignite anger in a person of one style, yet may not affect someone of a different style. For Twos, these pinches include:

Being taken for granted · Feeling unappreciated · Not being heard · Another acting in an interpersonally inappropriate way · Another being treated in an abusive manner

For more insights and information about conflict, please refer to the following: Chapter 4, "Managing Conflict," in *Bringing Out the Best in Yourself at Work* (McGraw-Hill, 2004) and Chapter 5, "Become an Excellent Communicator," in *What Type of Leader Are You?* (McGraw-Hill, 2007).

Development Stretches for Transforming Anger into an Opportunity for Growth

Share your likely pinches (anger triggers) with others at the beginning of your working relationship.

The pinches for Twos bear a striking similarity to one another: essentially, Twos like to be needed, acknowledged, and appreciated. However, because they tend to do for others in what appears to be an effortlessly spontaneous way, such as rising to meet a need and offering assistance, it may appear to others that Twos enjoy giving for its own sake. People often do not realize that Twos want to be explicitly thanked. Most Twos would not be able to tell someone else, particularly in a new working relationship, that they want to be appreciated and thanked. To say this might be embarrassing because of its personal tone in a business context and the perception of their being "needy." However, these Two pinches can be effectively communicated through anecdote and story. For example, after encouraging the other person to discuss his or her pinches, Twos can frame their pinches in this way: "One of my key values is that everyone gets treated with courtesy and respect. That means using 'please' when asking someone to do something, and explicitly saying 'thank you' to someone for a job completed or something they have done. I behave toward others this way and want to be treated this way myself. Once, I recommended a colleague for a project, and this person never explicitly said thank you for it. This is one of my core pinches."

Say something as soon as you are aware of feeling pinched or upset.

Twos may worry that if they raise the fact that they feel pinched, the other person may feel hurt or angry; Twos rarely want to elicit either reaction. The following perspective can be invaluable to Twos: when you share a pinch soon after it occurs, you are truly helping the other person to learn something about the impact of his or her behavior and you are helping your mutual relationship to grow. In addition, when you are forthcoming about feeling pinched, you are also helping yourself by learning to express your own needs early in a relationship.

When you start to behave in ways that indicate you are feeling pinched or distressed, do something physical if you can, such as working out or taking a walk.

Physical activity serves Twos well because when they do something physical that they enjoy, they are actually doing something for themselves rather than focusing their attention on the needs of others. When Twos care for themselves, they often need less affirmation and appreciation from other people.

Twos often find that physical activity helps to ground them during times of emotional duress. The act of doing something physical helps them to focus on their bodies rather than on their emotions or thoughts. This distance from their reactions often allows new perspectives on their pinches and crunches to emerge.

For more insights and information about conflict, please refer to the following: Chapter 4, "Managing Conflict," in *Bringing Out the Best in Yourself at Work* (McGraw-Hill, 2004) and Chapter 5, "Become an Excellent Communicator," in *What Type of Leader Are You?* (McGraw-Hill, 2007).

When you have a negative reaction and feel a pinch, ask yourself: ***What does my reaction to this situation or to the other person's behavior say about me as a Two and about the areas in which I can develop? How can working on my pinches and crunches help me to bring out the best in myself?***

This question makes Twos focus on themselves rather than on the other person. The issue becomes not what the other person needs to learn, but what the Two needs to examine about himself or herself. This change of attention can startle many Twos, and they may need to ask themselves the above question multiple times. The answers Twos most often give are these: *I need to be appreciated* or *I need to be needed and I'm not getting that response from this other person.* Whatever the initial answer to this question, it is very helpful for Twos to deepen their level of self-exploration and ask themselves these questions: *Why is appreciation so important to me? How would I be different if I didn't need to be needed and appreciated?* This line of questioning often leads Twos to explore the issue of whether they are usually giving to others in order to get something in return.

It is the tacit expectation of getting something back — for example, being honored, being considered indispensable, being praised, or even being revered — that is referred to by the term "manipulation." Manipulation means getting someone else to do something or shaping someone's behavior without his or her explicit knowledge or consent. Although Twos do not like to have this term applied to them, it is sometimes said that Twos give to get under the guise of appearing as though they are giving to give. This awareness can be both troubling and enlightening for most Twos.

For more insights and information about conflict, please refer to the following: Chapter 4, "Managing Conflict," in *Bringing Out the Best in Yourself at Work* (McGraw-Hill, 2004) and Chapter 5, "Become an Excellent Communicator," in *What Type of Leader Are You?* (McGraw-Hill, 2007).

TEAM DEVELOPMENT STRETCHES

There is a difference between a group and a team. A *group* is a collection of individuals who have something in common; a *team* is a specific type of group, one composed of members who share one or more *goals* that can be reached only when there is an optimal level of *interdependence* between and among team members.

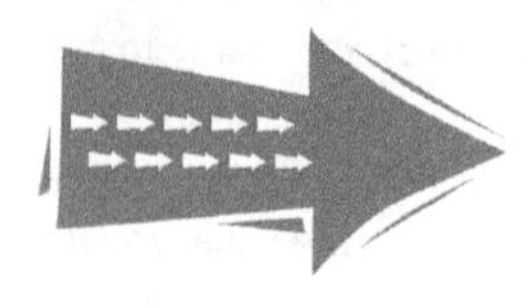

Team members also have *roles* — predictable patterns of behavior – within the team that are often related to their Enneagram styles. *Task roles* involve behaviors directed toward the work itself; *relationship roles* involve behaviors focused on feelings, relationships, and team processes, such as decision making and conflict resolution.

In addition, teams have unique yet predictable dynamics as they go through the four sequential stages of team development: *forming, storming, norming,* and *performing.* At each stage, there are questions the team must resolve before moving to the next stage.

TEAM STAGE	QUESTIONS
FORMING	*Who are we, where are we going, and are we all going there together?*
STORMING	*Can we disagree with one another in a constructive and productive way?*
NORMING	*How should we best organize ourselves and work together?*
PERFORMING	*How can we keep performing at a high level and not burn out?*

Twos: Development Stretches for Team Members and Team Leaders

Team Goals

Although you may prefer team goals that are *commonly shared and meaningful* and that fully utilize the talents of all members, other team members may need goals that are precise, practical, assigned to the team by those in authority (and thus might not be shared by all team members), and that rely on a few key players rather than fully utilizing everyone's talents. Allow yourself to be concrete and highly specific when you create team goals, and also to support the idea that some goals and tasks may depend on the capabilities of a few team players.

Team Interdependence

You may prefer to work in *highly to moderately interdependent teams* with a warm

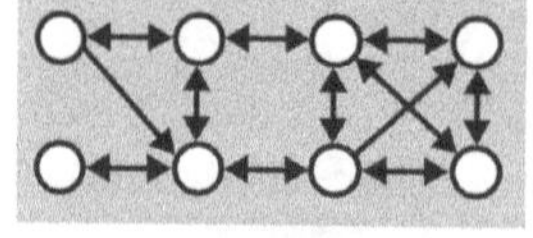

and supportive team environment. However, remind yourself that some teams need to work at a low level of interdependence to be effective, and that some teams are composed of members who dislike team environments that are too warm and supportive, perceiving these as coddling members and curtailing their independence. Work to support the level of interdependence the team needs, and work to develop the capacity to be effective in teams that may not offer the degree of support and warm interaction you desire.

For more insights and information about teams, please refer to the following: Chapter 5, "Creating High-Performing Teams," in *Bringing Out the Best in Yourself at Work* (McGraw-Hill, 2004) and Chapter 6, "Lead High-Performing Teams," in *What Type of Leader Are You?* (McGraw-Hill, 2007).

Team Roles

Task Roles

Your typical task-related team role is likely to involve the *solicitation of information* within the team through questions related to the team's topics of discussion — for example, what, how, why, when, and who; your likely relationship-related team role may be *encouraging participation* by soliciting (verbally and nonverbally) everyone's ideas and full participation. Stretch yourself to go beyond these typical roles and adopt the following additional team task and relationship roles:

Relationship Roles

New task role
Giving opinions by stating clearly what you think about items under discussion

New relationship role
Facilitating to move the process ahead by summarizing, synthesizing, probing, cajoling, charting, and other behaviors designed to get the tasks done and move forward

Team Dynamics

During the four stages of team development — *forming, storming, norming,* and *performing* — experiment with expanding your repertoire of behavior in the following ways:

FORMING	STORMING	NORMING	PERFORMING
Add a strong task focus to your current relationship focus by either stating what you believe is the team's central purpose so that others can agree or disagree, or by asking what others think about this issue and facilitating movement toward a common team purpose	Allow yourself to stay with team conflict longer than you normally would, encouraging yourself and other team members to both listen and express true feelings.	Maintain your strength in helping the team reach agreements, but make sure you also suggest ideas and are open to other people's responses to these.	Make sure you don't consistently volunteer to help others when they become overloaded or you will be the one needing help; experiment with allowing yourself to be a star performer.

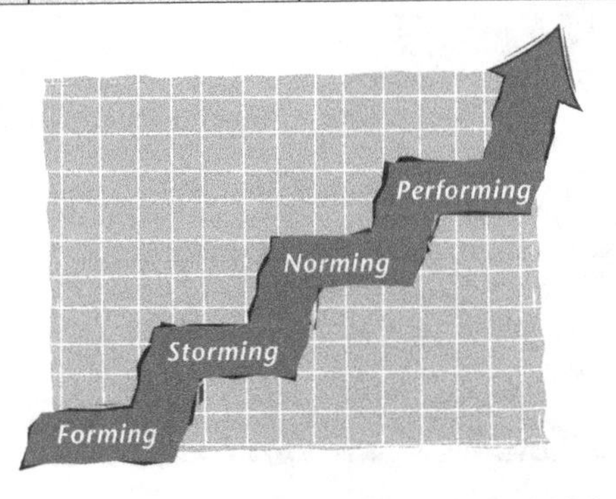

For more insights and information about teams, please refer to the following: Chapter 5, "Creating High-Performing Teams," in *Bringing Out the Best in Yourself at Work* (McGraw-Hill, 2004) and Chapter 6, "Lead High-Performing Teams," in *What Type of Leader Are You?* (McGraw-Hill, 2007).

Additional Team Development Stretches for Two Team Leaders

Step into visible leadership.

It is important for you to claim both the authority that goes with the leadership role and the personal influence you can have. Doing so makes it easier for others to follow your lead; it also creates more respect for the leadership role, and this increased level of recognition is important for both the team's success and your own professional growth. In public settings, refer to yourself as the leader of the team. Run your own team meetings rather than having someone else facilitate them. Pay attention to ways in which you minimize your leadership role.

Develop the team architecture to the same degree as the team processes.

Twos who are team leaders know how to set up processes that enable people to work together effectively, but they tend to put less emphasis on clear team structure, roles, and specific accountabilities. Greater clarity helps team members work more effectively and reduces unnecessary dependence on the team leader. Design the team architecture in the same way you design the team processes — that is, in a slightly *under*organized fashion, so that team members will still have the freedom to take initiative and be innovative.

Avoid doing too much of the day-to-day work.

Discipline yourself to neither offer assistance nor automatically say yes when asked. Each time you are about to involve yourself in detail work, say no and remind yourself that there is something more important you would be neglecting.

For more insights and information about teams, please refer to the following: Chapter 5, "Creating High-Performing Teams," in *Bringing Out the Best in Yourself at Work* (McGraw-Hill, 2004) and Chapter 6, "Lead High-Performing Teams," in *What Type of Leader Are You?* (McGraw-Hill, 2007).

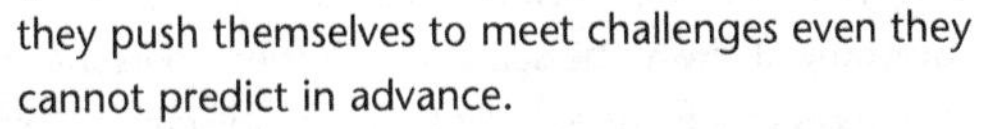

LEADERSHIP

The intense challenges of leadership are complex, demanding, unpredictable, exciting, and rewarding, and they require the ability to manage oneself and to interact effectively with hundreds of others in both stressful and exhilarating circumstances. For these reasons, leaders must spend time in honest self-reflection. Individuals who become extraordinary leaders grow in both evolutionary and revolutionary ways as they push themselves to meet challenges even they cannot predict in advance.

Excellent leadership comes in many forms, and no Enneagram style has a monopoly on greatness. However, your Enneagram style shows both your strengths as a leader and the areas that would most likely create obstacles to your success.

Enneagram Style Two leaders usually display this special gift: *motivation and service to others*. However, their greatest strength can also become their greatest weakness: in their dedicated efforts to give to everyone else, Two leaders lose touch with their own needs to the point of self-neglect, create dependency in others, and end up leaving the ones they most want to help because they become so frustrated by their inability to remove organizational obstacles.

Development Stretches to Enhance Your Leadership

Learn to say no!

Say no to work activities before you become overextended, get sick, sacrifice your family time, or become resentful.

Help the organization become less dependent on you.

Empower others to do their jobs, make their own decisions, and think through difficult issues without coming to you.

Bring more objectivity and less emotional reactivity into your leadership.

When you respond favorably to people who make you feel important and negatively to those who challenge you or your ideas, this may not lead to the best decisions. Focus more on strategy and less on people than you currently do.

For more insights and information about results orientation, please refer to the following: Chapter 2, "Drive for Results," in *What Type of Leader Are You?* (McGraw-Hill, 2007).

RESULTS ORIENTATION DEVELOPMENT STRETCHES

It is important to build credibility with customers by delivering sustained, high-quality results, continually driving for results, and reaching your potential. When you do this, you make gains in productivity, push the envelope of new product development, and support the organization as a leader in its field.

Focus as much on the work objectives as you do on people.
Because you will always be sensitive to others' personal needs, it is important to shift your emphasis and focus equally on work objectives. This will enable people to work more independently of you, and it will allow you to feel less obliged to make everything okay for everyone else.

Have the courage to deliver tough news.
People need to know where they stand, even at times when they may be under duress, whether for personal or work-related reasons. Be kind, clear, and compassionate, but make sure not to withhold negative information. Give constructive feedback.

Don't overextend yourself.
Do you know when you are overextending yourself to the point of exhaustion? When you're exhausted, you will not be performing at your best, and you may also react in ways that create barriers between you and others. Make sure you consider yourself as well as other people, acknowledging that you have needs for rest and support, and that you expect — and accept — that others can and will step up to tasks.

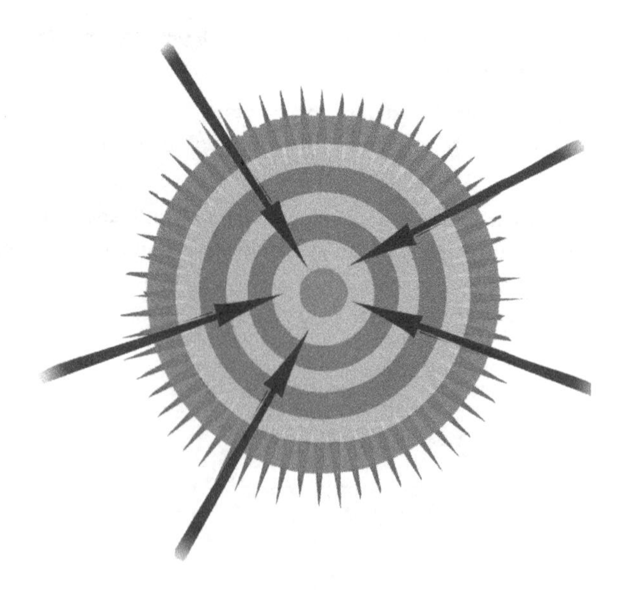

For more insights and information about strategy, please refer to the following: Chapter 4, "Know the Business: Think and Act Strategically," in *What Type of Leader Are You?* (McGraw-Hill, 2007).

STRATEGY DEVELOPMENT STRETCHES

Leaders and individual contributors must understand the actual business of their organizations and be able to think and act strategically in both big and small ways if their teams and organizations are to reach the highest levels of performance, effectiveness, and efficiency.

"Knowing the business" and "thinking and acting strategically" go hand in hand. Unless you know the business, you have no context for thinking and acting strategically. When you have this information, you need to be able to use it in a strategic way, working from a compelling and common vision, a customer-focused mission, a smart strategy, and effective goals and tactics aligned with that strategy.

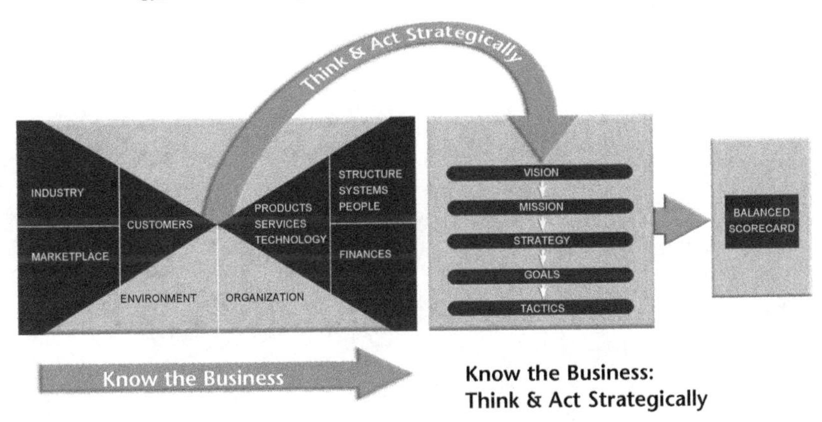

Know the Business: Think & Act Strategically

Challenge yourself to become an expert in all aspects of the business, particularly those not directly related to people.
A people orientation will always be your strength, so stretch your capabilities. Immerse yourself in the details of technology and undertake a thorough competitor analysis. Think about the impact of these on your business and share your analyses with bosses, peers, and employees.

Pay careful attention to finances.
Set the goal of knowing the financial aspects of the business. Once you have done this, ask yourself this question: *If I were going to take a conservative financial view of the key decisions I have made over the last year, would I make the same decisions?* Then think about the decisions facing you in the next three to six months and ask yourself these questions: *If I were to make these decisions from a primarily cost-effective perspective, what decisions would I make? How can I incorporate this fiscal perspective into my future decisions?*

For more insights and information about strategy, please refer to the following: Chapter 4, "Know the Business: Think and Act Strategically," in *What Type of Leader Are You?* (McGraw-Hill, 2007).

Make your strategic process explicit.

Write down your unit's or organization's vision so that it would be understandable to an intelligent 12-year-old. This will force you to make the vision statement clear and concise. Then, write down your team's mission, identifying your key customers and articulating the value you provide them. Next, write down the three to five key strategies that are the cornerstones for achieving the mission. Finally, write down three to five goals for each strategy and three to five tactics for each goal. All leaders need to provide this type of strategic process for their teams, and all team members need to be able to articulate the strategy with this level of clarity.

For more insights and information about decision making, please refer to the following: Chapter 7, "Make Optimal Decisions," in *What Type of Leader Are You?* (McGraw-Hill, 2007).

DECISION-MAKING DEVELOPMENT STRETCHES

We all make decisions on a daily basis, but we rarely think about the process by which we make them. The wisest decisions are made utilizing our heads (rational analysis and planning), our hearts (to examine values, feelings, and impact on people), and our guts (for taking action), with all three used in an integrated way. In addition, when you are making decisions at work, you need to consider three other factors: the organizational culture, the decision-making authority structure within the organization, and the context of the decision itself.

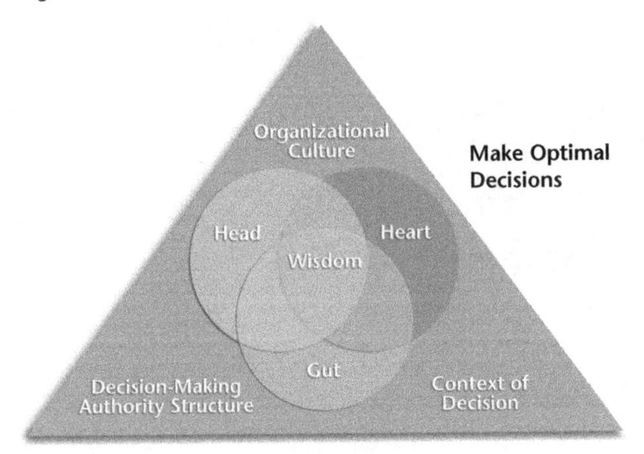

The following chart shows you how to develop each of your Centers of Intelligence (Head, Heart, and Gut) to assist you in making wise decisions.

Centers of Intelligence			
	Head Center	Heart Center	Body (Gut) Center
Activities for Twos That Develop Each Center	**Objective analysis** Do not let your personal feelings for other people bias your decisions; strive to be objective. **Astute insight** Base your decisions more on objective information than on perception. **Productive planning** Don't overplan when you're anxious or underplan when you're tired; don't overshedule yourself.	**Empathy** Examine your motivations for needing to know exactly what others are thinking and feeling. **Authentic relating** Be completely honest with others about your reasons for making a decision. **Compassion** Realize that offering too much compassion can make people unable to stand up for themselves.	**Taking effective action** Learn the art of timing so that you will know when to act, when to wait, and when to do nothing. **Steadfastness** Have the courage of your convictions so that you will neither back down nor become defensive when others disagree with your decisions. **Gut-knowing** Learn to trust your gut as much as your heart.

For more insights and information about organizational change, please refer to the following: Chapter 8, "Take Charge of Change," in *What Type of Leader Are You?* (McGraw-Hill, 2007).

ORGANIZATIONAL CHANGE DEVELOPMENT STRETCHES

In contemporary organizations, change has become a way of life. Companies exist in increasingly complex environments, with more competition, fewer resources, less time to market, higher customer expectations, increased regulation, more technology, and greater uncertainty. Organizations need to be flexible, innovative, cost-conscious, and responsive if they want to succeed. As a result, employees at all levels need to be able to embrace change and to function flexibly and effectively within their teams when an unforeseen direction must be taken.

Take Charge of Change

Manage your energy and stress levels.

When you first realize that you are overworking yourself or notice that you are chronically fatigued, stop. Get more rest, eat more healthfully, exercise more, and do something nice for yourself, preferably something that is not expensive. As a way of being nice to themselves, some Twos purchase items that are beyond their budgets, thus creating more stress.

Develop a more balanced approach to difficult issues.

When faced with extremely complex issues, you may feel more frustrated and emotional than usual. Examine why this is so — for example, it may relate to your sense that you are responsible for everyone and everything or that others are not supporting your efforts despite your consistent support of their endeavors. It can be difficult to acknowledge such beliefs, but once you do, it can be extremely freeing.

Develop the work in such a way that others can execute tasks without your guidance.

Without intending to do so, you may be making other people dependent on you. While this may make you feel needed and involved, people may begin to feel unable to perform a task without your direct participation. You can help people the most by allowing them to be independent.

For more insights and information about personal transformation, please refer to the following: Chapter 7, "Transforming Yourself," in *Bringing Out the Best in Yourself at Work* (McGraw-Hill, 2004).

TRANSFORMATION DEVELOPMENT STRETCHES

In order to move from *wanting so intently to be liked, trying to meet the needs of others, and attempting to orchestrate the people and events in their lives* to the understanding that *there is a profound purpose to everything that occurs that is completely separate from anything they try to do,* Twos can work toward these transformations:

Mental Transformation

Transform the mental pattern of **flattery** (the gaining of acceptance through thinking about how to give compliments or other forms of attention to others) *into the higher belief of* **free will** (the insight that acknowledging oneself and one's own needs leads to autonomy and freedom).

Mental Activity

When you realize you are complimenting someone frequently and/or giving him or her more continuous attention and focus than you truly want to give, think about one or more times when you were truly in tune with and able to acknowledge your own needs both to yourself and others. Recall those times and relive what was occurring within you. Pay particular attention to what you needed and how you expressed those needs, and also to any feelings of independence and liberation you experienced.

Emotional Transformation

Transform the emotional habit of **pride** (the inflation of self-esteem and self-importance derived from doing for and being needed by others and the deflation of esteem when this does not occur) *into the higher awareness of* **humility** (the feeling of self-acceptance and self-appreciation without either self-inflation, self-deflation, or deference to the opinions of others).

Emotional Activity

When you become aware of feeling prideful — feeling either elated about what you have done for others and how important you have become to a cause or a group, or feeling deflated because you were not appreciated enough or all of your efforts did not come to fruition — remember one or more times in your life where you experienced true humility. Humility is not the same as self-effacement or self-deprecation; it is more akin to having a modest and realistic appreciation and valuation of yourself without inflating your self-image because of your "good works," and without basing your self-worth on the opinions and reactions of others. Maintain your feeling of true humility, and carry it with you as you think about and interact with others.

For more insights and information about personal transformation, please refer to the following: Chapter 7, "Transforming Yourself," in *Bringing Out the Best in Yourself at Work* (McGraw-Hill, 2004).

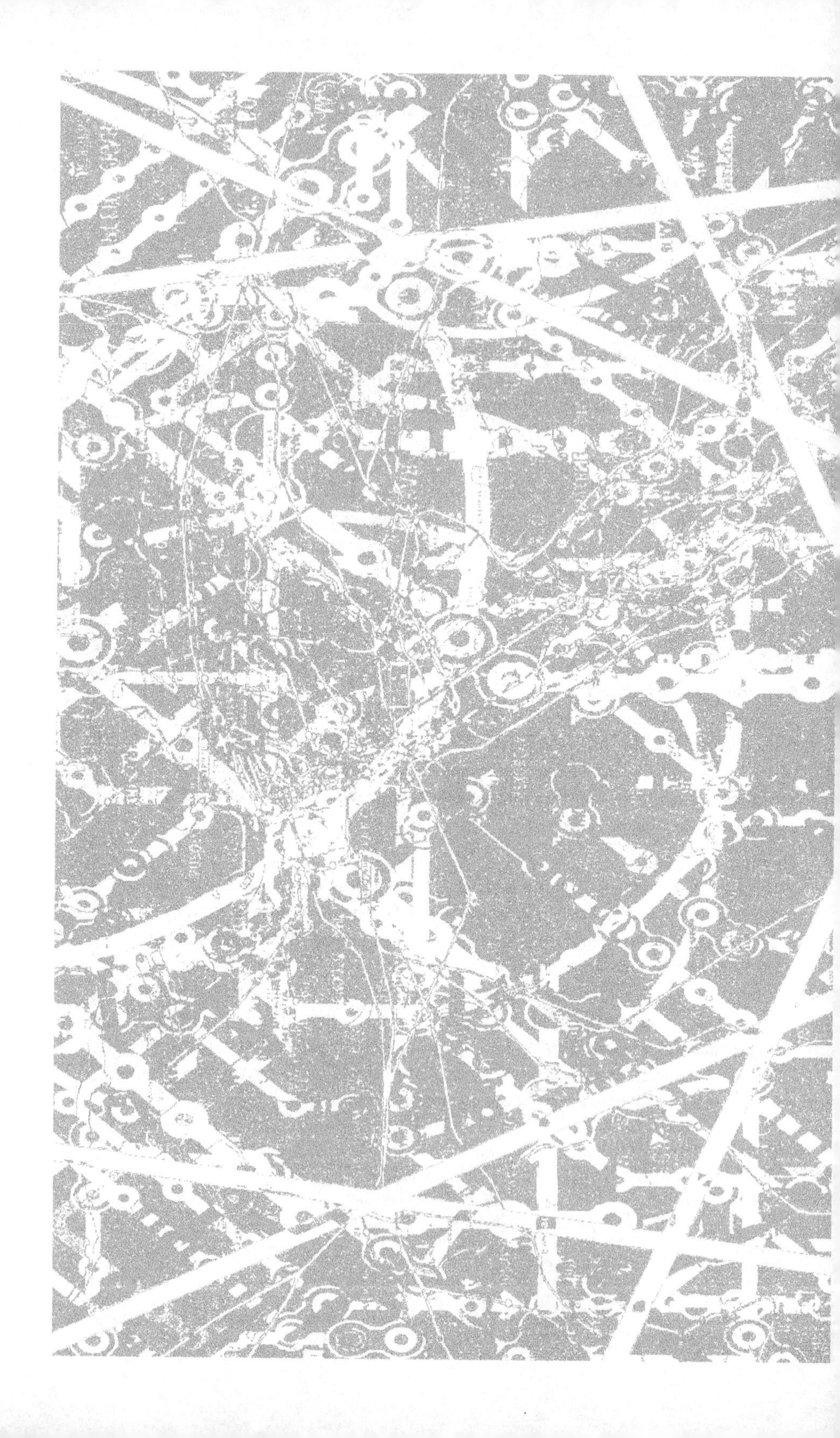

ENNEAGRAM STYLE THREE

ENNEAGRAM THREES

The search for success and the avoidance of failure

High energy, confident, and achievement oriented, Enneagram Threes focus on results they believe will bring them the respect of others and on efficient and effective plans for accomplishing these goals. As a result, they create a persona of confidence and success, but often at the expense of being completely genuine. They lose touch with their deeper feelings and sense of who they really are, confusing their "public" image with their real selves.

Although all Threes share a success orientation and constant need to have goals and plans, there are also differences among them. Some Threes are highly self-reliant, strive to be the model of a "good" person, and create an image of being authentic/having no image; other Threes create an image of being high status, having prestige, and being important as a result of their ability to perform and their credentials, position, and high-influence friends; and some Threes focus more on creating an image of being extremely attractive in a highly masculine or feminine way, having less need for visibility and a greater desire to support the success of important people in their lives.

The Three's interpersonal style is one of having strong, deliberate, and confident stage presence. They convey their ideas in a well-conceived and highly self-assured way, have strong social skills except when they are stressed — at which times they can be cold and abrupt — and often appear as if they were born to give public presentations.

While we can all be results-oriented and have difficulty differentiating between what we do or how we try to appear and who we really are, for Threes, the search for success and the avoidance of failure is their primary, persistent, and driving motivation.

DEVELOPMENT STRETCHES FOR THREES

INDIVIDUALS WHO ORGANIZE THEIR LIVES AROUND ACHIEVING SPECIFIC GOALS IN ORDER TO APPEAR SUCCESSFUL AND TO GAIN THE RESPECT AND ADMIRATION OF OTHERS

CONTENTS

SELF-MASTERY DEVELOPMENT STRETCHES

Self-Mastery — the ability to understand, accept, and transform your thoughts, feelings, and behavior, with the understanding that each day will bring new challenges that are opportunities for growth — is the foundation of all personal and professional development. Self-mastery begins with self-awareness, then expands to include the elements shown in the following graphic:

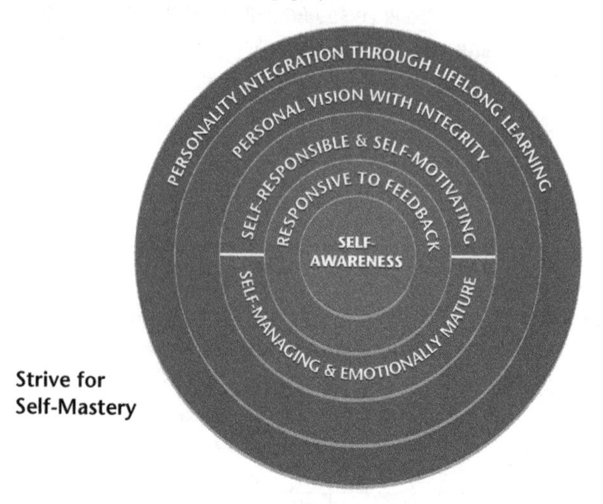

Strive for Self-Mastery

In this section on self-mastery, you will find the following:

- Three common issues for Threes related to self-mastery
- Three development stretches for working with the core issues of your Enneagram style, including one basic activity and one deeper activity for each stretch
- Three development stretches for working with your wings and arrow (stress-security) styles

Common Issues for Threes Related to Self-Mastery

Deeply exploring your inner thoughts, feelings, and experiences in order to become more genuine	Going more with the flow of events and experiences and being less driven to continuously try to make things happen	Learning the difference between *doing* and *being*, and appreciating yourself for who you are rather than for what you do

For more insights and information about self-mastery, please refer to the following: Chapter 7, "Transforming Yourself," in *Bringing Out the Best in Yourself at Work* (McGraw-Hill, 2004) and Chapter 3, "Strive for Self-Mastery," in *What Type of Leader Are You?* (McGraw-Hill, 2007).

Development Stretches for Working with the Core Issues of Your Enneagram Style

Take the time to get to know yourself.

Basic Activity

Make a commitment to spend at least 30 minutes each day just "being." This means not working or doing any activities in which you focus on something external (such as watching a film or going shopping). If you don't quite understand the idea of "being," ask three people who are very different from you what this concept means to them, and how they go about simply being. Experiment with some of the ideas they suggest.

Deeper Activity

It is important for Threes to regularly spend time with absolutely nothing on their agendas. There are several ways to do this — for example, spend 15 minutes a day or an hour a week with nothing on your schedule except being by yourself with no work, no interruptions (such as telephones or pagers), and no distractions (such as television). This time by yourself should be time to think about who you are, what you like and dislike, and what you most value.

Alternatively, you can use meditative techniques to help you stay focused on the present moment instead of thinking about what you have to do. Meditation calms the mind and body and settles the emotions. These practical guidelines can get you started. Find a quiet, private location and sit upright in a chair, on a couch, or on the floor for 15 minutes or more. With your eyes closed, focus on one item from the following list — your breath going in, down, up, and then out; numbers, starting from one and moving upward; or a simple image in your mind such as a lit candle, the sun, a white light, or some similar object.

You will find that it is almost impossible during this 15-minute period to stay focused on only what you have chosen. The goal, however, is just to notice when your attention shifts to other thoughts, feelings, bodily sensations, or noises in the environment, and then to simply shift your attention back to your intended focus.

If you need something more active to do instead of or in addition to the above activities, take a ten-minute walk each day during which you focus only on your physical experience. You might, for example, take inventory of your body as you walk: begin with your head, noting, such physical sensations as the level of clarity or congestion, the feeling of the wind on your face, the degree of tension or relaxation in your face, and so on. Move down through the neck to your shoulders. Threes often hold a great deal of tension in their shoulders, so it can be very helpful to consciously drop and relax your shoulders. Continue down your body and eventually focus on your feet, including the sensation of your feet touching the ground as you walk.

For more insights and information about self-mastery, please refer to the following: Chapter 7, "Transforming Yourself," in *Bringing Out the Best in Yourself at Work* (McGraw-Hill, 2004) and Chapter 3, "Strive for Self-Mastery," in *What Type of Leader Are You?* (McGraw-Hill, 2007).

Learn to avoid overidentifying with your work.

Basic Activity

Make a list of answers to this question: *Who am I?* Now place a check mark next to all the items that reflect roles you play, such as spouse, worker, and family member. How many items on your list are not roles? Now answer this question: *If I am not the roles I play, then who am I?* Keep adding to this list on a daily basis, and commit to appreciating that who you are is far more than just the roles you play.

Deeper Activity

Most Threes believe the following statement: "I am what I do and accomplish," and this belief causes them to overidentify with their work. When individuals overidentify with anything, whether work or another of life's roles, they tend to believe that this is who they really are. Overidentifying with only one aspect of ourselves limits us as human beings. In reality, people possess multiple facets, such as roles, attributes, behaviors, interests, talents, thoughts, feelings, physical characteristics, skills, and values as well as accomplishments.

The following activity can help Threes understand and overcome an overidentification with work. Make a precise list of at least 20 ways in which you identify with work — for example, how many hours a week you work, how much work you bring home nightly, and how you schedule yourself in general. Then, write down as many answers as you can think of to this question: *If I am not my work, then who am I?* Finally, ponder the next two questions for ten minutes every day: *Who am I, really? If I were valued for something other than my work accomplishments, what would that be?*

Acknowledge your weaknesses.

Basic Activity

When you are feeling concerned, anxious, or sad, can you admit this to someone else? Can you admit to and discuss your mistakes or failures? If your answer is yes, then practice doing this even more. If your answer is no, then seriously consider what *in you* keeps you from doing this. Imagine how you would feel if you could allow yourself to acknowledge and share more of your weaknesses. Commit to discussing at least one of your weaknesses or areas of anxiety with one new person each day.

For more insights and information about self-mastery, please refer to the following: Chapter 7, "Transforming Yourself," in *Bringing Out the Best in Yourself at Work* (McGraw-Hill, 2004) and Chapter 3, "Strive for Self-Mastery," in *What Type of Leader Are You?* (McGraw-Hill, 2007).

Deeper Activity

All of us have weaknesses, and Threes are no exception. Threes, however, are often more reluctant to reveal their flaws or Achilles' heels, even to themselves. The crux of the issue for Threes lies in the belief that they are valued only when they are seen as competent and successful. Because of this, they have learned to mask or otherwise hide their shortcomings.

The following activity can help with this issue. Make two long lists, heading them "Things I am good at" and "Things I am not good at." Discuss one item from the second list with at least one other person (and do so within the week). At first you may feel uncomfortable, but it gets easier with practice. You are also likely to have the opposite experience from what you might expect: rather than finding that people value you less because you're discussing your flaws, they will probably value you more because they will perceive you as more human and sincere. You may also find that your relationships with others become closer; interpersonal relationships usually grow when one or both parties reveal personal information to one another.

Feel free to add to these lists as you proceed. For the next three weeks, continue to share items from the second list with a new person each week and ask for reactions. Once you have done this, make a commitment to share one thing each day with someone else that suggests a flaw, weakness, or shortcoming you may have — for example, a statement such as *That's not my greatest strength* or *I wish I could be better at that.*

Development Stretches for Working with Your Wings and Arrow (Stress-Security) Styles

Wings are the Enneagram styles on either side of your core Enneagram style; arrow, or stress-security, styles are Enneagram styles shown with arrows pointing away or toward your core Enneagram style. Your wings and arrow styles don't change your core Enneagram style, but instead offer qualities that can broaden and enrich your patterns of thinking and feeling as well as enhance your behaviors. Your wings and arrow styles make you more complex and versatile because they provide more dimensions to your personality and serve as vehicles for self-development.

Integrate Your Two Wing

Motivate others.

Twos tend to focus on what will help and motivate others, whereas Threes focus more on what helps achieve goals and what helps themselves. When you approach a project or task, remind yourself again and again that it is crucial to enlist other people early on in the work. Ask yourself: *Who needs to be enlisted? What will motivate them to participate? What is the best approach to use with them? How can I help them to be successful and satisfied with the experience?*

2 3 4 WINGS FOR THREES

Dedicate yourself to the success of others.

Twos often take pleasure in assisting others to be successful, while Threes more often prefer to be the star attraction. Threes can ask their coworkers or those who work for them this question: *What can I do for you to help you be really successful?* In addition, Threes can purposely not take credit for work by spreading praise. For example, a Three can make a conscious effort to praise individuals and groups in front of interested bystanders. In addition, when Threes receive commendations, they can say, "Oh, but the real credit goes to [the team or to another person]."

Show more personal warmth and empathy.

Twos often display a great deal of empathy, while Threes can appear to others as more driven and less compassionate. When conversing with someone, ask yourself: *What are the various feelings this person might have?* When someone discusses a difficult or emotional situation with you, paraphrase what you hear, placing particular emphasis on the deeper feelings implicit in what the other person says. For example, if a person discusses an experience in which he or she was put down in public, you could say, "That person shouldn't have done that." While this is a supportive comment, it does not specifically address the person's feelings. A better response is this: "That must have felt horrible. You must be furious."

For more insights and information about integrating your wings and/or arrow styles (stress-security points), please refer to the following: Chapter 1, "What Type Are You?" and the conclusion, "Stretch Your Leadership Paradigms," in *What Type of Leader Are You?* (McGraw-Hill, 2007).

Integrate Your Four Wing

Show your emotions.

Fours tend to be visibly emotional, while Threes often come across as cool or more neutral. Tell stories about yourself to others, but make these stories not so much about your achievements as about events that have really mattered to you. Convey not only events, but also the feelings you had about them. For example, where you might normally say, "I got a promotion yesterday," you could say, "I'm so happy today — I got a promotion I really wanted. I can hardly believe it!"

Tap your creativity.

Fours tend to express their deep feelings and experiences through a variety of different art forms, while Threes generally keep their deeper feelings, if they are even aware of them, to themselves. Artistic expression involves experimentation and risk. Push yourself to try new avenues of expression, even if at first you are not very good at them. Over time, you will become more proficient, and even if you never become a Picasso or a Mozart, you may enjoy yourself and find an outlet for self-expression. Pick an artistic medium that you like, such as writing, painting, sculpture, dance, photography, or other avenues of expression. If nothing in particular appeals to you, just go to a local art store and select something that intrigues you. If you don't want to do that, take a class in an artistic field that seems interesting to you.

Every artist begins with a blank page, so simply start doing something. Begin writing, drawing, or taking photographs. After you become more comfortable with a particular artistic medium, you can pick a theme such as flowers, beauty, challenge, suffering, irony, generations, and so on. Find some way to express that theme. Try alternative ways to demonstrate that idea. Remember that you are doing this for yourself, not so that others can evaluate whether or not what you have done is good enough. Enjoy the process, and if the product also pleases you, that is merely a bonus!

For more insights and information about integrating your wings and/or arrow styles (stress-security points), please refer to the following: Chapter 1, "What Type Are You?" and the conclusion, "Stretch Your Leadership Paradigms," in *What Type of Leader Are You?* (McGraw-Hill, 2007).

Become a visionary.

Fours can be visionaries, whereas Threes tend to focus more on concrete goals. The ability to create compelling visions has been shown to be one of the most significant ways that leaders both enlist and align their followers to collectively create greatness in organizations. Visions convey direction at a higher level than goals and usually include purpose, values, and the meaning or rationale behind the overall direction. Goals are strategic objectives that are more tactical, tangible, and measurable. For example, Gandhi's vision might be stated as "the creation of a free and independent Indian state," whereas Gandhi had a goal that each person in India would be capable of making cloth — a goal that would free India of its dependence on British textiles.

Here are some ways that Threes can learn to create compelling visions:

1. For each goal and series of goals you want to accomplish, examine closely why you believe that goal or series of goals is important. When you communicate, emphasize the reason why the goals are important three times more than you emphasize the goals themselves.

2. Articulate the three to five core values that should drive people's actions. Include why these values are so important.

3. Learn to tell stories that teach an important message. Stories are a powerful way of enlisting others and are often remembered more than ideas alone. For example, an idea is this: Customer service is important. A comparable story is this: *I often travel for business and stay at a variety of hotels. There is one hotel, however, that I will go to great lengths to stay at. On my third stay, upon check-in, the reservationist acknowledged me by name before I reached the counter, the bellman said 'Welcome back,' and there was a basket of fruit waiting for me in my room. This hotel's service and courtesy only get better every time I stay there."*

For more insights and information about integrating your wings and/or arrow styles (stress-security points), please refer to the following: Chapter 1, "What Type Are You?" and the conclusion, "Stretch Your Leadership Paradigms," in *What Type of Leader Are You?* (McGraw-Hill, 2007).

Integrate Arrow Style Nine (Stress Point)

Learn the power of collaboration.

Threes value the contributions of others, but they listen primarily to those individuals who have demonstrated the ability to perform well. Although Nines do notice individual differences in performance levels, they also have a deep appreciation for the group harmony that grows out of collaboration and consensus. When Threes start to adopt some of the behaviors more typical of Nines, they often see such positive gains that they learn the power of collaboration. Threes can try the following: (1) spend three times more time getting to know your coworkers and teammates than you would normally do; (2) practice humility daily by behaving as if everyone with whom you interact has a contribution to make; (3) pay close attention to what others do and say; (4) mention something to each person with whom you interact that acknowledges or shows interest in them; (5) instead of giving your ideas and opinions early in a conversation, wait until everyone else has spoken; and (6) when a decision needs to be made, ask for a consensus decision by saying "Let's look at the alternatives and come up with a decision that we can all support."

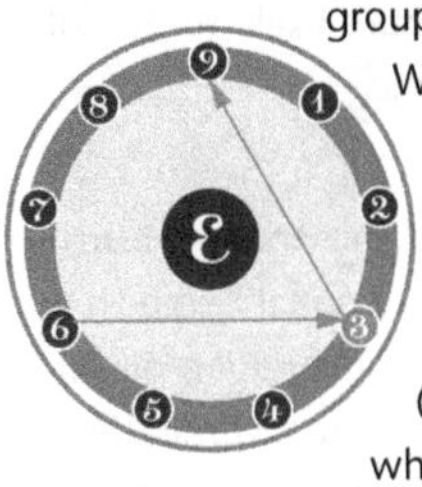

Learn to relax.

Threes are usually doers; truly relaxing by simply being does not come easily. Even when Threes go on vacation, they often plan the days in such detail that the vacation, while enjoyable, may not be truly relaxing. As a Three, you can learn from Nines, who really enjoy their leisure, by doing the following things: (1) getting plenty of sleep; (2) taking a vacation where the only advance planning involves the place, the mode of transportation, and the hotel; (3) treating yourself to a weekly massage; and (4) interrupting a project to take a half hour off to do something pleasurable and spontaneous. This last idea may be the most difficult, but if you can do it, it will show you that you can truly change a fundamental behavior.

Threes can also learn to relax by tuning into the natural flow of life, as Nines do. Contrast this with the Three's tendency to structure most activities. Become aware of when you are structuring something or developing a plan, and say this to yourself: *STOP. There I go, planning for something to happen. Let me just see what happens for the next 15 minutes if I don't plan.* In addition, ask yourself: *What word is the opposite of the word "doing"?* You may draw a blank, or your answer may be a word such as "being" or "allowing." Take the word that comes to you or use the word "being" and ask yourself: *How would I behave differently if I let this word guide far more of my daily behavior?*

For more insights and information about integrating your wings and/or arrow styles (stress-security points), please refer to the following: Chapter 1, "What Type Are You?" and the conclusion, "Stretch Your Leadership Paradigms," in *What Type of Leader Are You?* (McGraw-Hill, 2007).

Learn genuine humility.

Because Threes believe they must come across as confident and competent at all times, learning to become truly humble can be enlightening for them. Nines are often genuinely humble, believing that everyone is equally valuable, and they do not focus on status or accomplishments as the main determinant of someone's worth. Nines rarely come across as arrogant or conceited; they are more likely to be self-effacing, preferring not to draw too much attention to themselves.

By contrast, Threes can be perceived as having too high an opinion of themselves and sometimes as being prone to bragging about their accomplishments. To learn true humility, as a Three you can do several things: (1) notice when you begin to talk about what you have done or are about to do, and refocus the conversation on other people; (2) when you begin to feel excited about what you have just accomplished or feel uncomfortable because some of your efforts are not yielding the success you desire, tell yourself this: *My worth as a human being is not based on what I do, and neither is anyone else's;* and (3) spend time in the company of people you would not normally perceive as successful. Get to know them as people and try to discover what is special or unique about them aside from anything they may have accomplished. Focus on them instead purely as human beings.

Integrate Arrow Style Six (Security Point)

Put the team first.

At work, Threes usually stress the importance of results through individual performance. Sixes tend to emphasize the importance of teams and team performance. While Threes do appreciate teams and Sixes also strive for results, they place dramatically different emphases on these. You can learn to place a far greater value on teamwork and to create more effective teams by doing the following: (1) find a reason to value each team member and communicate this to that person; (2) refrain from making negative comments about team members to others; (3) promote other team members to your coworkers and bosses; and (4) defend other team members to those outside the team when needed.

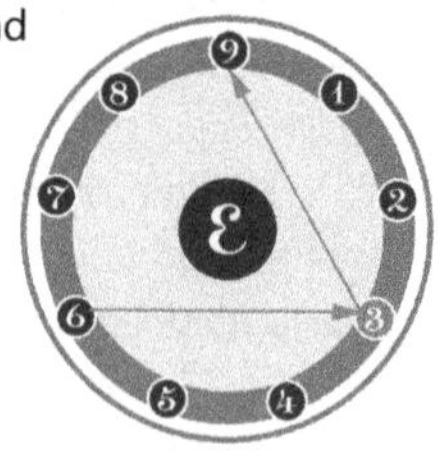

For more insights and information about integrating your wings and/or arrow styles (stress-security points), please refer to the following: Chapter 1, "What Type Are You?" and the conclusion, "Stretch Your Leadership Paradigms," in *What Type of Leader Are You?* (McGraw-Hill, 2007).

Push yourself to be completely honest.

Threes usually believe they are honest, but it is important for you to look at the notion of honesty in a new way. Threes often think of honesty as saying what is on their minds. Honesty and truth telling, however, involve the capacity to be totally honest with oneself and the willingness to be completely forthcoming with others. These comments should not be taken to mean that Threes are dishonest or that they even purposely lie; individuals of all nine Enneagram styles are capable of bending or not telling the truth. The issue for Threes is their tendency to shape information about themselves or their circumstances in a way that removes or deemphasizes the negative and accentuates the positive. This process of shaping a positive image tends to be more automatic than conscious. For example, a Three who is not selected for a promotion may say nothing about having even applied for the position. If others do know that the Three was not given the job, the Three may offer a rationale suggesting that the decision had nothing to do with his or her own capability.

Sixes, on the other hand, tend to be more forthcoming about their feelings and thoughts as well as more realistic about their strengths and weaknesses. The following activities can help Threes to become more forthcoming: (1) Spend time three times each day — morning, noon, and night — to ask yourself: *How do I really feel? What do I truly think?* (2) when you are unsuccessful at something, admit to yourself that you were not able to accomplish it and tell someone your real feelings about the situation; and (3) when you feel anxious before an event, admit your uncertainty to someone.

Honor your insights.

Sixes spend a great deal of time honing their perceptions and analyzing situations they encounter. Because of this, they often develop incisive and insightful minds. By contrast, Threes are usually so busy driving for action that they don't pay as much attention to their inner wisdom and insights. The easiest way for Threes to hone their insights is to structure time several times each day solely for self-reflection. The best time to do this is directly after an event or interaction has occurred. At these times, spend five minutes doing nothing but thinking, feeling, and reflecting. Ask yourself these questions: *What just happened here? How satisfied or dissatisfied do I feel about what just occurred? What was occurring at the most obvious level? What was occurring at several more levels of depth?*

It can be helpful to discuss your insights with someone else whom you believe is perceptive. In the discussion, you are likely to generate new insights you actually had but were unaware of until the conversation took place. The other person may also offer some valuable perspectives from which you can learn.

For more insights and information about integrating your wings and/or arrow styles (stress-security points), please refer to the following: Chapter 1, "What Type Are You?" and the conclusion, "Stretch Your Leadership Paradigms," in *What Type of Leader Are You?* (McGraw-Hill, 2007).

COMMUNICATION DEVELOPMENT STRETCHES

When you communicate with someone, three kinds of unintentional distortions may be present: speaking style, body language, and blind spots. *Speaking style* refers to your overall pattern of speaking. *Body language* includes posture, facial expressions, hand gestures, body movements, energy levels, and hundreds of other nonverbal messages. *Blind spots* are elements of your communication containing information about you that is not apparent to you but is highly visible to other people. We all unknowingly convey information through an amalgam of our speaking style, body language, and other inferential data.

The receivers of the messages you send also distort what they hear through their *distorting filters*. These are unconscious concerns or assumptions, often based on the listener's Enneagram style, that alter how someone hears what others say.

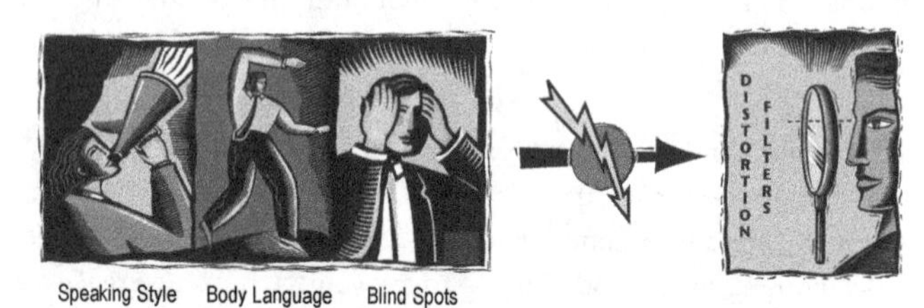

Change one communication style behavior at a time.

It is most effective to work on changing one behavior at a time, preferably in the following sequence: speaking style, body language, blind spots, and listening distorting filters. It is easiest to change the behaviors of which we are most aware, and this sequence represents the most common order of awareness, from most to least aware.

Threes: Speaking style

- Clear, efficient, logical, and well conceived
- Quick on their feet
- Avoid topics in which they have limited information
- Avoid topics that reflect negatively on them
- Use concrete examples
- Impatient with lengthy conversations

Threes: Body language

- Look put together
- Appear confident
- Breathe deeply into upper chest area
- Keep shoulders high
- Actions may appear staged for effect
- Look around regularly to check the reactions of others
- Let others know when their time is up

For more insights and information about communication, please refer to the following: Chapter 2, "Communicating Effectively," in *Bringing Out the Best in Yourself at Work* (McGraw-Hill, 2004) and Chapter 5, "Become an Excellent Communicator," in *What Type of Leader Are You?* (McGraw-Hill, 2007).

Threes: Blind spots

- Impatient when they perceive others as not capable
- Avoid discussing their own failings
- Appear driven
- Seem to rush or dismiss others
- May appear abrupt or insincere

Threes: Distorting filters when listening to someone else

- Whether the information will make them look good
- Whether the information will interfere with their goal achievement
- The apparent confidence and competence of the other person

Note: Some of the above characteristics may be positive, some negative, and some neutral or mixed. They are intended as an overview to allow you to select from among them.

Use e-mails to expand and adjust your language patterns.

- Review your e-mails before you send them for language and tone.
- Refer less often (both directly and implicitly) to your own actions and achievements.
- Use language that focuses more on the other people involved and less on yourself.
- Neither inflate nor understate the importance of your performance and actions when these are relevant to the communication.
- Use language that invites a response from the e-mail recipient.

For more insights and information about communication, please refer to the following: Chapter 2, "Communicating Effectively," in *Bringing Out the Best in Yourself at Work* (McGraw-Hill, 2004) and Chapter 5, "Become an Excellent Communicator," in *What Type of Leader Are You?* (McGraw-Hill, 2007).

FEEDBACK DEVELOPMENT STRETCHES

Honest, positive, and constructive *feedback* — direct, objective, simple, and respectful observations that one person makes about another's behavior — improves both relationships and on-the-job performance. When you offer feedback, the Feedback Formula, combined with the insights of the Enneagram, helps you tailor your delivery. When someone gives you feedback, the more receptive you are to hearing what is being said, the more likely it is that you will be able to discern what is useful and utilize what has been suggested.

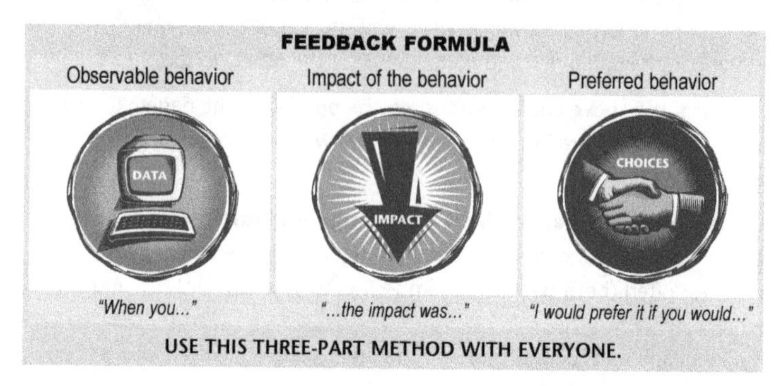

How Threes Can Enhance Their Ability to Deliver Feedback Effectively

When you offer feedback to someone, you want to be prepared and also to encourage the feedback recipient to be as receptive as possible. Remember that how and when you deliver feedback is just as important as what you actually say.

Use the three components of the **Feedback Formula** together with the following suggestions to plan and deliver the feedback.

- Maintain your focus, but also allow room for feelings, particularly those of the other person.
- Be clear and honest, and remember to be gentle.
- Stay focused on the desired result rather than using many small examples, which may derail your main point.
- Remember that other people may not drive themselves as hard as you drive yourself, and they may not identify with work as completely as you do, but this does not mean they do not value achievement or want to improve.

For more insights and information about feedback, please refer to the following: Chapter 3, "Giving Constructive Feedback," in *Bringing Out the Best in Yourself at Work* (McGraw-Hill, 2004) and Chapter 5, "Become an Excellent Communicator," in *What Type of Leader Are You?* (McGraw-Hill, 2007).

How Threes Can Be More Receptive When They Receive Feedback

- When someone gives you negative feedback, it may raise your concerns that you are failing in some way or that the other person has a negative impression of you. Instead of reacting in a defensive manner, remember that you yourself can hold someone in high regard and still have some constructive feedback to offer that person. If you can do this, so can others. In addition, remember that one item of negative feedback is not failure; it's simply one piece of information someone is offering you.
- Be as open to positive and negative feedback from people with whom you don't have a strong relationship or don't hold in high esteem as you are with individuals whom you know well and respect. Everyone has something to offer, and those who know us least well often have more objective information to share.
- Call forth all the patience you have when you receive any type of feedback. Sometimes the most useful information comes in the later parts of the discussion.

For more insights and information about feedback, please refer to the following: Chapter 3, "Giving Constructive Feedback," in *Bringing Out the Best in Yourself at Work* (McGraw-Hill, 2004) and Chapter 5, "Become an Excellent Communicator," in *What Type of Leader Are You?* (McGraw-Hill, 2007).

CONFLICT DEVELOPMENT STRETCHES

Relationships both at work and at home often involve some degree of conflict, which may be caused by a variety of factors and usually follows the pinch-crunch cycle below:

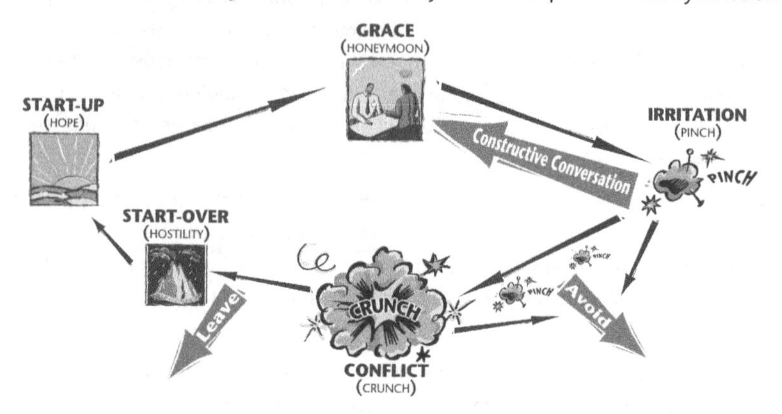

Whatever the root cause of the conflict, the Enneagram styles of the key parties involved will always be a factor in the conflict dynamics and resolution. The Enneagram enables each individual involved to make conflict resolution a constructive rather than destructive experience. The more people know themselves, understand their own responsibilities in the conflict interaction, engage in constructive self-management, and know how best to approach others through knowledge of the Enneagram, the greater the chances of a swift and effective outcome.

There are specific pinches (anger triggers) for each Enneagram style — that is, certain situations that will invariably ignite anger in a person of one style, yet may not affect someone of a different style. For Threes, these pinches include:

Being put in a position of likely failure · Not looking good professionally · Being blamed for the poor work of others · Not receiving credit for their work

Development Stretches for Transforming Anger into an Opportunity for Growth

Share your likely pinches (anger triggers) with others at the beginning of your working relationship.

At the beginning of a working relationship, engage the other person in a conversation about how you can both contribute to an effective and successful relationship. A helpful way to begin is to make an opening statement such as this: "Because we're just starting to work together, it would be really helpful for me to know about your preferred style of working with others, especially your likes and dislikes. That way, I can adjust my behavior accordingly when possible. I'd also like to share my preferences with you."

For more insights and information about conflict, please refer to the following: Chapter 4, "Managing Conflict," in *Bringing Out the Best in Yourself at Work* (McGraw-Hill, 2004) and Chapter 5, "Become an Excellent Communicator," in *What Type of Leader Are You?* (McGraw-Hill, 2007).

When it is your turn to share pinches, you might say, for example, "I work best with people who are highly capable and responsible. What I mean by this is that the individuals are highly skilled and work constantly to improve their performance and achieve high-quality results. I personally believe that what each of us accomplishes reflects positively or negatively on all of us. I dislike work situations in which I'm killing myself to get the job done, and when I look around, I see others not putting in nearly the same effort."

Say something as soon as you are aware of feeling pinched or upset.
As busy as a Three may be and as difficult as it may feel to discuss a pinch with someone, it is well worth the time. In fact, it will take less time and require less ongoing attention if pinches are discussed soon after they occur. A kind and straightforward introduction such as, "Do you have a minute to talk about a minor event that happened?" usually paves the way for a fruitful discussion.

When you start to behave in ways that indicate you are feeling pinched or distressed, do something physical if you can, such as working out or taking a walk.
Physical activity has a major benefit for Threes, as their focus on work ceases momentarily. However, to take full advantage of this "time-out" moment, try to engage in a physical activity that allows some time for self-reflection, such as walking, hiking, or yoga. Threes may be tempted to engage in highly competitive physical sports, such as tennis or basketball, but these sports may be so absorbing that there is little time left for feelings to emerge. Strenuous sports may also release so much of the anger that Threes no longer feel any need to deal with the issues. This may feel like a relief in the moment, but it does not really resolve the situation or give you the opportunity to take a look at yourself.

When you have a negative reaction and feel a pinch, ask yourself: *What does my reaction to this situation or to the other person's behavior say about me as a Three and about the areas in which I can develop? How can working on my pinches and crunches help me to bring out the best in myself?*
As a Three, it can be helpful to consider how the other person's behavior relates to your ability to succeed or fail; this issue is often the basis of a Three's negative reaction to others. Some related areas to examine include looking bad in front of others, feeling competitive with someone else, appearing less than fully competent, and disliking others who appear to be failures in some way (e.g., people whose projects haven't succeeded, whose appearances do not look put together, or whose personal styles do not exude confidence). Questions for Threes to ask themselves include these: *What is it about appearing to be successful that is so important to me? If this were not my ongoing intention, how would I be different, and how would my thoughts, feelings, and behavior change? What would happen if I were not so focused on impressing other people?*

For more insights and information about conflict, please refer to the following: Chapter 4, "Managing Conflict," in *Bringing Out the Best in Yourself at Work* (McGraw-Hill, 2004) and Chapter 5, "Become an Excellent Communicator," in *What Type of Leader Are You?* (McGraw-Hill, 2007).

TEAM DEVELOPMENT STRETCHES

There is a difference between a group and a team. A *group* is a collection of individuals who have something in common; a *team* is a specific type of group, one composed of members who share one or more *goals* that can be reached only when there is an optimal level of *interdependence* between and among team members.

Team members also have *roles* — predictable patterns of behavior – within the team that are often related to their Enneagram styles. *Task roles* involve behaviors directed toward the work itself; *relationship roles* involve behaviors focused on feelings, relationships, and team processes, such as decision making and conflict resolution.

In addition, teams have unique yet predictable dynamics as they go through the four sequential stages of team development: *forming, storming, norming,* and *performing.* At each stage, there are questions the team must resolve before moving to the next stage.

TEAM STAGE	QUESTIONS
FORMING	*Who are we, where are we going, and are we all going there together?*
STORMING	*Can we disagree with one another in a constructive and productive way?*
NORMING	*How should we best organize ourselves and work together?*
PERFORMING	*How can we keep performing at a high level and not burn out?*

Threes: Development Stretches for Team Members and Team Leaders

Team Goals

Although you may prefer team goals that are *extremely precise and measurable* and *most likely favor individual goals over team goals*, other team members may need team goals that are more purposeful and visionary. In addition, most teams function best when the team's goals are as highly emphasized as the individual goals. Allow yourself to be focused on the values and meaning of the team's goals and also to emphasize team-oriented goals as much or more than individual goals.

Team Interdependence

You may prefer to work in teams with *clear lines of interdependence that are appropriate to the task* and where all team members are highly focused and capable. Remind yourself, however, that too much clarity or responsibility can interfere with creativity and the development of new products and services, and that too much focus can burn people out and interfere with a team's ability to be flexible and responsive. Work to support the level of interdependence the team needs and to develop a more open and responsive attitude toward all team members, even those whom you believe are not as capable as you would like.

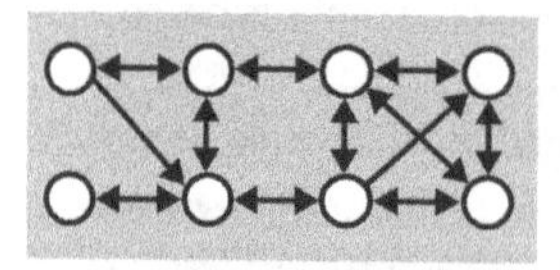

For more insights and information about teams, please refer to the following: Chapter 5, "Creating High-Performing Teams," in *Bringing Out the Best in Yourself at Work* (McGraw-Hill, 2004) and Chapter 6, "Lead High-Performing Teams," in *What Type of Leader Are You?* (McGraw-Hill, 2007).

Team Roles

Your typical task-related team role is likely to involve *defining goals and tracking tasks* for the team by helping articulate and clarify the team's concrete goals and deliverables, and by demonstrating your knowledge of how the team is progressing with regard to the work as well as what needs to be done to move the task forward. Your likely relationship-related team role may be *facilitating the team to move the process ahead* by summarizing, synthesizing, probing, charting, and other behaviors designed to help the team make progress. Stretch yourself to go beyond these typical roles and adopt the following additional team task and relationship roles:

Task Roles

New task role

Managing the agenda for the team, commenting and influencing (but not controlling) whether the important items are on the agenda, how the team is working through the agenda, and how the items are prioritized

Relationship Roles

New relationship role

Encouraging participation by verbally and nonverbally soliciting everyone's opinion and perspective

Team Dynamics

During the four stages of team development — *forming, storming, norming,* and *performing* — experiment with expanding your repertoire of behavior in the following ways:

FORMING	STORMING	NORMING	PERFORMING
Focus less on how others are responding to you and more on how effectively the team is developing, in terms of both how well members understand the team's overall purpose and task and how well they are getting to know one another.	Remind yourself that effectively dealing with differences related to the task and to relationships is fundamental to the team's ultimate success; encourage people to communicate about such issues, and be willing to offer your own reactions as well.	Maintain your strength in suggesting effective ways of working together, making sure you emphasize norms for working relationships as well as norms related to the team's tasks.	Be careful not to work so hard for extended periods of time that you become exhausted.

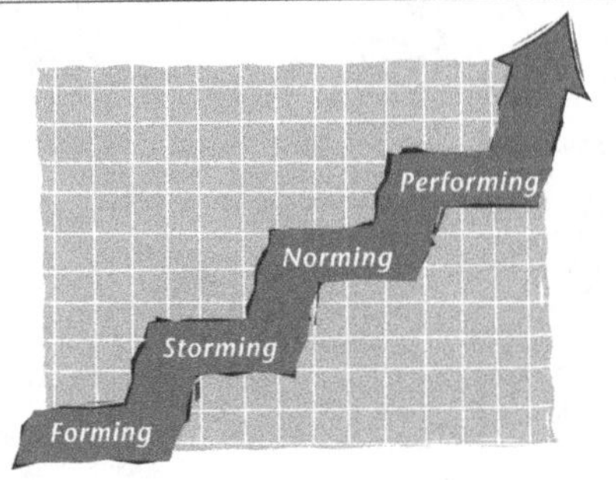

For more insights and information about teams, please refer to the following: Chapter 5, "Creating High-Performing Teams," in *Bringing Out the Best in Yourself at Work* (McGraw-Hill, 2004) and Chapter 6, "Lead High-Performing Teams," in *What Type of Leader Are You?* (McGraw-Hill, 2007).

Additional Team Development Stretches for Three Team Leaders

Enjoy the team more.

If you relax at work and enjoy the team more, team members will follow your lead and work more effectively and with less stress. When you explicitly emphasize both the task and the pleasure in working with others, so will your team.

Pay attention to human processes as much as to the work structure and processes.

Just as you pay attention to the team structure and how work flows between and among team members, give equal attention to the human processes as work — e.g., motivation, rewards, team morale, coaching and mentoring, and interpersonal relationships. Teams are actually comprised of two systems: the task system and the social system. The development of both systems allows them to reinforce each other; people work better at a task when the social system supports that task, and social systems work more effectively when the task system supports people in working together productively.

Restrain yourself from providing too much direction to the team.

While providing your team with clear direction is an asset, you also need to be clear about how much of the team's road map and route you should provide versus how much should be developed within the team itself. Too much direction given too early or too often impedes the team's ability to develop self-reliance and self-confidence. Share your ideas, but be genuinely open to others' reactions and to ideas. Involve team members more directly, and be willing to shift course as a result.

For more insights and information about teams, please refer to the following: Chapter 5, "Creating High-Performing Teams," in *Bringing Out the Best in Yourself at Work* (McGraw-Hill, 2004) and Chapter 6, "Lead High-Performing Teams," in *What Type of Leader Are You?* (McGraw-Hill, 2007).

LEADERSHIP DEVELOPMENT STRETCHES

The intense challenges of leadership are complex, demanding, unpredictable, exciting, and rewarding, and they require the ability to manage oneself and to interact effectively with hundreds of others in both stressful and exhilarating circumstances. For these reasons, leaders must spend time in honest self-reflection. Individuals who become extraordinary leaders grow in both evolutionary and revolutionary ways as they push themselves to meet challenges even they cannot predict in advance.

Excellent leadership comes in many forms, and no Enneagram style has a monopoly on greatness. However, your Enneagram style shows both your strengths as a leader and the areas that would most likely create obstacles to your success.

Enneagram Style Three leaders usually display this special gift: *obtaining results*. However, their greatest strength can also become their greatest weakness: in the relentless pursuit of accomplishment and success, Three leaders can become so focused on tasks that they forget the deeper human issues, including both their own feelings and those of people around them.

Development Stretches to Enhance Your Leadership

Pay more attention to the impact on people.

Your dual focus on goal achievement and efficiency can have the effect of minimizing the human side of work. Conduct a human-impact analysis each time you make a decision, and take the results very seriously.

Curtail your competitiveness.

Remember that not everything is a competition — something you must win or, at least, not lose. Make sure that rather than being debates, your conversations become collaborations as a result of your openness and receptivity.

Consciously tell the whole truth about yourself.

When you start trying to impress someone, consciously stop doing this. Become more familiar with the whole truth behind your facade of impressing others.

For more insights and information about leadership, please refer to the following: Chapter 6, "Leveraging Your Leadership," in *Bringing Out the Best in Yourself at Work* (McGraw-Hill, 2004) and the book, *What Type of Leader Are You?* (McGraw-Hill, 2007).

RESULTS ORIENTATION DEVELOPMENT STRETCHES

It is important to build credibility with customers by delivering sustained, high-quality results, continually driving for results, and reaching your potential. When you do this, you make gains in productivity, push the envelope of new product development, and support the organization as a leader in its field.

Provide more explicit expectations and directions.

While some who work with or for you may need only minimal guidance and communication beyond a simple understanding of the goals and objectives, others may want greater clarity and definition of tasks and even some guidance in developing an effective work plan. Having this latter work style does not mean that these individuals are any less competent or confident than you are; it simply means that they need a greater level of detail in order to proceed.

Treat your coworkers and bosses as if they were clients.

If you think of those with whom you work as clients, you will respond quickly, listen closely, and pay attention to their needs. Your graciousness and social skills will be at their best, and your tendency to focus primarily on tasks will be supplemented by an equal focus on people. This will also reduce the tendency you may have to be abrupt or to give the impression that you don't have enough time for others.

Ask yourself how you are feeling on a regular basis.

Threes often suspend their feelings when they work hard, believing that these will get in the way of achieving results. Because your focus on work may come at the expense of paying attention to your own needs and feelings, give yourself time each day to ask yourself these questions: *How am I feeling right at this very moment? Am I concerned about anything? Am I angry about something? What am I feeling happy about?* Paying attention to your feelings will help you be more genuine in your interactions with others, appear more human to your coworkers or employees, and enable you to feel more empathy when others approach you to discuss important issues.

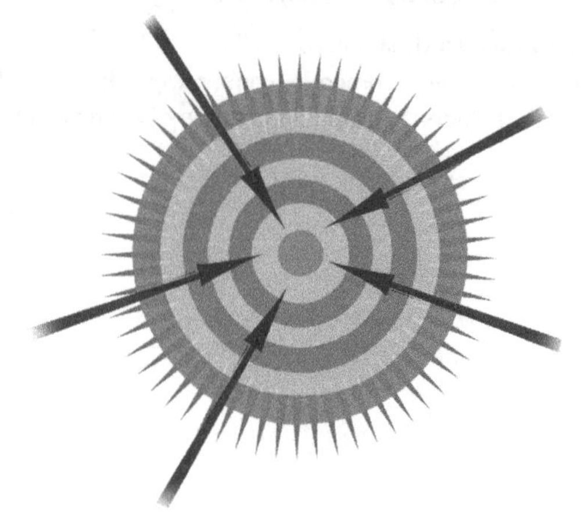

For more insights and information about results orientation, please refer to the following: Chapter 2, "Drive for Results," in *What Type of Leader Are You?* (McGraw-Hill, 2007).

STRATEGY DEVELOPMENT STRETCHES

Leaders and individual contributors must understand the actual business of their organizations and be able to think and act strategically in both big and small ways if their teams and organizations are to reach the highest levels of performance, effectiveness, and efficiency.

"Knowing the business" and "thinking and acting strategically" go hand in hand. Unless you know the business, you have no context for thinking and acting strategically. When you have this information, you need to be able to use it in a strategic way, working from a compelling and common vision, a customer-focused mission, a smart strategy, and effective goals and tactics aligned with that strategy.

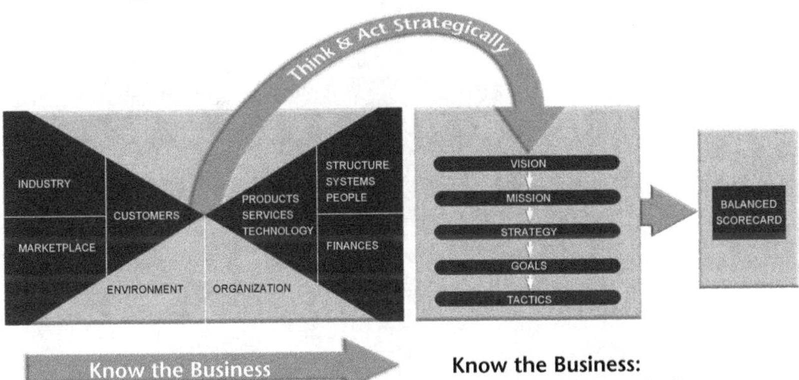

**Know the Business:
Think & Act Strategically**

Take your time to know the business.
Even though Threes learn quickly, knowing the business is a complex undertaking. To get a firm grounding in the business, give yourself three times longer than you expect. Once you have this deep understanding, you will be able to view environmental and organizational changes within their larger context, allowing you to be even more effective at adjusting goals when you take action.

Understand the vision, mission, and strategy, then work from all three.
When you work from goals rather than from vision, mission, and strategy, your success will be limited to the goals you have set. However, when your work comes from vision, mission, and strategy, those who work for or with you will be equipped with the tools they need to reformulate goals and drive tactics. This will create less dependency on you for your direct involvement, and more will be accomplished.

Communicate with everyone frequently.
The more the people who work with you or for you understand the business, the more effective they will be. Take the time to inform and enlist people at all levels of the organization. Doing so will motivate others and help them be better performers.

For more insights and information about strategy, please refer to the following: Chapter 4, "Know the Business: Think and Act Strategically," in *What Type of Leader Are You?* (McGraw-Hill, 2007).

DECISION-MAKING DEVELOPMENT STRETCHES

We all make decisions on a daily basis, but we rarely think about the process by which we make them. The wisest decisions are made utilizing our heads (rational analysis and planning), our hearts (to examine values, feelings, and impact on people), and our guts (for taking action), with all three used in an integrated way. In addition, when you are making decisions at work, you need to consider three other factors: the organizational culture, the decision-making authority structure within the organization, and the context of the decision itself.

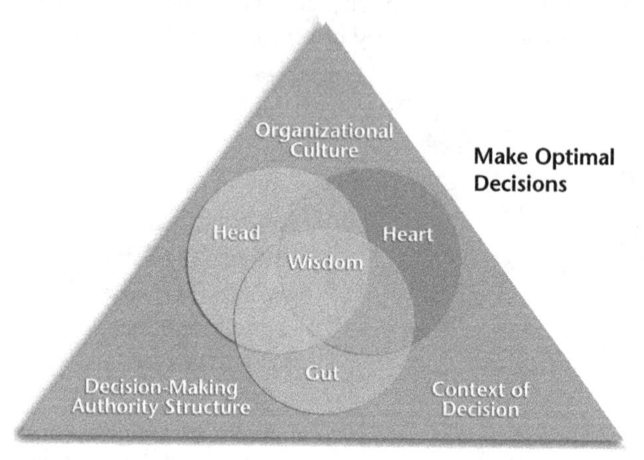

The following chart shows you how to develop each of your Centers of Intelligence (Head, Heart, and Gut) to assist you in making wise decisions.

	Centers of Intelligence		
	Head Center	**Heart Center**	**Body (Gut) Center**
Activities for Threes That Develop Each Center	**Objective analysis** Consider data, including feelings, that may not lead directly to the result you intend but that can help you make the best decision. **Astute insight** Make certain your desire for efficiency doesn't cause you to spend insufficient time analyzing the meaning of the data. **Productive planning** Be realistic about time frames, remembering to account for unforeseen obstacles.	**Empathy** Spend time considering your own feelings and those of others; factor them into your decisions. **Authentic relating** Share your real feelings (including anxieties) related to the decisions you must make; this will help dismantle the overly confident image you have created that serves as a barrier between you and others. **Compassion** Make decisions that are not just expedient but also compassionate.	**Taking effective action** Work on making most of your decisions less quickly so that new insights have time to percolate. **Steadfastness** Explore your deeper values and hold firm on values-based decisions. **Gut-knowing** Become more aware of your body's signals when considering alternatives.

For more insights and information about decision making, please refer to the following: Chapter 7, "Make Optimal Decisions," in *What Type of Leader Are You?* (McGraw-Hill, 2007).

ORGANIZATIONAL CHANGE DEVELOPMENT STRETCHES

In contemporary organizations, change has become a way of life. Companies exist in increasingly complex environments, with more competition, fewer resources, less time to market, higher customer expectations, increased regulation, more technology, and greater uncertainty. Organizations need to be flexible, innovative, cost-conscious, and responsive if they want to succeed. As a result, employees at all levels need to be able to embrace change and to function flexibly and effectively within their teams when an unforeseen direction must be taken.

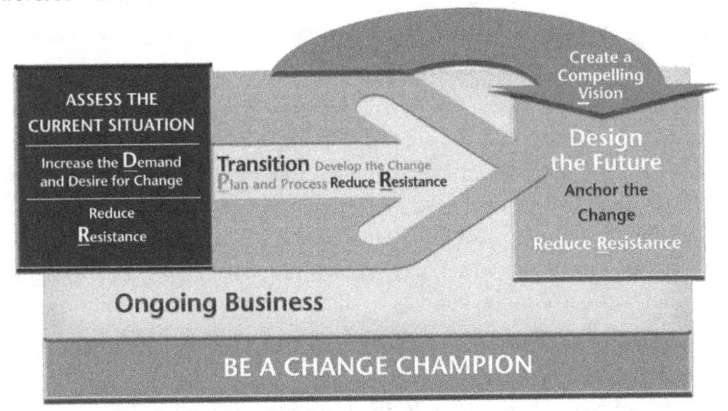

Take Charge of Change

Allow 35 percent more time than you anticipate.
Most Threes function efficiently and expect change initiatives to run smoothly. However, change efforts are far more complex than projects and involve many more people. It is unrealistic to expect everything to run according to plan. Make sure to build in a 35 percent contingency time.

Make sure your drive doesn't turn into overdrive.
You may be thinking: *How can I not go into overdrive when the work requires it?* Remember that other people get work done without going into overdrive, and so can you. When you see signs of overdrive, such as sleeplessness, anxiety, and anger, recognize that it's time to stop pushing yourself and others, to start enlisting help, and to take some time for rest and/or physical activity.

When you feel stressed, talk to someone you trust.
Threes can be enjoyable to be around when they are relaxed, but when they are under pressure, they seem to lose a great portion of their well-developed social skills. Ironically, this is the time when their social skills could serve them especially well. As soon as you feel frustration or stress, talk to someone you trust. Discuss how you really *feel*. Focus on what you can do — not on what someone else should do or on how the situation ought to be changed.

For more insights and information about organizational change, please refer to the following: Chapter 8, "Take Charge of Change," in *What Type of Leader Are You?* (McGraw-Hill, 2007).

TRANSFORMATION DEVELOPMENT STRETCHES FOR THREES

In order to move from *driving themselves to achieve goals in order to appear successful and to gain the respect and admiration of others* to the understanding that *there is a natural flow and order to everything that is completely independent of what they do,* Threes can work toward these transformations:

Mental Transformation

Transform the mental pattern of **vanity** (strategic thinking about how to create an idealized image based on being or appearing to be successful) *into the higher belief of* **hope** (the faith that you can be valued and appreciated for who you are rather than for what you do or accomplish).

Mental Activity

When you become aware that you are trying to impress others with how successful or desirable you are, stop for a moment and ask yourself, *What if I were not focusing on creating a positive image and thought of myself as valuable for who I truly am, not what I do?* Then try to remember one or more times when you actually believed in yourself, completely separate from any accomplishments. Stay in that thought, reliving what was occurring within you at that moment. Stay with this feeling of well-being about who you are, not what you do, for at least two minutes.

Emotional Transformation

Transform the emotional habit of **deceit** (the feeling that you must do everything possible to appear successful, hiding parts of yourself that do not conform to that image, and believing that your image is the real you) *into the higher awareness of* **truthfulness** (finding true self-acceptance through acknowledging both your successes and your failures, and realizing that your image is not your essence or true self).

Emotional Activity

When you realize you are not telling the complete truth to yourself or someone else, ask yourself, *What is the truth here? What am I really feeling and thinking, and how am I shading or changing my reporting of events so that I look good?* Then remember one or more times in your life when you told the whole truth and were completely accepting of yourself. Remember how you felt and what you experienced during those times. Keep replaying those truthful moments until you feel reconnected with the deeper part of yourself.

For more insights and information about personal transformation, please refer to the following: Chapter 7, "Transforming Yourself," in *Bringing Out the Best in Yourself at Work* (McGraw-Hill, 2004).

ENNEAGRAM STYLE FOUR

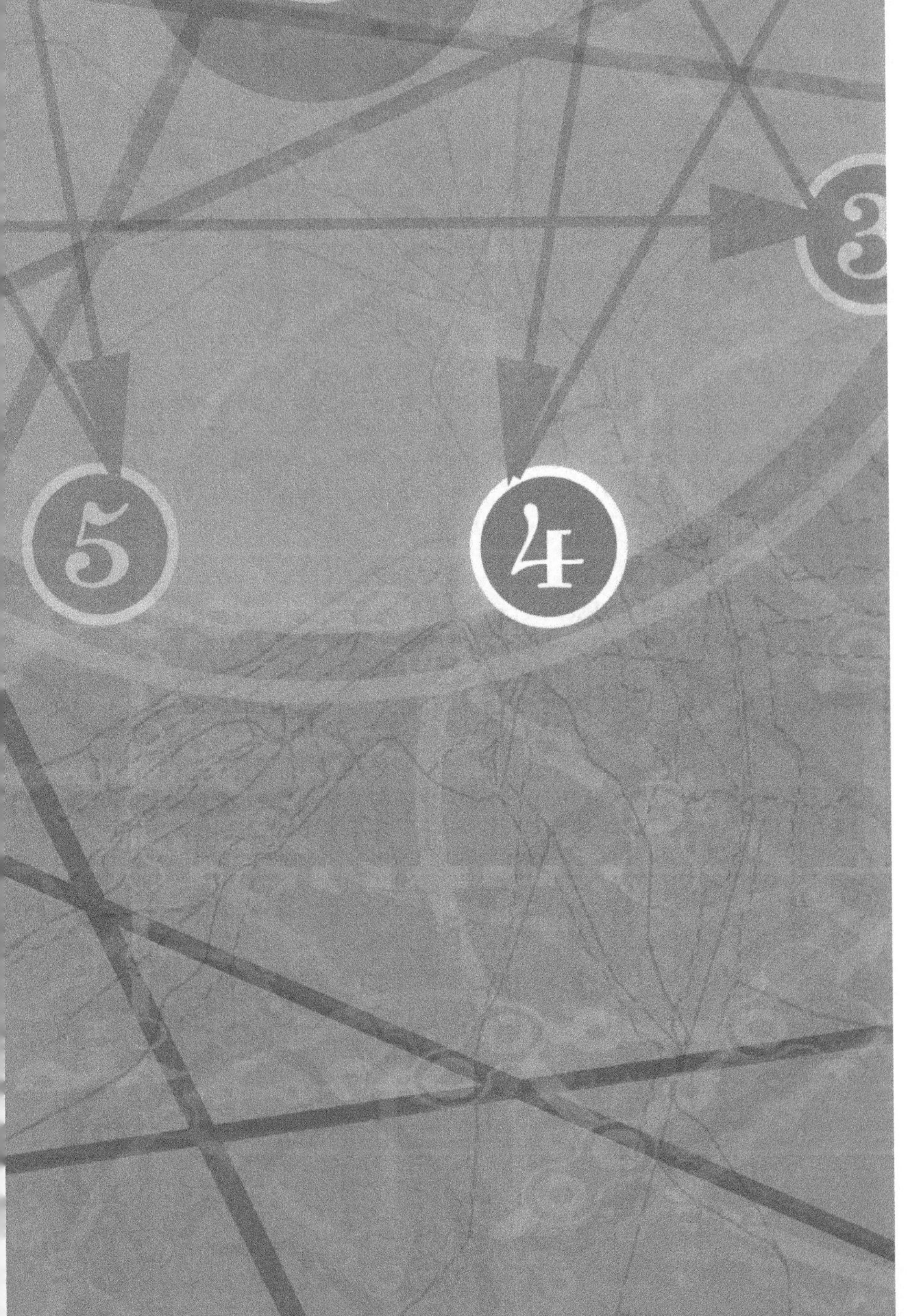

ENNEAGRAM FOURS

The search for deep experiences and emotional connection and the avoidance of rejection or feeling not-good-enough

Individualistic, emotionally sensitive, and creative, Fours seek deep meaning, authentic connections, and they tend to idealize that which seems unavailable, being especially attuned to what is missing in their complex worlds. Focusing on their internal experiences as a way of understanding and finding meaning, Fours seek to be deeply understood and want to be perceived as unique, special, or different.

Although all Fours have a special connection to suffering and have robust, complex inner lives full of nuance and symbolism, some Fours are hyper-active and risk-taking, silently enduring their suffering as a badge of virtue; some Fours are hypersensitive and more despairing, wanting to be accepted unconditionally for who they are; and some Fours exhibit a flair for the dramatic and engage in extreme competition with others in hopes of winning and taking center-stage, thus minimizing their sense of not being good enough.

The Four's interpersonal style combines an abundance of self-referencing speech — that is, the extensive use of words such as *I*, *me*, *my*, and *mine* as well as personal stories — and they often use emotion-laden and metaphoric language. It is as if their own inner worlds are the center of the universe, or at least, the center of their universe.

While we can all suffer at times and almost everyone wants to be understood, for Fours, the search for deep experiences and connection and the avoidance of rejection or feeling not-good-enough is their primary, persistent, and driving motivation.

DEVELOPMENT STRETCHES FOR FOURS

INDIVIDUALS WHO DESIRE DEEP CONNECTIONS BOTH WITH THEIR OWN INTERIOR WORLDS AND WITH OTHER PEOPLE, AND FEEL MOST ALIVE WHEN THEY AUTHENTICALLY EXPRESS THEIR PERSONAL EXPERIENCES AND FEELINGS

CONTENTS

SELF-MASTERY DEVELOPMENT STRETCHES

Self-Mastery — the ability to understand, accept, and transform your thoughts, feelings, and behavior, with the understanding that each day will bring new challenges that are opportunities for growth — is the foundation of all personal and professional development. Self-mastery begins with self-awareness, then expands to include the elements shown in the following graphic:

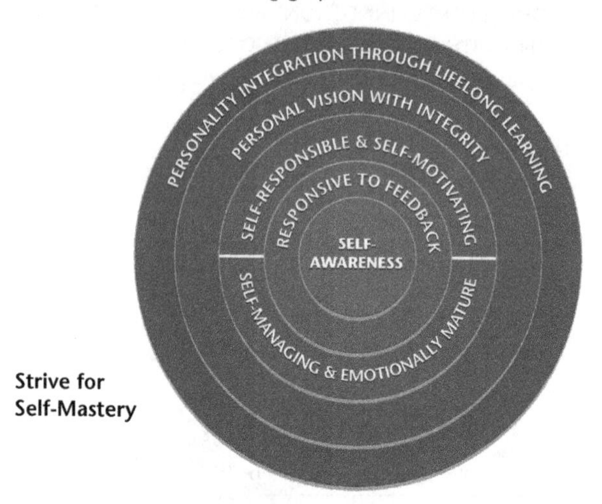

Strive for Self-Mastery

In this section on self-mastery, you will find the following:

- Three common issues for Fours related to self-mastery
- Three development stretches for working with the core issues of your Enneagram style, including one basic activity and one deeper activity for each stretch
- Three development stretches for working with your wings and arrow (stress-security) styles

Common Issues for Fours Related to Self-Mastery

Integrating objectivity with emotionality to find an equilibrium of your heart and mind	Finding a deep sense of self-worth without comparing yourself to others	Focusing simultaneously and equally on yourself and other people

For more insights and information about self-mastery, please refer to the following: Chapter 7, "Transforming Yourself," in *Bringing Out the Best in Yourself at Work* (McGraw-Hill, 2004) and Chapter 3, "Strive for Self-Mastery," in *What Type of Leader Are You?* (McGraw-Hill, 2007).

Development Stretches for Working with the Core Issues of Your Enneagram Style

Appreciate the ordinary.

Basic Activity

Do a task that you find tedious, paying attention to every aspect of it. Stay in the present moment while doing the task, not thinking about anyone or anything else, and find pleasure in it. Select a different mundane task each day and follow these same directions. Learning to appreciate the present will help you focus less on both the past and the future.

Deeper Activity

Because Fours tend to gravitate toward the unique and avoid the commonplace, they can grow enormously from focusing on and learning to appreciate the ordinary things in life. When the following activities are done every day, the results will be profound. First, make a long list of tasks you consider to be ordinary or boring — for example, doing paperwork, filing expense reports, or washing dishes. Each day, select one of these items and do it until you find pleasure in it.

Second, take a 15-minute walk every day and notice commonplace things in your environment. Reflect on each item and on what there is about it that you can deeply appreciate.

Third, when you are given a task that you perceive as being boring or insignificant, do it with relish, finding the joy and pleasure in it. You can do this by focusing on the actual activity rather than thinking about what you'd rather be doing instead or how boring the task is. Almost anything can be meaningful and interesting if your focus is on the present rather than on the past or the future.

Take pleasure in other people's positive qualities and accomplishments.

Basic Activity

A counterintuitive way to do this is to first take genuine pleasure in your own positive attributes. Do not use any caveats or "buts," such as "I'm smart, but he's smarter" or "I'm empathic, but I spend too much time thinking about myself." Simply enjoy who you are. Once you can do this, allow yourself to appreciate other people's qualities and achievements. Each day, think positively about yourself, then select another person to think positively about without making any comparisons to yourself.

For more insights and information about self-mastery, please refer to the following: Chapter 7, "Transforming Yourself," in *Bringing Out the Best in Yourself at Work* (McGraw-Hill, 2004) and Chapter 3, "Strive for Self-Mastery," in *What Type of Leader Are You?* (McGraw-Hill, 2007).

Deeper Activity

Fours consciously and unconsciously compare themselves to others. These comparisons can be about small things, such as an item of clothing that someone else is wearing, or large, such as the promotion of a friend or peer. This phenomenon of invidious comparison, or envy, results in Fours comparing themselves to others and then feeling superior or inferior to those individuals. When you notice you are comparing yourself to others (and this will become more apparent the more you pay attention to it), instead of feeling either superior or deficient, look at the person or situation again. If you initially felt inferior, continue looking at the person until you genuinely feel some pleasure for him or her. If you felt superior to the other person, continue looking and search for positive qualities in him or her that you truly admire.

Doing the above activity requires a commitment on your part. It means paying attention to yourself every day. Don't be surprised to find that you have to use this activity 15 times a day or more. The frequency of use really demonstrates to you that you are becoming more and more aware. When you use this process over several months, you will find that you compare yourself to others less often, you spend less time thinking about it when you do compare yourself to someone else, and that you can more easily change your feelings of envy and superiority into feelings of true appreciation.

Minimize your self-referencing behavior.

Basic Activity

Self-referencing behavior means that you tend to focus on yourself rather than other people — even if you are not aware of doing so — through word choice, storytelling, and the sharing of intense personal experiences and feelings. To challenge yourself every day, practice talking with one person and really listening to him or her, making no verbal references to yourself and not sharing any personal stories.

Deeper Activity

The self-referencing behavior of Fours comes in many forms, including e-mails, conversations, and even your inner thoughts and feelings. In order to eliminate self-referencing behavior, one must first recognize it — for example, the frequent use of the words *I, me, my,* and *mine*; the sharing of numerous personal stories and/or emotions; the redirection of a conversation back to oneself; the continuous thinking about one's own thoughts, feelings, and experiences; and, most importantly, a worldview that sees most events as emanating from or reverberating back to oneself, as if one is the hub in the center of a wheel and outside events are spokes to that hub.

Once Fours begin to recognize the extent to which they engage in self-referencing behavior, they can begin to minimize this behavior, one step at a time. E-mail is an easy first step, as we often write e-mail messages multiple times per day, and we are able to review them before sending them. Once your e-mail language becomes less self-referencing, your everyday conversations are likely to change as well.

A more difficult behavior to change is the redirection of conversations back to yourself. Not only is this behavior often unconscious, but many Fours do not even think of it as redirection. They think of it as showing empathy and personal warmth. If you want a greater understanding of your frequent telling of personal stories, refrain from telling personal stories to anyone for one day. As you do this, notice the number of times you have an impulse to say something personal about yourself and the amount of energy it takes for you to restrain yourself. Do this again for the second day and notice whether restraining yourself is becoming easier. Continue this activity for two more days or until not sharing personal stories feels easier. For the following two weeks, allow yourself to share only two or fewer stories per day. This activity will greatly reduce this aspect of your self-referencing behavior.

The most important thing to remember is that what occurs in life is not all about you or about any single person. Each person has his or her own universe of experience, and events do not occur in reference to only one person. This is particularly important to remember when you feel criticized or slighted by someone else; the other person's behavior may have nothing or very little to do with you. Saying the following words to yourself when you feel hurt, angry, or have in some way personalized someone's response to you can be very helpful: *This isn't all about me! What might be occurring related to this other person's experience?*

For more insights and information about self-mastery, please refer to the following: Chapter 7, "Transforming Yourself," in *Bringing Out the Best in Yourself at Work* (McGraw-Hill, 2004) and Chapter 3, "Strive for Self-Mastery," in *What Type of Leader Are You?* (McGraw-Hill, 2007).

Development Stretches for Working with Your Wings and Arrow (Stress-Security) Styles

Wings are the Enneagram styles on either side of your core Enneagram style; arrow, or stress-security, styles are Enneagram styles shown with arrows pointing away or toward your core Enneagram style. Your wings and arrow styles don't change your core Enneagram style, but instead offer qualities that can broaden and enrich your patterns of thinking and feeling as well as enhance your behaviors. Your wings and arrow styles make you more complex and versatile because they provide more dimensions to your personality and serve as vehicles for self-development.

Integrate Your Three Wing

Stay in charge of yourself.

Most Threes have learned how to keep their feelings from interfering with what they need to do, while Fours often become immobilized when their emotions become intense. When Fours feel extremely emotional, with feelings whirling around inside, they can practice staying on task by saying to themselves: *I am feeling very emotional, but I am not going to allow my feelings to take me over. What tasks need my attention right now?* Each time you feel your emotions taking over, ask the question once again.

Step into the professional limelight.

Threes usually like being in the professional limelight. Although Fours typically seek personal attention in interpersonal situations, the professional spotlight can make them self-conscious and apprehensive. Take some risks that put you at front and center stage, and try to do so in a way that does not preempt the stature or influence of other people. For example, volunteer for leadership roles on projects or professional organizations when these opportunities arise. Give presentations to large audiences and learn to truly enjoy the experience. Find ways to have your name mentioned in the newspaper or on radio or television, and continually improve your ability to perform.

Focus on work.

Threes focus on work and getting their goals achieved most of the time, and they do this when they are distressed as a way to keep their concerns from interfering with what they want to accomplish. Fours can also be work focused, but they have difficulty being so when they are emotionally concerned about something. At these times, the Four's emotions tend to play and replay themselves so that Fours can end up in what feels like a swirl of emotional activity. Learning to bypass emotions at will helps Fours maintain their focus and restore their equilibrium.

The next time you feel you are about to have an emotional experience that may derail you from moving forward, acknowledge your feelings, but also say this to yourself: *I can choose to dive into my emotions, and I can also choose to keep focused and start doing something instead. What will I choose to pursue?*

For more insights and information about integrating your wings and/or arrow styles (stress-security points), please refer to the following: Chapter 1, "What Type Are You?" and the conclusion, "Stretch Your Leadership Paradigms," in *What Type of Leader Are You?* (McGraw-Hill, 2007).

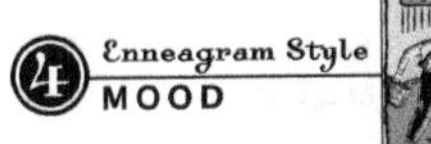

Integrate Your Five Wing

Become more objective.

The Five's objective approach can provide an excellent counterbalance to the Four's

more subjective orientation. Fours can practice a more objective approach by emphasizing the facts of a situation and taking a less personal focus when responding to others. For example, when an event occurs, Fours can ask themselves: *What are the actual facts of this situation, as opposed to my interpretation of the facts or my feelings about them?* When Fours respond to someone, they can minimize their use of personal references and feeling words. For example, when a Four feels like saying "I didn't like that decision because it violates my values about how others should be treated," the Four can express this more objectively, saying instead, "It would be helpful to examine this decision in light of certain value propositions, such as how people are treated." In addition, Fours can invoke the Five perspective by asking themselves this: *How would a Five approach this situation?* This increased objectivity can also help Fours respond in a less intense emotional manner and assist them in staying calm in a crisis.

Set clear boundaries.

Most Fives have learned how to establish clear boundaries between themselves and others, whereas Fours often have difficulty identifying the line that clarifies where they end and the other person begins. This boundary between people includes expectations, roles, information sharing, feelings, physical space, responsibilities, and so forth. Fours can learn to establish clearer boundaries by following these guidelines:

1. Discuss mutual expectations at the start of a relationship or when difficulties arise between you and another person.
2. Discuss and negotiate the various roles you perform with the person(s) directly affected — for example, coworker, subordinate, leader, spouse, parent, friend.
3. Share less information about yourself with others and discuss information about someone else with a third party rarely and only with permission.
4. Create a permeable filter between you and others so that when someone gives you feedback or you feel someone has rejected you, rather than immediately absorbing negative information, you can filter or sort through what is accurate and real versus what is your subjective interpretation of events.
5. Maintain three to six more inches of personal space between you and others than you normally would, and don't touch people unless they touch you first.

For more insights and information about integrating your wings and/or arrow styles (stress-security points), please refer to the following: Chapter 1, "What Type Are You?" and the conclusion, "Stretch Your Leadership Paradigms," in *What Type of Leader Are You?* (McGraw-Hill, 2007).

Value your mind.

Fives know how to value their minds; they must learn to also value the wisdom of the heart. By contrast, Fours typically value their emotional reactions and experiences but place lesser emphasis on their minds, even if they have highly developed analytical skills. There is, however, a unique wisdom in both the mind and the heart (as well as the body). Fours often use their analytical powers to analyze their feelings and experiences, but they can also use their minds for other purposes.

Try to use your mental functioning for analytical planning — for example, the next time you need to make a decision, develop a methodical process for how you will make the decision and design an implementation plan. Similarly, the next opportunity you have to see a work of art, go to an excellent play, watch a good film, or listen to a fine piece of music, in addition to enjoying the experience, also analyze the component parts the artist used that contributed to the quality of what you saw or heard.

For more insights and information about integrating your wings and/or arrow styles (stress-security points), please refer to the following: Chapter 1, "What Type Are You?" and the conclusion, "Stretch Your Leadership Paradigms," in *What Type of Leader Are You?* (McGraw-Hill, 2007).

Integrate Arrow Style Two (Stress Point)

Retain your optimism.

Twos tend to have an optimistic view of people and events; in an identical situation, however, Fours notice what is missing. In essence, Twos sense potential, while Fours are keenly aware of the gap between the potential of a situation and the reality. Fours can regain this optimistic quality by saying to themselves, at appropriate times: *I'm looking at this situation as if the glass is half empty. Let me see it now as half full.* Instead of feeling disappointed in others, as Fours can when an event or interaction has not met their ideal, Fours can focus on what has gone well and appreciate the potential for improvement.

Be easy and comfortable to deal with.

Twos tend to adjust their personas to other people, and the result is that they are typically agreeable, likeable, and easy to deal with. Fours, by contrast, are often more controversial because they are generally more interested in expressing their authentic self than in being pleasing to others. This latter quality, combined with the moodiness or emotional unpredictability of many Fours, sometimes causes others to perceive Fours as difficult to deal with. Every morning, Fours can say to themselves: *Today, I am going to make myself really easy to deal with!* From this principle, spend the day being easy and comfortable to deal with.

When you become involved with a difficult situation, ask yourself: *Am I being easy to deal with right now?* If the answer is no, change your behavior. This does not mean you should refrain from saying what you think or how you feel. It suggests, instead, that you listen fully to others first, reduce the intensity of your speaking style and body language, and treat the other person as though you hold him or her in high regard.

Focus on others.

Twos and Fours are, in many ways, two different sides of the same coin. Both styles are based in the Heart Center and have strong feeling responses. Twos and Fours also share a worldview, which is that the world is full of both joyful possibilities and suffering. Twos, however, focus on others and try to keep other people from suffering, while Fours focus more on themselves and their own experiences, including their own distress. By focusing more on others than on oneself, Fours can move beyond their own framework into the worlds of other people.

When you start to go inward and realize that you are likely to spend a great deal of time dwelling on your own responses, stop yourself and ask these questions: *What is someone else [preferably someone directly involved in the event that has triggered your emotional reaction] experiencing? What does he or she need?*

For more insights and information about integrating your wings and/or arrow styles (stress-security points), please refer to the following: Chapter 1, "What Type Are You?" and the conclusion, "Stretch Your Leadership Paradigms," in *What Type of Leader Are You?* (McGraw-Hill, 2007).

Integrate Arrow Style One (Security Point)

Take care of business.

Ones usually take care of tasks quickly because they interpret this rapid response as acting responsibly. Fours, on the other hand, tend to follow their interests first, putting off tasks that they perceive as uninteresting or mundane in order to do tasks that they find creative and meaningful. Fours can overcome this tendency to let the smaller things pile up by doing the following: (1) creating a plan for accomplishing tasks; (2) allotting a specific time each day to handle routine tasks; (3) taking care of routine tasks immediately so they don't pile up; and (4) regarding mundane tasks as developmental opportunities — that is, finding pleasure and satisfaction in ordinary work.

Practice precision.

Fours often think of themselves as precise and detail focused, but if they compare themselves to Ones, Fours often find that they can grow a great deal by emulating the precision and accuracy of Ones. Fours may see what is missing in the big picture but fail to notice errors in the details. To practice the art of precision, you can reread the e-mails (or other documents) you write at least three times before you send them. First, review what you have written for accuracy of meaning. Next, review it for spelling, grammar, and sentence structure. Finally, review the entire document for typographical errors or any other items that could be changed to make it better. Fours can also go to restaurants and systematically ask themselves the following questions: *Does everything match, such as the tables and chairs, artwork, menu graphics? Are there any typographical errors or misspellings on the menu? Is the quality of service impeccable?* When Fours practice systematically paying attention to details such as these, they usually integrate this into multiple aspects of their lives.

Be more assertive in sharing what you think.

Because Ones believe they are correct most of the time and are not particularly other-directed, they usually voice their opinions without either second-guessing themselves or being concerned with how someone else will respond to them. Fours, by contrast, may hold strong views, but they may hesitate to say what they think or feel, wondering if another thought or reaction will emerge or being concerned that others might challenge them personally. Fours can benefit from being more forthcoming and acting with more certainty by asking themselves this question: *What do I believe is true or accurate, knowing that I might change my opinion at a later point?* Once they are clear on what they believe at this moment, even if this might change later, Fours can practice courage and forthrightness and simply say what they think. This can be very freeing.

For more insights and information about integrating your wings and/or arrow styles (stress-security points), please refer to the following: Chapter 1, "What Type Are You?" and the conclusion, "Stretch Your Leadership Paradigms," in *What Type of Leader Are You?* (McGraw-Hill, 2007).

COMMUNICATION DEVELOPMENT STRETCHES

When you communicate with someone, three kinds of unintentional distortions may be present: speaking style, body language, and blind spots. *Speaking style* refers to your overall pattern of speaking. *Body language* includes posture, facial expressions, hand gestures, body movements, energy levels, and hundreds of other nonverbal messages. *Blind spots* are elements of your communication containing information about you that is not apparent to you but is highly visible to other people. We all unknowingly convey information through an amalgam of our speaking style, body language, and other inferential data.

The receivers of the messages you send also distort what they hear through their *distorting filters.* These are unconscious concerns or assumptions, often based on the listener's Enneagram style, that alter how someone hears what others say.

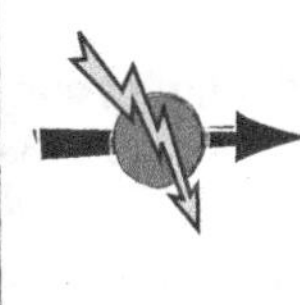

DISTORTION FILTERS

Change one communication style behavior at a time.

It is most effective to work on changing one behavior at a time, preferably in the following sequence: speaking style, body language, blind spots, and listening distorting filters. It is easiest to change the behaviors of which we are most aware, and this sequence represents the most common order of awareness, from most to least aware.

Fours: Speaking style

- Use words such as *I, me, my,* and *mine* frequently
- Talk about self
- Discuss feelings
- Share personal and/or painful stories
- Ask personal questions
- Word choice may be deliberate

Fours: Body language

- Intense
- Urgent
- Appear to be focused inward, as if analyzing the words they say
- Communicate that they want undivided attention
- Eyes may appear moist or sad

For more insights and information about communication, please refer to the following: Chapter 2, "Communicating Effectively," in *Bringing Out the Best in Yourself at Work* (McGraw-Hill, 2004) and Chapter 5, "Become an Excellent Communicator," in *What Type of Leader Are You?* (McGraw-Hill, 2007).

Fours: Blind spots

- Pull the conversation back to themselves using self-referencing behavior
- Need to fully complete a conversation even when the other person no longer wants to discuss an issue
- May appear dramatic or contrived
- May appear withdrawn, aloof, or condescending

Fours: Distorting filters when listening to someone else

- Personal rejection
- Being slighted or demeaned
- Not wanting to appear defective
- Being misunderstood

Note: Some of the above characteristics may be positive, some negative, and some neutral or mixed. They are intended as an overview to allow you to select from among them.

Use e-mails to expand and adjust your language patterns.

- Review your e-mails before you send them for language and tone.
- Reduce the number of self-referencing words (i.e., *I, my, me, mine,* and *myself*).
- Use language that is less personalized and more objective.
- Tell fewer anecdotes about yourself.
- Focus the content of your e-mails more on others than on yourself.

For more insights and information about communication, please refer to the following: Chapter 2, "Communicating Effectively," in *Bringing Out the Best in Yourself at Work* (McGraw-Hill, 2004) and Chapter 5, "Become an Excellent Communicator," in *What Type of Leader Are You?* (McGraw-Hill, 2007).

FEEDBACK DEVELOPMENT STRETCHES

Honest, positive, and constructive *feedback* — direct, objective, simple, and respectful observations that one person makes about another's behavior — improves both relationships and on-the-job performance. When you offer feedback, the Feedback Formula, combined with the insights of the Enneagram, helps you tailor your delivery. When someone gives you feedback, the more receptive you are to hearing what is being said, the more likely it is that you will be able to discern what is useful and utilize what has been suggested.

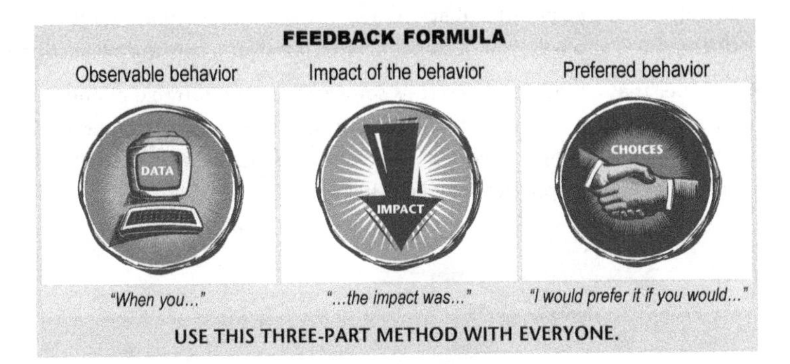

How Fours Can Enhance Their Ability to Deliver Feedback Effectively

When you offer feedback to someone, you want to be prepared and also to encourage the feedback recipient to be as receptive as possible. Remember that how and when you deliver feedback is just as important as what you actually say.

Use the three components of the Feedback Formula together with the following suggestions to plan and deliver the feedback.

- Be empathic, but be careful not to get your own feelings so involved that you presume you know what the other person feels.
- Maintain your truthfulness, but add a positive tone and include positive comments.
- Pay attention to the other person, but try to match that person's intensity, mood, and energy rather than trying to get him or her to match yours.
- Remember that even with your best efforts to be genuine, truthful, and empathic, your intentions will be misunderstood at times.

For more insights and information about feedback, please refer to the following: Chapter 3, "Giving Constructive Feedback," in *Bringing Out the Best in Yourself at Work* (McGraw-Hill, 2004) and Chapter 5, "Become an Excellent Communicator," in *What Type of Leader Are You?* (McGraw-Hill, 2007).

How Fours Can Be More Receptive When They Receive Feedback

- When someone gives you negative feedback, it may elicit your concerns about being misunderstood, being rejected, or not being good enough. If you are aware of your tendency to do this, it will help you to be more open to what the other person has to say.
- Become more receptive to positive feedback; allow yourself to embrace positive feedback that you agree with and then to internalize it. Fours tend to absorb negative feedback without deciphering whether or not they agree with it but summarily discard positive feedback. When you learn to integrate positive feedback, it will also help you become more responsive to constructive feedback.
- Remember that almost everyone feels somewhat uncomfortable offering negative or positive feedback. If you focus on supporting the person giving you feedback to do the best job possible, it will help you to become less focused on yourself and more responsive to what is being said.

For more insights and information about feedback, please refer to the following: Chapter 3, "Giving Constructive Feedback," in *Bringing Out the Best in Yourself at Work* (McGraw-Hill, 2004) and Chapter 5, "Become an Excellent Communicator," in *What Type of Leader Are You?* (McGraw-Hill, 2007).

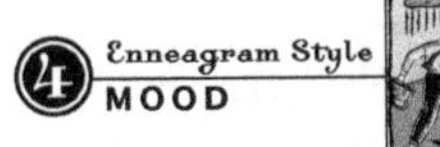

CONFLICT DEVELOPMENT STRETCHES

Relationships both at work and at home often involve some degree of conflict, which may be caused by a variety of factors and usually follows the pinch-crunch cycle below:

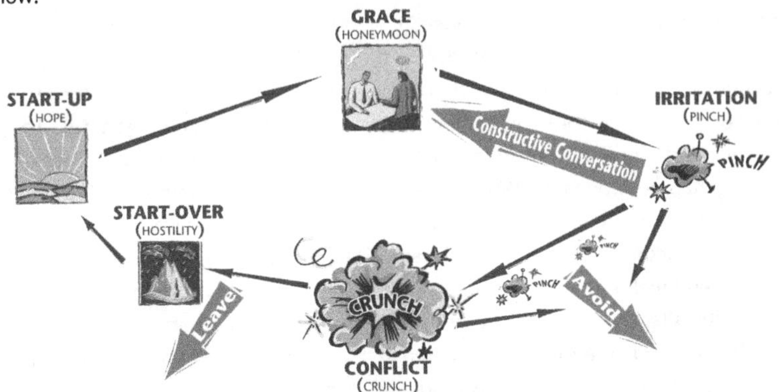

Whatever the root cause of the conflict, the Enneagram styles of the key parties involved will always be a factor in the conflict dynamics and resolution. The Enneagram enables each individual involved to make conflict resolution a constructive rather than destructive experience. The more people know themselves, understand their own responsibilities in the conflict interaction, engage in constructive self-management, and know how best to approach others through knowledge of the Enneagram, the greater the chances of a swift and effective outcome.

There are specific pinches (anger triggers) for each Enneagram style — that is, certain situations that will invariably ignite anger in a person of one style, yet may not affect someone of a different style. For Fours, these pinches include:

Being ignored or slighted · Being asked to do something contrary to his or her values · An event that elicits the Four's envy

For more insights and information about conflict, please refer to the following: Chapter 4, "Managing Conflict," in *Bringing Out the Best in Yourself at Work* (McGraw-Hill, 2004) and Chapter 5, "Become an Excellent Communicator," in *What Type of Leader Are You?* (McGraw-Hill, 2007).

Development Stretches for Transforming Anger into an Opportunity for Growth

Share your likely pinches (anger triggers) with others at the beginning of your working relationship.

Because Fours like to establish a connection early in a working relationship, it can be quite easy to add the topic of pinches into these early conversations. A Four might say: "Something I find very helpful in a relationship is for both of us to be honest about what we know from past experiences that has and has not worked well. That way, we can get to know each other better and learn what to do and what not to do. I'd be happy to go first." When discussing such pinches as being slighted or feeling envious, Fours are likely to feel that this is too personal and revealing at the early stages of a working relationship. However, a Four can say, "I tend to work well with others when I feel respected and included in conversations or meetings that directly or indirectly affect my work. The other thing that means a lot to me is responsiveness. When I send an e-mail or call someone, I really appreciate a prompt response — within a day or two. I know this is not always possible, but even a quick response such as 'I am really busy and will get back to you later this week' is very helpful."

Say something as soon as you are aware of feeling pinched or upset.

When they feel pinched, Fours tend either to say nothing or to say something quite spontaneously. It is almost impossible, even for them, to predict which will be the case. Because Fours are so sensitive to pinches, it is important for them to express feeling pinched as soon as possible. However, this needs to be done in a way that does not put the other person on the spot. For example, a Four who is asked to do a task without financial compensation may say in a blunt manner: "What about me? What do I get out of this?" While this is certainly an honest response, it can be off-putting to some people. Another way to say the same thing without creating an adverse reaction might be: "Although I understand why you are asking me to do this, I feel uncomfortable about being asked to do something like this without any compensation. Can we discuss some alternatives?" To avoid giving a response that may be perceived as too aggressive, Fours can use the age-old technique of taking three deep breaths. This gives them a chance to regroup and decide what to say about the pinch. Alternatively, Fours may prefer some time away to think before they say something. This is fine, but they should not let too much time go by, lest another pinch occurs and builds on the first one.

For more insights and information about conflict, please refer to the following: Chapter 4, "Managing Conflict," in *Bringing Out the Best in Yourself at Work* (McGraw-Hill, 2004) and Chapter 5, "Become an Excellent Communicator," in *What Type of Leader Are You?* (McGraw-Hill, 2007).

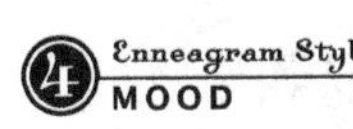

When you start to behave in ways that indicate you are feeling pinched or distressed, do something physical if you can, such as working out or taking a walk. Many Fours find the thought of an impending conflict to be discouraging and depressing. As a result, lethargy may set in, with Fours concentrating their attention on the reverberations of their feelings and the related mental analysis of why a particular thing has happened. Even when Fours exercise regularly, they may put this aside during moments of distress. Give yourself the message to take care of yourself, with some form of physical activity included as part of this. Exercise also serves to keep the Four's feelings and thoughts moving and flowing, countering the tendency to recirculate feelings and thought patterns relating to the upsetting experience.

When you have a negative reaction and feel a pinch, ask yourself: *What does my reaction to this situation or to the other person's behavior say about me as a Four and about the areas in which I can develop? How can working on my pinches and crunches help me to bring out the best in myself?*

Fritz Perls, the father of Gestalt therapy, explained that depression is often caused by anger that is turned inward. Fours can benefit from this concept, because depression — ranging from mild to severe — is a familiar feeling for most Fours. When Fours become depressed, it can be extremely helpful for them to ask themselves: *If my depression is masking my anger, what am I really mad about?* When Fours pursue this question in depth, the answers can be illuminating and enlightening. What frequently emerges are issues related to rejection, envy, and feelings of being defective in some way.

Growth for Fours does not come from the outside — for example, getting others to be less rejecting, reducing the immediate feeling of envy by increasing one's credentials, changing one's image, or encouraging others to treat the Four as special in some way. While these tactics may reduce a Four's anxiety momentarily, they do not support genuine long-term growth. For Fours, real growth occurs when they explore their sensitivity to rejection, understand the role that envy (continuous invidious comparison) plays in their lives, and accept that everyone is special and no one is any more defective or flawless than anyone else.

For more insights and information about conflict, please refer to the following: Chapter 4, "Managing Conflict," in *Bringing Out the Best in Yourself at Work* (McGraw-Hill, 2004) and Chapter 5, "Become an Excellent Communicator," in *What Type of Leader Are You?* (McGraw-Hill, 2007).

TEAM DEVELOPMENT STRETCHES

There is a difference between a group and a team. A *group* is a collection of individuals who have something in common; a *team* is a specific type of group, one composed of members who share one or more *goals* that can be reached only when there is an optimal level of *interdependence* between and among team members.

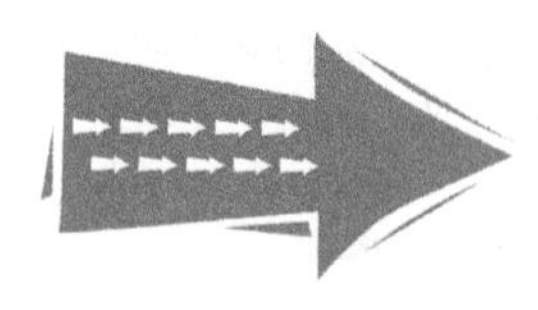

Team members also have *roles* — predictable patterns of behavior – within the team that are often related to their Enneagram styles. *Task roles* involve behaviors directed toward the work itself; *relationship roles* involve behaviors focused on feelings, relationships, and team processes, such as decision making and conflict resolution.

In addition, teams have unique yet predictable dynamics as they go through the four sequential stages of team development: *forming, storming, norming,* and *performing.* At each stage, there are questions the team must resolve before moving to the next stage.

TEAM STAGE	QUESTIONS
FORMING	*Who are we, where are we going, and are we all going there together?*
STORMING	*Can we disagree with one another in a constructive and productive way?*
NORMING	*How should we best organize ourselves and work together?*
PERFORMING	*How can we keep performing at a high level and not burn out?*

Fours: Development Stretches for Team Members and Team Leaders

Team Goals

Although you may prefer team goals that are *significant, challenging, and broad in scope yet contain specific benchmarks,* other team members may need goals that are more precise, concrete, and smaller in scope. Allow yourself to also include goals that will help operationalize the larger goals into more concrete work products. This will help others be more productive as well as assist you in determining your deliverables.

Team Interdependence

Although you may prefer to work in teams that are *interdependent as long as there is also room for independence* and the environment allows for self-expression and

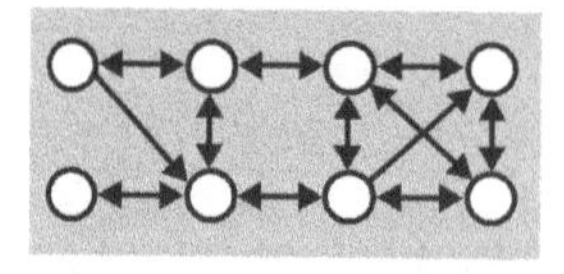

creativity, remind yourself that different teams need to work at a variety of levels of interdependence in order to be effective. The optimum level may or may not include latitude for individual members to work independently. In addition, teams vary both in their need to be interdependent and in comfort levels regarding self-expression and creativity. Work to support the level of interdependence your team needs, as well as to develop your capacity to be effective in teams that don't offer the degree of independence you like or exhibit the willingness to spend time with emotional expressiveness.

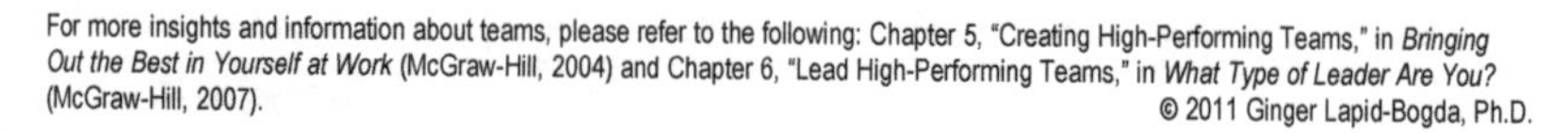
For more insights and information about teams, please refer to the following: Chapter 5, "Creating High-Performing Teams," in *Bringing Out the Best in Yourself at Work* (McGraw-Hill, 2004) and Chapter 6, "Lead High-Performing Teams," in *What Type of Leader Are You?* (McGraw-Hill, 2007).

Team Roles

Your typical task-related team role is likely to involve *managing the agenda* within the team by offering comments and influencing the team with regard to whether the important items are on the agenda, how the team is working through the agenda together, and how effectively the items are prioritized. Your likely relationship-related team role may be *expressing feelings* by sharing your own emotional reactions and personal experiences or by helping others to do this.

Task Roles

Stretch yourself to go beyond these typical roles and adopt the following additional team task and relationship roles:

Relationship Roles

New task role

Defining goals and tracking tasks, stating clearly what you believe are the team's concrete goals and deliverables and offering your opinions about how the team is progressing with the work and what it needs in order to move forward

New relationship role

Providing perspective by stating complex issues in a larger and more objective context so that alternative views and courses of action can be considered

Team Dynamics

During the four stages of team development — *forming, storming, norming,* and *performing* — experiment with expanding your repertoire of behavior in the following ways:

FORMING	STORMING	NORMING	PERFORMING
Instead of focusing only on your own reactions to the team's purpose and how the team might function most effectively, solicit the opinions and feelings of others as well.	Maintain your willingness to help the team resolve the conflicts that arise, but also be willing to share your own thoughts and feelings.	Keep your willingness to suggest new ways of working together, and be more open to norms that may curtail your degrees of freedom if these norms are in the team's best interest.	Enjoy the closeness and effectiveness of the team at this stage; be careful of overextending yourself or of feeling too disheartened when team members leave or the team disbands.

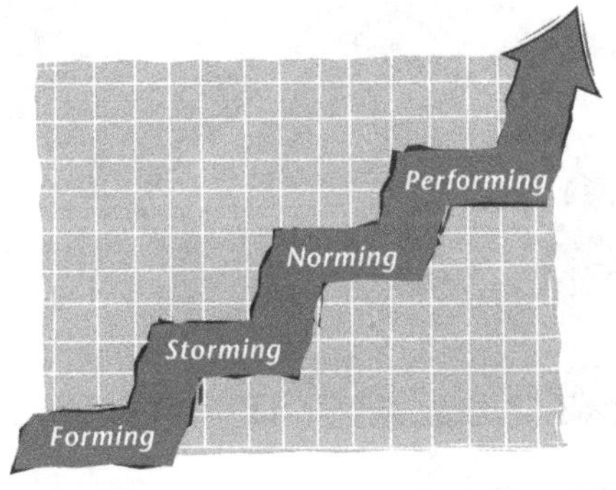

For more insights and information about teams, please refer to the following: Chapter 5, "Creating High-Performing Teams," in *Bringing Out the Best in Yourself at Work* (McGraw-Hill, 2004) and Chapter 6, "Lead High-Performing Teams," in *What Type of Leader Are You?* (McGraw-Hill, 2007).

Additional Team Development Stretches for Four Team Leaders

Put your strength in working with team processes into perspective.

While it is important to honor and utilize your sensitivity to underlying team issues, it is equally important to remember that issues need only be discussed to the extent that they no longer impede the team's progress, not to the point at which every issue has been thoroughly examined. Practice your ability to facilitate issue identification and resolution using methods that are efficient as well as effective.

When you feel deeply discouraged, use this as a signal to work on changing your perspective.

When you feel discouraged, this can permeate and demoralize your team. Whenever you begin to feel disheartened and concerned, intercept these reactions by gathering an ad hoc team of trusted advisors. They can help you gain a different perspective and assist you in developing innovative ways of addressing the organizational factors triggering your concerns.

Be more playful.

Fours can be intense and serious as team leaders. While these are not necessarily negative characteristics, they do need to be balanced with some lighthearted fun. Find the humor in adverse circumstances, laugh at the absurdity of situations that you might normally perceive as negative, and try to balance your seriousness with some levity.

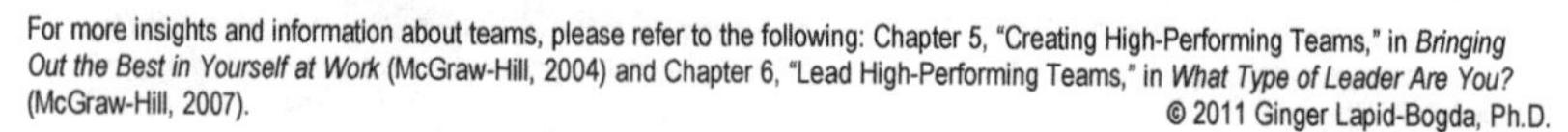
For more insights and information about teams, please refer to the following: Chapter 5, "Creating High-Performing Teams," in *Bringing Out the Best in Yourself at Work* (McGraw-Hill, 2004) and Chapter 6, "Lead High-Performing Teams," in *What Type of Leader Are You?* (McGraw-Hill, 2007).

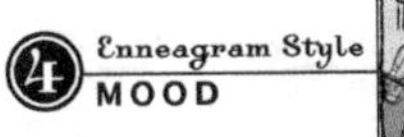

LEADERSHIP DEVELOPMENT STRETCHES

The intense challenges of leadership are complex, demanding, unpredictable, exciting, and rewarding, and they require the ability to manage oneself and to interact effectively with hundreds of others in both stressful and exhilarating circumstances. For these reasons, leaders must spend time in honest self-reflection. Individuals who become extraordinary leaders grow in both evolutionary and revolutionary ways as they push themselves to meet challenges even they cannot predict in advance.

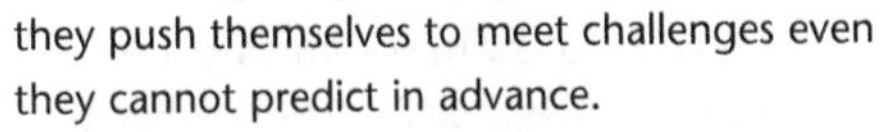

Excellent leadership comes in many forms, and no Enneagram style has a monopoly on greatness. However, your Enneagram style shows both your strengths as a leader and the areas that would most likely create obstacles to your success.

Enneagram Style Four leaders usually display this special gift: *the pursuit of one's passion.* However, their greatest strength can also become their greatest weakness: in their unending quest for meaning and connection, Four leaders can become encumbered by interior mood swings, leaving those around them to focus primarily on the leader instead of on the work.

Development Stretches to Enhance Your Leadership

Focus on others more than on yourself.

Use personal stories and the words *I, me, my,* or *mine* only ten percent as much as you currently do. Think about how others feel, not how you would respond if you were in their position.

Turn down your intensity.

In both what you say and how you say it, cut your intensity level in half. Let conversations end before you want them to, don't feel a need to constantly hold the other person's attention, and learn to express yourself in less dramatic ways.

Learn to forgive and let go.

Learn to think, feel, experience, and then move on, rather than dwelling on difficulties or holding something against another person for a long period of time. Followers need this sort of balance in their leaders.

For more insights and information about leadership, please refer to the following: Chapter 6, "Leveraging Your Leadership," in *Bringing Out the Best in Yourself at Work* (McGraw-Hill, 2004) and the book, *What Type of Leader Are You?* (McGraw-Hill, 2007).

RESULTS ORIENTATION DEVELOPMENT STRETCHES

It is important to build credibility with customers by delivering sustained, high-quality results, continually driving for results, and reaching your potential. When you do this, you make gains in productivity, push the envelope of new product development, and support the organization as a leader in its field.

Follow your mind as well as your heart.

Most Fours tend to follow their own inner experience and feelings first and then use their analytical function to make sense of their reactions. They also have a tendency to overemphasize the feelings of others — for example, structuring work or job responsibilities around someone's preferences rather than around what is best for the organization. The key is not to ignore your own and others' personal experiences, but rather to use your objective reasoning in conjunction with your sensitivity.

Give people what they need, not what you think they need.

While being empathic and sensitive to others is a strength, it is important to differentiate how you might react in a given situation from how the other person actually feels. The best way to do this is either to ask others directly how they feel or what they want or to tell them what you imagine they may want and then solicit their confirmation or disconfirmation. In addition, don't withhold negative feedback from people for fear they may be hurt by it or get angry at you. If you frame the feedback in objective terms, at the same time maintaining your positive regard for the individual, the person is likely to respond in a constructive way.

Make the finer details of project plans more explicit.

Although some people can work easily from a common vision, shared goals, and key milestones, others may need more explicit information and direction. Thus, laying out more detailed plans and coordinating them with others can be extremely helpful to everyone. This is true whether you are a coworker or a team leader.

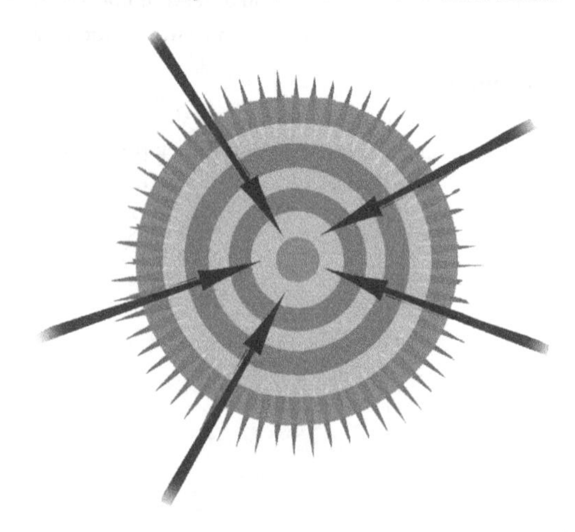

For more insights and information about results orientation, please refer to the following: Chapter 2, "Drive for Results," in *What Type of Leader Are You?* (McGraw-Hill, 2007).

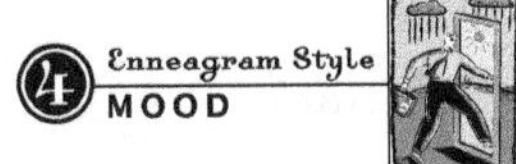

STRATEGY DEVELOPMENT STRETCHES

Leaders and individual contributors must understand the actual business of their organizations and be able to think and act strategically in both big and small ways if their teams and organizations are to reach the highest levels of performance, effectiveness, and efficiency.

"Knowing the business" and "thinking and acting strategically" go hand in hand. Unless you know the business, you have no context for thinking and acting strategically. When you have this information, you need to be able to use it in a strategic way, working from a compelling and common vision, a customer-focused mission, a smart strategy, and effective goals and tactics aligned with that strategy.

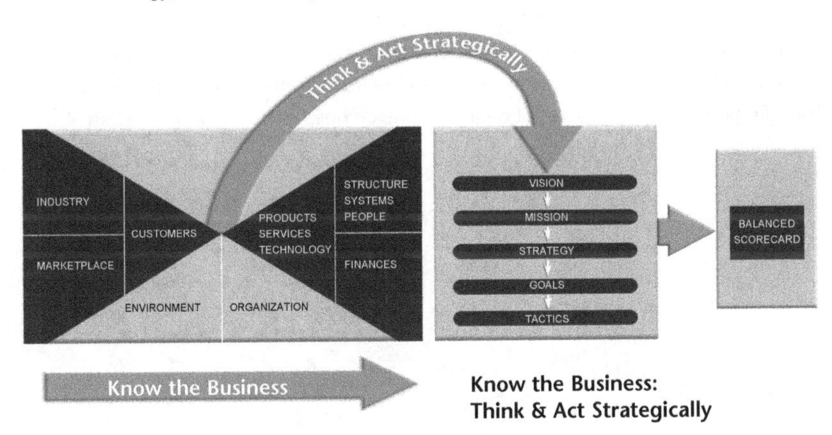

Know the Business: Think & Act Strategically

Be very clear about what you want to communicate.

Rather than being overly complex, challenge yourself to be as clear and straightforward as you possibly can, especially when you speak in front of groups. In that situation, write down in advance exactly what you want to say, and practice your speech in front of others who will give you honest feedback. Ask them these questions: *Can you repeat my main point in two sentences? Did my words inspire you to move forward? Do you have a clear sense of what action to take as a result of what I said?* If the answer to any of these questions is no, keep revising your speech until you get an affirmative response to all three questions.

For more insights and information about strategy, please refer to the following: Chapter 4, "Know the Business: Think and Act Strategically," in *What Type of Leader Are You?* (McGraw-Hill, 2007).

Be honest in identifying what you don't like doing, and then give your full attention to those areas.

Write down the parts of your job that you truly enjoy. Review this list, and think about how you approach these tasks and how you feel when you do them. Make a second list of the responsibilities you find dull or uninteresting. Review each item, and ask yourself this question: *How can I bring the same enthusiasm, satisfaction, and overall approach to these tasks that I bring to those activities I enjoy?*

Create and work from a vision, mission, and strategy; keep your eye on strategies and their implementation.

Write down your team's vision, mission, and strategies. List your goals beneath each strategy, and place your tactics beneath each goal. Putting all of this on paper will clarify your strategic elements, showing you what might be missing and needing more thought, and giving you something to discuss with those you work with or lead. Remember that this level of detail helps everyone, including you, function at a higher level of performance.

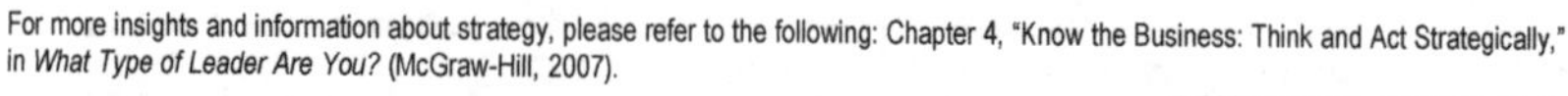
For more insights and information about strategy, please refer to the following: Chapter 4, "Know the Business: Think and Act Strategically," in *What Type of Leader Are You?* (McGraw-Hill, 2007).

DECISION-MAKING DEVELOPMENT STRETCHES

We all make decisions on a daily basis, but we rarely think about the process by which we make them. The wisest decisions are made utilizing our heads (rational analysis and planning), our hearts (to examine values, feelings, and impact on people), and our guts (for taking action), with all three used in an integrated way. In addition, when you are making decisions at work, you need to consider three other factors: the organizational culture, the decision-making authority structure within the organization, and the context of the decision itself.

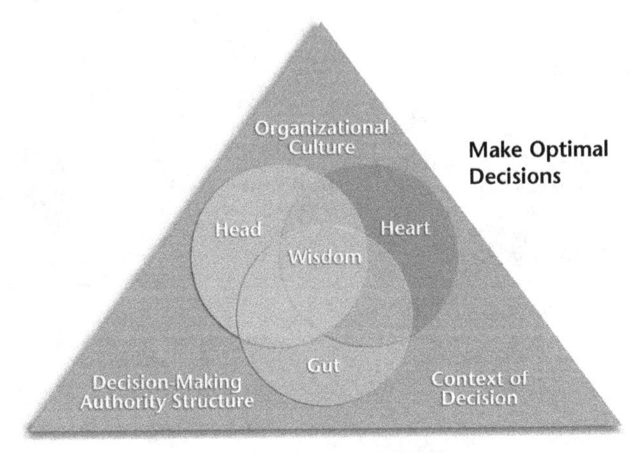

The following chart shows you how to develop each of your Centers of Intelligence (Head, Heart, and Gut) to assist you in making wise decisions.

Centers of Intelligence			
	Head Center	**Heart Center**	**Body (Gut) Center**
Activities for Fours That Develop Each Center	**Objective analysis** Don't let your personal experiences and feelings bias your view of the facts; become more objective in your decision making. **Astute insight** Develop insights of the mind in addition to insights of the heart. Ask yourself: *What do I think is true?* in addition to *What do I feel is true?* **Productive planning** Think through your decisions using a logical as well as an intuitive approach; if you get two different answers, ask yourself which decision will provide the best result.	**Empathy** Examine your perceptions of what other people are feeling about issues and decisions; make sure you are not projecting your own emotional reactions onto others. **Authentic relating** Let others tell you their real thoughts and feelings about a decision; be open to whatever is said. **Compassion** Remember that excessive emotionality does not help either you or others when making decisions.	**Taking effective action** Don't let feelings immobilize and prevent you from making a decision; action is one way to move through emotional reactions. **Steadfastness** Being adamant and overly tenacious about a decision rarely enlists people, but neither does being overly compliant or passive. Find the middle ground. **Gut-knowing** Ask yourself on a regular basis what your gut reactions are to these questions: *What do I really want? What should I do here?*

For more insights and information about decision making, please refer to the following: Chapter 7, "Make Optimal Decisions," in *What Type of Leader Are You?* (McGraw-Hill, 2007).

ORGANIZATIONAL CHANGE DEVELOPMENT STRETCHES

In contemporary organizations, change has become a way of life. Companies exist in increasingly complex environments, with more competition, fewer resources, less time to market, higher customer expectations, increased regulation, more technology, and greater uncertainty. Organizations need to be flexible, innovative, cost-conscious, and responsive if they want to succeed. As a result, employees at all levels need to be able to embrace change and to function flexibly and effectively within their teams when an unforeseen direction must be taken.

Take Charge of Change

Say supportive statements to yourself every day.
Because Fours can be very hard on themselves, it is important for you to make positive self-statements on a daily basis, at a minimum of six times per day. Statements such as "You did a very good job on that" and "How wonderful that you enjoy your children so much" are fine, as long as you actually believe what you say. When you do this multiple times a day for three months, you will find that your negative self-talk becomes less pervasive.

Develop effective filters for both positive and negative information about yourself.
Fours tend to absorb negative information they receive about themselves with a limited ability to filter out what they believe is false. In addition, when Fours hear positive information, they often hear it but then discard it without integrating any of it into their sense of self. It is important for you to develop well-functioning filters that allow you to absorb positive and negative information *only after* you have decided you agree with it. Every time someone tells you something about yourself, ask yourself this before you take it in or discard it: *Do I really agree with this information?*

Develop a way to manage your feelings that works for you.
Some Fours keep journals or write poetry. Others play musical instruments, sing, dance, or paint. Some Fours simply talk with friends and family. What is important is that you have an outlet for emotional expression and that you do not keep your feelings locked inside.

For more insights and information about organizational change, please refer to the following: Chapter 8, "Take Charge of Change," in *What Type of Leader Are You?* (McGraw-Hill, 2007).

TRANSFORMATION DEVELOPMENT STRETCHES

In order to move from their *desire for deep connections — both with their own interior worlds and with other people — and the sense that they are most alive when they authentically express their personal experiences and feelings* to the understanding that *everyone and everything is connected at the deepest levels,* Fours can work toward these transformations:

Mental Transformation

Transform the mental pattern of **melancholy** (thinking continually about what is missing, with accompanying thoughts of being disconnected or separated from others) *into a higher belief in the* **original source** (the insight that nothing is missing and that everything and everybody are ultimately deeply connected, because we all emanate from the same source).

Mental Activity

When you become aware that you are noticing what is missing or lacking in a situation and underplaying or ignoring what is positive, try to remember one or more times when you perceived both the positive and the negative in a situation and truly appreciated what you had as well as your deep connection with everything and everyone. Try to remember both ordinary moments and big events. Allow those times to come back into your mind, and relive what was occurring within you at those times for a minimum of three minutes.

Emotional Transformation

Transform the emotional habit of **envy** (consciously or unconsciously comparing oneself repeatedly with others in large and small ways, with accompanying feelings of deficiency or superiority) *into the higher awareness of* **balance** (experiencing emotions in such a clear and centered way that thoughts, feelings, and actions emanate from the inner self).

Emotional Activity

When you find that you're comparing yourself to others, remember one or more times in your life when you didn't compare yourself or anything in your situation to anyone or anything else. Remember how you felt during those times — it's likely that things seemed to be going well without any effort whatsoever, and that your thoughts, feelings, and actions were balanced, clear, and working in harmony. Keep replaying those moments in your mind and heart until you feel fully reconnected with the experiences.

For more insights and information about personal transformation, please refer to the following: Chapter 7, "Transforming Yourself," in *Bringing Out the Best in Yourself at Work* (McGraw-Hill, 2004).

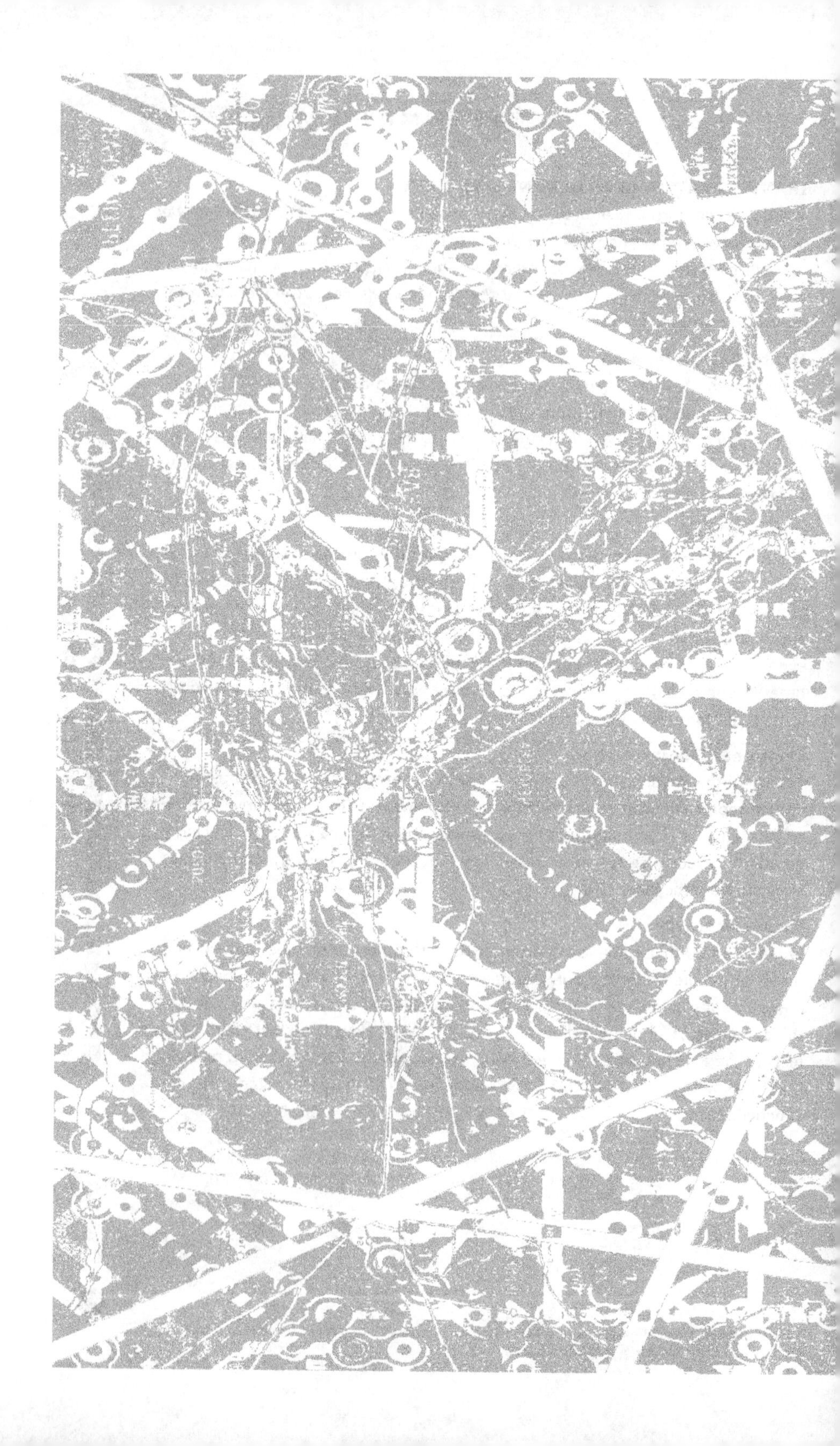

ENNEAGRAM STYLE FIVE

ENNEAGRAM FIVES

The search for knowledge and wisdom and the avoidance of intrusion and loss of energy

Emotionally detached, private, self-controlled, and highly independent — autonomous may be a more accurate description — Fives have an insatiable need to know, particularly about areas that interest or concern them. Fully understanding how everything works and fits together helps Fives believe that they are on the path to wisdom, but just as important, accumulating knowledge helps them feel prepared for the inevitable surprises they would prefer to not experience. The quest for privacy is a constant among Fives, although the areas they consider private vary widely. Some Fives like to share their knowledge, while others consider this proprietary. Some Fives are highly private about what they do in their spare time, while others consider their age, marital status, and other such personal information to be in the confidential realm.

All Fives automatically detach from their feelings in the actual moment of an emotional experience, reactivating some of these feelings later, at a more convenient and private time. Fives also compartmentalize or isolate aspects of their lives from other parts. However, the content of what Fives compartmentalize can differ widely. Some Fives compartmentalize their work life from their home life; others keep their friends separated from one another; and other Fives keep themselves isolated from other people.

In addition, most Fives are extremely wary of intrusions on their physical space, their time and energy, and demands for intense interpersonal interactions. Some keep extremely controlled boundaries and are attached to their seclusion, coming out for more engagement at specifically selected moments; others are more outgoing and social — though the content of their conversations tends to be information and facts that interest them — and are so drawn to lofty ideals that they can lose interest in everyday life; and some Fives engage primarily with the few others they completely trust and with whom they feel a special bond.

The Five's interpersonal style is highly self-contained, with little animation in either their voice tone or body language. They may appear forthcoming about giving information and others less so, but all Fives appear remote to some degree. Some Fives may be engaging in a way that attracts others and others less so, but all Fives make it obvious that there are clear boundaries on what they will discuss and how they will discuss it.

While we can all be emotionally detached and many people enjoy interesting information, for Fives, the search for knowledge and wisdom and the avoidance of intrusion and loss of energy is their primary, persistent, and driving motivation.

DEVELOPMENT STRETCHES FOR FIVES

INDIVIDUALS WHO THIRST FOR KNOWLEDGE AND USE EMOTIONAL DETACHMENT AS A WAY OF KEEPING INVOLVEMENT WITH OTHERS TO A MINIMUM

CONTENTS

SELF-MASTERY DEVELOPMENT STRETCHES

Self-Mastery — the ability to understand, accept, and transform your thoughts, feelings, and behavior, with the understanding that each day will bring new challenges that are opportunities for growth — is the foundation of all personal and professional development. Self-mastery begins with self-awareness, then expands to include the elements shown in the following graphic:

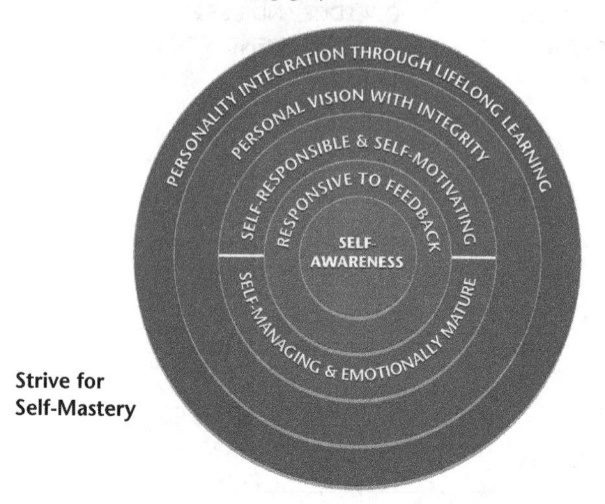

Strive for Self-Mastery

In this section on self-mastery, you will find the following:

- Three common issues for Fives related to self-mastery
- Three development stretches for working with the core issues of your Enneagram style, including one basic activity and one deeper activity for each stretch
- Three development stretches for working with your wings and arrow (stress-security) styles

Common Issues for Fives Related to Self-Mastery

Engaging emotionally in real time rather than automatically disengaging from your emotional responses	Sharing more of yourself — including your thoughts, feelings, and personal experiences — with others	Being a central part of events, interpersonal interactions, and organizations, rather than staying on the periphery

For more insights and information about self-mastery, please refer to the following: Chapter 7, "Transforming Yourself," in *Bringing Out the Best in Yourself at Work* (McGraw-Hill, 2004) and Chapter 3, "Strive for Self-Mastery," in *What Type of Leader Are You?* (McGraw-Hill, 2007).

Development Stretches for Working with the Core Issues of Your Enneagram Style

Allow yourself to need others.

Basic Activity

Each week, think of one thing you can't provide completely for yourself and that you therefore need from others. Then think of someone who might be able to provide this for you, and ask that person if he or she will do so. What matters most is not whether the person says yes but that you have identified a need and asked for it to be met.

Deeper Activity

Because Fives value their autonomy and have come to believe that they really don't need other people very much, it can be enlightening to realize that you either do — or could — need others far more than you currently think. Take a piece of paper and fold it in half. On the left side, write down at least ten ways in which you currently do or could need others, if you allowed yourself to do so (e.g., a need for intellectual rapport). On the right side, write down ten ways in which you hold yourself back from getting your needs met by others (e.g., not knowing how to start a conversation).

Some of the ways in which you hold yourself back may be related to specific needs listed on the left-hand side. When this is the case, draw a line between these related items from the two lists. For example, not knowing how to start a conversation would be a likely barrier to engaging in an intellectual conversation.

The next day, select one of the needs from your first list and make a commitment to take action to get this need met. A very logical and helpful first step would be to remove the relevant barriers from the second list. Continue working on this one need for a full week. The second week, select another need from your list and follow the same process. Take action on a new item from your needs list each week until you have completed the entire list. If any new needs or barriers come to your attention, feel free to add these to your lists.

Connect with and express your feelings.

Basic Activity

For two or three days, every hour on the hour, ask yourself this question: *What am I feeling right now?* Don't settle for a one-word answer. Then ask yourself this: *And what else am I feeling?* After three days, continue asking yourself both questions, but do so at those times when you are aware that you are becoming extremely analytical. These moments of extreme analysis may be covering over your feelings.

For more insights and information about self-mastery, please refer to the following: Chapter 7, "Transforming Yourself," in *Bringing Out the Best in Yourself at Work* (McGraw-Hill, 2004) and Chapter 3, "Strive for Self-Mastery," in *What Type of Leader Are You?* (McGraw-Hill, 2007).

Deeper Activity

In their thirst to know everything they possibly can, Fives also tend to take a more cerebral view of the world of feelings. They have learned how to disconnect from their feelings the moment that these actually occur so that they can bring them up for examination later, at a time of their choosing. This way of dealing with feelings makes Fives believe that they are able to understand their feelings, and it also makes them feel less vulnerable and more in control.

Fives disconnect from their feelings in various ways. Some, for example, simply start thinking intensely about something else when their feelings arise; some Fives may hold their breath until the feelings subside; and others may pull their attention into their heads and begin to observe themselves as if they were objects to study. For all Fives, however, the process of emotional disconnection is so automatic and habitual that they are usually unaware they are doing it. The very first step in the development process for Fives is to pay close attention to exactly how and when they disconnect from their feelings.

For one week, simply observe the ways in which you disconnect from your feelings. Write down these observations in very precise terms, but don't attempt to change your behavior yet. There will be numerous times each day that you do this; consequently, one week will give you ample information. The following week, practice not doing the behaviors you noted doing when you disconnect from your feelings. As you do this, make sure you breathe deeply; this will help your feelings to surface. Continue to practice allowing yourself to connect with your feelings until it becomes easy for you to do so. At this point, you can choose either to remain connected to your feelings or to disconnect from them at will.

For more insights and information about self-mastery, please refer to the following: Chapter 7, "Transforming Yourself," in *Bringing Out the Best in Yourself at Work* (McGraw-Hill, 2004) and Chapter 3, "Strive for Self-Mastery," in *What Type of Leader Are You?* (McGraw-Hill, 2007).

Once you have learned how to experience your emotions at the time they actually occur, you will also become more aware of the variety of feelings you have. The next step is to share these feelings with others. It is easiest to begin by discussing some feelings you have had recently with individuals whom you know well and trust. For one week, select three different people with whom to talk. An effective conversation opener is "Do you have a minute? I want to get your reactions to some feelings I had recently." Feel free to talk about anything you like as long as you are sharing emotions — for example, *I've been wondering if I should take a vacation abroad* is a thought, whereas *I want to take a vacation abroad, but I'm terribly worried about leaving my sick mother* is a feeling. Do the above activity for two more weeks, selecting different individuals each week. Once you feel comfortable discussing recent feelings, then practice discussing feelings in the present. Choose three people per week — you can choose the same people if you wish — and share spontaneous feelings, such as *That project was so much fun* or *I really didn't like the way the meeting we attended was run.*

Continue this phase of the activity for two more weeks, selecting different individuals each week. Finally, you are ready to practice communicating your feelings with people whom you know less well. Select two people each week with whom you will practice. Choose to communicate either recent or spontaneous feelings with each of them. There is no reason to bare your heart to this person — simply make sure that you take the risk and get practice in revealing information about your feelings to him or her. A good conversation starter might be "Do you have a few minutes to talk about the project? I'm feeling more and more nervous that we may not make our deadline" or "Wasn't that a great meeting? I felt so pleased when they honored our team for its accomplishments."

Increase your capacity to engage rather than to withdraw.

Basic Activity

When you attend any sort of social gathering, force yourself to stand or sit right in the middle of where people are interacting. When you do this, look at other people and smile, which will encourage them to approach you. When someone approaches you, engage in interaction by asking a question or offering some information about yourself.

For more insights and information about self-mastery, please refer to the following: Chapter 7, "Transforming Yourself," in *Bringing Out the Best in Yourself at Work* (McGraw-Hill, 2004) and Chapter 3, "Strive for Self-Mastery," in *What Type of Leader Are You?* (McGraw-Hill, 2007).

Deeper Activity

Everyone has cycles of engagement and withdrawal, but Fives tend to withdraw from others far more than they engage. In fact, Fives tend to disengage as a matter of habit. Some Fives literally or figuratively sit outside of groups they belong to. Others say very little in social encounters or leave events early. Still others give monosyllabic answers to questions, thereby giving the impression that they prefer not to converse.

The first step in learning to engage is to actually want to engage with others. The second step involves specific actions that foster engagement. To begin with, Fives need to consider why they would want to engage with others and to find some compelling reasons to do so. Otherwise, there will be no motivation to change behavior. Once you feel that you do want to learn how to engage more frequently with others, make three lists, side by side. In the first column, write down how you will benefit if you do engage with others more frequently. In the second column, write down what you believe you may be missing because of your pattern of withdrawal. In the third column, write down the specific things you do that allow you to disengage from interaction — for example, bringing work with you to meetings, not communicating with others unless they ask you a question, or standing literally outside of groups.

Over the next two weeks, observe other people as they interact with others. When you observe individuals who seem very effective in their interactions, pay attention to the details of their behavior — where they stand or sit, what they say and how they say it, their timing, their body language, and so on. Next, experiment with trying some of these behaviors yourself, and notice the effects of your new behaviors both on you and on your interactions with others.

After you have done this for two weeks, select someone you know well who appears to be able to engage effectively, and ask this person for some tips on how to engage others. Open up with a simple statement to him or her such as "I've noticed you're quite skilled at networking, and this is something I'm exploring how to do more effectively. Can you give me a few tips on what you've learned about doing this?" Then try each of these suggested behaviors yourself.

For more insights and information about self-mastery, please refer to the following: Chapter 7, "Transforming Yourself," in *Bringing Out the Best in Yourself at Work* (McGraw-Hill, 2004) and Chapter 3, "Strive for Self-Mastery," in *What Type of Leader Are You?* (McGraw-Hill, 2007).

Development Stretches for Working with Your Wings and Arrow (Stress-Security) Styles

Wings are the Enneagram styles on either side of your core Enneagram style; arrow, or stress-security, styles are Enneagram styles shown with arrows pointing away or toward your core Enneagram style. Your wings and arrow styles don't change your core Enneagram style, but instead offer qualities that can broaden and enrich your patterns of thinking and feeling as well as enhance your behaviors. Your wings and arrow styles make you more complex and versatile because they provide more dimensions to your personality and serve as vehicles for self-development.

Integrate Your Four Wing

Explore the world of feelings.

While Fours are familiar with the nuances of the world of feeling and often express feelings spontaneously, Fives usually stay away from the emotional realm and its direct expression. Consequently, Fives can use the strengths and skills of their wing style Four to familiarize themselves with their feelings and further develop their emotional repertoire. They can do this by asking themselves this question each time they think, do, or say something important to them: *What am I feeling right now?* If a thought emerges instead of a feeling, such as "I'm thinking about my work," the next question to ask is this: *Yes, but what am I feeling about it?*

After answering the last question, it can be helpful for Fives to pinpoint where in their bodies they experience sensations when they have this feeling — for example, a constriction in the chest area, a knot or a sensation in the pit of the stomach, or an ache in the shoulder. These physical cues can be helpful later on in identifying feelings. For example, anger may come with a clenched jaw and a tightening of the lower arms. On some future occasion when you may not immediately know your exact feelings, recognition of your body sensations may make you realize, *Oh, I must be feeling angry. What am I angry about?*

Develop your artistic expression.

Emotions are often the subject of artistic expression and artistic expression can help us understand the feelings we have. When Fives combine the expression of their feelings with the abilities of their keen minds, their artistry can be exquisite — whether they express themselves through writing (such as plays, prose, or poetry), the visual arts (e.g., photography, film, painting, drawing, or sculpture), or the performing arts (theater, dance, and other physical modes). Select an artistic medium that appeals to you. Then ponder some event or situation that elicited strong feelings in you. Allow yourself to consider the feelings deeply in all their nuances, and allow symbols to emerge that represent these feelings. Symbols can be images, colors, lines, shapes, words, movement, or anything else that represents the deeper meaning of your experience. Then, use these symbols to express your artistic sensibility.

For more insights and information about integrating your wings and/or arrow styles (stress-security points), please refer to the following: Chapter 1, "What Type Are You?" and the conclusion, "Stretch Your Leadership Paradigms," in *What Type of Leader Are You?* (McGraw-Hill, 2007).

Connect with others on a deep level.

Fours relish engaging others on a deep level because connecting in this way invigorates Fours. They most often do this through the mutual sharing of stories about emotional lives and personal experiences. Fives, by contrast, keep such information to themselves, sharing this information only with individuals whom they have known a very long time (decades rather than years or months) and whom they trust. When Fives learn to connect emotionally with other people who are not extremely close friends, it pushes them to stay with their own and other people's feelings in real time and to find the wisdom in people's personal experiences.

Fives can practice connecting deeply with individuals with whom they could imagine having a closer relationship, thus fast-forwarding the relationship-building process. The best way to practice this is to take advantage of the opportunities that present themselves weekly. When you observe someone you know looking either happier or more concerned than normal, and the two of you are in a position to have a private discussion, all you have to do is make this statement: *I noticed that you seem to be concerned [or happy] about something.* Normally, the person will start telling you about his or her experience. As the person is speaking, simply ask a few questions for more insight, or share your reactions to what he or she is saying.

For more insights and information about integrating your wings and/or arrow styles (stress-security points), please refer to the following: Chapter 1, "What Type Are You?" and the conclusion, "Stretch Your Leadership Paradigms," in *What Type of Leader Are You?* (McGraw-Hill, 2007).

Integrate Your Six Wing

Focus on the group.

While Fives often behave more like individual players in a group context, Sixes concentrate more on the group. Fives can also learn to do this when they are in groups or on teams by asking themselves these questions: *How can I contribute more to the group? What is it that the group needs from me, and how can I contribute in this way? How can I demonstrate my loyalty and commitment to the group?*

4 5 6 WINGS FOR FIVES

When Fives participate in groups or teams, other people often focus on them because they seem hesitant or withdrawn. Their solitude either elicits efforts from others to draw them out of their shells or attracts people to them who are puzzled by the Five's silence and air of mystery. Ironically, when Fives become more involved and energetic in groups, people often focus less on them; as a consequence, Fives end up feeling fewer demands from others, rather than more.

Increase your interactions with others.

Sixes often talk easily with others because they tend to ask relevant questions and respond to others with details, thus giving the impression that they are interested in the conversation. They usually smile or lean toward the other person, both of which indicate their engagement with the person. Fives can do this, too, by (1) asking open-ended questions of others rather than yes-no questions — for example, by asking, "What did you think of the meeting?" rather than "Did you like the meeting?" (2) making their comments or answers to questions about three sentences in length (Fives tend to give very short or extremely long answers), and (3) leaning toward the other person.

Develop your intuition.

Because Fives and Sixes are both styles based in the Head Center, individuals of both styles often rely on their logic and analytical abilities. However, Sixes also utilize their intuition, which is based on feelings and gut reactions as much as on mental processing. This more holisitic intuition is generally more reliable than insights based on reason alone. To develop intuition based on the integration of the head, heart, and gut, you need to do three things: (1) ask yourself how you truly and deeply feel about a situation; (2) ask your gut the following question: *What is the real truth of the situation?* and (3) combine the above answers with what your logic says about the situation. If you get three answers that are not aligned with one another, ask your gut for the reason behind this lack of alignment.

For more insights and information about integrating your wings and/or arrow styles (stress-security points), please refer to the following: Chapter 1, "What Type Are You?" and the conclusion, "Stretch Your Leadership Paradigms," in *What Type of Leader Are You?* (McGraw-Hill, 2007).

ENNEAGRAM FIVES

Integrate Arrow Style Seven (Stress Point)

Become more spontaneous.

Sevens tend to be spontaneous by saying what comes to mind, acting quickly on impulse, and engaging with others with a minimal degree of self-consciousness. Fives, on the other hand, more typically calculate and consider what they will say, control the actions they take, and are often reserved or guarded in their interactions with others. Practice being more spontaneous by first doing so with those whom you know best, eventually using the same behavior in widening circles of friends and acquaintances as you become more comfortable with spontaneity. Select an event or interaction each day and say to yourself: *I will let my guard down at this time and just do or say what comes to me at the time.* At the end of the day, reflect on this experience and ask yourself these questions: *How did I do? Was I spontaneous? What happened because of this that was positive? Did anything negative occur as a result?* Continue the above activity daily; you will likely find that you become more and more spontaneous with increased practice and reflection.

Allow your energy to flow.

Fives tend to contain and restrain their energy because they believe that energy exists in a limited supply, and therefore must be guarded. Sevens, in contrast, usually allow their energy to flow from them to the outside and from the outside into them. The Seven style is based more on the notion that there is an abundance of energy that can be exchanged with others and the environment, and that this exchange only increases the total amount of energy available. This paradigm shift can be a challenge for Fives, but if they try to act as if energy flowing between themselves and others creates more energy, even for a few minutes at a time, they may experience a very new way of being in the world. For example, when giving a speech, really look at the audience and take in the positive responses they may give you. When you are giving information to others, ask them to give you their thoughts and ideas in return.

Have more fun.

Sevens can be extremely playful, while Fives usually appear serious or reserved. Many Fives can be joyful around people they know well and trust, although this usually occurs outside the work setting. Because Fives already know how to be playful in one context, all they have to do is experiment with being playful in a new context — at work and/or with people they don't know quite as well. Make a commitment to doing this one time per week. Once you are more comfortable doing this, you are likely to find that it comes more naturally and more regularly.

For more insights and information about integrating your wings and/or arrow styles (stress-security points), please refer to the following: Chapter 1, "What Type Are You?" and the conclusion, "Stretch Your Leadership Paradigms," in *What Type of Leader Are You?* (McGraw-Hill, 2007).

Integrate Arrow Style Eight (Security Point)

Claim your personal power.

Most Eights claim their personal power readily. When they step into a room, others sense their presence. At times, they appear to fill up more space than other people. Fives, by contrast, often prefer to stay somewhat invisible in groups, so their body language and speaking styles reflect this.

To claim more personal power in the presence of others, Fives need to overcome the tendency to stay figuratively smaller than they are. You can practice this using a number of techniques:

1. Look at the other person or persons the entire time you are interacting. You can smile, frown, or do whatever comes naturally, but make sure you do not give any indication that you have somehow checked out of the conversation.
2. Make your presence known early in the conversation by making a statement (not asking a question).
3. Keep breathing deeply the entire time you are interacting, making sure not to breathe only in a shallow manner. Deep breathing fills your entire body with energy and often emits a larger sense of presence than does shallow breathing.
4. Make short comments about other people's ideas.
5. Make clear and practical suggestions about how to organize or do something relevant to the conversation.
6. Pay attention to the conversations that occur by using your eyes — follow different speakers with your eyes and give head nods to good ideas.

Assert yourself.

Eights can act assertive at will, without having to muster the confidence first. Fives, in contrast, do not assert themselves as easily and often have to plan and strategize for doing so. When it comes to marketing themselves, Eights are likely to tell you what you may need to know and how they can provide these services, whereas Fives may have all the necessary skills and tools yet have difficulty suggesting that you might want to use their services. Fives can be left wondering why their ample abilities go underappreciated, when the issue may well be that Fives are not articulating their skills and abilities effectively.

For more insights and information about integrating your wings and/or arrow styles (stress-security points), please refer to the following: Chapter 1, "What Type Are You?" and the conclusion, "Stretch Your Leadership Paradigms," in *What Type of Leader Are You?* (McGraw-Hill, 2007).

The following practice can be a stretch, yet a useful one for Fives. Every week, make a list of things you want to do that others have control over. Select one person from that list each week and initiate a conversation. After exchanging some initial pleasantries, tell this person what you want and why he or she should select you as the person to do it. Don't say: *I want to be the next supervisor in this group.* Instead, say: *I know you are considering several people for the supervisory position. I would like you to know that given my strong technical background and my ability to work with and gain commitment from all types of people, I want you to give my candidacy serious consideration. I know I can deliver what you want, and I am committed to doing so.* This way of talking sounds assertive, confident, and compelling.

Take up more space.

Eights have such a strong physical presence that others are usually quite aware of them even when Eights are silent. When Eights walk, they often take up so much physical space that others move in order not to be in their way. Fives, by contrast, often prefer to remain more physically invisible; the result is that they take up less physical space than they are entitled to, often making way for other people when they walk.

Fives can experiment with taking up more space than they normally do through two activities. First, when you are walking on the sidewalk and someone appears to be walking toward you using the same space on the sidewalk as you are, don't move out of the other person's way; keep walking forward. The person will move out of your way, even if he or she does so at the last minute. Second, when you are in a meeting (or at a social gathering) and you are not the person speaking, keep breathing deeply and maintain your physical presence, and give your full attention to all conversations and interactions — just as you would if you were the speaker. This will allow you to fill the space completely.

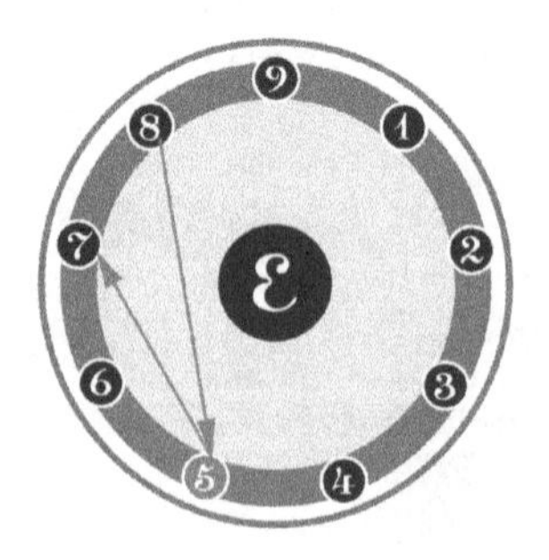

For more insights and information about integrating your wings and/or arrow styles (stress-security points), please refer to the following: Chapter 1, "What Type Are You?" and the conclusion, "Stretch Your Leadership Paradigms," in *What Type of Leader Are You?* (McGraw-Hill, 2007).

COMMUNICATION DEVELOPMENT STRETCHES

When you communicate with someone, three kinds of unintentional distortions may be present: speaking style, body language, and blind spots. *Speaking style* refers to your overall pattern of speaking. *Body language* includes posture, facial expressions, hand gestures, body movements, energy levels, and hundreds of other nonverbal messages. *Blind spots* are elements of your communication containing information about you that is not apparent to you but is highly visible to other people. We all unknowingly convey information through an amalgam of our speaking style, body language, and other inferential data.

The receivers of the messages you send also distort what they hear through their *distorting filters*. These are unconscious concerns or assumptions, often based on the listener's Enneagram style, that alter how someone hears what others say.

Speaking Style Body Language Blind Spots

Change one communication style behavior at a time.

It is most effective to work on changing one behavior at a time, preferably in the following sequence: speaking style, body language, blind spots, and listening distorting filters. It is easiest to change the behaviors of which we are most aware, and this sequence represents the most common order of awareness, from most to least aware.

Fives: Speaking style

- Speak tersely *or* in lengthy discourse
- Highly selective word choice
- Limited sharing of personal information
- Share thoughts rather than feelings

Fives: Body language

- Appear self-contained and self-controlled, with unanimated body language
- Prefer 50 percent more physical distance between themselves and others when conversing than the cultural norm for physical space
- May appear to be observing themselves as they speak and interact
- Offer few facial cues regarding their reactions to people and ideas

For more insights and information about communication, please refer to the following: Chapter 2, "Communicating Effectively," in *Bringing Out the Best in Yourself at Work* (McGraw-Hill, 2004) and Chapter 5, "Become an Excellent Communicator," in *What Type of Leader Are You?* (McGraw-Hill, 2007).

Fives: Blind spots

- May not exhibit warmth
- May appear aloof or remote
- May use too few words and so may not be understood by others
- May say too much and lose listeners
- May appear condescending or elitist

Fives: Distorting filters when listening to someone else

- Unexpected demands and expectations from others
- Feeling inadequate
- Emotionality from the other person that feels overwhelming
- Whether or not the Five trusts the other person to maintain privacy
- Physical proximity that feels too close

Note: Some of the above characteristics may be positive, some negative, and some neutral or mixed. They are intended as an overview to allow you to select from among them.

Use e-mails to expand and adjust your language patterns.

- Review your e-mails before you send them for language and tone.
- Elaborate more on each idea if you have written a brief e-mail.
- Make your e-mail more concise if you have written a long e-mail.
- Include your feelings as well as your thoughts.
- If you want the e-mail recipient to do something specific, be explicit about your wishes near the beginning of the e-mail.

For more insights and information about communication, please refer to the following: Chapter 2, "Communicating Effectively," in *Bringing Out the Best in Yourself at Work* (McGraw-Hill, 2004) and Chapter 5, "Become an Excellent Communicator," in *What Type of Leader Are You?* (McGraw-Hill, 2007).

FEEDBACK DEVELOPMENT STRETCHES

Honest, positive, and constructive *feedback* — direct, objective, simple, and respectful observations that one person makes about another's behavior — improves both relationships and on-the-job performance. When you offer feedback, the Feedback Formula, combined with the insights of the Enneagram, helps you tailor your delivery. When someone gives you feedback, the more receptive you are to hearing what is being said, the more likely it is that you will be able to discern what is useful and utilize what has been suggested.

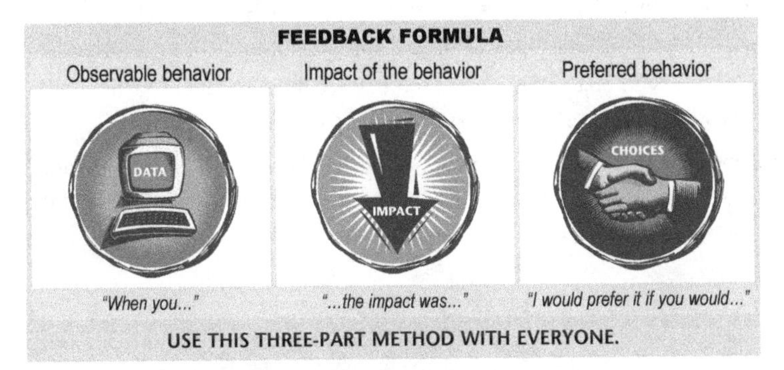

How Fives Can Enhance Their Ability to Deliver Feedback Effectively

When you offer feedback to someone, you want to be prepared and also to encourage the feedback recipient to be as receptive as possible. Remember that how and when you deliver feedback is just as important as what you actually say.

Use the three components of the **Feedback Formula** together with the following suggestions to plan and deliver the feedback.

- Maintain your precision, but do not be so concise that the other person does not understand what you are saying.
- Continue to rigorously think through your approach, but be careful not to overload the feedback recipient with information.
- Continue to be clear about your task, but also invite an emotional response from the other person.
- Remember that the feedback recipient may not want a clearly defined, logical approach and may prefer an integrated, thinking-feeling interaction.

For more insights and information about feedback, please refer to the following: Chapter 3, "Giving Constructive Feedback," in *Bringing Out the Best in Yourself at Work* (McGraw-Hill, 2004) and Chapter 5, "Become an Excellent Communicator," in *What Type of Leader Are You?* (McGraw-Hill, 2007).

How Fives Can Be More Receptive When They Receive Feedback

- When someone is about to give you positive or negative feedback, you may give that person nonverbal cues that you don't want to receive the feedback — for example, through limited eye contact or stepping back. The person's timing might not be right, or you may be anticipating that the other person is expecting an emotional response you are not prepared to offer. Remind yourself that people may not think to ask you if the timing is right, but they may still have some valuable insights to offer that might not be shared if they think you are not interested.
- Practice giving positive and negative feedback to others. This will give you the opportunity to objectively understand that feedback has great value, thus making you more receptive when you're the recipient.
- Remember that even though you may like feedback that is very logical and delivered concisely, it may actually be most useful to you to receive feedback that includes feelings and that contains some detail.

For more insights and information about feedback, please refer to the following: Chapter 3, "Giving Constructive Feedback," in *Bringing Out the Best in Yourself at Work* (McGraw-Hill, 2004) and Chapter 5, "Become an Excellent Communicator," in *What Type of Leader Are You?* (McGraw-Hill, 2007).

CONFLICT DEVELOPMENT STRETCHES

Relationships both at work and at home often involve some degree of conflict, which may be caused by a variety of factors and usually follows the pinch-crunch cycle below:

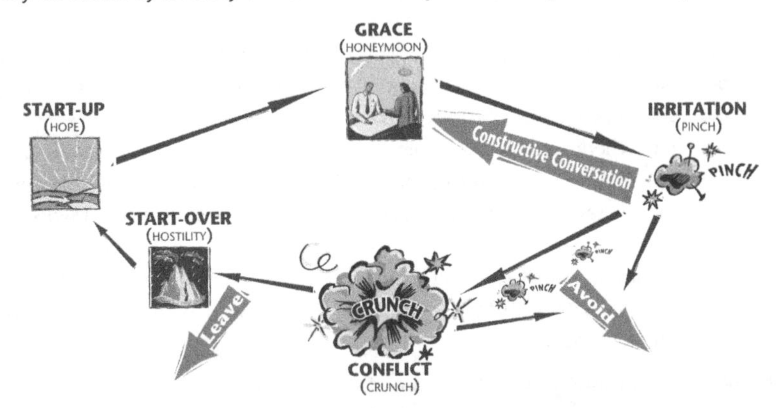

Whatever the root cause of the conflict, the Enneagram styles of the key parties involved will always be a factor in the conflict dynamics and resolution. The Enneagram enables each individual involved to make conflict resolution a constructive rather than destructive experience. The more people know themselves, understand their own responsibilities in the conflict interaction, engage in constructive self-management, and know how best to approach others through knowledge of the Enneagram, the greater the chances of a swift and effective outcome.

There are specific pinches (anger triggers) for each Enneagram style — that is, certain situations that will invariably ignite anger in a person of one style, yet may not affect someone of a different style. For Fives, these pinches include:

Someone's disclosing the Five's private information to another person · Being surprised or taken off-guard · Dishonesty in another person, including the other person not delivering a quality work product at the agreed upon time · Situations that feel out of control · Overwhelming tasks · Being expected to offer an emotional response before the Five desires to do so

For more insights and information about conflict, please refer to the following: Chapter 4, "Managing Conflict," in *Bringing Out the Best in Yourself at Work* (McGraw-Hill, 2004) and Chapter 5, "Become an Excellent Communicator," in *What Type of Leader Are You?* (McGraw-Hill, 2007).

Development Stretches for Transforming Anger into an Opportunity for Growth

Share your likely pinches (anger triggers) with others at the beginning of your working relationship.

This type of self-disclosure early on in a working relationship can be a stretch for many Fives, but it also has many benefits. The level of disclosure can be simple as this: "Let's talk about how we work best with others so that our relationship begins on a productive note. There are only a few things that are very important. I like work to be well managed and under control, and I dislike surprises. By 'surprises' I mean things like unnecessary or last-minute requests, as well as demands that I work beyond certain hours when I have already made other plans. I also don't like to be surprised by information that you may know but not have shared that can help me understand the organization or the project better. I like to work with others when we keep each other informed."

Say something as soon as you are aware of feeling pinched or upset.

This is actually a great way to minimize surprises for both you and the other person. In the initial conversation to discuss working styles, simply suggest that you both agree to discuss any pinches that may occur as you work together. A simple statement such as "Let's agree to discuss any pinches or glitches as they occur so that we can continue to have a productive work relationship" will almost always be well received by the other person. With this agreement in mind, make a commitment to take the initiative and to share any concern, even a small one, soon after it arises. This is not an intrusion on the other person, because he or she has already agreed to this plan. The biggest issue is for Fives to actually say something, since this means they will need to acknowledge that something has disturbed them and stay connected to their feelings, as well as assert themselves and approach the other person.

When you start to behave in ways that indicate you are feeling pinched or distressed, do something physical if you can, such as working out or taking a walk.

In disconnecting from their feelings and disengaging from other people, Fives use different techniques. For example, some Fives stop breathing deeply and begin to breathe only as far as their necks. Other Fives simply focus all their attention on their minds and engage in a flurry of thought. Still others may compartmentalize a distressing event by placing it in their minds as a categorized mental idea.

Compartmentalization is the process by which a person puts information, experiences, and even personal behavior into mental categories or "boxes," each separated from the other. One person, a high-level manager, bought a house but never told anyone (lest they come over unannounced), and was married for eight years but kept it a secret from work colleagues and friends (lest the marriage not work out). It did not!

For more insights and information about conflict, please refer to the following: Chapter 4, "Managing Conflict," in *Bringing Out the Best in Yourself at Work* (McGraw-Hill, 2004) and Chapter 5, "Become an Excellent Communicator," in *What Type of Leader Are You?* (McGraw-Hill, 2007).

Whichever process Fives use to disconnect and disengage, their choice of technique invariably puts them less in touch with their bodies and their feelings. Physical activity of any type usually reestablishes the connection between mind and body; it often reconnects Fives with their feelings as well, because feelings correspond to sensations located in the body.

When you have a negative reaction and feel a pinch, ask yourself: ***What does my reaction to this situation or to the other person's behavior say about me as a Five and about the areas in which I can develop? How can working on my pinches and crunches help me to bring out the best in myself?***

Because most Fives crave knowledge and understanding, pursuing this type of self-discovery often suits them very well. The crucial consideration is to answer this question in both an emotional and an objective way. The emotional aspect involves the exploration of feelings and the treatment of these as equal in importance to thoughts. To answer the questions above objectively, Fives must take stock of themselves — not only from their own perspective, but from the perspectives of others as well. A helpful question to ask yourself is this: *I understand my reaction as a Five in this way, but how would individuals from the other eight styles perceive it? What can I learn from these alternative points of view?* Very often, the self-discovery leads Fives to understand the ways in which they disconnect from their emotional lives and disengage both from other people and from experiences.

For more insights and information about conflict, please refer to the following: Chapter 4, "Managing Conflict," in *Bringing Out the Best in Yourself at Work* (McGraw-Hill, 2004) and Chapter 5, "Become an Excellent Communicator," in *What Type of Leader Are You?* (McGraw-Hill, 2007).

TEAM DEVELOPMENT STRETCHES

There is a difference between a group and a team. A *group* is a collection of individuals who have something in common; a *team* is a specific type of group, one composed of members who share one or more *goals* that can be reached only when there is an optimal level of *interdependence* between and among team members.

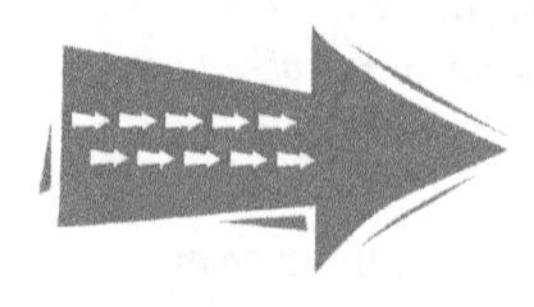

Team members also have *roles* — predictable patterns of behavior – within the team that are often related to their Enneagram styles. *Task roles* involve behaviors directed toward the work itself; *relationship roles* involve behaviors focused on feelings, relationships, and team processes, such as decision making and conflict resolution.

In addition, teams have unique yet predictable dynamics as they go through the four sequential stages of team development: *forming, storming, norming,* and *performing.* At each stage, there are questions the team must resolve before moving to the next stage.

TEAM STAGE	QUESTIONS
FORMING	*Who are we, where are we going, and are we all going there together?*
STORMING	*Can we disagree with one another in a constructive and productive way?*
NORMING	*How should we best organize ourselves and work together?*
PERFORMING	*How can we keep performing at a high level and not burn out?*

Fives: Development Stretches for Team Members and Team Leaders

Team Goals

Although you may prefer team goals that are extremely *precise, concrete, useful,* and *manageable,* other team members may need goals that are more lofty, compelling, and values based. Allow yourself to also see the big picture and be vision oriented when you create team goals.

Team Interdependence

Although you may prefer to work in teams with *low interdependence and high degrees of individual autonomy*, where all team members are capable and efficient, remind yourself that some teams need to work at a medium to high interdependence to be effective, and that not all team members will be as efficient as you would like. Work to support the level of interdependence the team needs, even if this means giving up some of the autonomy you prefer, and work to develop patience with team members who are not highly efficient or who take longer than others to demonstrate their capabilities.

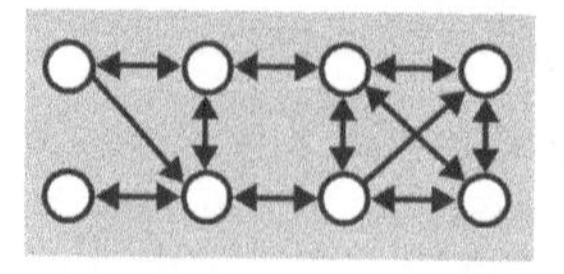

For more insights and information about teams, please refer to the following: Chapter 5, "Creating High-Performing Teams," in *Bringing Out the Best in Yourself at Work* (McGraw-Hill, 2004) and Chapter 6, "Lead High-Performing Teams," in *What Type of Leader Are You?* (McGraw-Hill, 2007).

Team Roles

Your typical task-related team role is likely to involve *managing resources* within the team by paying attention to and monitoring the team's resources, such as time, money, staffing, and materials. Your likely relationship-related team role may be *providing perspective* by stating or reframing complex issues either in a larger and more complex context or in a simpler and more straightforward way, so that alternative views and courses of action can be considered. Stretch yourself to go beyond these typical roles and adopt the following additional team task and relationship roles:

Task Roles

New task role

Defining the larger purpose, stating or helping the team clarify its charter and larger intention

New relationship role

Expressing feelings by sharing your own emotional reactions with other team members and helping others do the same

Relationship Roles

Team Dynamics

During the four stages of team development — *forming, storming, norming,* and *performing* — experiment with expanding your repertoire of behavior in the following ways:

FORMING	STORMING	NORMING	PERFORMING
Add a strong relationship focus to your current task focus by encouraging team members to get to know one another and to learn what skills and strengths each person brings to the team's task.	Allow yourself to become more comfortable with team conflict by allowing yourself to feel your feelings about the team's progress in real time, and also by supporting yourself and other team members in listening to and expressing true feelings.	Be willing to suggest ways in which the team members can work together more effectively, and be open to suggestions that may curtail some of your autonomy but are beneficial for the team as a whole.	Volunteer to help others when they become overloaded, ask for help when you need it yourself, and keep sharing your knowledge.

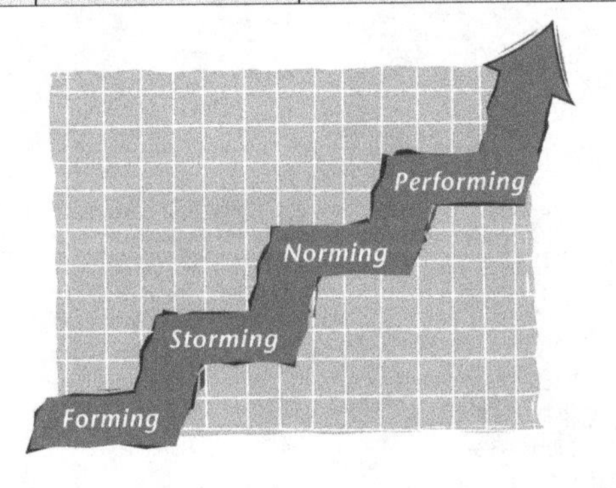

For more insights and information about teams, please refer to the following: Chapter 5, "Creating High-Performing Teams," in *Bringing Out the Best in Yourself at Work* (McGraw-Hill, 2004) and Chapter 6, "Lead High-Performing Teams," in *What Type of Leader Are You?* (McGraw-Hill, 2007).

Additional Team Development Stretches for Five Team Leaders

Express your feelings by using more than just words.

Fives usually control their body language and rely on words to communicate, but your team needs more information from you than this. Videotape yourself talking about something that is important to you. Watch the tape with a coach or someone you respect, soliciting his or her feedback about how you come across. Finally, practice communicating your feelings during a staff meeting, with an emphasis on making your words and body language congruent.

Be explicit about needing time to consider your true reactions.

It is perfectly fine for you to tell individuals or groups that you want time to think about a situation. Both you and they deserve to work from your most heartfelt and well-considered responses. In fact, being clear about your need to take time to consider your reactions is preferable to acting as though you have no response at all. During your time of reflection, go beyond an initial identification of feelings by asking yourself: *Yes, but why do I feel that way?* The deeper you go, the more deeply you will connect with your truest feelings. You may or may not choose to share these with others, but at least you will know what they are.

Learn to read body language clearly.

Pay as much attention to others' body language as to their words so you can become expert at reading nonverbal cues. An excellent way to learn this skill is to watch 15 minutes of a DVD you have not seen before, with the sound on mute. As you watch, write down what you think is occurring, what you imagine the characters are feeling, and what you believe to be the film's general feeling or atmosphere. Then review the same segment with the sound on. Assess your accuracy in reading the nonverbal behavior. If you were not very accurate, watch the segment again to determine what you missed. Repeat this activity with the same and/or other DVDs until you feel more knowledgeable in the art of reading body language.

For more insights and information about teams, please refer to the following: Chapter 5, "Creating High-Performing Teams," in *Bringing Out the Best in Yourself at Work* (McGraw-Hill, 2004) and Chapter 6, "Lead High-Performing Teams," in *What Type of Leader Are You?* (McGraw-Hill, 2007).

LEADERSHIP DEVELOPMENT STRETCHES

The intense challenges of leadership are complex, demanding, unpredictable, exciting, and rewarding, and they require the ability to manage oneself and to interact effectively with hundreds of others in both stressful and exhilarating circumstances. For these reasons, leaders must spend time in honest self-reflection. Individuals who become extraordinary leaders grow in both evolutionary and revolutionary ways as they push themselves to meet challenges even they cannot predict in advance.

Excellent leadership comes in many forms, and no Enneagram style has a monopoly on greatness. However, your Enneagram style shows both your strengths as a leader and the areas that would most likely create obstacles to your success.

Enneagram Style Five leaders usually display this special gift: *the importance of objectivity*. However, their greatest strength can also become their greatest weakness: in their tendency to be self-contained and their unending thirst for intellectual understanding, Five leaders run the risk of not being appreciated for all of their talents, as well as of not fully integrating an emotional component into their organization.

Development Stretches to Enhance Your Leadership

Focus on team interdependence.

Pay attention to helping your team optimize their hand-offs to one another and increase their coordination, rather than focusing on how to optimize the competency and autonomy of each individual.

Stop strategizing and start acting.

Thinking is not the same as doing, and strategizing is not the same as taking action. Err on the side of action and if you're not sure what to do, seek the counsel of others whom you respect — but make sure you move to action quickly.

Pay more attention to politics.

Know the political players and learn how to influence them in productive ways, rather than excessive strategizing and dismissing, ignoring, or not paying enough attention to political relationships.

For more insights and information about leadership, please refer to the following: Chapter 6, "Leveraging Your Leadership," in *Bringing Out the Best in Yourself at Work* (McGraw-Hill, 2004) and the book, *What Type of Leader Are You?* (McGraw-Hill, 2007).

ENNEAGRAM FIVES

RESULTS ORIENTATION DEVELOPMENT STRETCHES

Think before you act — but act, act, act.

Thinking, researching, and planning are essential elements for achieving excellent results. Just remember that taking action is equally important. Take action twice as quickly as you do now. Review your past three projects and answer this question: *What could I have done to move each project along more quickly?* Think about someone at work whom you admire and who takes effective action quickly. Observe what this person does or, better yet, ask the person how he or she moves to action so readily.

Ask the big questions.

At all points in the project, ask yourself these questions: *Why are we doing this project? How does this project align with the vision and strategy both of the organization and of the business unit?*

Communicate continuously.

Because Fives tend to keep their thought processes and ideas to themselves, you can stretch and grow by constantly sharing ideas with others at work. Even if you increase the frequency of your communication fivefold, it might still be too little. You need to communicate to other people on an ongoing basis, and you also need to make sure that the communication is reciprocal.

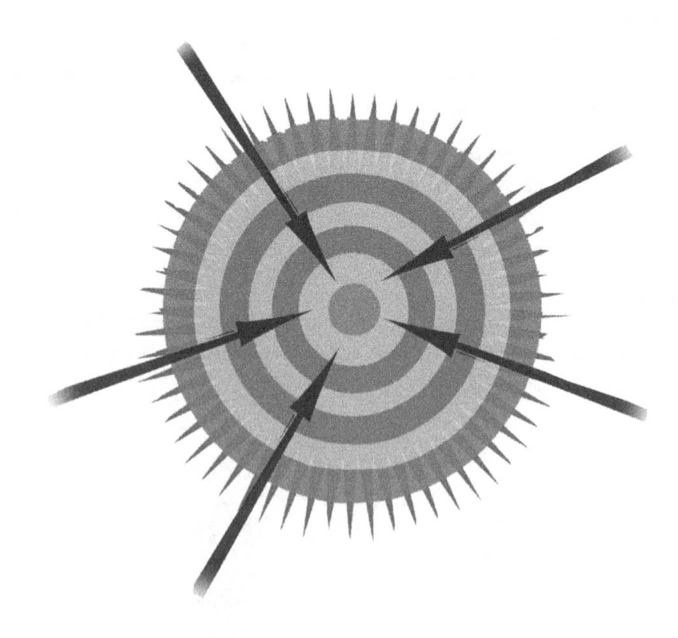

For more insights and information about results orientation, please refer to the following: Chapter 2, "Drive for Results," in *What Type of Leader Are You?* (McGraw-Hill, 2007).

STRATEGY DEVELOPMENT STRETCHES

Leaders and individual contributors must understand the actual business of their organizations and be able to think and act strategically in both big and small ways if their teams and organizations are to reach the highest levels of performance, effectiveness, and efficiency.

"Knowing the business" and "thinking and acting strategically" go hand in hand. Unless you know the business, you have no context for thinking and acting strategically. When you have this information, you need to be able to use it in a strategic way, working from a compelling and common vision, a customer-focused mission, a smart strategy, and effective goals and tactics aligned with that strategy.

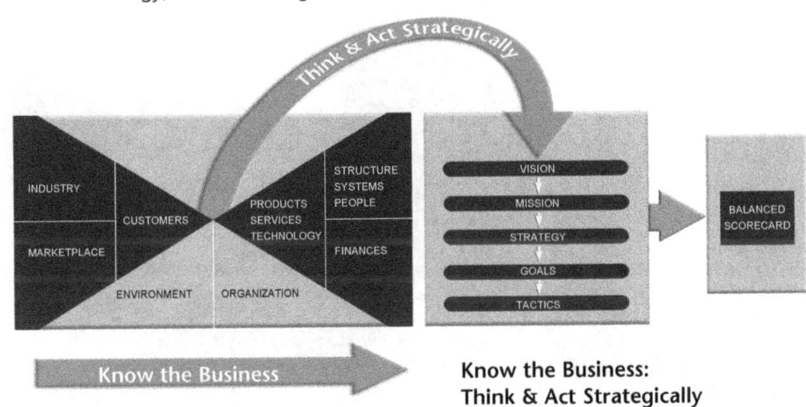

Know the Business: Think & Act Strategically

Use your feelings and gut reactions as much as your intellect.

The deepest part of knowledge — that is, insight and wisdom — does not come from intellect alone. Increasing your capacity to trust your feelings will mean first allowing yourself to experience your emotions in real time and in depth. Work on not automatically detaching emotionally, even though this will push you beyond your comfort zone.

In addition, pay attention to your gut reactions. Instead of analyzing as much as you do, ask yourself this question: *What does my gut say about this situation?* Allow a spontaneous answer to emerge. When you have developed your emotional capacity and your gut instincts, you will likely discover that your overreliance on mental data will decrease because you will also have access to these other sources of information.

Push yourself to develop a vision.

Make sure you have a clear, purposeful, and values-based vision for your work, and that this vision is aligned with the vision of other team members. This requires time, but you will find that it is time and energy well spent.

Talk with people.

Learn to use others as information sources and sounding boards. Doing this will not only help you to create a better information base, but it will also make others feel like partners in the process of knowing the business and thinking and acting strategically.

For more insights and information about strategy, please refer to the following: Chapter 4, "Know the Business: Think and Act Strategically," in *What Type of Leader Are You?* (McGraw-Hill, 2007).

DECISION-MAKING DEVELOPMENT STRETCHES

We all make decisions on a daily basis, but we rarely think about the process by which we make them. The wisest decisions are made utilizing our heads (rational analysis and planning), our hearts (to examine values, feelings, and impact on people), and our guts (for taking action), with all three used in an integrated way. In addition, when you are making decisions at work, you need to consider three other factors: the organizational culture, the decision-making authority structure within the organization, and the context of the decision itself.

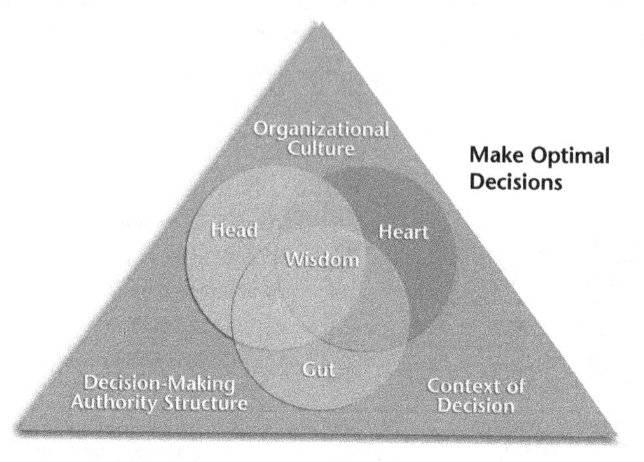

The following chart shows you how to develop each of your Centers of Intelligence (Head, Heart, and Gut) to assist you in making wise decisions.

Centers of Intelligence			
	Head Center	**Heart Center**	**Body (Gut) Center**
Activities for Fives That Develop Each Center	**Objective analysis** Remember that logical analysis is not necessarily objective; logic can have its own bias, depending on the logic used. **Astute insight** Make sure your insights include information about feelings as well as facts. **Productive planning** Don't overplan or overstrategize; remember, it is not always possible to know everything before you develop a plan.	**Empathy** Learn to feel your own feelings in real time, not after the fact. This will enable you to read other people's feelings more accurately and to use this information in decision making. **Authentic relating** Create fewer communication barriers between yourself and others; people will then give you more truthful information. **Compassion** Tell people how you reached your decision, and also share your feelings about it. Be kind when delivering tough information.	**Taking effective action** Make decisions in a timely manner, using information from your mind, heart, and gut. **Steadfastness** Hold firm on decisions you have made using your mind, heart, and gut in an integrated way; be flexible and reconsider decisions you have made using your mind only. **Gut-knowing** Learn to read your body's signals so you can trust your gut; doing so will enable you to make better and faster decisions.

For more insights and information about decision making, please refer to the following: Chapter 7, "Make Optimal Decisions," in *What Type of Leader Are You?* (McGraw-Hill, 2007).

ORGANIZATIONAL CHANGE DEVELOPMENT STRETCHES

In contemporary organizations, change has become a way of life. Companies exist in increasingly complex environments, with more competition, fewer resources, less time to market, higher customer expectations, increased regulation, more technology, and greater uncertainty. Organizations need to be flexible, innovative, cost-conscious, and responsive if they want to succeed. As a result, employees at all levels need to be able to embrace change and to function flexibly and effectively within their teams when an unforeseen direction must be taken.

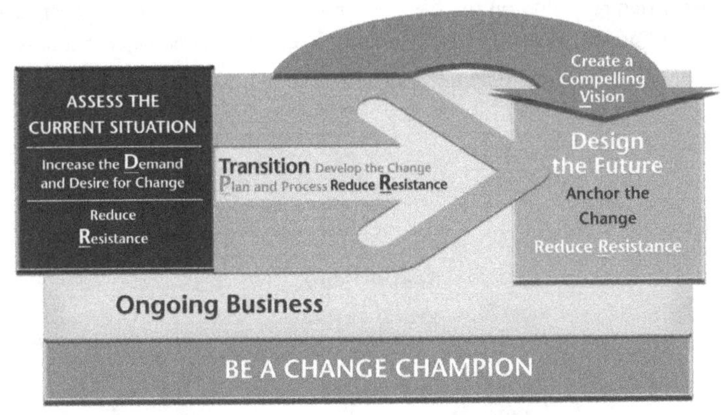

Take Charge of Change

Share stories.

If people are feeling apprehensive, share a story about a situation in which people felt concern about a change but in fact experienced a positive outcome. If people are feeling angry, share a story about a situation that ignited people's positive and negative passions, with those passions then transformed into energy for taking positive action. The stories do not need to be long, but they need to be compelling. Story sharing is helpful whether or not you are a leader, because stories draw people together. Make sure each story you tell has a positive message.

Allow feelings to be shared, including yours.

During any large change, people — yourself included — have a variety of different feelings that will change over time. Legitimize the expression of feelings by asking simple questions such as "How do you feel about this?" Encourage others to share feelings by sharing your own reactions. If you are feeling optimistic about the change, share a real experience that elicited this feeling in you; if you are feeling concerned, share that as well. Just make sure that both your intention and the message are designed to help others accept their own feelings and move toward support of the change.

For more insights and information about organizational change, please refer to the following: Chapter 8, "Take Charge of Change," in *What Type of Leader Are You?* (McGraw-Hill, 2007).

Share yourself.

Change can be hard on everyone, even when people support the new direction. Employees at all levels in the organization need you to be there for them. It is important that you share yourself by listening fully without distraction and then also speaking your truth. The latter means going several levels below your obvious reactions to find the deeper responses. For example, a Five leader, in explaining to a key manager why she was being passed over to lead a change initiative, was prepared to tell her that the decision had been made on the basis of the manager's lack of experience. However, when reflecting on the decision, the Five realized that the deeper reason was that he thought the promotion would have placed the manager in a no-win situation, that he believed in her, and that he had another position in mind for her.

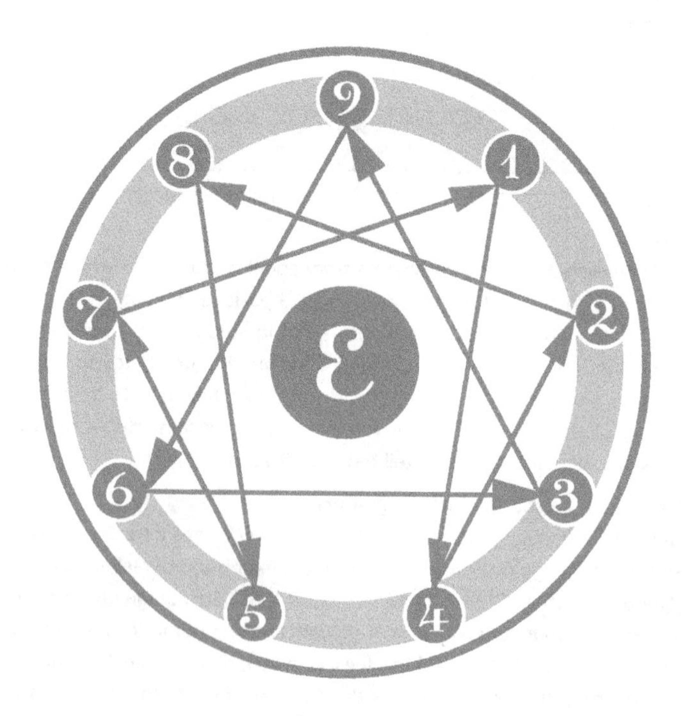

For more insights and information about organizational change, please refer to the following: Chapter 8, "Take Charge of Change," in *What Type of Leader Are You?* (McGraw-Hill, 2007).

TRANSFORMATION DEVELOPMENT STRETCHES

In order to move from *thirsting for knowledge and using emotional detachment as a way of keeping involvement with others to a minimum* to the understanding that *there is a universal wisdom that comes from the full integration of the intellect, emotions, and experience*, Fives can work toward these transformations:

Mental Transformation

Transform the mental pattern of **stinginess** (a scarcity paradigm that leads to an insatiable thirst for intellectual knowing, a reluctance to share — knowledge, time, space, and personal information — and to strategizing about how to control one's environment) *into the higher belief of* **omniscience** (the insight that only through direct personal experience and complete engagement can one know all things).

Mental Activity

When you become aware that you are thirsting for and withholding information, distancing yourself from direct experience, or engaging in extended strategizing about how to control your environment, remember one or more times when you understood that true wisdom can be achieved only through complete engagement with your direct experience. Allow those times to come back into your thinking, and relive what was occurring within you at those moments.

Emotional Transformation

Transform the emotional habit of **avarice** (the intense desire to guard everything related to oneself — information, physical and emotional privacy, energy, and resources — combined with the automatic detachment from feelings) *into the higher awareness of* **nonattachment** (the firsthand experience that detachment — from feelings, people, and experience — is not nonattachment, and that one must fully engage and become attached to something before one can be truly nonattached and able to appreciate something without coveting it).

Emotional Activity

When you become aware that you are withholding anything from others — for example, your knowledge, time, physical space, and feelings — remember one or more times in your life when you were fully sharing and present to others. Remember the circumstances and how you felt, and what you experienced during those times. Keep replaying those completely engaged moments until you feel fully reconnected with the experiences.

For more insights and information about personal transformation, please refer to the following: Chapter 7, "Transforming Yourself," in *Bringing Out the Best in Yourself at Work* (McGraw-Hill, 2004).

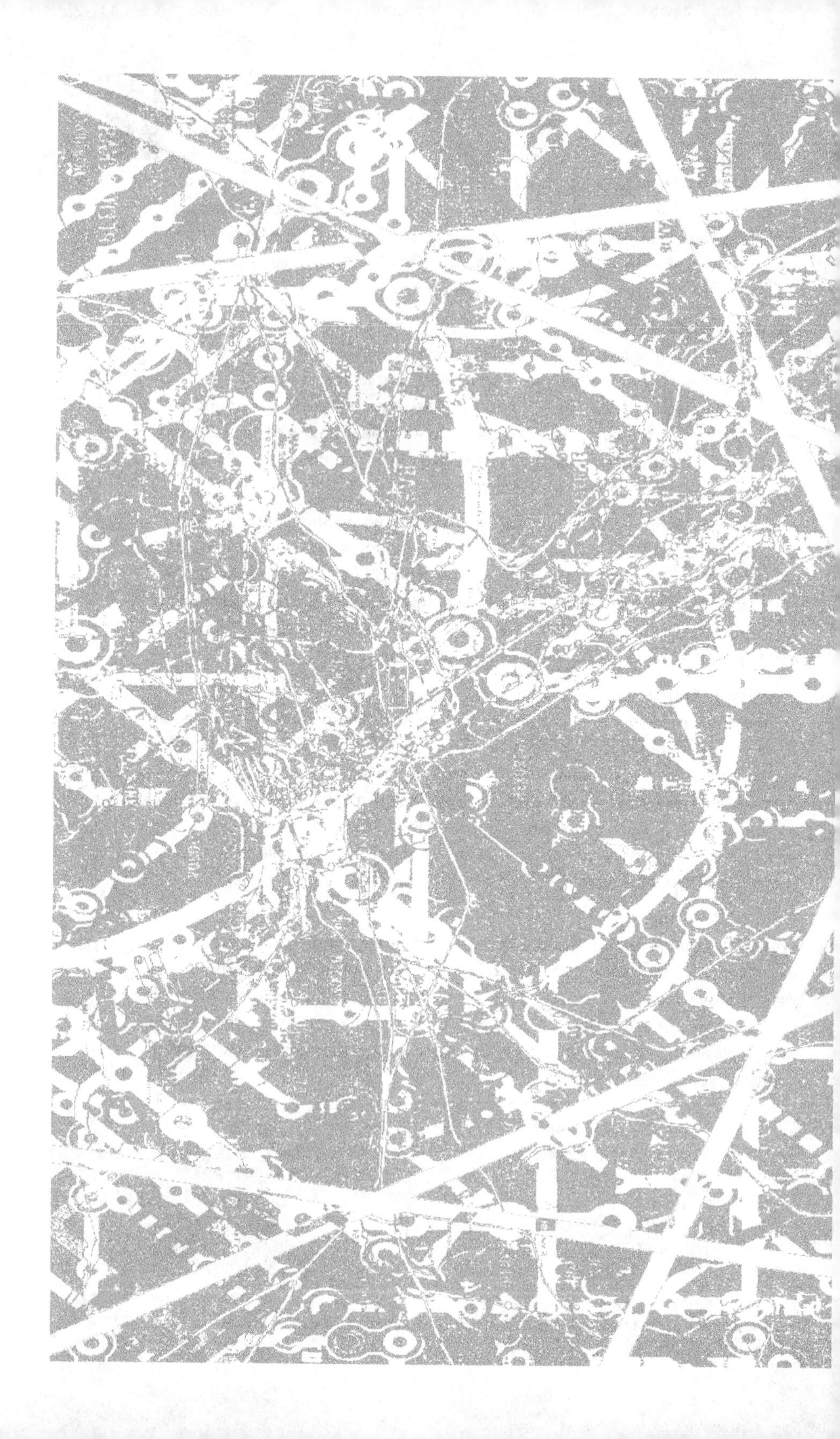

ENNEAGRAM STYLE SIX

ENNEAGRAM SIXES

The search for meaning, certainty, and trust, and the avoidance of negative scenarios from occurring

Sharp-minded, insightful, and loyal, Sixes are issue identifiers and problem solvers, with a mental-emotional antenna that is finely attuned to anticipate problems before they occur so that alternative paths and contingency plans can be created. This is done to ensure the best possible outcome and prevent the worst from happening. Although the above description applies to all Sixes, Sixes are complex individuals who run the gamut from phobic Sixes, who are overtly and palpably fearful, to counter-phobic Sixes, who often mask their fear by taking dramatic risks — often, but not always, physical ones — that adrenalize them and prove to themselves and others, at least for the moment, that they are not fearful. Many Sixes display characteristics of the phobic and the counter-phobic Six.

All Sixes worry as a habit of mind, although some Sixes call it instantaneous anticipatory planning or problem solving, and other Sixes do this so naturally that they no longer notice it. There are also key differences among Sixes. Some Sixes deal with their concerns by becoming warm, inviting, and by developing strong and loyal social alliances as a way to feel safe; other Sixes become extraordinarily dutiful and try to know and adhere to the "rules" as a way to not get in trouble by going astray; and still other Sixes — the highly counter-phobic Sixes — unconsciously turn against their fear with demonstrations of strength as a way to convince themselves and others of their bravery. In reality, most phobic Sixes have some counter-phobic qualities — for example, they can become aggressive toward authority or authority figures — and most counter-phobic Sixes do display fears and concerns to those they trust or through their non-verbal behavior.

Sixes have a variety of interpersonal styles, but most are warm; loyal; appear genuine, displaying a relative lack of pretentiousness; candid; agile in expressing concerns; and willing to talk truthfully about themselves.

While we can all worry, be insightful, and want to feel well-prepared for the various scenarios life offers, for Sixes, the search for meaning, certainty, and trust, and the avoidance of negative scenarios from occurring is their primary, persistent, and driving motivation.

DEVELOPMENT STRETCHES FOR SIXES

INDIVIDUALS WHO HAVE INSIGHTFUL MINDS AND CREATE ANTICIPATORY OR WORST-CASE SCENARIOS TO HELP THEMSELVES FEEL PREPARED IN CASE SOMETHING GOES WRONG

CONTENTS

SELF-MASTERY DEVELOPMENT STRETCHES

Self-Mastery — the ability to understand, accept, and transform your thoughts, feelings, and behavior, with the understanding that each day will bring new challenges that are opportunities for growth — is the foundation of all personal and professional development. Self-mastery begins with self-awareness, then expands to include the elements shown in the following graphic:

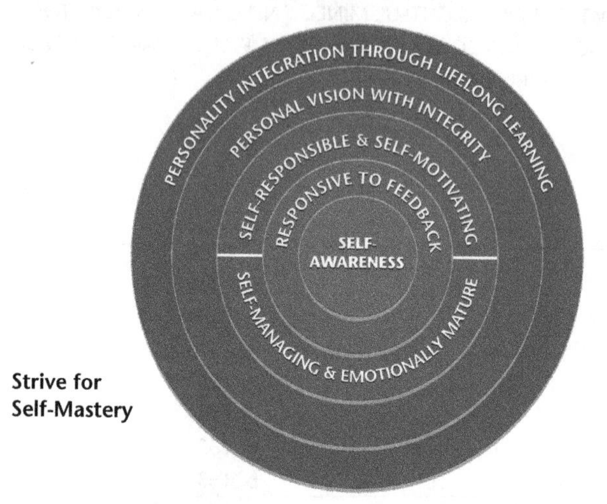

Strive for Self-Mastery

In this section on self-mastery, you will find the following:

- Three common issues for Sixes related to self-mastery
- Three development stretches for working with the core issues of your Enneagram style, including one basic activity and one deeper activity for each stretch
- Three development stretches for working with your wings and arrow (stress-security) styles

Common Issues for Sixes Related to Self-Mastery

Learning to differentiate between an insight and a projection (something based on imagination)	Trusting your own inner authority rather than looking to someone or something outside yourself for meaning and certainty	Having faith in yourself and others to be able to handle whatever occurs

For more insights and information about self-mastery, please refer to the following: Chapter 7, "Transforming Yourself," in *Bringing Out the Best in Yourself at Work* (McGraw-Hill, 2004) and Chapter 3, "Strive for Self-Mastery," in *What Type of Leader Are You?* (McGraw-Hill, 2007).

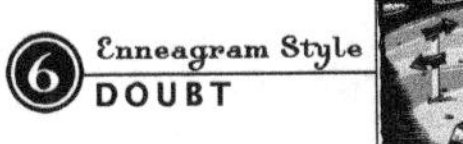

Development Stretches for Working with the Core Issues of Your Enneagram Style

Shift your focus from half empty to half full.

Basic Activity

Each morning, start your day with 15 minutes of thinking about everything that is going well and is problem free. You can look at items in your home, objects you see on your way to work, and aspects of yourself. This practice will actually begin to change some of your brain's pathways.

Deeper Activity

Because Sixes tend to focus on what could go wrong, it can be said that they usually view the glass as being half empty. To change your focus from worrying about the negative, you have to consciously shift your focus and view the glass as being half full. To do this, you need to purposely think of all the things that are right, effective, and in place. For example, if you are planning a business trip, instead of being worried that the cab may forget to pick you up, that you may miss the airplane, or that a presentation you'll be giving may not go well, think instead about how well organized the cab company usually is, how important it is for your safety that airports have expanded their security procedures, and how useful others will find the information that you will be covering in your presentation.

The following activity can also help you to focus more on positive scenarios. For two weeks, spend ten minutes at the end of each day making a list of all the things that have gone right that day. Then, for the next two weeks, make a list each morning of at least five things that will occur that day that are likely to go well.

The following month, take ten minutes each evening and make a list of everything that has gone well during the day. Next to each item, write down exactly what you did that contributed to the success. At the end of the month, you should see your focus shift to include positive as well as negative scenarios, and your self-confidence will increase because you better understand your role in creating positive outcomes.

Trust your own authority.

Basic Activity

Make a list of all the times you have followed your own advice and found it to be advice well taken. Next to each item, write down all of the benefits that you have accrued from following your own advice. Think of this self-advice as the wisdom of your own inner authority. Each time you feel confused about what to do, ask yourself this question: *If I were going to follow my own inner authority, what advice would it give me?* Then follow that advice.

For more insights and information about self-mastery, please refer to the following: Chapter 7, "Transforming Yourself," in *Bringing Out the Best in Yourself at Work* (McGraw-Hill, 2004) and Chapter 3, "Strive for Self-Mastery," in *What Type of Leader Are You?* (McGraw-Hill, 2007).

Deeper Activity

It is not unusual for Sixes to seek the counsel of other people, and often several people, before making a decision. With high self-doubt, Sixes may actually trust an outside authority's judgment over their own, even in the face of facts that would indicate that the Six's own assessment is superior. Sixes thus sometimes give their power to someone else when they really need to trust themselves.

Ironically, Sixes often give others excellent advice, then turn around and ask someone else for advice on the exact same matter. The following technique works well with Sixes because it tricks the mind into releasing its own wise inner authority. When you think you need to solicit the counsel of someone else on a particular topic, stop and ask yourself this question: *What do I think about this?* If your answer is "I don't know," ask yourself: *Well, if I did know what to do about this issue, what would it be?* Usually, the self-advice that is elicited is worth following. Another variation on this technique is to ask yourself, *If someone else were coming to me with a similar request for advice, what advice would I give?*

Differentiate between an insight and a pure projection.

Basic Activity

Can you tell the difference between an insight and a pure projection? Do you know when you are being really perceptive (an insight) versus purely projecting (making something up entirely in your own mind so that instead of reflecting reality, this view instead reflects what you think, feel, or want to do)? Spend 15 minutes each morning making a list of your uncensored thoughts about what you believe will happen that day. At the end of the day, review your list. For each item on the list, answer these questions: *Was this an insight, a pure projection, or a mixture of the two? How can I tell the difference?* After you have practiced this activity for several weeks, answering the question *How can I tell the difference?* will give you useful information.

For more insights and information about self-mastery, please refer to the following: Chapter 7, "Transforming Yourself," in *Bringing Out the Best in Yourself at Work* (McGraw-Hill, 2004) and Chapter 3, "Strive for Self-Mastery," in *What Type of Leader Are You?* (McGraw-Hill, 2007).

Deeper Activity

One of the most difficult tasks for Sixes is to learn to differentiate between an insight and a projection. Insights are astute perceptions that are accurate and therefore actionable. Projections are also perceptions, but they reflect the psyche of the perceiver more than the truth about the person or thing being observed. What can make differentiating between the two even more difficult is that sometimes ideas are projections but are also accurate, and so they are insights. Thus, Sixes actually need to discern among pure projections, pure insights, and ideas that are both projections and insights.

Two activities can help Sixes with this discernment. The first is to recognize that pure insights are really keenly intuitive perceptions and almost always have very little emotion attached to them by the perceiver. Consequently, the more emotion you feel with a perception, the more likely it is to be a projection; the less emotion, the more likely it is to be an insight, something you can trust to be real.

When you discover a perception that you sense is a projection or at least partly a projection, the best way to test it is to ask yourself this question: *Is what I have just thought true in any way about me?* For example, if you think someone is not being truthful with you, ask yourself this question: *How am I not being truthful with that person?* Once you have discovered how you are not being honest with the other person, ask yourself this: *Now that I understand how I am not being honest, are there any other reasons to suggest that this person is not being honest with me?*

The second way to test a projection is to ask others for feedback about the thought you have had. If you check with several people who have no particular reason for bias, you can confirm or disconfirm the veracity of the thought. Over time, this will help you to understand the pattern of your projections and the nature of your insights.

For more insights and information about self-mastery, please refer to the following: Chapter 7, "Transforming Yourself," in *Bringing Out the Best in Yourself at Work* (McGraw-Hill, 2004) and Chapter 3, "Strive for Self-Mastery," in *What Type of Leader Are You?* (McGraw-Hill, 2007).

Development Stretches for Working with Your Wings and Arrow (Stress-Security) Styles

Wings are the Enneagram styles on either side of your core Enneagram style; arrow, or stress-security, styles are Enneagram styles shown with arrows pointing away or toward your core Enneagram style. Your wings and arrow styles don't change your core Enneagram style, but instead offer qualities that can broaden and enrich your patterns of thinking and feeling as well as enhance your behaviors. Your wings and arrow styles make you more complex and versatile because they provide more dimensions to your personality and serve as vehicles for self-development.

Integrate Your Five Wing

Slow down your mental processes.

Sixes typically think and analyze with great speed, particularly when they are concerned or anxious, but also when they are excited and hopeful. Fives, on the other hand, tend to use a slower and more deliberate analytical route, and this allows them to ponder the possibilities more methodically. Sixes can try different methods to slow down their mental processes. The first method is to simply notice the rapidity of your mental processing and to say this to yourself: *You're thinking really fast right now. Just take one idea at a time and give it full consideration.*

567 WINGS FOR SIXES

The second method involves breathing. When Sixes (or individuals of any other Enneagram style) begin to think, feel, or act quickly, their breathing tends to be shallow and rapid; for example, they breathe only as far as their necks and in about two seconds per breath, rather than breathing deeply into their diaphragms and allowing ten or more seconds per breath. Slowing down and deepening your breathing often results in a slower mental processing rate.

Plan for what you want to happen.

Sixes plan constantly, but the planning typically involves the prevention or avoidance of negative outcomes. While Fives plan in this manner too, they also plan for desired outcomes. To do the same, Sixes need to change their focus from what they don't want to have happen to what they do want to have occur. In a given situation, Sixes need to notice when they are planning to avert a specific outcome and ask themselves: *What do I want to have happen in this situation?* It may take some effort, as the Six's mind will tend to answer in the negative — for example, *I don't want this to happen* or *I want this not to happen*. However, as soon as the Six can articulate the affirmative goal — *I want this to occur* — he or she can then use the planning process to focus on a positive result.

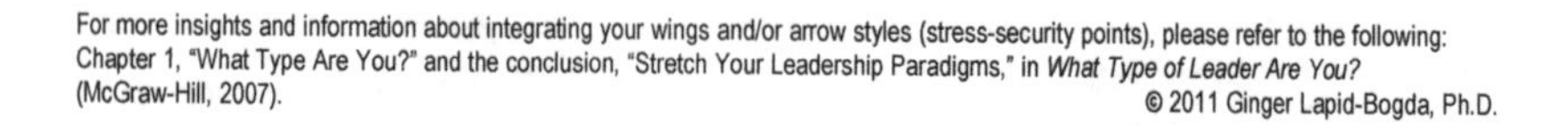
For more insights and information about integrating your wings and/or arrow styles (stress-security points), please refer to the following: Chapter 1, "What Type Are You?" and the conclusion, "Stretch Your Leadership Paradigms," in *What Type of Leader Are You?* (McGraw-Hill, 2007).

Practice self-containment.

Fives are almost always highly self-contained, rarely exhibiting visibly reactive responses to what others say and do. Sixes, on the other hand, are extremely easy to read (through both words and body language) because they often react so quickly. Although this expressiveness can be an asset, under certain circumstances Sixes may spontaneously say something they regret afterward, or take swift action and later wish they had considered their response before acting.

It is always beneficial to have the choice of whether to be expressive or to not show precisely what you are thinking and feeling. The best way to do this is to learn to calm yourself *at will*. When you feel calm, you have more behavioral choices available, because calmness is the opposite of reactivity. If you practice calming yourself when you are not in the throes of a reaction, you will be able to use this technique more easily when you are distressed about something. A simple self-statement that you repeat to yourself, breathing in while you say it, is very helpful. Select one from among these that appeals to you: *There is meaning and certainty in the world; I'm fine and everything will be fine; I'll be able to handle this; I can count on both myself and others.*

Integrate Your Seven Wing

Learn to have spontaneous fun.

Sixes need to ask themselves this important question: *How often do I enjoy myself in a spontaneous way?* Sixes often have trouble relaxing and enjoying themselves in a spontaneous manner, because they tend to spend their time either demonstrating their loyalty and being dutiful, or else engaging in worrying and planning in an attempt to prevent anticipated negative scenarios. Sevens, in contrast, can switch readily from work to spontaneous interaction, and if an interesting idea or activity comes to mind, they are usually able to pursue that endeavor and be fully engaged. Sixes can do this by taking the following actions. Once a day, do something completely unplanned and enjoyable for 30 minutes. This can be a walk, a ride, a visit to a bookstore or museum, a conversation with a friend, or anything else purely enjoyable to you. During this time, whenever a worry or obligation comes to your mind, simply say to yourself: *Okay — I can deal with that later.* Do this activity daily until you can freely enjoy it without any intervening thoughts that cause you to feel guilty or worried. Once this occurs, increase the amount of daily and/or weekly time you spend in spontaneous fun.

For more insights and information about integrating your wings and/or arrow styles (stress-security points), please refer to the following: Chapter 1, "What Type Are You?" and the conclusion, "Stretch Your Leadership Paradigms," in *What Type of Leader Are You?* (McGraw-Hill, 2007).

Focus on positive possibilities.

Although Sixes and Sevens both focus on future possibilities and on planning for these scenarios, they do so from different perspectives: Sixes tend to focus on negative possibilities and how to prevent them from occurring, while Sevens focus more on positive possibilities and how to increase the probability of a positive outcome. This is akin to viewing the glass as half empty versus half full. When Sixes become aware that they are focusing on the negative possibility in a situation, they can say this to themselves: *Let me act like a Seven for a moment. What would be a possible positive scenario? What would it take to make that happen? What are some other positive outcomes? How can I plan for one of these?*

Get wildly creative.

Sixes can be highly creative, in part due to their fertile imaginations. Sevens are often creative most of the time, the result of the fluid boundaries of their mental processing whereby seemingly unrelated ideas, pictures, experiences, and more become connected in new ways. Because of this, Sevens can have wild imaginations, censoring their ideas after the fact rather than before. Sixes can learn from Sevens to let go and dream seemingly impossible dreams.

To experiment with this, try brainstorming with a "mind map," a tool for creative problem solving. Simply draw a two-inch circle in the center of a piece of paper, and write one word in the center of the circle that interests you. Look at the word and let another word or an idea come to you, with no censoring whatsoever from you. Draw a line from the circle in any direction, and write that word or phrase on the line. Let any other word or idea come to you. If it is related at all to the word on the first line you drew, draw a line from the first line on which to write the new word or phrase. Repeat the above process for ten minutes, allowing new ideas in with no censorship and connecting the new words to whichever line or lines they seem related.

For more insights and information about integrating your wings and/or arrow styles (stress-security points), please refer to the following: Chapter 1, "What Type Are You?" and the conclusion, "Stretch Your Leadership Paradigms," in *What Type of Leader Are You?* (McGraw-Hill, 2007).

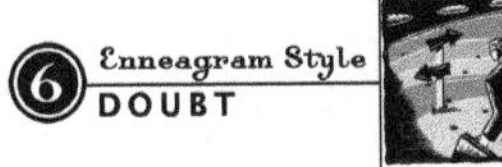

Integrate Arrow Style Three (Stress Point)

Focus on results.

While Sixes often fret about which course of action to take, thinking through different options and their possible negative consequences, Threes tend to focus on the results they want and then drive their behavior toward those goals. A certain amount of stress can be helpful to Sixes, because time pressure with the need for a result can help them bypass their tendency toward procrastination fueled by doubt. Instead of thinking about what they will be able to do and what could go wrong, Sixes can focus on the specific goal required and ask themselves, *What is the most effective and efficient way to achieve this specific goal?* If they are unable to answer that question, Sixes can "trick" themselves by asking this: *If it were someone other than me in this situation, what would I suggest that he or she do?* Sixes are often far better at giving concrete, clear, and focused advice to others than to themselves.

Take action.

Preparing to act and then taking action can be likened to the three steps of shooting a pistol: *ready, aim, fire.* Sixes tend to take action by inaction, or *ready, aim, ready, aim*, not quite getting to *fire*. Threes, by comparison, tend to *aim, fire, aim, fire*. From Threes, Sixes can learn to take the action of *fire* more frequently. They can do this by changing their inner dialogue from *No action is better than the wrong action* to *Some action is better than no action.* In fact, when Sixes begin to procrastinate or equivocate, they can say this to themselves: *Some action is better than no action, because action is needed here.*

Take credit for what you contribute.

Sixes are prone to not call attention to themselves or to what they have achieved. When asked what they did that contributed to the success of a project or a team endeavor, Sixes are likely to say, "The team did it." In fact, Sixes have a great deal of difficulty in determining their own individual contributions. Although Threes may also say that credit goes to the team, they have little difficulty in identifying their own contributions.

As a Six, you may be totally unaware of your own contributions, even when these have been outstanding. You can become more aware of these by doing the following: Directly after a successful activity or project, write down three things you did that contributed to the result. Next, ask three different people who are aware of your work what they believe your contributions to have been, and write these down on the paper with your original list.

For more insights and information about integrating your wings and/or arrow styles (stress-security points), please refer to the following: Chapter 1, "What Type Are You?" and the conclusion, "Stretch Your Leadership Paradigms," in *What Type of Leader Are You?* (McGraw-Hill, 2007).

Compare the two lists, noticing the ways in which you tend to discount or ignore your contributions — for example, you may have forgotten what these were immediately after identifying them, minimized them to yourself by saying "Yes, but…," or immediately turned to thinking about what other individuals or the team as a whole contributed. Each day, select one of the items on your list and repeat this item to yourself at least 15 times that day. Repeat the above process with a new item each day until you have done this for all items.

Integrate Arrow Style Nine (Security Point)

Learn to relax.

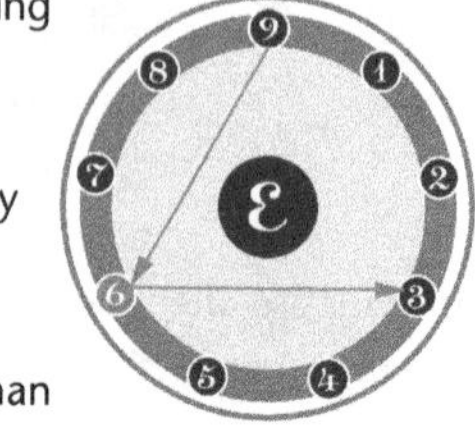

This is easier said than done, especially for Sixes, but increasing your access to Security Point Nine can be a helpful way for you to learn to relax. While it can be very difficult for Sixes to stop the activity in their minds long enough to relax, they can learn to do so by doing what Nines tend to do easily. Simply start doing something relaxing that you enjoy very much, and continue doing it for a longer period of time than you would normally allow yourself. It doesn't matter what you choose as long as you enjoy it, find the activity relaxing, and do it for an extended period of time. For example, take a long walk, go shopping, soak in a bath, talk with friends, watch television, even clean the house — whatever you enjoy doing. When you do something like this for a period of time and relax as you do it, your mind will begin to move at a slower pace. In addition, a prolonged relaxing activity can serve as a substitute for mental processing. It is difficult to think while watching television or talking with friends.

Spend time "going with the flow."

Sixes tend to think through what they will do ahead of time and do so with great rigor. Nines typically know how to "go with the flow," which means that they do not necessarily plan everything out in advance. One event or action leads to another without effort, with one moment merging into the next without the Nine's prethinking or being concerned. This behavior can be learned, and although it may feel awkward at first, doing it over time can be enjoyable.

Allow yourself one half hour in which you are alone and have nothing planned or structured to do. Don't do anything until something occurs to you that you truly want to do because you would enjoy it, not because you should do it, someone expects you to do it, or you have to do it before you do something else. When something emerges that you want to do, then do it as long as you want to. Then, allow that activity to guide you into doing something else you want to do because you would enjoy it. Again, continue this activity until something else emerges that you would like to do, and follow this pattern until your half hour is up.

For more insights and information about integrating your wings and/or arrow styles (stress-security points), please refer to the following: Chapter 1, "What Type Are You?" and the conclusion, "Stretch Your Leadership Paradigms," in *What Type of Leader Are You?* (McGraw-Hill, 2007).

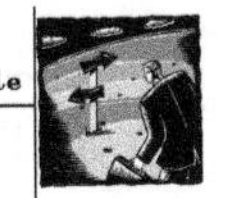

Continue this practice daily until you look forward to this time of going with the flow. Once you feel a sense of pleasure and mastery in this, go through the same process while interacting with others. For example, go shopping for a half hour, but allow yourself to interact with others as long as you want to, following where the interaction and conversation takes you. When you no longer want to continue the interaction, go to another store or interact with another person.

Give yourself permission to be out in nature more regularly.
Being out in nature and simply enjoying it (rather than thinking too much) has a way of calming both the senses and the mind. Once a day, give yourself permission to be in nature — for example, walking, jogging, or sitting — and to simply enjoy the experience. Once you have become accustomed to doing this, allow yourself to go out in nature just whenever you feel like it, rather than doing this activity on a daily schedule. Nines simply stop what they're doing and take some time off to be outside, whereas Sixes often enjoy nature but do so only after their work is complete or when they have it on their schedule.

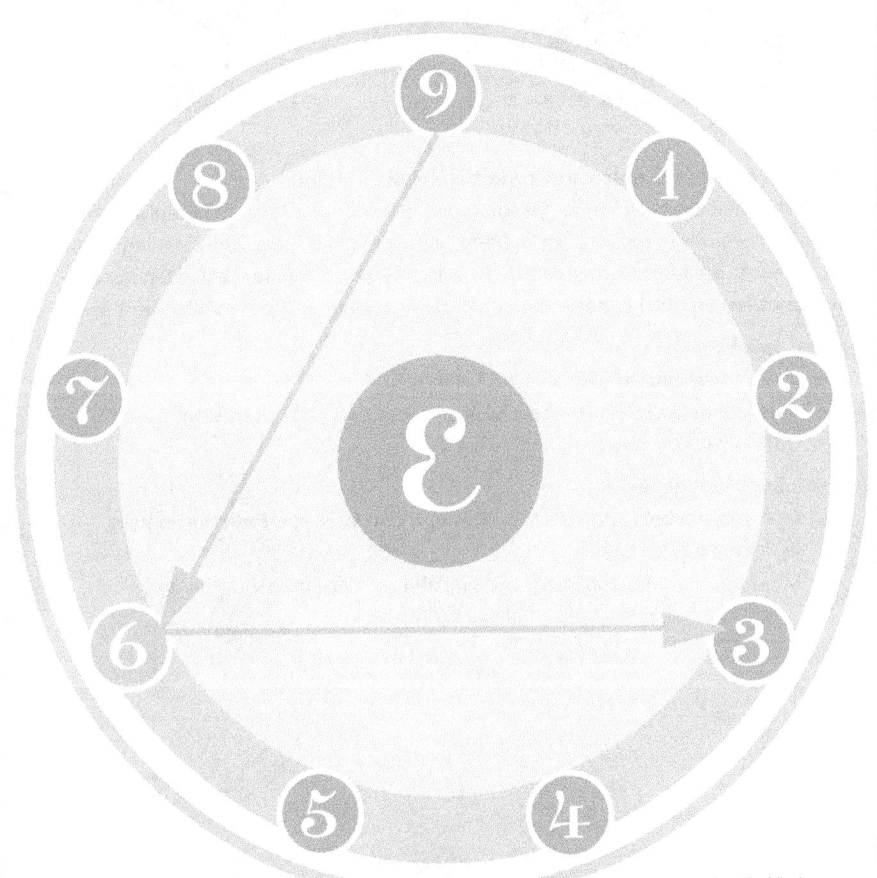

For more insights and information about integrating your wings and/or arrow styles (stress-security points), please refer to the following: Chapter 1, "What Type Are You?" and the conclusion, "Stretch Your Leadership Paradigms," in *What Type of Leader Are You?* (McGraw-Hill, 2007).

COMMUNICATION DEVELOPMENT STRETCHES

When you communicate with someone, three kinds of unintentional distortions may be present: speaking style, body language, and blind spots. *Speaking style* refers to your overall pattern of speaking. *Body language* includes posture, facial expressions, hand gestures, body movements, energy levels, and hundreds of other nonverbal messages. *Blind spots* are elements of your communication containing information about you that is not apparent to you but is highly visible to other people. We all unknowingly convey information through an amalgam of our speaking style, body language, and other inferential data.

The receivers of the messages you send also distort what they hear through their *distorting filters*. These are unconscious concerns or assumptions, often based on the listener's Enneagram style, that alter how someone hears what others say.

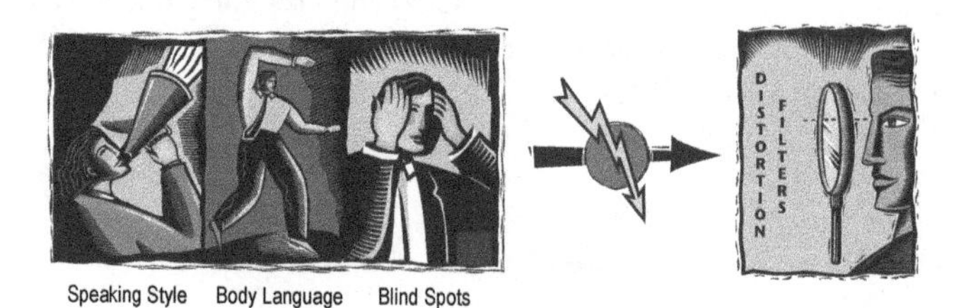

Change one communication style behavior at a time.

It is most effective to work on changing one behavior at a time, preferably in the following sequence: speaking style, body language, blind spots, and listening distorting filters. It is easiest to change the behaviors of which we are most aware, and this sequence represents the most common order of awareness, from most to least aware.

Sixes: Speaking style

- Begin conversations with analytical comments
- Alternate between syncopated, hesitant speech and bold, confident speech
- Discuss worries, concerns, and "what ifs"

Sixes: Body language

- Gaze may be bold and direct, or eyes may dart back and forth horizontally, as if scanning for danger
- May appear warm, engaging, and empathic, or face may show worry
- Quick, nonverbal reactions to perceived threats

For more insights and information about communication, please refer to the following: Chapter 2, "Communicating Effectively," in *Bringing Out the Best in Yourself at Work* (McGraw-Hill, 2004) and Chapter 5, "Become an Excellent Communicator," in *What Type of Leader Are You?* (McGraw-Hill, 2007).

Sixes: Blind spots

- The Six's negative scenarios appear to others as negativism, pessimism, and a "can't do" orientation
- Self-doubt and worry can cause others to question the Six's competence
- No matter how hard the Six tries to mask the worry, it is still apparent

Sixes: Distorting filters when listening to someone else

- Determining whether the other person is using his or her authority properly or improperly
- Projecting own thoughts and feelings onto the other person, but being unaware of doing so
- Questioning whether the other person can be trusted

Note: Some of the above characteristics may be positive, some negative, and some neutral or mixed. They are intended as an overview to allow you to select from among them.

Use e-mails to expand and adjust your language patterns.

- Review your e-mails before you send them for language and tone.
- When you are distressed, make sure to include the recipient's name at the start of the e-mail; this will communicate more warmth.
- Collect your thoughts and feelings and send one e-mail only on topics of concern until you receive a response from the recipient; sending a series of e-mails usually conveys uncertainty and anxiety.
- Reduce the number of words and phrases that connote fear, concern, and worry.
- Imply in your e-mail that the e-mail recipient will effectively handle the issues raised.

For more insights and information about communication, please refer to the following: Chapter 2, "Communicating Effectively," in *Bringing Out the Best in Yourself at Work* (McGraw-Hill, 2004) and Chapter 5, "Become an Excellent Communicator," in *What Type of Leader Are You?* (McGraw-Hill, 2007).

FEEDBACK DEVELOPMENT STRETCHES

Honest, positive, and constructive *feedback* — direct, objective, simple, and respectful observations that one person makes about another's behavior — improves both relationships and on-the-job performance. When you offer feedback, the Feedback Formula, combined with the insights of the Enneagram, helps you tailor your delivery. When someone gives you feedback, the more receptive you are to hearing what is being said, the more likely it is that you will be able to discern what is useful and utilize what has been suggested.

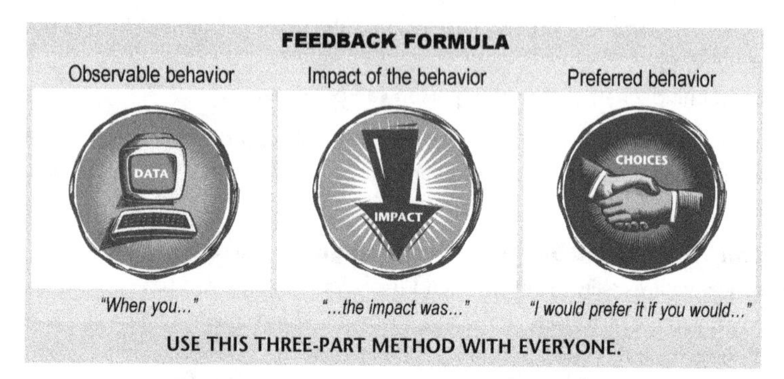

How Sixes Can Enhance Their Ability to Deliver Feedback Effectively

When you offer feedback to someone, you want to be prepared and also to encourage the feedback recipient to be as receptive as possible. Remember that how and when you deliver feedback is just as important as what you actually say.

Use the three components of the **Feedback Formula** together with the following suggestions to plan and deliver the feedback.

- Keep your focus on planning what you will say, but also work to calm yourself before the feedback discussion.
- Maintain your attention to details and also keep sight of the big picture.
- Retaining your strength in anticipating potential scenarios is helpful, but try to balance the negative possibilities with positive ones.
- Honor your insights, but avoid assuming that your thoughts are accurate; treat them as hypotheses, and seek the answers from the feedback recipient.
- Remember that once you have given the feedback, you will need to allow the feedback recipient to take responsibility to achieve a positive outcome, rather than believing that the burden of resolving the situation rests on your shoulders.

For more insights and information about feedback, please refer to the following: Chapter 3, "Giving Constructive Feedback," in *Bringing Out the Best in Yourself at Work* (McGraw-Hill, 2004) and Chapter 5, "Become an Excellent Communicator," in *What Type of Leader Are You?* (McGraw-Hill, 2007).

How Sixes Can Be More Receptive When They Receive Feedback

- When someone gives you negative feedback, it may ignite your doubt and worry. At such times, it is best to acknowledge your worry rather than fight it, because suppressing your worry often makes it stronger. Simply notice that you are going into "worry mode" and say this to yourself: *There I go, into worry. Let me be open to what this person has to say.*
- When someone offers you positive feedback, you may have a tendency to discount it or to not remember it later. To help you integrate and retain the positive feedback you receive, either paraphrase the information for the other person to confirm or write it down on a piece of paper so you can review it later.
- Remember that feedback always says as much about the person giving it as it does about the recipient. If you listen with this in mind, it will help you to be more receptive and will also give you more data with which to compare your own perceptions and speculations.

For more insights and information about feedback, please refer to the following: Chapter 3, "Giving Constructive Feedback," in *Bringing Out the Best in Yourself at Work* (McGraw-Hill, 2004) and Chapter 5, "Become an Excellent Communicator," in *What Type of Leader Are You?* (McGraw-Hill, 2007).

CONFLICT DEVELOPMENT STRETCHES

Relationships both at work and at home often involve some degree of conflict, which may be caused by a variety of factors and usually follows the pinch-crunch cycle below:

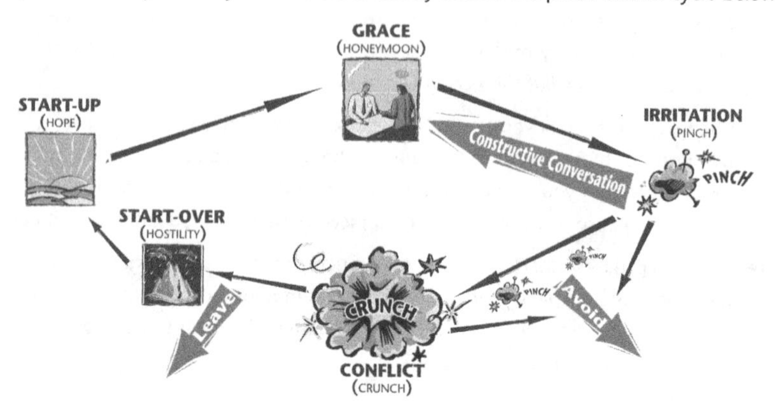

Whatever the root cause of the conflict, the Enneagram styles of the key parties involved will always be a factor in the conflict dynamics and resolution. The Enneagram enables each individual involved to make conflict resolution a constructive rather than destructive experience. The more people know themselves, understand their own responsibilities in the conflict interaction, engage in constructive self-management, and know how best to approach others through knowledge of the Enneagram, the greater the chances of a swift and effective outcome.

There are specific pinches (anger triggers) for each Enneagram style — that is, certain situations that will invariably ignite anger in a person of one style, yet may not affect someone of a different style. For Sixes, these pinches include:

Pressure from someone else · Lack of genuineness from the other person · Another's lack of commitment · Abusive use of authority

For more insights and information about conflict, please refer to the following: Chapter 4, "Managing Conflict," in *Bringing Out the Best in Yourself at Work* (McGraw-Hill, 2004) and Chapter 5, "Become an Excellent Communicator," in *What Type of Leader Are You?* (McGraw-Hill, 2007).

Development Stretches for Transforming Anger into an Opportunity for Growth

Share your likely pinches (anger triggers) with others at the beginning of your working relationship.

This is simply a good, practical suggestion, and most Sixes recognize a good idea when they hear it. Sit down with the new person with whom you are working and talk about work in a casual manner. Toward the end of the discussion, raise the issue of mutual expectations by saying something like, "Let's talk about our mutual expectations so we can get this working relationship off to an excellent start." The discussion can cover goals, roles, accountabilities, and so forth. After discussing these topics, the idea of pinches can be introduced in the following way: "I've learned that if people discuss working issues that bother or pinch them, it can be really helpful in preventing misunderstandings. Perhaps we can share some of our pinches from other working relationships so we can understand what will work well for us here." When the time comes to share pinches, Sixes can note that they don't respond well to pressure from others (i.e., numerous phone calls to check progress) because they usually have excellent memories. Sixes can add that because they put pressure on themselves to follow through, pressure from others feels doubly stressful.

Say something as soon as you are aware of feeling pinched or upset.

Once you have both agreed to share pinches when they occur, there is little need to worry when either you or the other person initiates a conversation about a pinch. Keep in mind that the pinch will likely be a low-level frustration that can be easily remedied. The sharing of pinches as they occur, along with subsequent productive conversations, builds mutual rapport, loyalty, and teamwork.

When you start to behave in ways that indicate you are feeling pinched or distressed, do something physical if you can, such as working out or taking a walk.

Walking and other sorts of physical activity help Sixes to ease their concerns and calm their active minds. In a pinch, and especially in a crunch, physical exertion serves to get Sixes back into their bodies and away from being overly focused on thoughts and emotions. There is often a sense of relaxation and freedom that comes from physical exercise, particularly outdoor activities. When more relaxed, Sixes can often conceive of new ways to perceive and handle potentially difficult situations.

For more insights and information about conflict, please refer to the following: Chapter 4, "Managing Conflict," in *Bringing Out the Best in Yourself at Work* (McGraw-Hill, 2004) and Chapter 5, "Become an Excellent Communicator," in *What Type of Leader Are You?* (McGraw-Hill, 2007).

When you have a negative reaction and feel a pinch, ask yourself: *What does my reaction to this situation or to the other person's behavior say about me as a Six and about the areas in which I can develop? How can working on my pinches and crunches help me to bring out the best in myself?*

Like Fives, most Sixes seek to understand themselves in most areas of their lives. For Sixes, however, the caution in answering the above questions is to refrain from over-analyzing themselves and to work instead on simply observing their inner processes and reactions. One instructive way for them to do this is to pay special attention to both the content of their reactions and the process they go through during times of pinches and crunches. For example, a pinched Six may focus on events that have the underlying content of loyalty, trustworthiness, dependability, authority, or other factors. In taking note of their thought processes, Sixes may realize that each time they replay an event in their minds that has raised these issues, their emotions accelerate or they remember numerous past events that created the same feelings in them, further agitating and heightening their feelings.

To take this a step further, it can be helpful for Sixes to consider what sets off their anticipation of and planning for worst-case scenarios. All repetitive behavior serves a purpose, although the exact purpose may not be obvious at first. Sixes can ask themselves these types of questions: *What function does envisioning worst-case scenarios really play in my life? What is the underlying purpose of my tendency to project my thoughts and fears onto others? What makes loyalty so important to me, and how does being loyal help me avoid feelings and having to deal with them? Although I focus on trusting others, what would I learn if I focused more on trusting myself?*

For more insights and information about conflict, please refer to the following: Chapter 4, "Managing Conflict," in *Bringing Out the Best in Yourself at Work* (McGraw-Hill, 2004) and Chapter 5, "Become an Excellent Communicator," in *What Type of Leader Are You?* (McGraw-Hill, 2007).

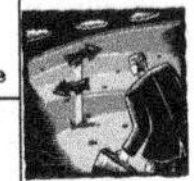

TEAM DEVELOPMENT STRETCHES

There is a difference between a group and a team. A *group* is a collection of individuals who have something in common; a *team* is a specific type of group, one composed of members who share one or more *goals* that can be reached only when there is an optimal level of *interdependence* between and among team members.

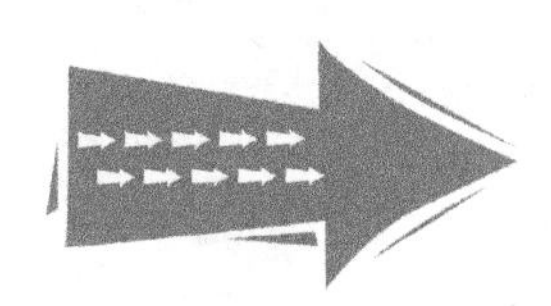

Team members also have *roles* — predictable patterns of behavior – within the team that are often related to their Enneagram styles. *Task roles* involve behaviors directed toward the work itself; *relationship roles* involve behaviors focused on feelings, relationships, and team processes, such as decision making and conflict resolution.

In addition, teams have unique yet predictable dynamics as they go through the four sequential stages of team development: *forming, storming, norming,* and *performing.* At each stage, there are questions the team must resolve before moving to the next stage.

TEAM STAGE	QUESTIONS
FORMING	*Who are we, where are we going, and are we all going there together?*
STORMING	*Can we disagree with one another in a constructive and productive way?*
NORMING	*How should we best organize ourselves and work together?*
PERFORMING	*How can we keep performing at a high level and not burn out?*

Sixes: Development Stretches for Team Members and Team Leaders

Team Goals

Although you may prefer team goals that are *substantial and meaningful* for both the team and individual team members, other team members may need goals that are more circumscribed and specific and are focused more on individual contributions than on team goals. Allow yourself to also be concrete and precise when you create team goals and to support the idea that individual goals are just as important as team goals.

Team Interdependence

You may prefer *moderately to highly interdependent teams* where members work

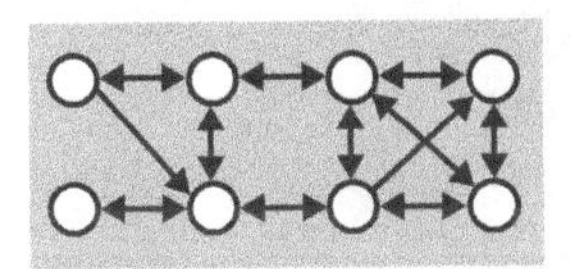

together in a like-minded, competency-focused, and loyalty-driven team atmosphere. However, you need to remind yourself that some teams need to work at a lower level of interdependence to be most effective, and that some are composed of members who dislike team environments where there is a high degree of interconnection or where they perceive the price of loyalty to be the inability to disagree with the team's direction or the ideas of other team members. Work to support the level of interdependence the team needs, and work to develop the capacity to be comfortable in teams that may not offer the degree of loyalty and cohesion you desire.

For more insights and information about teams, please refer to the following: Chapter 5, "Creating High-Performing Teams," in *Bringing Out the Best in Yourself at Work* (McGraw-Hill, 2004) and Chapter 6, "Lead High-Performing Teams," in *What Type of Leader Are You?* (McGraw-Hill, 2007).

Team Roles

Your typical task-related team role is likely to involve *evaluating information* within the team by reacting to and evaluating or questioning ideas and information presented by others; your likely relationship-related team role is *playing devil's advocate* by articulating obstacles that need to be considered or overcome before the team moves to action. Stretch yourself to go beyond these typical roles and adopt the following additional team task and relationship roles:

Task Roles

New task role

Generating and elaborating on ideas, bringing up new ideas and providing additional ideas based on ideas already under discussion

New relationship role

Relieving tension by using humor or other behavior — for example, telling brief stories — to reduce team tension

Relationship Roles

Team Dynamics

During the four stages of team development — *forming, storming, norming,* and *performing* — experiment with expanding your repertoire of behavior in the following ways:

FORMING	STORMING	NORMING	PERFORMING
Become more active during this stage rather than primarily watching the team's dynamics — for example, make suggestions for how the team should proceed and help team members get to know one another.	Allow yourself to notice issues other than those related to power and authority; experiment with encouraging people to discuss issues and feelings, and be willing to discuss your own reactions.	Maintain your strength in helping the team to reach working agreements, and make sure the ideas you suggest and/or support are designed to allow individual autonomy as much as team coordination.	Continue keeping others focused on deliverables and acknowledging the contributions of team members, making sure to acknowledge — both to yourself and others — your own contributions as well.

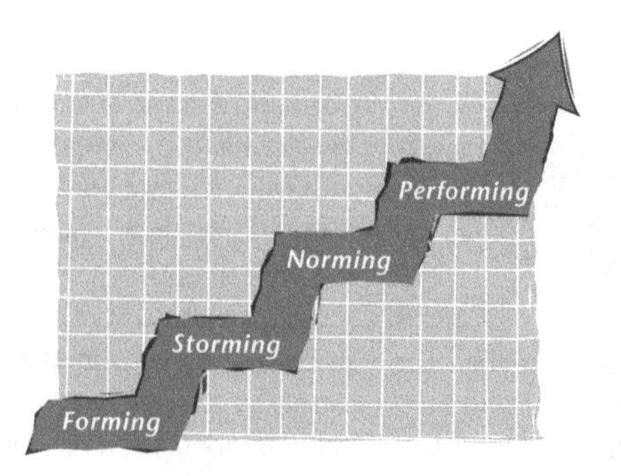

For more insights and information about teams, please refer to the following: Chapter 5, "Creating High-Performing Teams," in *Bringing Out the Best in Yourself at Work* (McGraw-Hill, 2004) and Chapter 6, "Lead High-Performing Teams," in *What Type of Leader Are You?* (McGraw-Hill, 2007).

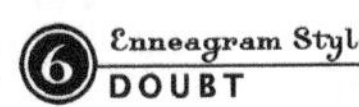

Additional Team Development Stretches for Six Team Leaders

Become increasingly comfortable with power and authority.

Examine your relationship to power and authority, with a focus on understanding that most authority figures are not completely positive or negative but usually a mixture of both.

Take a piece of paper and make three columns, heading these "positive authority figures," "negative authority figures," and "mixed authority figures" (both positive and negative). Make a list of all your prior bosses and place each name in the appropriate column. Next to each name, write down that person's most prominent leadership qualities. Then review each column. Do you have more names in the positive column, more in the negative, more in the mixed, or some other pattern? For each individual in the positive column, write down some of his or her negative qualities; for each individual in the negative column, write down some of his or her positive qualities. Then, write down your own name, listing your positive and negative leadership traits. You will find that most leaders have both positive and negative attributes.

Say positive things about yourself to yourself.

You may have a tendency to underestimate yourself and to understate your positive qualities. Write down all your positive attributes, both as a leader and a person. Make this list at least 20 items or more. Pick one item each day to focus on and to appreciate in yourself. Look in the mirror a minimum of three times per day and say out loud: *I really like that I am*...[fill in the blank with your word or phrase of the day].

Ask for positive feedback from others.

Don't go fishing for compliments, but do seek genuine positive feedback in order to understand how others perceive your favorable attributes. During the first week, select three people whom you know well and respect, and ask each of them to give you one item of positive feedback regarding something they believe you might not know about yourself. Write it down. During the second week, select three more individuals and follow the above process. Continue this for two more weeks so that you have at least twelve items of positive feedback. Review these nightly to remind and encourage yourself to appreciate your assets.

For more insights and information about teams, please refer to the following: Chapter 5, "Creating High-Performing Teams," in *Bringing Out the Best in Yourself at Work* (McGraw-Hill, 2004) and Chapter 6, "Lead High-Performing Teams," in *What Type of Leader Are You?* (McGraw-Hill, 2007).

LEADERSHIP DEVELOPMENT STRETCHES

The intense challenges of leadership are complex, demanding, unpredictable, exciting, and rewarding, and they require the ability to manage oneself and to interact effectively with hundreds of others in both stressful and exhilarating circumstances. For these reasons, leaders must spend time in honest self-reflection. Individuals who become extraordinary leaders grow in both evolutionary and revolutionary ways as they push themselves to meet challenges even they cannot predict in advance.

Excellent leadership comes in many forms, and no Enneagram style has a monopoly on greatness. However, your Enneagram style shows both your strengths as a leader and the areas that would most likely create obstacles to your success.

Enneagram Style Six leaders usually display this special gift: *insight and planning*. However, Six leaders' greatest strength can also become their greatest weakness: through their tendency to doubt both themselves and others, together with their sharp insights about themselves, others, and their environment, Six leaders can create a work climate of either great safety and loyalty or of distrust — or of both, in a back-and-forth pattern.

Development Stretches to Enhance Your Leadership

Deal with your authority issues.

Take a serious look at your history with bosses and authority figures, particularly in those cases where your reactivity to authority may have hurt your career and/or those with whom you work. Try to learn from your past experiences.

Learn to manage your anxiety.

Manage your anxiety by learning its early warning signs and then deescalating it (by walking, talking, or whatever works well for you) rather than fueling it with worst-case scenario development. Remember that fretting is not problem solving.

Cultivate worthy adversaries.

With the same fervor with which you seek loyalty from those with whom you work, also cultivate worthy adversaries from the ranks of your peers and subordinates. These individuals are most likely to push your growth and development as a leader.

For more insights and information about leadership, please refer to the following: Chapter 6, "Leveraging Your Leadership," in *Bringing Out the Best in Yourself at Work* (McGraw-Hill, 2004) and the book, *What Type of Leader Are You?* (McGraw-Hill, 2007).

RESULTS ORIENTATION DEVELOPMENT STRETCHES

It is important to build credibility with customers by delivering sustained, high-quality results, continually driving for results, and reaching your potential. When you do this, you make gains in productivity, push the envelope of new product development, and support the organization as a leader in its field.

Each time you think of a worst-case scenario, think of a best-case scenario as well.
It will be almost impossible for you not to anticipate problems, but you should use your scenario-planning skills at the same time to also create positive scenarios. Discipline yourself to create a viable, positive scenario in addition to — not instead of — a negative scenario. When you do this as a regular part of the planning process, eventually both positive and negative alternatives will come easily to you.

Use best-case scenario planning with the team before introducing worst-case scenarios.
It is best to begin planning with best-case scenarios rather than worst-case ones; the former motivates people to move forward, while the latter can deplete their energy and focus. After the positive possibilities have been discussed, consideration of the worst-case scenarios will be very helpful for grounding the decisions and plans in reality.

Stay calm in a crisis.
When things go awry, and they will, people will look to you for ideas, plans, alternatives, and calmness. There is nothing wrong with conveying a sense of urgency to resolve problems. However, it is best to do so in a calm and deliberate manner. Sometimes it helps to take a walk before responding or to say some calming words to yourself — e.g., *It's worked out before, and so it will this time* or *I know that I'm going into my Six worrying, and I can choose either to continue to worry or to stop it if I want to.*

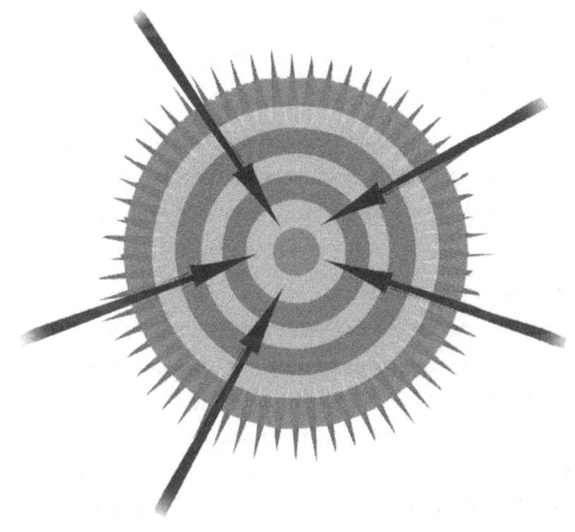

For more insights and information about results orientation, please refer to the following: Chapter 2, "Drive for Results," in *What Type of Leader Are You?* (McGraw-Hill, 2007).

STRATEGY DEVELOPMENT STRETCHES

Leaders and individual contributors must understand the actual business of their organizations and be able to think and act strategically in both big and small ways if their teams and organizations are to reach the highest levels of performance, effectiveness, and efficiency.

"Knowing the business" and "thinking and acting strategically" go hand in hand. Unless you know the business, you have no context for thinking and acting strategically. When you have this information, you need to be able to use it in a strategic way, working from a compelling and common vision, a customer-focused mission, a smart strategy, and effective goals and tactics aligned with that strategy.

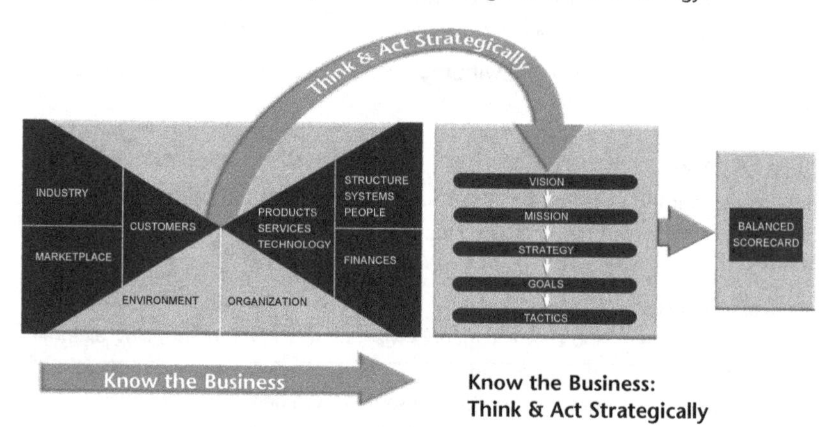

Know the Business: Think & Act Strategically

Take projects or jobs that will be productive stretches for you.
Don't undersell yourself and take on work that is too easy for you, as doing so won't push you to expand your capabilities. On the other hand, be careful not to be so attracted to the risk and excitement of a new challenge that you take on a project or job that is more complex than your prior experience would suggest is a good career move. Give yourself the time to fully develop your skills.

Make sure you develop a vision and strategy before moving to goals and tactics.
Although you may feel more comfortable working with the concrete areas of missions, goals, and tactics, staying within this comfort zone will hurt your chances to rise in the organization. At higher levels, you will need to lead from vision and strategy.

Frame your responses in positive ways.
Instead of responding to the ideas of others with reasons why something may not work, respond first with how the ideas *could* work, then add your thoughts about potential problems. Although Sixes are often thought of as more pessimistic than optimistic, they can also be thought of as optimists with a strong sense of reality. When you think of a worst-case scenario, instead of verbalizing it, ask yourself this question: *I know what I am trying to prevent from happening, but what is my hope of what* can *happen?*

For more insights and information about strategy, please refer to the following: Chapter 4, "Know the Business: Think and Act Strategically," in *What Type of Leader Are You?* (McGraw-Hill, 2007).

DECISION-MAKING DEVELOPMENT STRETCHES

We all make decisions on a daily basis, but we rarely think about the process by which we make them. The wisest decisions are made utilizing our heads (rational analysis and planning), our hearts (to examine values, feelings, and impact on people), and our guts (for taking action), with all three used in an integrated way. In addition, when you are making decisions at work, you need to consider three other factors: the organizational culture, the decision-making authority structure within the organization, and the context of the decision itself.

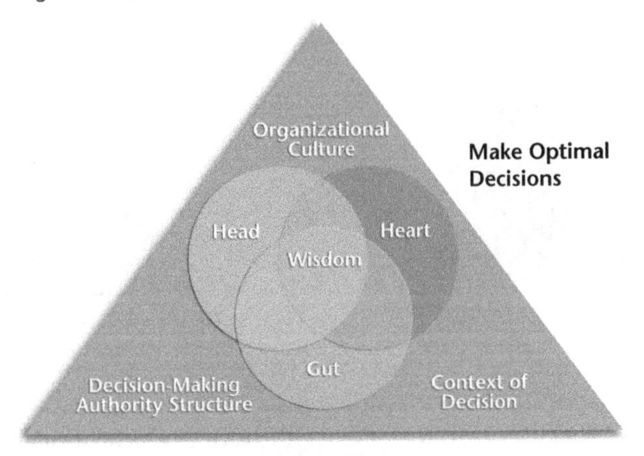

The following chart shows you how to develop each of your Centers of Intelligence (Head, Heart, and Gut) to assist you in making wise decisions.

	Centers of Intelligence		
	Head Center	**Heart Center**	**Body (Gut) Center**
Activities for Sixes That Develop Each Center	**Objective analysis** Slow down your analysis of data related to a decision, particularly when you are anxious or notice that you are repeating the same thoughts. **Astute insight** Learn to differentiate your projections from objective insights by honestly examining your own feelings and motivations. This will help you clarify your intentions and allow you to make better decisions. **Productive planning** Plan for both positive and negative scenarios and know when to stop planning and take action.	**Empathy** Remain empathic even when someone's behavior bothers, hurts, or angers you. **Authentic relating** Be true to yourself even when you need or want something from the other person; don't engage in ingratiating behavior. **Compassion** Be as compassionate to yourself as you are to others; factor you into your decision making.	**Taking effective action** Make decisions that are good risks, not just exciting ones; take action using your gut as a way to bypass overanalysis. **Steadfastness** When you are sure of a decision, believe in yourself and hold your ground in the face of opposition; make sure you do this in an approachable rather than reactive manner. **Gut-knowing** When you are unsure of what to do, engage in physical activity (such as walking) and ask your gut for the best alternative.

For more insights and information about decision making, please refer to the following: Chapter 7, "Make Optimal Decisions," in *What Type of Leader Are You?* (McGraw-Hill, 2007).

ORGANIZATIONAL CHANGE DEVELOPMENT STRETCHES

In contemporary organizations, change has become a way of life. Companies exist in increasingly complex environments, with more competition, fewer resources, less time to market, higher customer expectations, increased regulation, more technology, and greater uncertainty. Organizations need to be flexible, innovative, cost-conscious, and responsive if they want to succeed. As a result, employees at all levels need to be able to embrace change and to function flexibly and effectively within their teams when an unforeseen direction must be taken.

Take Charge of Change

Take reasonable risks.

Pay attention to your own feelings, making sure you do not refuse to take a prominent role in a change effort simply because you feel anxious about its likelihood of success. All change efforts involve uncertainty. At the same time, don't agree to get highly involved in a change initiative primarily on the basis of the thrill factor. If you do, you may end up in a situation in which it will be nearly impossible to succeed.

Develop realistic relationships with your bosses.

Many Sixes focus on their bosses, becoming highly concerned if their bosses appear to have a negative reaction to something the Six does. Although it would be nice if all bosses were consistently supportive, this is not realistic. It is important to give your boss the latitude to raise concerns without your reacting as though the relationship were in jeopardy.

Learn to perceive resistance as simply another problem to be solved.

Resistance to change is normal, inevitable, and even desirable. You want people to disagree, preferably in a constructive way, because opposing ideas often generate better ways of doing things. In addition, resistance that is not dealt with directly during the change process usually surfaces again at a later date, sometimes in a more serious form. Treating resistance as a problem to be solved will help you reduce your emotional reactivity and increase your chances of a productive outcome.

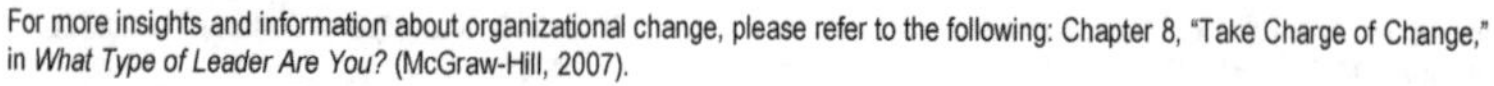
For more insights and information about organizational change, please refer to the following: Chapter 8, "Take Charge of Change," in *What Type of Leader Are You?* (McGraw-Hill, 2007).

TRANSFORMATION DEVELOPMENT STRETCHES

In order to move from *creating anticipatory or worst-case scenarios using your insights to help yourself understand what might happen and feel prepared in case something goes wrong* to the understanding that *there is meaning and support in the world,* Sixes can work toward these transformations:

Mental Transformation

Transform the mental pattern of **cowardice** (thoughts of doubt and worry that cause you to continually create anticipatory or worst-case scenarios) *into the higher belief of* **faith** (the belief that both you and others can capably meet life's challenges, and that there is some certainty and meaning in the world).

Mental Activity

When you become aware that you are plagued with self-doubt and worry and are creating worst-case scenarios, remember one or more times when a situation or outcome was uncertain yet you had complete trust in yourself and others to rise to the challenges in a constructive and meaningful way. Allow those times to come back into your thinking, and relive what was occurring within you at those moments.

Emotional Transformation

Transform the emotional habit of **fear** (feelings of anxiety, deep concern, and panic that the worst will occur, that others cannot be trusted, and that you are not up to the challenges that present themselves) *into the higher awareness of* **courage** (the feeling of being able to overcome fear through fully conscious action, rather than turning to either inaction or to action designed to prove that you have no fear).

Emotional Activity

When you become aware that you're feeling fear, anxiety, and deep concern or panic, remember one or more times in your life when you were courageous and were able to overcome your fears in a fully conscious and calm way. Remember the circumstances and your feeling of being capable of taking action, and recall what you experienced during those times. Keep replaying those completely engaged moments until you feel fully reconnected with the experiences.

For more insights and information about personal transformation, please refer to the following: Chapter 7, "Transforming Yourself," in *Bringing Out the Best in Yourself at Work* (McGraw-Hill, 2004).

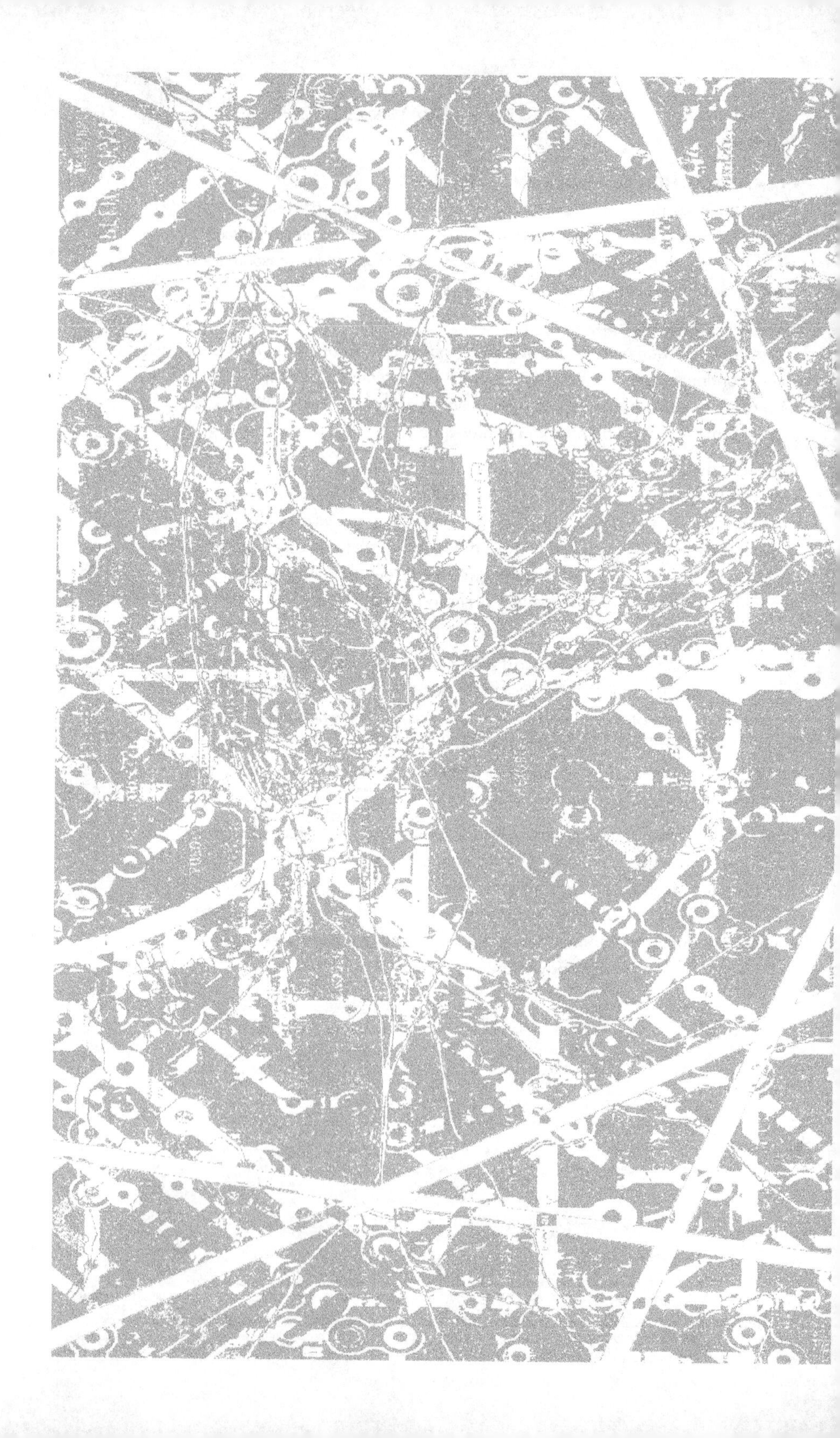

ENNEAGRAM STYLE SEVEN

ENNEAGRAM SEVENS

The search for pleasure and stimulation and the avoidance of pain and discomfort

Spontaneous, engaging, and multitasking to an extreme, Sevens are upbeat, energetic, and need to feel that they have all options possible open to them. Elaborate future planners, dreamers and visionaries, Sevens generate enthusiasm, push boundaries, and avoid painful experiences by conjuring up new ideas, engaging with people or activities that excite them, and by rationalizing negative experiences through a positive reframing of events.

Almost all Sevens have difficulty focusing on one thing at a time, as their attention shifts from one idea, activity, or person to the next that grabs their interest, and they also have a contagious sense of optimism that comes from a sense that everything is possible. Some Sevens create extensive social networks, a kind of collective surrogate family that gives them the support to make the best of every opportunity; other Sevens restrain their desire to have everything as a way to sacrifice themselves in the service of the group; and still other Sevens are unabashed dreamers, looking to everything new to stimulate and excite them.

Their interpersonal style can be described as fast-talking and even faster thinking, with a mental process that moves 1000 miles per hour and jumps from topic to topic. While some Sevens are quiet, most Sevens say what's on their minds as soon as they think it. And although their ideas may seem loosely connected to the rest of us, Sevens make these associative connections instantly and share them in rapid fire, using voices filled with enthusiasm and energy.

While we can all be creative thinkers, enjoy the rush of adrenalin, and prefer pleasure to pain, for Sevens, the search for pleasure and stimulation and the avoidance of pain and discomfort is their primary, persistent, and driving motivation.

DEVELOPMENT STRETCHES FOR SEVENS

INDIVIDUALS WHO CRAVE THE STIMULATION OF NEW IDEAS, PEOPLE, AND EXPERIENCES, AVOID PAIN, AND CREATE ELABORATE PLANS THAT WILL ALLOW THEM TO KEEP ALL OF THEIR OPTIONS OPEN

CONTENTS

SELF-MASTERY DEVELOPMENT STRETCHES

Self-Mastery — the ability to understand, accept, and transform your thoughts, feelings, and behavior, with the understanding that each day will bring new challenges that are opportunities for growth — is the foundation of all personal and professional development. Self-mastery begins with self-awareness, then expands to include the elements shown in the following graphic:

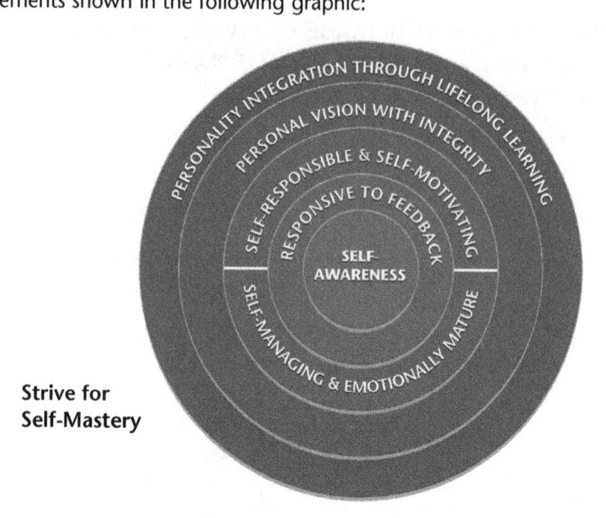

In this section on self-mastery, you will find the following:

- Three common issues for Sevens related to self-mastery
- Three development stretches for working with the core issues of your Enneagram style, including one basic activity and one deeper activity for each stretch
- Three development stretches for working with your wings and arrow (stress-security) styles

Common Issues for Sevens Related to Self-Mastery

Being able to focus mentally, emotionally, and physically at will	Feeling genuine and consistent empathy for others	Accepting and integrating the reality of pain and discomfort along with pleasure

For more insights and information about self-mastery, please refer to the following: Chapter 7, "Transforming Yourself," in *Bringing Out the Best in Yourself at Work* (McGraw-Hill, 2004) and Chapter 3, "Strive for Self-Mastery," in *What Type of Leader Are You?* (McGraw-Hill, 2007).

Development Stretches for Working with the Core Issues of Your Enneagram Style

Listen fully to others.

Basic Activity

After you have had a conversation with someone, ask the person these questions: *What percentage of the time were you talking, and what percentage was I talking? At any time during the conversation did you feel I was interrupting, not listening, or appearing distracted?* Do this at least once a day with different people. Listen fully to the answers without giving counterarguments or explanations for what you did or did not do. Your task is to have someone reflect your behavior back to you, whether you agree with the reflection or not.

Deeper Activity

Sevens usually listen more with their heads than their hearts; listening fully, however, means listening with both your head and your heart. When you are listening to others, ask yourself this question: *What are they saying about what they think and how they feel?* In addition, Sevens often believe that they know what the other person is saying before the person has completed his or her thoughts, so they often stop listening and/or interrupt the other person. To help yourself listen more fully, allow at least three seconds between the time the other person finishes speaking and the time you begin to speak.

It can also be helpful to paraphrase both the content and the feeling of what you have just heard. A paraphrase is a restatement of what someone has said, and it includes both the thoughts and the feelings that the person has communicated. For example, when a colleague says, "This place is so disorganized," you can paraphrase this as follows: "You sound very frustrated. What happened?" When you do paraphrase, be sure to listen to the other person's affirmation or disconfirmation of your paraphrasing. This feedback can be of great help to you in increasing the accuracy of your listening skills. For example, the colleague in the above scenario might respond, "No, I'm beyond frustrated — I'm furious! They told me I'd be receiving a raise, but no one can find my paperwork." It is common, as in this example, for a paraphrased statement to lead to a deeper level of communication between two individuals.

Stay focused by learning to go inward.

Basic Activity

The biggest challenge for you will be to focus on your physical sensations and emotional reactions. For an hour each day, practice bringing your focus to both your emotions and your physical sensations. Once you have developed the ability to do this, practice this inner focusing on a regular basis, particularly at times when you feel either highly stimulated or anxious.

For more insights and information about self-mastery, please refer to the following: Chapter 7, "Transforming Yourself," in *Bringing Out the Best in Yourself at Work* (McGraw-Hill, 2004) and Chapter 3, "Strive for Self-Mastery," in *What Type of Leader Are You?* (McGraw-Hill, 2007).

Deeper Activity

Staying focused on one thing at a time can be one of the most difficult tasks for Sevens, because the Seven's mind and attention tend to move quickly from one area of interest to another. The following exercise is very helpful and can be applied to every area of your life. In everything you do — for example, considering an idea, eating a meal, experiencing a feeling, having a conversation, or engaging in any activity — try to notice when your attention becomes diverted from that activity, thought, or feeling. Then bring your attention back to it, and stay focused on it for at least one more minute. As you become proficient at refocusing your attention, expand the areas of your life in which you do this, and also prolong the amount of time in which you give consciously concentrated time and attention to the experiences.

One structured way to practice this skill is to spend eight minutes every morning simply focusing. First, sit or stand with minimal body movement and focus on an object you see, hear, or smell in your environment. Concentrate only on that object for two full minutes; if your attention becomes diverted to anything else, just notice this shift and bring your attention back to the original object. For the next two minutes, focus on something inside yourself, such as a feeling, a bodily sensation, or your breathing. Follow the same process as the first part: try to stay focused for two minutes, and simply observe attention shifts and return to your intended focus. Next, follow the same two-minute procedure with an external object as your point of focus. For the final two minutes, focus again on something inside yourself.

Focusing may be difficult for you at first, but with practice you will find that it will become easier and more enjoyable. This should become a daily practice.

Note: A kitchen timer or a watch with an alarm may be useful to keep track of the two-minute intervals.

Develop your emotional repertoire.

Basic Activity

Using the categories of *mad, glad, sad,* and *afraid,* make lists of all the events in the past year in which you have felt each of these emotions. Analyze your lists to determine which of these four feelings you tend to experience most and least often. Spend one hour thinking about how you can expand your emotional repertoire by eliciting feelings in the emotional categories you experience least often. Write down your answers. This activity will help you to relate more deeply both to yourself and to others.

For more insights and information about self-mastery, please refer to the following: Chapter 7, "Transforming Yourself," in *Bringing Out the Best in Yourself at Work* (McGraw-Hill, 2004) and Chapter 3, "Strive for Self-Mastery," in *What Type of Leader Are You?* (McGraw-Hill, 2007).

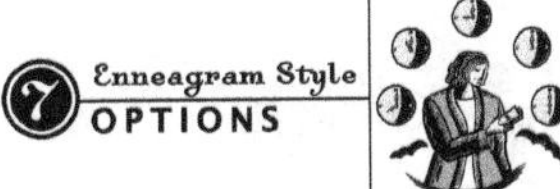

Deeper Activity

Expanding one's emotional repertoire and developing a deeper empathy for other people can be a major challenge for many Sevens. While Sevens can be very emotionally engaging and tend to express positive feelings easily, they often close off their access to the emotions of fear, anger, and particularly sadness by thinking interesting thoughts or pursuing stimulating activities. Unfamiliarity with their own feelings can hinder Sevens from being able to deeply empathize with the emotions of other people. Several approaches can be helpful to the Seven in changing this pattern. It is important to be patient with yourself, keeping in mind that the development of a deeper emotional repertoire is a long-term process.

First, the previous activity on staying focused can be very easily applied to emotions. Second, the Emotional Index in Chapter 1, "Discovering Your Enneagram Style," of *Bringing Out the Best in Yourself at Work,* can be useful for identifying your current repertoire in the four basic emotional groups — *mad, sad, glad,* and *afraid.* Once you have identified your emotional repertoire, you can work to increase the range by doing the following: allow yourself to feel more emotions in the categories in which you had a low number of marks and/or allow yourself to feel your emotions more fully, thus increasing your intensity levels in all four emotional groups.

Third, you can increase your emotional repertoire by talking about your feelings in depth, as well as by listening to other people talk about their feelings. Fourth, you can go to movies or plays that evoke emotions, then discuss the experiences with a confidant afterward.

Note that sadness is the emotion that Sevens often have the most difficulty allowing themselves to feel. Part of the foundation of the Seven personality is the seeking of pleasure and the avoidance of pain — and sadness is emotional pain. Here are some ideas that can help you to stop avoiding pain, which is a natural part of the human experience. First, make a list of all the things that elicit sadness in you. You may find that it is not very long at first, but keep this list and add to it every day. Once you begin to pay attention to your own feelings, you may be surprised to find that a number of feelings related to pain are lurking below the surface. Second, whenever you feel even the slightest twinge of sadness, make sure that you keep breathing normally and deeply. Shallow breathing typically cuts people off from their feelings, while deeper breathing tends to allow feelings to become strong enough that we can recognize them.

For more insights and information about self-mastery, please refer to the following: Chapter 7, "Transforming Yourself," in *Bringing Out the Best in Yourself at Work* (McGraw-Hill, 2004) and Chapter 3, "Strive for Self-Mastery," in *What Type of Leader Are You?* (McGraw-Hill, 2007).

Development Stretches for Working with Your Wings and Arrow (Stress-Security) Styles

Wings are the Enneagram styles on either side of your core Enneagram style; arrow, or stress-security, styles are Enneagram styles shown with arrows pointing away or toward your core Enneagram style. Your wings and arrow styles don't change your core Enneagram style, but instead offer qualities that can broaden and enrich your patterns of thinking and feeling as well as enhance your behaviors. Your wings and arrow styles make you more complex and versatile because they provide more dimensions to your personality and serve as vehicles for self-development.

Integrate Your Six Wing

Acknowledge authority.

While Sevens may say that they acknowledge authority, they most often act as though they are their own bosses, either by befriending authority figures, which equalizes the relationship, or by ignoring authorities in the sense that Sevens tend to do what they themselves think best. Acknowledging authority goes beyond recognizing that someone has a specific role; it means accepting the fact that someone has power over you, allowing their directives to supersede your own preferred direction, and conceding, especially to yourself, that they have the right to do this. Sixes, by contrast, usually respect and accept the role of authority figures, the one caveat being bosses who appear abusive or arbitrary. Sevens can take stock of their authority relationships by asking themselves some hard questions:

1. *As you think of all your prior bosses, how would you describe the pattern of your relationships with each of them?*
2. *If you notice that you have tended to befriend some of your bosses, what have these friendships allowed you to do or protected you from?*
3. *Which of your bosses do you think would say that you did not grant them the full authority of their roles?*
4. *How do you really feel when your boss does not act warmly toward you?*
5. *Why does a boss's warmth and acceptance feel so important to you?*

Face your fears.

While Sixes and Sevens are both Mental Center styles, Sixes are often more conscious of feeling fearful than are Sevens. The Seven's fear or anxiety (a mild form of fear) may actually trigger the defocusing process of the Seven as he or she searches for something interesting or stimulating as a way of avoiding fear. Sixes tend to face their fears more directly, and Sevens can benefit from doing this, too. When you feel at all uncomfortable, nervous, or unsettled or when you are uncomfortable and your attention becomes diverted from what you were doing, thinking, feeling, or saying, ask yourself this question: *What am I feeling fearful about?* Be vigilant in your response by not taking the answer *Nothing* at face value, and by asking yourself probing questions, such as this: *Underneath that fear, what am I feeling fearful or worried about?*

For more insights and information about integrating your wings and/or arrow styles (stress-security points), please refer to the following: Chapter 1, "What Type Are You?" and the conclusion, "Stretch Your Leadership Paradigms," in *What Type of Leader Are You?* (McGraw-Hill, 2007).

Pursue deep levels of insight.

Because Sixes spend so much time thinking about and examining issues and dynamics, trying to understand them and develop plans to support positive outcomes and prevent negative ones, they often develop deep insights. Sevens, by contrast, try to grasp the key issues, spend less time on uncomfortable issues, and then move on. As a result, Sevens may miss the deeper perspectives offered by a more thorough analysis. Sevens can train themselves to go deeper by asking themselves, then answering, these questions when issues arise: *What additional perspectives might I be missing? How do I feel about this situation, and what do my reactions illuminate about me that could be altering my perspective? How can I understand this situation from the point of view of everyone involved, not just my own?* Having specific questions to answer is important for this reason: the Seven's mind moves very quickly and jumps from idea to idea automatically. Having specific questions to answer helps you to focus your mind and reach a deeper level of insight. Make sure you give the greatest consideration and time to the areas that arise that create discomfort in you. These are the issues from which you can gain the greatest insight.

For more insights and information about integrating your wings and/or arrow styles (stress-security points), please refer to the following: Chapter 1, "What Type Are You?" and the conclusion, "Stretch Your Leadership Paradigms," in *What Type of Leader Are You?* (McGraw-Hill, 2007).

Integrate Your Eight Wing

Step into leadership.

Eights tend to be authoritative in their leadership style, while Sevens tend to be more facilitative. In general, Eights are often more comfortable than other styles with being in roles of authority and having power; Sevens, on the other hand, often exhibit more ambivalence about being in leadership roles. In addition to doing the earlier activity on acknowledging authority, Sevens can begin to act with more powerful assertion themselves by doing some of the things that Eights do.

Like all of the Mental Center styles, Sevens tend to breathe into their heads but often not lower into their bodies. Power, however, often comes from the belly area. Experiment first with breathing into your belly, right below your navel, and continue to do this for extended periods of time. Next, practice walking and moving "from" your belly, still breathing deeply into this area. Finally, you can interact with others while you are breathing in this deep way. Talking from the abdomen actually conveys assertion and power far more than does talking from the head or heart area alone.

Ground your action.

It can be helpful to think of the metaphor of grounding an electric wire. Sevens can be full of electric energy, but they may need to ground their action so that an unintended explosion does not occur. Eights, on the other hand, are typically more deliberate and intentional when they take action. Here are some analyses to consider before taking action:

1. What are the likely intended and unintended consequences of this action?
2. Who are the individuals with power and influence that need to be brought on board before this action can be successful?
3. Where is resistance to this action likely to occur? What can be done, and by whom, to overcome these concerns?
4. Do all of the resources exist to make this happen?
5. What alternative courses of action might enlist those with influence more fully, minimize potential resistance, use fewer resources, and/or achieve a more potent outcome?

Talk less so you will influence others more.

Most Sevens talk frequently, saying whatever they are thinking about various topics in rapid succession. Because of this, others may not know which ideas are the most significant ones or when is the right time to comment on an idea. By contrast, most Eights weigh what they will say, determine when they will say it, and consider the best timing for their comments, thus maximizing their influence. When Sevens learn to do this, they will increase their ability to influence others.

For more insights and information about integrating your wings and/or arrow styles (stress-security points), please refer to the following: Chapter 1, "What Type Are You?" and the conclusion, "Stretch Your Leadership Paradigms," in *What Type of Leader Are You?* (McGraw-Hill, 2007).

The easiest way to learn to do this is to restrain yourself in conversations, waiting to say something until you have heard comments from others. While you are waiting and listening, ask yourself this question: *Given what I'm hearing and what I'm thinking, what is the one thing I most want people to respond to?* Once you have the answer, make your statement in one sentence. When you do so, look at other people directly without staring, making sure you are not looking away as you gather your thoughts. Do not re-explain your ideas if others do not comment immediately. Simply wait. If they are confused, let them ask you questions, but keep your answers brief. When you want to influence others, less is more.

Integrate Arrow Style One (Stress Point)

Complete your tasks early.

While Ones tend to focus on tasks to completion, Sevens usually focus on multiple tasks simultaneously, completing those that hold their interest and not finishing others unless there is an impending deadline. During these times, a crisis often ensues as Sevens try to meet their abundant commitments. There are numerous ways to fulfill all of them. A difficult yet effective way is to take one task at a time to completion rather than multitasking. A second alternative is to accept fewer tasks or to minimize nonessential (although pleasurable or stimulating) activities when there is work to be completed.

Third, Sevens can begin tasks far sooner than they normally would; for example, if you think a task should take one week and your tendency is to start it just two days before the deadline, then begin the task four days before the deadline. A fourth alternative is to start and continue the least interesting tasks first. Sevens often choose the interesting tasks first and delay the more boring work until later. Reversing this can help Sevens get both the interesting and monotonous tasks accomplished.

Finally, ask someone whose work you value (and is not another Seven) to look over your completed product and to give you feedback about whether the job looks complete to him or her. Sometimes, Sevens may perceive a project as complete, yet another person may suggest areas where further work is needed.

For more insights and information about integrating your wings and/or arrow styles (stress-security points), please refer to the following: Chapter 1, "What Type Are You?" and the conclusion, "Stretch Your Leadership Paradigms," in *What Type of Leader Are You?* (McGraw-Hill, 2007).

Take the time to do things right.

Taking the time to do things right involves a great deal of pre-thinking and consideration of ideas. Ones tend to be deliberate and deliberative in their approach to tasks, considering the best and highest quality ways to accomplish a goal. Sevens tend to be more spontaneous and propelled toward action, and they sometimes do not give careful consideration to their actions. The following activity is easy to do. First, select a project for which you are responsible. Develop a plan in writing that you think will work. Pick two people whom you respect and who are very different both from you and from each other. Sit down with each separately, tell the person your project goal, and ask how he or she would approach the work. Listen carefully and take notes. Have each person look at your plan and give you feedback about it, both positive and negative. Then, consider what each has said, and revise your plan accordingly. Continue this process with additional work for which you are responsible until this way of considering alternatives comes naturally to you as you develop your plans.

Pay attention to details on a regular basis.

Although many Sevens would say they do pay attention to detail, they often do this at the last minute or with the final product rather than paying attention to detail throughout the course of a project. Ones, however, attend to detail at each step so that they end up with a quality product without any last-minute frenzy of activity. Sevens can do this by focusing on each task, taking the time to examine the details at each step. This can include checking for correct grammar and typographical errors in written pieces, sending e-mails as reminders of meetings or as summations of conversations, and more. While this may seem to some Sevens to be a poor use of time — based on the Seven's assumption that these items will take care of themselves, are not that important, or can be dealt with at a later time — addressing details early on in fact ensures the quality of the final product.

For more insights and information about integrating your wings and/or arrow styles (stress-security points), please refer to the following: Chapter 1, "What Type Are You?" and the conclusion, "Stretch Your Leadership Paradigms," in *What Type of Leader Are You?* (McGraw-Hill, 2007).

Integrate Arrow Style Five (Security Point)

Spend time alone.

Fives often spend time alone and can even feel alone by choice when in the presence of others. Sevens, in comparison, tend to spend time alone only after they have expended all their energy, and this takes quite a while. As one Seven said, "Yes, I spend a lot of time alone — about two days every three months, and then everyone wonders what's happened to me." Truly spending time alone on a frequent basis can really benefit Sevens as they learn to focus their energy and delve into their own growing self-awareness. It is difficult to become more self-aware when you are constantly doing something, thinking in quick succession about topics, and interacting with others. Once a week, spend three full hours by yourself doing something relaxing while reflecting and paying attention to your feelings and thought processes. The discipline of doing this will allow you to access far more of your interior world.

Contain your energy.

Sevens tend to be exuberant and energetic, allowing their energy to follow their interests. In a sense, they are like rivers that continually pour forth water. Fives, on the other hand, contain their energy, giving it out at will and recharging their batteries at regular intervals. They are more like lakes. To practice containing energy, Sevens need to pay attention to the moment when they begin to put their energy forward — that is, outside themselves — by talking, thinking, doing something, or interacting with others. At these times, instead of putting the energy forward or external, bring it back inside yourself. Breathing deeply at these times will help, as will keeping your body from moving around. Ideally, Sevens can learn to contain their energy or put it forth, but to do so at their choice of time and place.

Acquire knowledge in depth.

While both Fives and Sevens relish learning about areas that interest them, Fives are more likely to pursue in-depth knowledge and Sevens to pursue information in breadth. Thus, Fives will have deep reservoirs of information, whereas Sevens will grasp the essentials of a topic and then learn as much as they can about related areas. Both ways of pursuing knowledge are valuable, but Sevens can benefit from going more deeply into their areas of interest. To do this, simply spend twice as long as you would normally reading about and discussing the areas that interest you. When you are learning about a new area, and you feel you are finished learning what you need to know, take the same amount of time you just spent and pursue the same topic at a deeper level.

For more insights and information about integrating your wings and/or arrow styles (stress-security points), please refer to the following: Chapter 1, "What Type Are You?" and the conclusion, "Stretch Your Leadership Paradigms," in *What Type of Leader Are You?* (McGraw-Hill, 2007).

COMMUNICATION DEVELOPMENT STRETCHES

When you communicate with someone, three kinds of unintentional distortions may be present: speaking style, body language, and blind spots. *Speaking style* refers to your overall pattern of speaking. *Body language* includes posture, facial expressions, hand gestures, body movements, energy levels, and hundreds of other nonverbal messages. *Blind spots* are elements of your communication containing information about you that is not apparent to you but is highly visible to other people. We all unknowingly convey information through an amalgam of our speaking style, body language, and other inferential data.

The receivers of the messages you send also distort what they hear through their *distorting filters*. These are unconscious concerns or assumptions, often based on the listener's Enneagram style, that alter how someone hears what others say.

Change one communication style behavior at a time.

It is most effective to work on changing one behavior at a time, preferably in the following sequence: speaking style, body language, blind spots, and listening distorting filters. It is easiest to change the behaviors of which we are most aware, and this sequence represents the most common order of awareness, from most to least aware.

Sevens: Speaking style

- Quick and spontaneous, with words released in a flurry
- Tell engaging stories
- Make jokes to defuse tension
- Shift from topic to topic instantaneously
- Upbeat and charming
- Avoid negative topics about themselves
- Reframe negative information, giving it a positive context

Sevens: Body language

- Smiling and bright-eyed
- Sharp tone of voice when angry
- Highly animated face and numerous hand and/or arm gestures
- May walk around and/or pace while speaking
- Easily distracted by external stimuli or internal thoughts

For more insights and information about communication, please refer to the following: Chapter 2, "Communicating Effectively," in *Bringing Out the Best in Yourself at Work* (McGraw-Hill, 2004) and Chapter 5, "Become an Excellent Communicator," in *What Type of Leader Are You?* (McGraw-Hill, 2007).

Sevens: Blind spots

- They may not have absorbed all the information and knowledge they believe they have mastered
- Fail to see that their own behavior causes others to take them less seriously
- Constant shifting of ideas and animated body language is distracting to others

Sevens: Distorting filters when listening to someone else

- Feeling their competence is being questioned or demeaned
- Think they know what the other person is going to say, so they stop listening and/or interrupt
- Believing that limits may be placed on them
- Being forced into a long-term commitment they do not want

Note: Some of the above characteristics may be positive, some negative, and some neutral or mixed. They are intended as an overview to allow you to select from among them.

Use e-mails to expand and adjust your language patterns.

- Review your e-mails before you send them for language and tone.
- Elaborate on problems or concerns as well as on positive information.
- Use complete sentences.
- Pay attention to punctuation; this makes the e-mail easier to read.
- Focus on the e-mail recipient and what he or she is doing as well as on yourself.

For more insights and information about communication, please refer to the following: Chapter 2, "Communicating Effectively," in *Bringing Out the Best in Yourself at Work* (McGraw-Hill, 2004) and Chapter 5, "Become an Excellent Communicator," in *What Type of Leader Are You?* (McGraw-Hill, 2007).

FEEDBACK DEVELOPMENT STRETCHES

Honest, positive, and constructive *feedback* — direct, objective, simple, and respectful observations that one person makes about another's behavior — improves both relationships and on-the-job performance. When you offer feedback, the Feedback Formula, combined with the insights of the Enneagram, helps you tailor your delivery. When someone gives you feedback, the more receptive you are to hearing what is being said, the more likely it is that you will be able to discern what is useful and utilize what has been suggested.

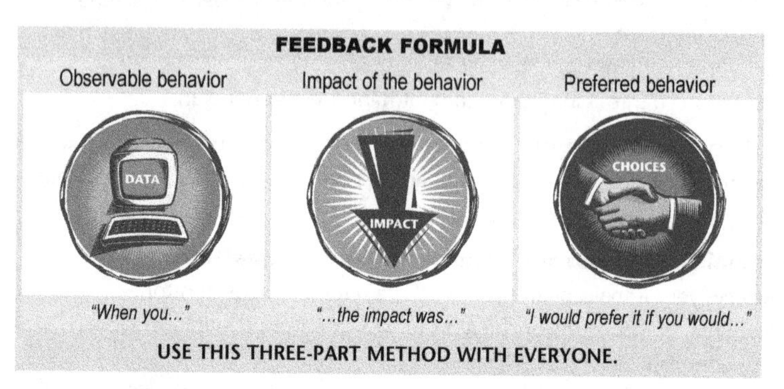

How Sevens Can Enhance Their Ability to Deliver Feedback Effectively

When you offer feedback to someone, you want to be prepared and also to encourage the feedback recipient to be as receptive as possible. Remember that how and when you deliver feedback is just as important as what you actually say.

Use the three components of the **Feedback Formula** together with the following suggestions to plan and deliver the feedback.

- Maintain your optimism, but be careful not to let that obscure what the feedback recipient needs to hear.
- Use your ability to provide context and perspective carefully so that the central issue does not get lost.
- Do bring in related information, but keep your focus so that the feedback recipient does not get sidetracked.
- Remember that although you can think fast and are able to multitask, the feedback recipient may need to focus on one topic until it has been discussed completely before moving to another topic.

For more insights and information about feedback, please refer to the following: Chapter 3, "Giving Constructive Feedback," in *Bringing Out the Best in Yourself at Work* (McGraw-Hill, 2004) and Chapter 5, "Become an Excellent Communicator," in *What Type of Leader Are You?* (McGraw-Hill, 2007).

How Sevens Can Be More Receptive When They Receive Feedback

- When someone takes the time to offer you feedback, minimize distractions during the conversations — for example, no cell phones, no walking around, no doing unrelated work.
- Although you may appear to others to want only positive feedback, you may actually pay more attention to negative feedback. Pay equal attention to both, making sure that you neither dismiss positive feedback nor reframe or overexplain negative feedback. It is important for you to just listen, asking questions for clarification when necessary.
- Remember that everyone needs both positive and negative feedback in order to learn and grow, and that this is especially important for Sevens, who sometimes get so caught up in their own thinking processes and reactions that they may miss being able to accurately read other people's reactions.

For more insights and information about feedback, please refer to the following: Chapter 3, "Giving Constructive Feedback," in *Bringing Out the Best in Yourself at Work* (McGraw-Hill, 2004) and Chapter 5, "Become an Excellent Communicator," in *What Type of Leader Are You?* (McGraw-Hill, 2007).

CONFLICT DEVELOPMENT STRETCHES

Relationships both at work and at home often involve some degree of conflict, which may be caused by a variety of factors and usually follows the pinch-crunch cycle below:

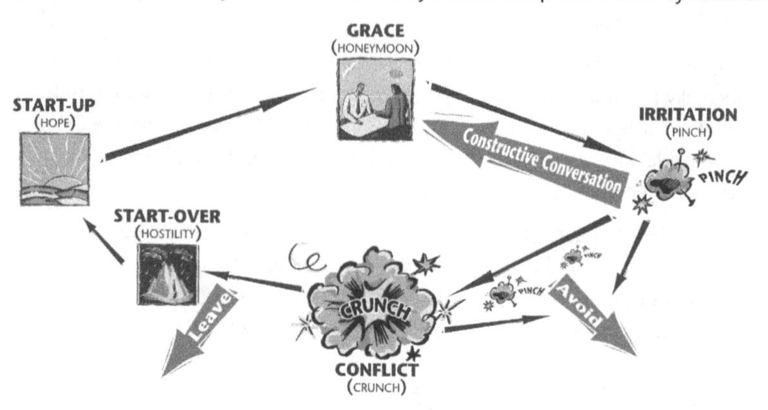

Whatever the root cause of the conflict, the Enneagram styles of the key parties involved will always be a factor in the conflict dynamics and resolution. The Enneagram enables each individual involved to make conflict resolution a constructive rather than destructive experience. The more people know themselves, understand their own responsibilities in the conflict interaction, engage in constructive self-management, and know how best to approach others through knowledge of the Enneagram, the greater the chances of a swift and effective outcome.

There are specific pinches (anger triggers) for each Enneagram style — that is, certain situations that will invariably ignite anger in a person of one style, yet may not affect someone of a different style. For Sevens, these pinches include:

Having to do boring and mundane tasks · Feeling dismissed or not taken seriously · Unjust criticism · Not being listened to; not having their ideas responded to

For more insights and information about conflict, please refer to the following: Chapter 4, "Managing Conflict," in *Bringing Out the Best in Yourself at Work* (McGraw-Hill, 2004) and Chapter 5, "Become an Excellent Communicator," in *What Type of Leader Are You?* (McGraw-Hill, 2007).

Development Stretches for Transforming Anger into an Opportunity for Growth

Share your likely pinches (anger triggers) with others at the beginning of your working relationship.
Sevens need to take the time to do this step and to make sure they communicate their pinches in some detail. Although it may feel like a waste of time to discuss mutual expectations before any conflict has occurred, it doesn't take much time and is well worth the effort. It also provides an opportunity to get to know the other person better.

When you discuss your pinches, make sure you are highly explicit. Sevens often talk quickly and may leave out certain details that seem obvious; consequently, slowing down the pace of discussion can be helpful to the other person. It is safest to assume that nothing is obvious. In a new work relationship, even the obvious is worth stating clearly.

Another reminder for Sevens during this initial conversation is to listen thoroughly to the other person and then ask for clarification of what has been said. Because their minds move so quickly, Sevens may not always fully understand what the other person means, even if they believe that they do. For instance, if the other person mentions that timeliness is one of his or her pinches, the Seven can ask, "Can you give me some examples of what you mean by timeliness?"

Say something as soon as you are aware of feeling pinched or upset.
Because Sevens often avoid situations and conversations that are either uncomfortable or possibly painful, they may avoid saying anything about feeling pinched. This avoidance may even be unconscious; Sevens may simply start thinking about something that interests them and not even be aware of feeling pinched. The first step for Sevens is to acknowledge that they are feeling upset. Sevens can usually do this by paying closer attention to themselves. Another technique for Sevens is to try to notice when their minds switch from topic to topic and to say to themselves: *I just changed mental gears. Am I feeling pinched or uncomfortable about something?* Once Sevens realize that something is distressing them, they need to make a commitment to say something to the other person. It sometimes helps Sevens to do this when they realize that even if the discussion may be uncomfortable, the conversation will usually be far more difficult if they wait until more pinches have built up.

For more insights and information about conflict, please refer to the following: Chapter 4, "Managing Conflict," in *Bringing Out the Best in Yourself at Work* (McGraw-Hill, 2004) and Chapter 5, "Become an Excellent Communicator," in *What Type of Leader Are You?* (McGraw-Hill, 2007).

When you start to behave in ways that indicate you are feeling pinched or distressed, do something physical if you can, such as working out or taking a walk.

Physical activity helps release some of the anxiety and built-up energy that Sevens often experience when they feel pinched. The Seven's mental activity often increases during times of distress; physical activity helps Sevens focus more on their bodies, and it therefore often slows down their thought processes and helps them to clear their minds. After doing something physical, it is particularly helpful to Sevens to stop, be still, and focus on their feelings and reactions for an extended period of time. The following question can also be helpful: *What did the person actually do that caused the pinch, as opposed to my interpretation about what he or she did?*

When you have a negative reaction and feel a pinch, ask yourself: *What does my reaction to this situation or to the other person's behavior say about me as a Seven and about the areas in which I can develop? How can working on my pinches and crunches help me to bring out the best in myself?*

Sevens can benefit by asking themselves the above questions over and over again. The reason for this is that Sevens may start to answer the question but then do one of two things: 1) stop seeking answers after their first response because their first answer may be insightful or interesting to them, or 2) begin by thinking about themselves but then drift into thinking about what the other person did or should have done, and what might be wrong with that individual. Sometimes the first answer is the best answer; however, more often than not, continued self-questioning peels back the layers of the onion, and subsequent answers often produce deeper personal insights. Sevens also need to focus on their own issues rather than unconsciously derailing their own self-development by focusing primarily on the other person's perceived actions.

Learning to focus is fundamental to the development of Sevens. When Sevens become aware that they are having difficulty staying focused on one idea, task, person, or feeling, it is very helpful to ask: *What am I feeling right now? Am I feeling anxious, angry, or sad? What is the real source of these feelings?* Determining the answers to such questions can profoundly affect and transform a Seven.

For more insights and information about conflict, please refer to the following: Chapter 4, "Managing Conflict," in *Bringing Out the Best in Yourself at Work* (McGraw-Hill, 2004) and Chapter 5, "Become an Excellent Communicator," in *What Type of Leader Are You?* (McGraw-Hill, 2007).

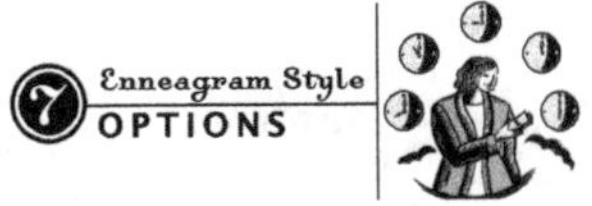

TEAM DEVELOPMENT STRETCHES

There is a difference between a group and a team. A *group* is a collection of individuals who have something in common; a *team* is a specific type of group, one composed of members who share one or more *goals* that can be reached only when there is an optimal level of *interdependence* between and among team members.

Team members also have *roles* — predictable patterns of behavior – within the team that are often related to their Enneagram styles. *Task roles* involve behaviors directed toward the work itself; *relationship roles* involve behaviors focused on feelings, relationships, and team processes, such as decision making and conflict resolution.

In addition, teams have unique yet predictable dynamics as they go through the four sequential stages of team development: *forming, storming, norming,* and *performing.* At each stage, there are questions the team must resolve before moving to the next stage.

TEAM STAGE	QUESTIONS
FORMING	*Who are we, where are we going, and are we all going there together?*
STORMING	*Can we disagree with one another in a constructive and productive way?*
NORMING	*How should we best organize ourselves and work together?*
PERFORMING	*How can we keep performing at a high level and not burn out?*

Sevens: Development Stretches for Team Members and Team Leaders

Team Goals

Although you may prefer team goals that are extremely *stimulating, energizing, visionary, and action oriented,* other team members may need goals that are more focused, specific, prioritized, and conceived through thoughtful analysis before the team takes action. Allow yourself to also be concrete and precise when you create team goals, and to support the idea of thoroughly discussing and prioritizing them before implementation.

Team Interdependence

Although you may prefer to work in *teams with fluid roles* with a democratic, stimulating and productive team culture, remind yourself that most teams need clarity

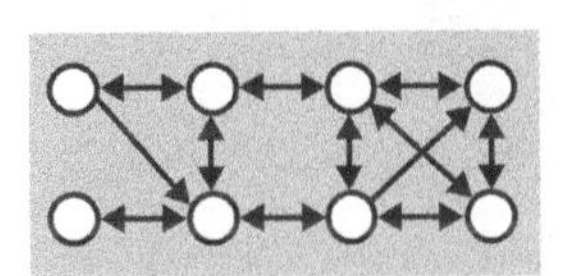

regarding the level and types of interdependencies between and among team members in order to be effective, and that the optimal level of team interdependence may not allow for highly fluid individual roles. In addition, some teams are composed of members who neither want to discuss every issue among themselves nor want to be highly stimulated all the time. Work to support the level of interdependence the team needs, and work to develop the capacity to be effective in teams that may not be as egalitarian or stimulating as you prefer.

For more insights and information about teams, please refer to the following: Chapter 5, "Creating High-Performing Teams," in *Bringing Out the Best in Yourself at Work* (McGraw-Hill, 2004) and Chapter 6, "Lead High-Performing Teams," in *What Type of Leader Are You?* (McGraw-Hill, 2007).

Team Roles

Your typical task-related team role is likely to involve *generating and elaborating on ideas* within the team by bringing up new ideas or providing additional input on ideas already under discussion; your likely relationship-related team role may be *relieving tension* by using humor or other behavior designed to reduce team tension. Stretch yourself to go beyond these typical roles and adopt the following additional team task and relationship roles:

Task Roles

New task role

Structuring tasks, making suggestions about how to organize the team's work

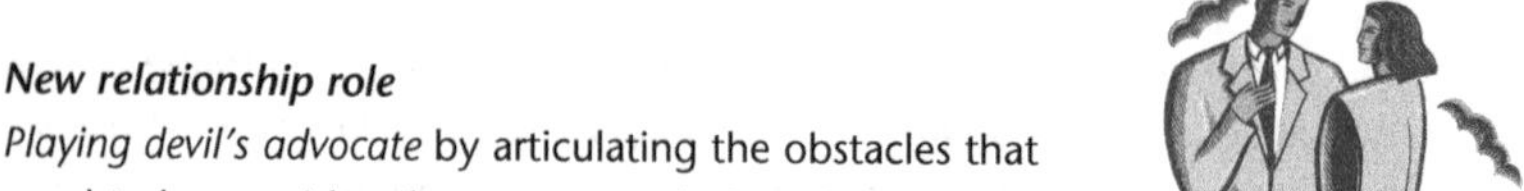

New relationship role

Playing devil's advocate by articulating the obstacles that need to be considered or overcome before the team can move forward

Relationship Roles

Team Dynamics

During the four stages of team development — *forming, storming, norming,* and *performing* — experiment with expanding your repertoire of behavior in the following ways:

FORMING	STORMING	NORMING	PERFORMING
Pay as much attention to the development of relationships between and among team members as you do to helping the team articulate its vision; remember that others may need more structure to their work than you do in order to be effective.	Allow yourself to become more comfortable with team conflict and to understand its benefits for the team's development, being careful not to defuse serious situations through humor or distracting stories that derail the team from resolving important issues.	Maintain your strength in helping the team reach agreements that will support and not impair creativity, but make sure that your own needs for freedom of movement do not limit you from supporting team norms that most team members need in order to work together effectively.	Make sure your priorities are fully aligned with those of the team.

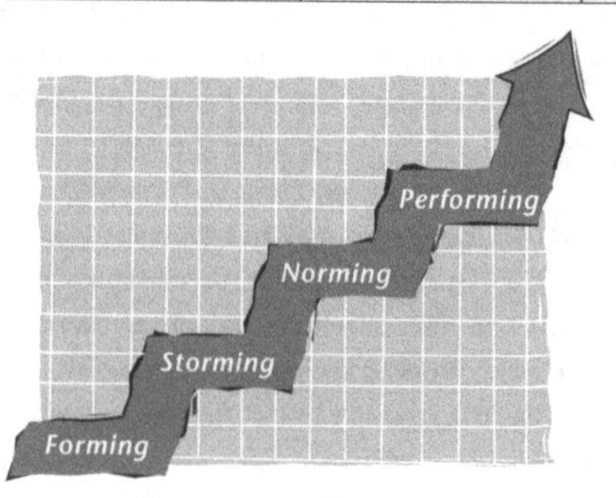

For more insights and information about teams, please refer to the following: Chapter 5, "Creating High-Performing Teams," in *Bringing Out the Best in Yourself at Work* (McGraw-Hill, 2004) and Chapter 6, "Lead High-Performing Teams," in *What Type of Leader Are You?* (McGraw-Hill, 2007).

Additional Team Development Stretches for Seven Team Leaders

Accept that your job is to lead from a clearly defined leadership role.
Although you may prefer teams that are egalitarian, they can still be egalitarian when you are in a clear leadership role. Embrace the leadership role from the start. Many Seven team leaders may act more like team members in the beginning; this can make the inevitable and necessary shift to a more authoritative role difficult.

Create more team structure and processes than you yourself need.
Encourage your team to tell you how much structure they need beyond what you currently provide. In honoring these requests, you'll create more safety in the group and will likely see an increase in the team's innovation and productivity.

Know when to stop.
This suggestion applies to many areas of a Seven team leader's development. Do you know when to stop sharing your own ideas and start listening to others? Do you know when to stop creating new ideas and focus on the most important ones already developed? Do you know when to disengage from a fascinating conversation because there are critical meetings to attend or items on your desk that need action? In general, it is helpful to think in terms of shortening everything you are involved in to one-third. For example, talk one-third of the time, and listen two-thirds. Stop when one-third of the ideas have been generated and decide which of the ideas are the most actionable. Limit your work conversations to one-third of their usual length.

For more insights and information about teams, please refer to the following: Chapter 5, "Creating High-Performing Teams," in *Bringing Out the Best in Yourself at Work* (McGraw-Hill, 2004) and Chapter 6, "Lead High-Performing Teams," in *What Type of Leader Are You?* (McGraw-Hill, 2007).

LEADERSHIP DEVELOPMENT STRETCHES

The intense challenges of leadership are complex, demanding, unpredictable, exciting, and rewarding, and they require the ability to manage oneself and to interact effectively with hundreds of others in both stressful and exhilarating circumstances. For these reasons, leaders must spend time in honest self-reflection. Individuals who become extraordinary leaders grow in both evolutionary and revolutionary ways as they push themselves to meet challenges even they cannot predict in advance.

Excellent leadership comes in many forms, and no Enneagram style has a monopoly on greatness. However, your Enneagram style shows both your strengths as a leader and the areas that would most likely create obstacles to your success.

Enneagram Style Seven leaders usually display this special gift: *innovation and flexibility*. However, Seven leaders' greatest strength can also become their greatest weakness: with their tendency to be highly creative and to pursue multiple options, Seven leaders can move rapidly in so many directions that their followers may become exhausted, unfocused, and frustrated.

Development Stretches to Enhance Your Leadership

Slow your pace.

Slow your speed to 50 percent of your natural rate, speaking half as fast about half as many items. Breathe twice as deeply for twice as long.

Find the truth in a criticism.

Instead of defending against a criticism by rationalizing, blaming, or critiquing the critique, ask instead: *What is really true about the criticism, and what can I learn from it?*

Complete your tasks.

Follow through on every task you start, and don't start a task unless you know are 100 percent committed to take it to completion.

For more insights and information about leadership, please refer to the following: Chapter 6, "Leveraging Your Leadership," in *Bringing Out the Best in Yourself at Work* (McGraw-Hill, 2004) and the book, *What Type of Leader Are You?* (McGraw-Hill, 2007).

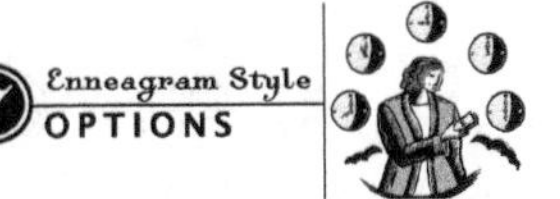

RESULTS ORIENTATION DEVELOPMENT STRETCHES

It is important to build credibility with customers by delivering sustained, high-quality results, continually driving for results, and reaching your potential. When you do this, you make gains in productivity, push the envelope of new product development, and support the organization as a leader in its field.

Stay focused.

When you move quickly from idea to idea and activity to activity, this can create an upsetting frenzy for those around you, even if they find the ideas and activities stimulating. Practice staying focused three times as long as you currently do, and learn to tame your mind when it jumps around, bringing it back to the original thought.

Create the work plan at the right level of detail.

Sevens tend to be good planners, but the plan tends to be at the big idea and execution level, with many of the steps in between getting less attention. Make sure that in developing a collaborative work plan, you describe all tasks, milestones, and deliverables along the way in sufficient detail, and hold yourself and others accountable for following through.

Get things done in advance.

Although Sevens will get most, if not all, of their work done either on time or only a little late, they may have to work long hours at the last minute (and require coworkers to do the same) in order to meet their commitments. Remember that you tend to overcommit to interesting work, that unexpected demands will always arise that need your attention, and that not everyone (including you) can get his or her best work done at the zero hour. Make a commitment to get every piece of work for which you are responsible completed three days before the deadline.

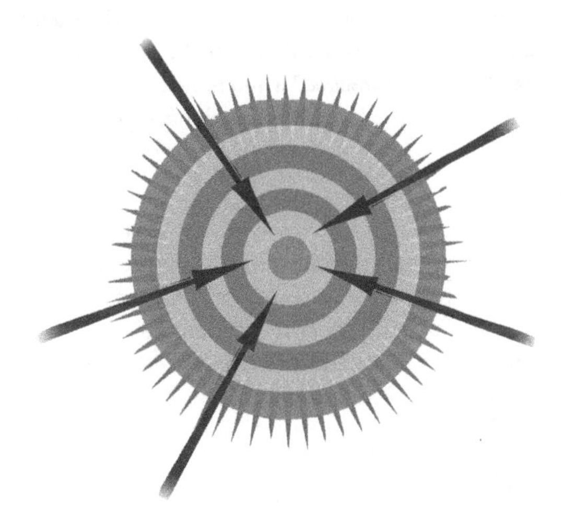

For more insights and information about results orientation, please refer to the following: Chapter 2, "Drive for Results," in *What Type of Leader Are You?* (McGraw-Hill, 2007).

STRATEGY DEVELOPMENT STRETCHES

Leaders and individual contributors must understand the actual business of their organizations and be able to think and act strategically in both big and small ways if their teams and organizations are to reach the highest levels of performance, effectiveness, and efficiency.

"Knowing the business" and "thinking and acting strategically" go hand in hand. Unless you know the business, you have no context for thinking and acting strategically. When you have this information, you need to be able to use it in a strategic way, working from a compelling and common vision, a customer-focused mission, a smart strategy, and effective goals and tactics aligned with that strategy.

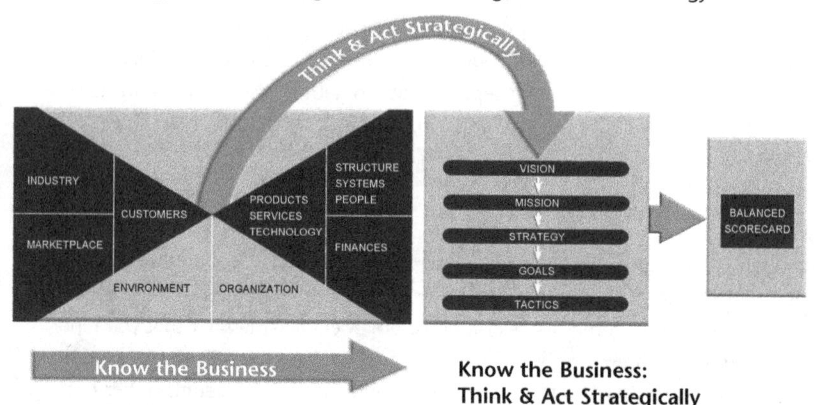

Know the Business: Think & Act Strategically

Go for depth.

You may be a quick study, but it's important to become a deep study as well. Every time you scan a piece of written information, go back and read the item in its entirety. At first you may feel frustrated, but after you have finished fully examining each piece of information, ask yourself this question: *What have I learned from reviewing this item in depth that I missed the first time around?* If you have an affirmative answer, this is good. If you don't think you have learned anything new, go back and review the item again.

Stay the course.

Once your team has developed a shared vision, do not waver from it. Write it down and keep it posted near your desk so you will have a reminder to stay on course. If you have an impulse to rework the vision within two years of its development, remind yourself that this may simply be related to your excitement about new possibilities, and that changing the vision may not benefit the organization. In order for you and others to have a solid sense of direction, a vision requires constancy.

For more insights and information about strategy, please refer to the following: Chapter 4, "Know the Business: Think and Act Strategically," in *What Type of Leader Are You?* (McGraw-Hill, 2007).

Similarly, when you think of new ideas for strategies, goals, and tactics, make sure you focus on possible changes in tactics before you even consider changing goals or strategies. When you have new ideas, let those with whom you discuss them know that they are merely ideas, not directives for a shift in action, and that your intent is solely to discuss their viability.

Slow down.

The two preceding developmental stretches will be easier to do if you also slow down. That means making a conscious effort to speak less quickly and staying with an idea and considering it from many angles before discussing it with others. It also means concentrating on the task at hand and not getting distracted by external stimuli — for example, extraneous noise or a beautiful tree outside the window. Most importantly, slowing down requires focusing your attention inward and asking yourself these questions: *What am I feeling (as opposed to thinking)? What body sensations am I experiencing? Can I simply focus inside myself without thinking about anything or being distracted by something external?*

For more insights and information about strategy, please refer to the following: Chapter 4, "Know the Business: Think and Act Strategically," in *What Type of Leader Are You?* (McGraw-Hill, 2007).

DECISION-MAKING DEVELOPMENT STRETCHES

We all make decisions on a daily basis, but we rarely think about the process by which we make them. The wisest decisions are made utilizing our heads (rational analysis and planning), our hearts (to examine values, feelings, and impact on people), and our guts (for taking action), with all three used in an integrated way. In addition, when you are making decisions at work, you need to consider three other factors: the organizational culture, the decision-making authority structure within the organization, and the context of the decision itself.

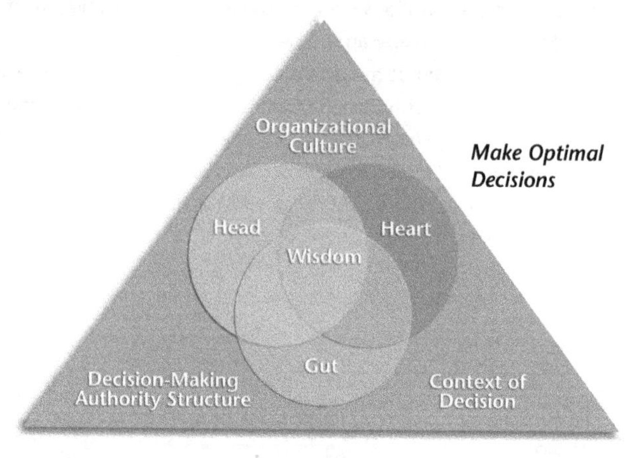

The following chart shows you how to develop each of your Centers of Intelligence (Head, Heart, and Gut) to assist you in making wise decisions.

Centers of Intelligence			
	Head Center	**Heart Center**	**Body (Gut) Center**
Activities for Sevens That Develop Each Center	**Objective analysis** Make sure you really have all the data, not just the highlights. **Astute insight** To have insight takes time and reflection; allow yourself both of these in order to get a deeper view of the issues. **Productive planning** Make a decision and a plan, and stick to them; focus your mind.	**Empathy** Examine your feelings and read your internal cues; this will help you to read others' body language. **Authentic relating** Relate through more than your mind alone; when you relate through your heart as well, your decisions will be better. **Compassion** Think about the potential impact on people of every alternative you consider.	**Taking effective action** Slowing your pace will help you make wise decisions, not just decisions that intrigue or stimulate you. **Steadfastness** Become confident in your depth of knowledge and in your capacity to feel; this confidence will enable you to make the best decisions and to stand by them. **Gut-knowing** Bypass your tendency to overthink and overplan by developing your gut-knowing. When considering options, ask yourself: *Which of these options does my gut tell me will lead to the best outcome?*

For more insights and information about decision making, please refer to the following: Chapter 7, "Make Optimal Decisions," in *What Type of Leader Are You?* (McGraw-Hill, 2007).

ORGANIZATIONAL CHANGE DEVELOPMENT STRETCHES

In contemporary organizations, change has become a way of life. Companies exist in increasingly complex environments, with more competition, fewer resources, less time to market, higher customer expectations, increased regulation, more technology, and greater uncertainty. Organizations need to be flexible, innovative, cost-conscious, and responsive if they want to succeed. As a result, employees at all levels need to be able to embrace change and to function flexibly and effectively within their teams when an unforeseen direction must be taken.

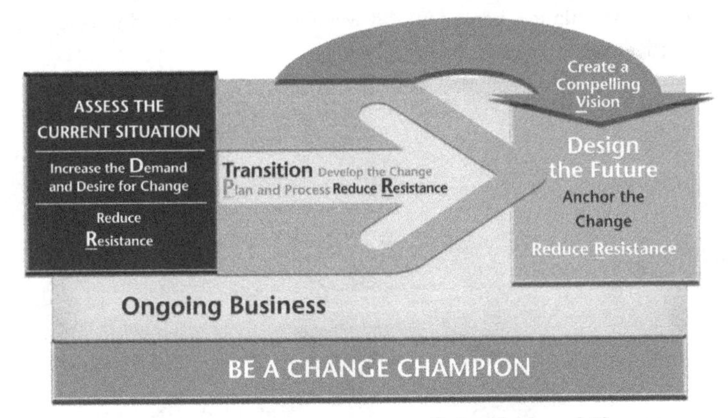

Take Charge of Change

Make it your job to keep everyone focused on the three most important priorities.

You may think it is your job to continuously create innovative ideas and to encourage others to do the same. However, after the future direction has been decided upon, your job is to lead the change effort by helping others focus on the most essential priorities. If you intentionally limit yourself to the three most important priorities, your ability to focus will improve, and the initiative will be far more successful.

Learn to say no to new ways of doing things.

As interesting and potentially useful as new ideas may be, the continuous accumulation of ideas may derail the change initiative. Once a plan and process have been agreed to, make only minor adjustments. When you learn to say no, you are also saying yes to staying on course.

For more insights and information about organizational change, please refer to the following: Chapter 8, "Take Charge of Change," in *What Type of Leader Are You?* (McGraw-Hill, 2007).

Learn to read resistance accurately.

Unless you are absolutely sure of whether an individual or group supports the change effort, solicit more information. Make certain that you understand the issues and feelings involved, as well as the intensity of the resistance or support. Gather a group of advisors — preferably people whose styles are different from yours — and ask them for their perceptions. When you do this over the course of several change projects, your ability to accurately read both resistance and support will grow. In addition, you are likely to realize that while resistance may not always appear rational, it always has some rationale behind it. This will help you to respond to resistance in more effective ways.

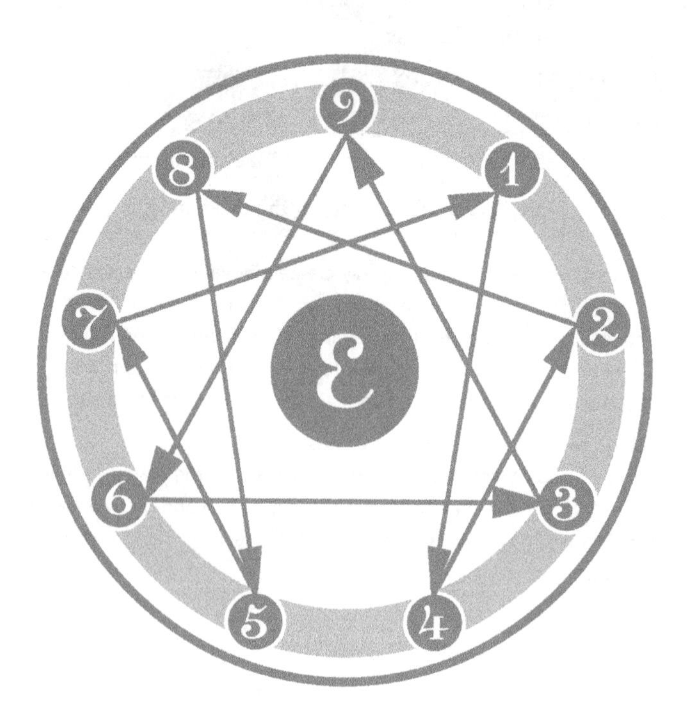

For more insights and information about organizational change, please refer to the following: Chapter 8, "Take Charge of Change," in *What Type of Leader Are You?* (McGraw-Hill, 2007).

TRANSFORMATION DEVELOPMENT STRETCHES FOR SEVENS

In order to move from *craving the stimulation of new ideas, people, and experiences, avoiding pain, and creating elaborate plans that allow them to keep all options open* to the understanding that *a complete sense of self comes from accepting and integrating the positive and negative in life and that there is a bigger plan that already exists,* Sevens can work toward these transformations:

Mental Transformation

Transform the mental pattern of **planning** (the mental process by which the mind goes into "hyper gear," moving in rapid succession from one thing to another) *into the higher belief of* **work** (the ability to direct the focus of one's mental attention to the work at hand, and to control and sustain that focus).

Mental Activity

When your mind starts moving in rapid succession from one thing, person, or idea to another, remember one or more times when you were able to sustain your mental focus and change the focus of your thoughts at will. Allow those times to come back into your thinking, and relive what was occurring within you at those moments. Sustain your focus as you remember these incidents for several minutes.

Emotional Transformation

Transform the emotional habit of **gluttony** (the insatiable, unrelenting thirst for new stimulation of all kinds — people, things, ideas, and experiences) *into the higher awareness of* **sobriety** (the feeling of being a full and complete person, which comes from pursuing and integrating painful and uncomfortable experiences as well as pleasurable and stimulating ones).

Emotional Activity

When you become aware of constantly needing new stimulation, remember one or more times in your life when you felt integrated and complete as a person because you were able to absorb the difficult as well as the pleasurable aspects of an important event. Remember the circumstances, how you felt, and what you experienced during those times. Keep replaying each of those moments until you feel fully reconnected with the experience.

For more insights and information about personal transformation, please refer to the following: Chapter 7, "Transforming Yourself," in *Bringing Out the Best in Yourself at Work* (McGraw-Hill, 2004).

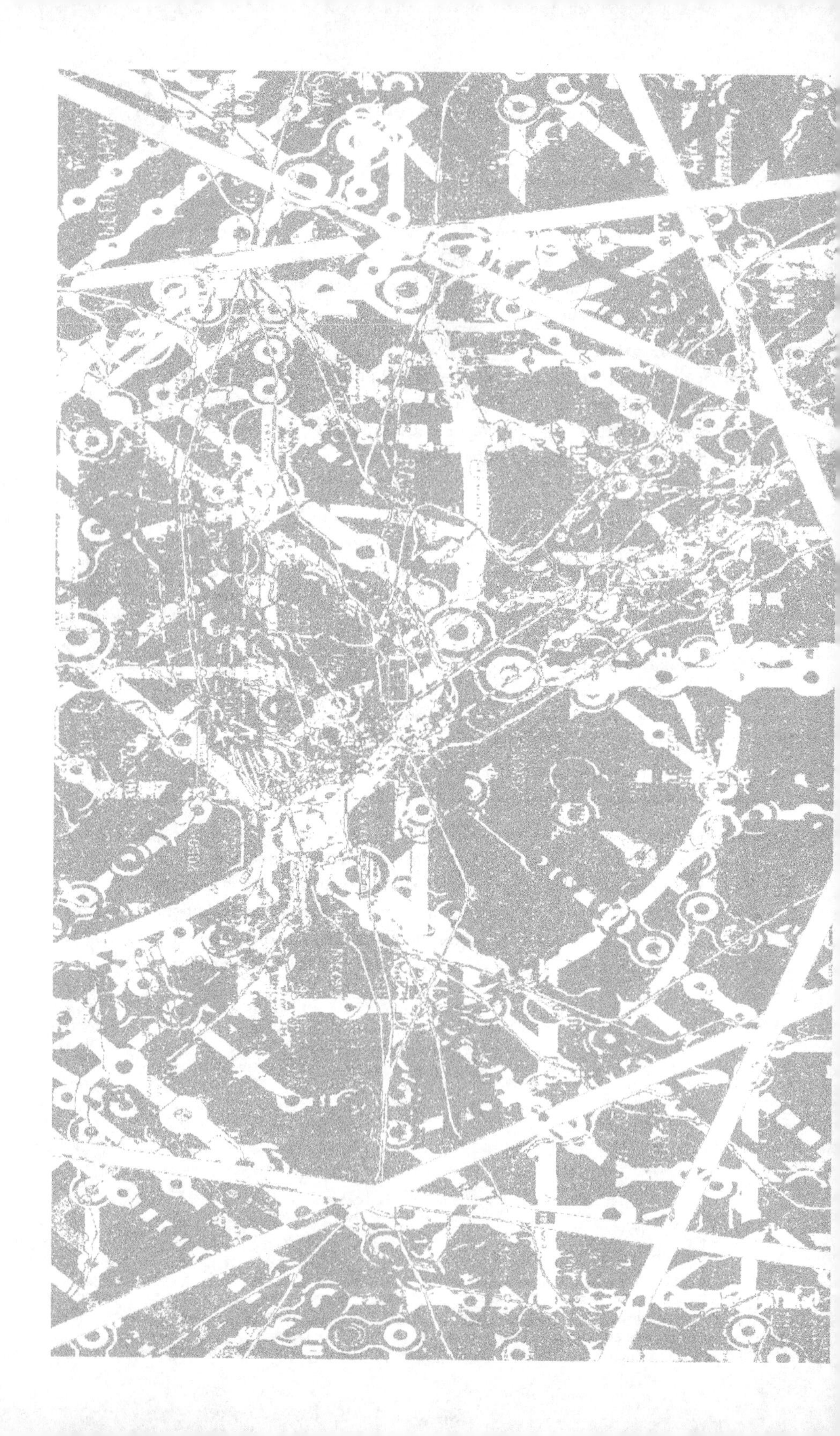

ENNEAGRAM STYLE EIGHT

ENNEAGRAM EIGHTS

The search for control and justice and the avoidance of vulnerability

Assertive, bold, and confident, Eights are highly independent, with a tendency to both protect and control people and events around them and a deep commitment to truth, justice, and equity or fairness. Most Eights are excessive in some way, particularly when they feel anxious or vulnerable. Because they strongly prefer to not show this side of themselves to others, perceiving such feelings as signaling weakness, Eights mask their tender side by engaging in excessiveness in a variety of forms: over-work, too much or too little exercise, erratic or unhealthy eating, and other forms of over-consumption, such as incessant shopping or the purchasing of items — often expensive ones — that they don't really need.

Eights want to get their needs and desires met, want to make big things happen quickly, much akin to moving mountains, and most have a big presence even when they are saying little. Eights can also appear somewhat different from one another. Some Eights are quiet with a low threshold for frustration and an ability to survive and gain control in almost any situation; other Eights are social rebels and protective of others to an extreme; and some Eights are highly emotional, extraordinarily passionate, and enjoy being more center stage.

The Eight's interpersonal style is assertive, and they use voice modulation and non-verbal behavior for effect and impact. For example, they may use a strident voice, direct eye contact, and move closer to others as a way to take charge or make their point, or they may use a softer voice tone, warm eye contact, and a smile to appear gracious, hospitable, or non-threatening.

While we can all highly value truth-telling and pursue justice, want to make big things happen, and have issues with not appearing weak, for Eights, the search for control and justice and the avoidance of vulnerability is their primary, persistent, and driving motivation.

DEVELOPMENT STRETCHES FOR EIGHTS

INDIVIDUALS WHO PURSUE THE TRUTH, LIKE TO KEEP SITUATIONS UNDER CONTROL, WANT TO MAKE IMPORTANT THINGS HAPPEN, AND TRY TO HIDE THEIR VULNERABILITY

CONTENTS

SELF-MASTERY DEVELOPMENT STRETCHES

Self-Mastery — the ability to understand, accept, and transform your thoughts, feelings, and behavior, with the understanding that each day will bring new challenges that are opportunities for growth — is the foundation of all personal and professional development. Self-mastery begins with self-awareness, then expands to include the elements shown in the following graphic:

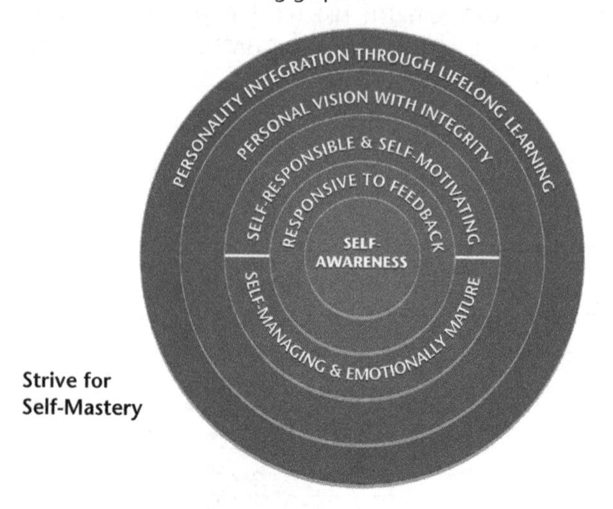

Strive for Self-Mastery

In this section on self-mastery, you will find the following:

- Three common issues for Eights related to self-mastery
- Three development stretches for working with the core issues of your Enneagram style, including one basic activity and one deeper activity for each stretch
- Three development stretches for working with your wings and arrow (stress-security) styles

Common Issues for Eights Related to Self-Mastery

Being forthcoming about your deep vulnerabilities	Allowing others to exercise autonomy and control	Being receptive and responsive to input from others rather than moving to immediate, unilateral action

For more insights and information about self-mastery, please refer to the following: Chapter 7, "Transforming Yourself," in *Bringing Out the Best in Yourself at Work* (McGraw-Hill, 2004) and Chapter 3, "Strive for Self-Mastery," in *What Type of Leader Are You?* (McGraw-Hill, 2007).

Development Stretches for Working with the Core Issues of Your Enneagram Style

Take care of yourself physically.

Basic Activity

Get enough sleep on a regular basis, eat healthfully and in moderation, and exercise regularly. The more you take care of yourself physically, instead of wearing yourself down to the point of exhaustion, the less emotionally reactive you will be.

Deeper Activity

More often than not, Eights take action continuously and often run themselves down, becoming like a car running out of gas or oil. We all do this to some degree, but Eights tend to do it regularly and excessively. When they get run down, they often come to a complete stop; it can take weeks or even months for them to recharge their batteries. Worse, Eights may not even realize they are becoming run down until they have become very ill. Physical awareness and exhaustion prevention are crucial issues for most Eights, as they have a tendency to go into denial related to their physical limitations until it is too late.

First, make sure to get a full night's rest every night and to eat healthfully every day. Second, take time daily to ask yourself, *Am I running myself down?* If the answer is yes, then take time that same day to do something that will replenish your reserves. If your answer is *not yet,* do not take this to mean you can and should keep pushing yourself. Instead, stop and relax for at least an hour or more. Don't wait until you are forced to stop by the limitations of your own body. When you take care of yourself regularly, you will be calmer and more patient, and you will get agitated less easily. This will give you more genuine self-control so that when something occurs that you don't like, you will be able to respond to it in a less intense and more constructive way.

Exercise can also be very helpful. However, when Eights exercise, they tend do so excessively — for example, not exercising for a month, then going to the gym for two-hour workouts for a full week, then getting no exercise at all for another month. Exercise regularly and in moderation. Not only will you feel better physically, but you'll also release some of the physical energy that accumulates in your body.

Slow down your impulse to take action.

Basic Activity

Each time you feel the impulse to take action — for example, giving an opinion, suggesting or demanding that someone else do something, or in any way mobilizing forward action — stop yourself and think: *What is going on inside me that makes me want to move forward so quickly? What will happen if I don't take action right now?*

For more insights and information about self-mastery, please refer to the following: Chapter 7, "Transforming Yourself," in *Bringing Out the Best in Yourself at Work* (McGraw-Hill, 2004) and Chapter 3, "Strive for Self-Mastery," in *What Type of Leader Are You?* (McGraw-Hill, 2007).

Deeper Activity

In almost every situation, Eights take direct and rapid action. This tendency, combined with the Eight's authoritative stance, often leads others to think of Eights as controlling or dominating. The easiest way to alter this behavior is to be alert to each time you are about to suggest a course of action — whether it is a strategic action to take, a way of organizing a committee, or a choice of restaurant — and stop yourself. The most difficult response at these times, and probably the most useful for your growth, would be to say nothing at all for several minutes and simply see what happens. At first, others may look to you for direction, but if you say nothing, they will eventually begin to voice their opinions. If you feel compelled to say something, then ask the other individuals involved, "What do you think is best?" Make sure that your response or reaction to someone else's suggestion involves either asking for more information about the thoughts behind the suggestion, or making a suggestion that builds on the other person's idea.

If you want to practice this new behavior every day, you can do the following exercise: when you arrive at work, write down one item you will need to act on that day. Ask at least two people for their advice, and consider their suggestions before you act. Each day, select a new item for which you will solicit the opinions of others. While you may think that asking other people for their opinions will make you appear indecisive, it is far more likely to make you look like a person who both respects others and makes important decisions by thoughtfully weighing alternatives.

Share your feelings of vulnerability.

Basic Activity

How many times have you allowed yourself to feel sad or to cry in the last year? How many times have you become angry? It is likely that you have been angry far more often than sad. Can you identify areas of vulnerability that your anger may be masking? Even if your anger has been the result of another person being treated poorly or someone not stepping up to perform a task for which they are responsible, can you identify an area of your own vulnerability that this is activating?

For more insights and information about self-mastery, please refer to the following: Chapter 7, "Transforming Yourself," in *Bringing Out the Best in Yourself at Work* (McGraw-Hill, 2004) and Chapter 3, "Strive for Self-Mastery," in *What Type of Leader Are You?* (McGraw-Hill, 2007).

Deeper Activity

The notion of being vulnerable or sharing vulnerabilities can be very anxiety producing for many Eights. While feelings related to anger or joy may come readily, feelings of sadness or fear can be more difficult to acknowledge, as these feelings are often more indicative of uncertainty and vulnerability.

The first step for Eights is to acknowledge to themselves that they are feeling vulnerable. One way to do this is to examine the deeper issues that may lurk behind the feelings of anger. When you begin to experience a surge of anger, ask yourself this: *What vulnerability could my anger be protecting or covering?*

Eights can also use their drive to action as a possible clue to their softer feelings, such as weakness, anxiety, or hurt. When you find yourself ready to act quickly on something, ask yourself these questions: *Before I move to action, what am I trying to prevent from occurring? What does this indicate about feelings I would prefer not to expose?*

For more insights and information about self-mastery, please refer to the following: Chapter 7, "Transforming Yourself," in *Bringing Out the Best in Yourself at Work* (McGraw-Hill, 2004) and Chapter 3, "Strive for Self-Mastery," in *What Type of Leader Are You?* (McGraw-Hill, 2007).

Development Stretches for Working with Your Wings and Arrow (Stress-Security) Styles

Wings are the Enneagram styles on either side of your core Enneagram style; arrow, or stress-security, styles are Enneagram styles shown with arrows pointing away or toward your core Enneagram style. Your wings and arrow styles don't change your core Enneagram style, but instead offer qualities that can broaden and enrich your patterns of thinking and feeling as well as enhance your behaviors. Your wings and arrow styles make you more complex and versatile because they provide more dimensions to your personality and serve as vehicles for self-development.

Integrate Your Seven Wing

Lighten up.

More often than not, Eights approach their work and life with great intensity as they try to transform ideas into action and make things work. Sevens, on the other hand, tend to lighten intense situations through their use of humor and their ability to reframe difficult situations in ways that highlight the positive aspects. Eights can learn to do this by pausing intermittently during times when they would otherwise be driving toward action. During these intervals, you should ask yourself these two questions*: What is occurring in this situation that is positive or engaging? What can I notice that is interesting or amusing?*

Free yourself.

While Eights often perceive themselves as free because they tend to follow their own inner direction, there is another type of freedom that involves being free from the intensity of drive, purpose, and action that compels many Eights. For example, Eights may drive themselves to complete an arduous task at the expense of their physical well-being. They can also become workaholics, much to the detriment of their personal and home lives. Sevens, by contrast, may be in the midst of an important work project, yet take time for a visit to the gym, an art museum, or a meal with an interesting person. This can allow them to go back to work with a refreshed outlook.

Eights can learn this Seven behavior by paying attention to the ways in which they drive themselves too hard. Fatigue, body tension, and poor eating habits are often clues that can be used to free yourself from the burden of having to get the work done immediately. At these times, you can say to yourself: *Let me take a real break from the work. What can I do that I would enjoy and find relaxing?* When Eights learn to free themselves from a continuously high-pressure work style, they often find that they put less pressure on others as well.

Enjoy your creativity.

Being creative means letting go of control and allowing yourself to perceive things in a new way. Sevens do this quite easily, because they experiment with new ideas and are willing to try new approaches that stimulate them even when they don't know in advance whether these will produce the best results. Eights tend to be more self-controlled and controlling of situations, both of which can interfere with creativity. Find something you've always wanted to do — for example, take an art class, learn to play a musical instrument, take singing lessons, learn to write screenplays, or travel somewhere you've always wanted to go. When you've selected something to do, do it without preconceived ideas about what it will be like, how you will experience it, or what the result will be. Simply do what you have chosen with the curiosity of a child, letting your creativity emerge spontaneously.

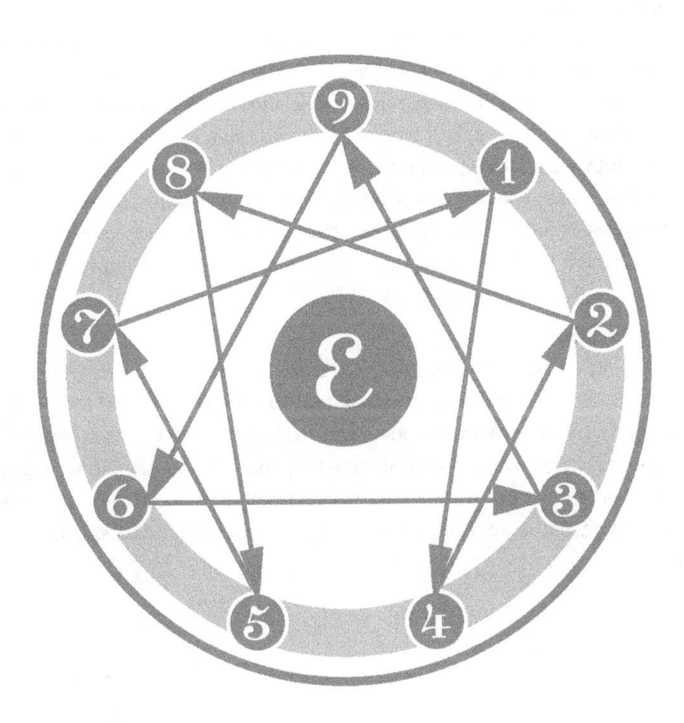

For more insights and information about integrating your wings and/or arrow styles (stress-security points), please refer to the following: Chapter 1, "What Type Are You?" and the conclusion, "Stretch Your Leadership Paradigms," in *What Type of Leader Are You?* (McGraw-Hill, 2007).

Integrate Your Nine Wing

Listen to multiple points of view.

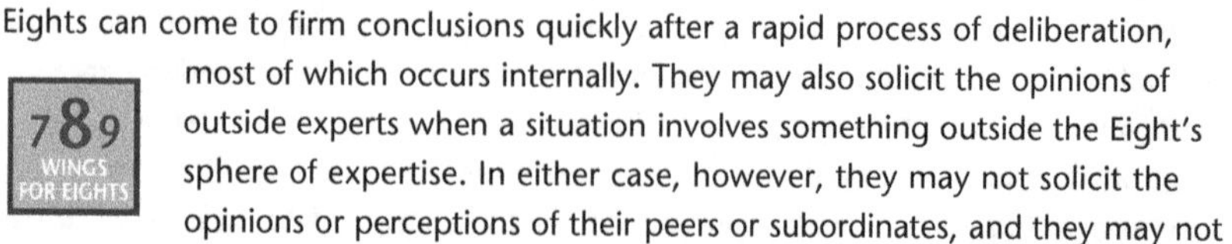

Eights can come to firm conclusions quickly after a rapid process of deliberation, most of which occurs internally. They may also solicit the opinions of outside experts when a situation involves something outside the Eight's sphere of expertise. In either case, however, they may not solicit the opinions or perceptions of their peers or subordinates, and they may not be readily open to opposing points of views. Nines, however, more typically solicit and consider multiple points of view and try to integrate these ideas with their own. Eights can do this by soliciting the views of others before reaching a conclusion, asking this question: *What do you think are the critical issues involved in this situation, and what course of action would you suggest?* When the other person is talking, the challenge for Eights will be to fully listen for understanding before assessing the merits of what the other person has said.

Practice the art of being calm.

While Eights can be very intense, energetic, and quick to respond, Nines tend to ponder ideas and reflect on what they have heard, generally doing so in a calm and relaxed manner. Calmness starts from the inside, and a simple way to begin is to breathe deeply and regularly. This type of breathing often calms a person quickly and increases receptivity. Another technique that often works is to think of someplace or something that makes you feel serene and at ease — for example, you can imagine being on a beach or in the mountains, or perhaps eating a large ice cream sundae or a piece of chocolate cake. Once you have done this, keep this feeling with you as you approach your interactions and work.

Learn to be receptive.

Nines are usually receptive to people, experiences, and ideas and take their time to react, while Eights often make nearly instantaneous assessments and then respond immediately. To become more receptive, you will first need to go inside yourself and examine your reactions. Once you have done this, you can then say this to yourself: *Just because I have a certain reaction doesn't mean I know all I need to know. Let me put my reactions aside, not share them, and then fully listen to what the other person is trying to tell me.*

For more insights and information about integrating your wings and/or arrow styles (stress-security points), please refer to the following: Chapter 1, "What Type Are You?" and the conclusion, "Stretch Your Leadership Paradigms," in *What Type of Leader Are You?* (McGraw-Hill, 2007).

Integrate Arrow Style Five (Stress Point)

Take time out.

Eights often move to their Stress Point Five when they have expended so much energy on getting things under control and moving forward, with no time taken for themselves, that they have become exhausted. However, when Eights learn to take more time for themselves at more frequent and regular intervals, they don't have to reach the place of physical or mental overload in order to take time out and recharge their batteries. The following simple idea is extremely helpful. Once a week, without fail, take three hours for yourself. Put this on your schedule and hold to it, no matter what may arise at work to demand your attention. During these three hours, do something that you truly enjoy that relaxes you — for example, a short golf game, a walk in the woods, or reading a good book. You will find that this time- out recharges your batteries and reduces your tendency to go into overdrive.

Conserve your energy.

Eights tend to expend all their energy until they have no more, while Fives typically conserve their resources, expending no more than is necessary in a given situation. When Eights begin to think of their energy as a natural resource and apply the same conservation principles, they can interrupt their cycle of working to exhaustion, resting, then working to exhaustion again. We conserve electricity by turning lights off when we are not in a room. Similarly, Eights can turn off their incessant expenditure of energy when they are not required to do so, such as when they are alone or when someone else in the group can take charge; this latter idea requires Eights to hold their suggestions back until someone else comes forward.

We conserve water by not letting the faucet run while brushing our teeth. Similarly, Eights can refrain from multitasking and working on several projects simultaneously. Try to take one task at a time or not to accept several large projects at the same time.

Honor your mind.

Most Eights honor fine minds but tend to underestimate their own intellects. Even when they become high-level leaders in organizations and receive feedback for their ability to think strategically, most Eights will say that they have been successful because of their tenacity and incessant hard work, not as a result of their strategic intellects. This often surprises other people. Fives, by contrast, honor their own intellects and are not surprised when others view them as intellectually agile. Eights can learn to honor their minds by asking themselves these questions: *If others perceive me as having a well-honed intellect, why don't I? What would happen if I did accept that my intellect is a great strength? How would I be different? What gets in the way of my seeing what others see in me?*

For more insights and information about integrating your wings and/or arrow styles (stress-security points), please refer to the following: Chapter 1, "What Type Are You?" and the conclusion, "Stretch Your Leadership Paradigms," in *What Type of Leader Are You?* (McGraw-Hill, 2007).

Integrate Arrow Style Two (Security Point)

Acknowledge the best in others.

While Eights most often do recognize talent in others, it is often highly talented and capable people to whom they give their attention. Twos, on the other hand, are more prone to perceiving and acknowledging the strengths of most people, and they try to motivate others through support and encouragement. When Eights perceive someone as not living up to his or her potential, they may be encouraging at first, but they can then move to displeasure and even confrontation. The following daily activity can assist Eights in seeing the best in others. Whenever you interact with someone, think of at least two positive attributes that the person possesses, then keep these qualities in mind as you interact with this individual. With people you don't particularly like or respect, force yourself to think of three positive qualities. After doing this activity for two weeks, practice giving one sincere compliment to a minimum of two people each day.

Allow your warmth to show.

Eights can be extremely warm to others, but they may not demonstrate this on a continual basis for a number of reasons, such as fatigue, overwork, distress with the other person's behavior, and the pressures of work. Twos, by contrast, tend to show their warmth and concern for others in a more ongoing way. Much of this care is shown through body language in particular, with sincere smiling and eye contact giving the sense of the Two being fully present and receptive.

Practice this aspect of the Two's behavior in front of the mirror at home, looking directly into the mirror and smiling while thinking about specific individuals with whom you work. Simultaneously, make eye contact with yourself, and keep your gaze looking receptive. If you don't know how to do this, imagine yourself listening with great interest to someone whom you like very much. This is the way your eyes will look when you are showing warmth and receptivity. At work, smile and have your eyes show your receptivity when you interact with others.

Nurture your generous spirit.

Eights can be quite generous, but they often worry that this could make them appear "soft" or cause others to take advantage of them. Twos, however, perceive giving to others as a strength rather than a weakness. Allow yourself to give to others twice each day, and simply enjoy the pleasure of giving. You can do this if you allow yourself to be generous without harboring the related worries of how you will be perceived or what someone might do in return.

For more insights and information about integrating your wings and/or arrow styles (stress-security points), please refer to the following: Chapter 1, "What Type Are You?" and the conclusion, "Stretch Your Leadership Paradigms," in *What Type of Leader Are You?* (McGraw-Hill, 2007).

COMMUNICATION DEVELOPMENT STRETCHES

When you communicate with someone, three kinds of unintentional distortions may be present: speaking style, body language, and blind spots. *Speaking style* refers to your overall pattern of speaking. *Body language* includes posture, facial expressions, hand gestures, body movements, energy levels, and hundreds of other nonverbal messages. *Blind spots* are elements of your communication containing information about you that is not apparent to you but is highly visible to other people. We all unknowingly convey information through an amalgam of our speaking style, body language, and other inferential data.

The receivers of the messages you send also distort what they hear through their *distorting filters*. These are unconscious concerns or assumptions, often based on the listener's Enneagram style, that alter how someone hears what others say.

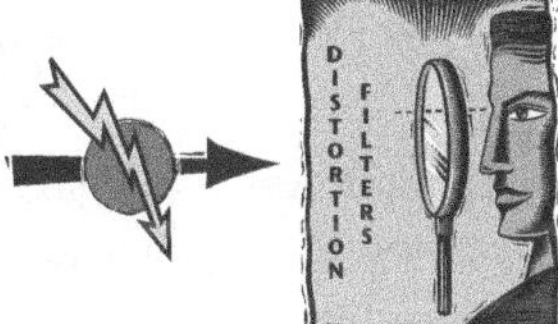

Speaking Style Body Language Blind Spots

Change one communication style behavior at a time.

It is most effective to work on changing one behavior at a time, preferably in the following sequence: speaking style, body language, blind spots, and listening distorting filters. It is easiest to change the behaviors of which we are most aware, and this sequence represents the most common order of awareness, from most to least aware.

Eights: Speaking style

- ➢ Bold and authoritative
- ➢ Big picture and strategic
- ➢ Statements designed to structure or control a situation
- ➢ Impatient with detail
- ➢ Raise the intensity of language until they get a response from the other person
- ➢ May display anger directly
- ➢ May use profanity or body-based humor
- ➢ May say very little
- ➢ Blame others if they feel blamed

Eights: Body language

- ➢ Have a strong physical presence, even when they are silent
- ➢ Modulate voice tone for maximum impact
- ➢ Give strong and easy-to-read nonverbal cues
- ➢ Appear grounded and solid, as if rooted to the earth
- ➢ Make intense, direct eye contact

For more insights and information about communication, please refer to the following: Chapter 2, "Communicating Effectively," in *Bringing Out the Best in Yourself at Work* (McGraw-Hill, 2004) and Chapter 5, "Become an Excellent Communicator," in *What Type of Leader Are You?* (McGraw-Hill, 2007).

ENNEAGRAM EIGHTS

Eights: Blind spots

- ➢ Many people, not just timid individuals, are intimidated by Eights
- ➢ Their energy is far stronger than they realize, even when they are holding back
- ➢ Not everyone is capable of grasping the big picture as quickly as Eights are
- ➢ Their vulnerability may show at times when they are not aware of it

Eights: Distorting filters when listening to someone else

- ➢ Feeling they should protect others they believe truly need protection
- ➢ Feeling disdain for someone whom they perceive as weak
- ➢ Perceiving control related issues — for example, the other person is trying to control the Eight or the conversation seems out of control
- ➢ Perceived lack of truthfulness from the other person
- ➢ Feeling blamed

Note: Some of the above characteristics may be positive, some negative, and some neutral or mixed. They are intended as an overview to allow you to select from among them.

Use e-mails to expand and adjust your language patterns.

- ➢ Review your e-mails before you send them for language and tone.
- ➢ Change any thoughts or statements that convey ways to organize, structure, and control events to statements that are less directive and more contingent.
- ➢ Acknowledge and invite a response from the other person.
- ➢ Include more variation in your sentence structure.
- ➢ Instead of using primarily declarative sentences with only nouns and verbs, use more adjectives and adverbs.
- ➢ Be more personal and less formal.

For more insights and information about communication, please refer to the following: Chapter 2, "Communicating Effectively," in *Bringing Out the Best in Yourself at Work* (McGraw-Hill, 2004) and Chapter 5, "Become an Excellent Communicator," in *What Type of Leader Are You?* (McGraw-Hill, 2007).

FEEDBACK DEVELOPMENT STRETCHES

Honest, positive, and constructive *feedback* — direct, objective, simple, and respectful observations that one person makes about another's behavior — improves both relationships and on-the-job performance. When you offer feedback, the Feedback Formula, combined with the insights of the Enneagram, helps you tailor your delivery. When someone gives you feedback, the more receptive you are to hearing what is being said, the more likely it is that you will be able to discern what is useful and utilize what has been suggested.

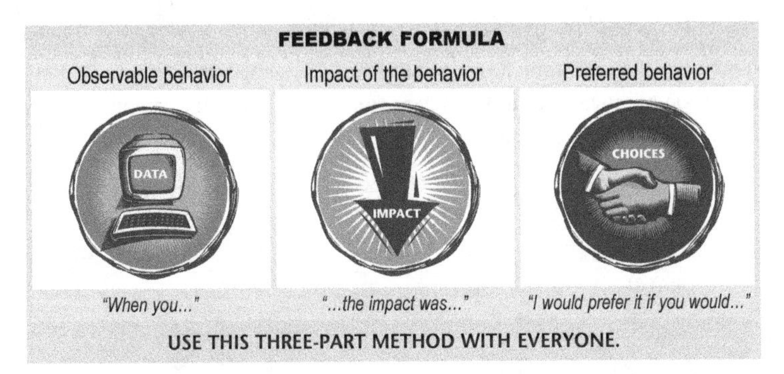

How Eights Can Enhance Their Ability to Deliver Feedback Effectively

When you offer feedback to someone, you want to be prepared and also to encourage the feedback recipient to be as receptive as possible. Remember that how and when you deliver feedback is just as important as what you actually say.

Use the three components of the **Feedback Formula** together with the following suggestions to plan and deliver the feedback.

- Consider in advance what you want to say.
- Maintain your ability to stay focused on the key points, but do so in a receptive way.
- Keep your skill in steering your full attention to the task, but downplay your energy level so the other person does not feel overwhelmed.
- Have some ideas about what to do, but allow the feedback recipient to make the first suggestions.
- Wait patiently for responses; smiling and making easy jokes are also helpful.
- Retain your truthfulness, but include a positive component.
- Remember that while you like to deal with issues head-on as these occur, the feedback recipient may want to deal with the issues in his or her own timeframe and way.

For more insights and information about feedback, please refer to the following: Chapter 3, "Giving Constructive Feedback," in *Bringing Out the Best in Yourself at Work* (McGraw-Hill, 2004) and Chapter 5, "Become an Excellent Communicator," in *What Type of Leader Are You?* (McGraw-Hill, 2007).

How Eights Can Be More Receptive When They Receive Feedback

- When someone gives you negative feedback, it may make you feel vulnerable, a feeling you probably dislike. Even positive feedback may cause you to react in this way. Feedback gives you the opportunity to practice experiencing your softer side.
- The person offering the feedback always has a little more control of the conversation than the person receiving the feedback, because the feedback giver knows what he or she is about to say and has some delivery plan in mind. If you try to take control of the situation, you may miss some valuable information.
- Remember that everyone has a point of view. It is important to take in these various perspectives, because a bigger truth will be available to you when you take everything into account.

For more insights and information about feedback, please refer to the following: Chapter 3, "Giving Constructive Feedback," in *Bringing Out the Best in Yourself at Work* (McGraw-Hill, 2004) and Chapter 5, "Become an Excellent Communicator," in *What Type of Leader Are You?* (McGraw-Hill, 2007).

CONFLICT DEVELOPMENT STRETCHES

Relationships both at work and at home often involve some degree of conflict, which may be caused by a variety of factors and usually follows the pinch-crunch cycle below:

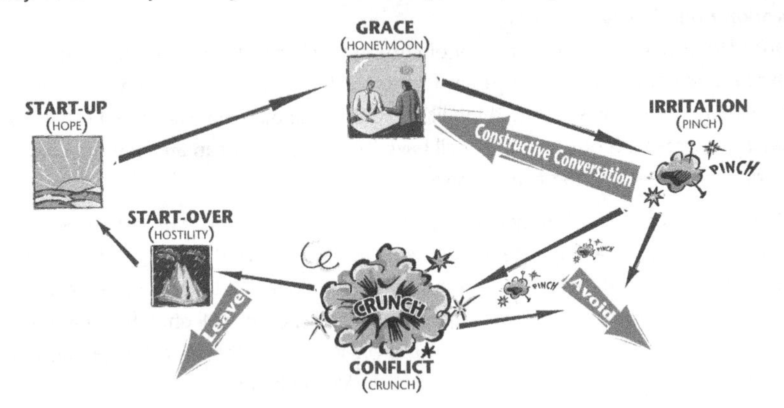

Whatever the root cause of the conflict, the Enneagram styles of the key parties involved will always be a factor in the conflict dynamics and resolution. The Enneagram enables each individual involved to make conflict resolution a constructive rather than destructive experience. The more people know themselves, understand their own responsibilities in the conflict interaction, engage in constructive self-management, and know how best to approach others through knowledge of the Enneagram, the greater the chances of a swift and effective outcome.

There are specific pinches (anger triggers) for each Enneagram style — that is, certain situations that will invariably ignite anger in a person of one style, yet may not affect someone of a different style. For Eights, these pinches include:

Injustice · Others not dealing directly with the issues · Others not taking responsibility for their own behavior · Being blindsided · Another's lack of truthfulness

For more insights and information about conflict, please refer to the following: Chapter 4, "Managing Conflict," in *Bringing Out the Best in Yourself at Work* (McGraw-Hill, 2004) and Chapter 5, "Become an Excellent Communicator," in *What Type of Leader Are You?* (McGraw-Hill, 2007).

Development Stretches for Transforming Anger into an Opportunity for Growth

Share your likely pinches (anger triggers) with others at the beginning of your working relationship.

Once Eights understand the value of discussing pinches early on in a work relationship, it becomes quite easy for them to start such a conversation in a natural and direct way. They may say something like, "Let's talk about what we know bothers us when we work with others" or "We all have things we know can annoy us when we work with others, and these are mine!"

One aspect to consider is how to explain the pinches. Many Eight pinches have a moral tone to them — injustice, lack of directness, lack of truthfulness, and failure to take responsibility. When these are shared with someone else in the context of a new working relationship, however, giving examples and specifics will often be more useful than stating only the value or moral issue itself. The reason for this is that people may agree with a value but have a very different understanding of what it means or what it looks like in action. There are many kinds of injustice, for example, and one person's sense of justice may be quite different from another's. It is therefore important for Eights to take time to discuss both their pinches and those of the other person in some depth.

Say something as soon as you are aware of feeling pinched or upset.

Eights need to remind themselves to do this, and to not discount little pinches as unworthy of mentioning. No pinch is too small to share; further, sharing even small pinches has the secondary effect of helping both parties learn how to have productive conversations about their concerns. This early positive experience increases the likelihood of positive outcomes when future, and possibly more severe, pinches occur. The skills have been developed, the process for having the conversation is clear, and both parties are more likely to anticipate a constructive outcome.

In addition, it is very important that Eights not let their feelings of displeasure build up. The force that often comes with the sharing of accumulated, unexpressed pinches can overwhelm the other person under normal circumstances. When this built-up anger or frustration combines with the typical power and intensity of most Eights, the other person is doubly overwhelmed.

For more insights and information about conflict, please refer to the following: Chapter 4, "Managing Conflict," in *Bringing Out the Best in Yourself at Work* (McGraw-Hill, 2004) and Chapter 5, "Become an Excellent Communicator," in *What Type of Leader Are You?* (McGraw-Hill, 2007).

When you start to behave in ways that indicate you are feeling pinched or distressed, do something physical if you can, such as working out or taking a walk. Physical activity provides an excellent way to release some of the pent-up and rising anger that many Eights experience. Aerobic activities in particular provide constructive outlets for the excess energy that Eights often feel. In addition, when Eights feel deeply angry and frustrated, they can become sedentary and lethargic. Exercise allows Eights to become reenergized.

When you have a negative reaction and feel a pinch, ask yourself: ***What does my reaction to this situation or to the other person's behavior say about me as an Eight and about the areas in which I can develop? How can working on my pinches and crunches help me to bring out the best in myself?***

A long, hard look at these questions always gives a tremendous amount of useful information to Eights, many of whom truly want to understand themselves better. The answers almost invariably lead Eights into the territory that is most uncomfortable for them — their deep, often hidden, vulnerabilities. Issues such as the need to control, the insistence on justice, and the desire to tackle the largest challenges and move things forward in significant ways almost always lead to the underlying issue of vulnerability.

In addition, the issue of intimidation is an important one for Eights to think about. Most Eights do not understand why others are often intimidated by them, and they do not believe that they are intimidating to others. It can be helpful to ask several people whom you respect why they think others might be intimidated by you, and then to ask them this: "Are you intimidated by me in any way at all?" The answers to these questions may be surprising and illuminating.

Next, ask yourself this question: *Do I ever consciously try to intimidate anyone else?* For example, as you think about nonwork situations in which you interact with strangers (at the gas station, grocery store, and so on), do you recall ever having raised your voice, stepped forward, or engaged in other assertive behaviors when you were displeased? At work, do you assert your opinions over opposing points of view — for example, speaking without waiting for the other person to finish his or her thoughts — in an attempt to have your will prevail? Try to be completely honest in answering these questions.

For more insights and information about conflict, please refer to the following: Chapter 4, "Managing Conflict," in *Bringing Out the Best in Yourself at Work* (McGraw-Hill, 2004) and Chapter 5, "Become an Excellent Communicator," in *What Type of Leader Are You?* (McGraw-Hill, 2007).

TEAM DEVELOPMENT STRETCHES

There is a difference between a group and a team. A *group* is a collection of individuals who have something in common; a *team* is a specific type of group, one composed of members who share one or more *goals* that can be reached only when there is an optimal level of *interdependence* between and among team members.

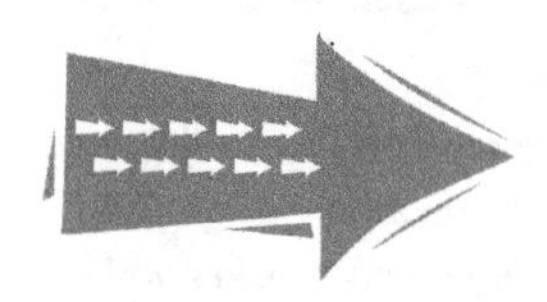

Team members also have *roles* — predictable patterns of behavior – within the team that are often related to their Enneagram styles. *Task roles* involve behaviors directed toward the work itself; *relationship roles* involve behaviors focused on feelings, relationships, and team processes, such as decision making and conflict resolution.

In addition, teams have unique yet predictable dynamics as they go through the four sequential stages of team development: *forming, storming, norming,* and *performing.* At each stage, there are questions the team must resolve before moving to the next stage.

TEAM STAGE	QUESTIONS
FORMING	*Who are we, where are we going, and are we all going there together?*
STORMING	*Can we disagree with one another in a constructive and productive way?*
NORMING	*How should we best organize ourselves and work together?*
PERFORMING	*How can we keep performing at a high level and not burn out?*

Eights: Development Stretches for Team Members and Team Leaders

Team Goals

Although you may prefer team goals that *reflect the big picture and move the organization forward,* other team members may need goals that are more specific and smaller in scope and that include more detailed directions. Allow yourself to also be more practical and specific when you create team goals, as well as to support the idea that in order for goals to be highly actionable, some team members may need to have far more detail than you do.

Team Interdependence

You may prefer to work in teams where the *interconnections allow team members to have a sufficient amount of their own territory* and where the other members are effective and enjoyable to work with. Remind yourself that some teams need to work at a level of interdependence required by the work they must do, and that this degree of interdependence may be more or less than you prefer. In addition, some work is not conducive to allowing members their own territory because it involves a high degree of coordinated activity. Work to support the level of interdependence the team needs, as well as to develop the capacity to be effective in teams that may not offer the degrees of personal space you desire or where you don't find all the members enjoyable to work with.

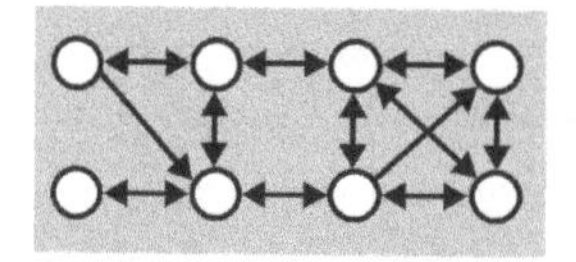

For more insights and information about teams, please refer to the following: Chapter 5, "Creating High-Performing Teams," in *Bringing Out the Best in Yourself at Work* (McGraw-Hill, 2004) and Chapter 6, "Lead High-Performing Teams," in *What Type of Leader Are You?* (McGraw-Hill, 2007).

Team Roles

Your typical task-related team role is likely to involve *defining the team's larger purpose* by stating or helping the team clarify its charter and purpose; your likely relationship-related team role may be *challenging others* by confronting, questioning, and asking direct questions or making direct statements that change the focus or direction of the team. Stretch yourself to go beyond these typical roles and adopt the following additional team task and relationship roles:

Task Roles

New task role

Managing resources, paying attention to and monitoring the team's resources (such as time, money, staffing, and materials)

New relationship role

Harmonizing team interactions by helping team members get along, feel comfortable, connect with others, and achieve consensus

Relationship Roles

Team Dynamics

During the four stages of team development — *forming, storming, norming,* and *performing* — experiment with expanding your repertoire of behavior in the following ways:

FORMING	STORMING	NORMING	PERFORMING
Rather than helping direct the team early on or pulling back in a wait-and-see stance, work collaboratively with other team members to clarify the team's direction, and make a special effort to help team members get to know one another.	Maintain your ability to help teams deal with conflict in a forthright and respectful way.	Maintain your strength in helping the team reach agreements; remember to make suggestions involving issues that go beyond the ways in which people can be heard or what the authority dynamics are — for example, suggest ideas about work product, timeliness, and agenda development.	Stay fully engaged with the team even when there are ebbs and flows in productivity; work to help the team members reach high levels of performance instead of disengaging from the team.

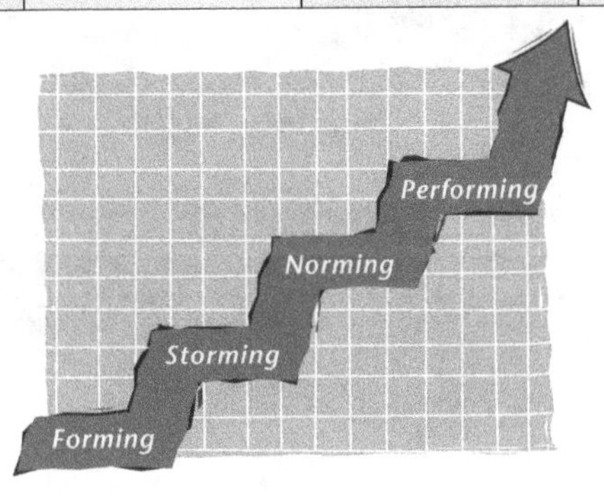

For more insights and information about teams, please refer to the following: Chapter 5, "Creating High-Performing Teams," in *Bringing Out the Best in Yourself at Work* (McGraw-Hill, 2004) and Chapter 6, "Lead High-Performing Teams," in *What Type of Leader Are You?* (McGraw-Hill, 2007).

Additional Team Development Stretches for Eight Team Leaders

Organize your team at the optimal level of structure and process.

In collaboration with your team, discuss the current team structure and processes. Ask for members' reactions to the way in which the team is organized, solicit their ideas for improvement, and then organize accordingly.

Be more consistent in your attention to detail.

Most Eight leaders do not like to delve into detail unless they absolutely have to. When they do, Eights can be relentless. Be more balanced and consistent in your approach; become more involved than you normally would be when work is running smoothly, and become less micromanaging when things feel out of control.

Examine your issues with dependency and autonomy.

This stretch can be challenging, because you may not see yourself as creating dependency or as offering too much autonomy to those whom you regard highly. Start by asking yourself this question: *How have I become overly reliant on my own strength?* Next, ask yourself this question: *How am I overly reliant on my autonomy?* Discuss your answers with someone whom you know well and respect. Finally, examine how you may be demonstrating these same tendencies in your team leadership by asking yourself these questions: *How am I causing some members to become dependent on my strength? How am I acting overly reliant on the strength of a few team members? What is the downside of my giving some team members so much autonomy?*

For more insights and information about teams, please refer to the following: Chapter 5, "Creating High-Performing Teams," in *Bringing Out the Best in Yourself at Work* (McGraw-Hill, 2004) and Chapter 6, "Lead High-Performing Teams," in *What Type of Leader Are You?* (McGraw-Hill, 2007).

LEADERSHIP DEVELOPMENT STRETCHES

The intense challenges of leadership are complex, demanding, unpredictable, exciting, and rewarding, and they require the ability to manage oneself and to interact effectively with hundreds of others in both stressful and exhilarating circumstances. For these reasons, leaders must spend time in honest self-reflection. Individuals who become extraordinary leaders grow in both evolutionary and revolutionary ways as they push themselves to meet challenges even they cannot predict in advance.

Excellent leadership comes in many forms, and no Enneagram style has a monopoly on greatness. However, your Enneagram style shows both your strengths as a leader and the areas that would most likely create obstacles to your success.

Enneagram Style Eight leaders usually display this special gift: *making important things happen.* However, Eight leaders' greatest strength can also become their greatest weakness: with their strategic ability, authoritative leadership, and ability to both sense and support greatness in others, Eight leaders can create exemplary organizations, but they can also deplete themselves and create intimidating, underperforming work environments in the process.

Development Stretches to Enhance Your Leadership

Never yell at work!

As frustrated as you may feel and even if you are not directing a raised voice toward a particular person, the price paid for yelling (fear and/or disrespect) is never worth it.

Be careful about blaming others.

When something for which you are responsible does not succeed as planned, take care that your tone of voice, line of questioning, and general approach do not make others feel blamed. The perception of being blamed shuts down candid conversation and effective problem solving.

Consider opposing points of view.

Ask yourself every day: *Who and what am I not listening to?*

For more insights and information about leadership, please refer to the following: Chapter 6, "Leveraging Your Leadership," in *Bringing Out the Best in Yourself at Work* (McGraw-Hill, 2004) and the book, *What Type of Leader Are You?* (McGraw-Hill, 2007).

RESULTS ORIENTATION DEVELOPMENT STRETCHES

It is important to build credibility with customers by delivering sustained, high-quality results, continually driving for results, and reaching your potential. When you do this, you make gains in productivity, push the envelope of new product development, and support the organization as a leader in its field.

Empower others to take action.

Because you move to action quickly and others are accustomed to following your lead (whether or not you are the team leader), the more you do, the less others are inclined to take action on their own. If you want to encourage other people to take initiative, you need to act less often and less quickly. When you use this approach on an ongoing basis, others will eventually rise to the occasion. For example, don't always be the first to issue an opinion; in this way, you can help reduce people's reliance on you as a thought leader. When someone else suggests a good idea, affirm the person, and ask him or her to explain the idea in more detail.

Put yourself in charge of working well with everyone.

It has been said that Eights do not suffer fools gladly, nor do they like being around people they perceive as incompetent or as not taking responsibility for their own behavior. However, since we can all be "fools" sometimes, and very few people always take full responsibility for their own behavior, it is important to learn to be more accepting or, at the least, to not give people the impression that you don't want to make time for them. Try to find something you appreciate in people whom you find troubling; this will help you to respond to them in a warmer way.

Have more fun.

This may be the biggest challenge of all for Eights, who tend to be serious at work, especially when the work demands are high (and this always seems to be the case when Eights are involved). However, because Eights can be so demanding and intense, it is even more important that they and those following them also relax and enjoy themselves. Others will usually follow your lead, both because they admire you and because they don't want to get on your bad side. If you are extremely serious, other people will be too; if you can relax more, others will also be more relaxed, and this will improve their productivity.

For more insights and information about results orientation, please refer to the following: Chapter 2, "Drive for Results," in *What Type of Leader Are You?* (McGraw-Hill, 2007).

STRATEGY DEVELOPMENT STRETCHES

Leaders and individual contributors must understand the actual business of their organizations and be able to think and act strategically in both big and small ways if their teams and organizations are to reach the highest levels of performance, effectiveness, and efficiency.

"Knowing the business" and "thinking and acting strategically" go hand in hand. Unless you know the business, you have no context for thinking and acting strategically. When you have this information, you need to be able to use it in a strategic way, working from a compelling and common vision, a customer-focused mission, a smart strategy, and effective goals and tactics aligned with that strategy.

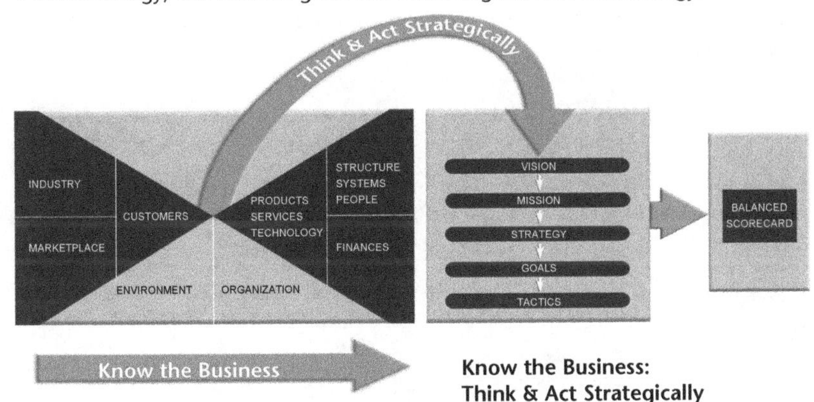

Know the Business: Think & Act Strategically

Develop your sense of humor.
You may think you already have a well-developed sense of humor, but ask yourself this question: *Do I use my sense of humor at work as a way to laugh at myself and my expectations?* If you can laugh at your foibles, you will work less excessively and enjoy yourself more at work.

Become more flexible.
Make a list of all your strongest beliefs, opinions, and ideas. Next, ask yourself: *If I were to react less intensely and become more open-minded about anything on this list, would I perceive myself as being less strong?* If your answer is no, proceed to the next paragraph. However, if you answered yes, tell yourself this: *Being flexible is not the same as being weak, and having fixed opinions does not mean being strong. While too much flexibility is a weakness, so is too much rigidity.* Repeat these statements until you believe them.

Once you are more receptive to new ideas, review each item on your list and answer this question for each item: *What do I need to do to be even more open-minded about this?* Finally, select three of the items and take the actions you have identified as ways to help you become more open.

For more insights and information about strategy, please refer to the following: Chapter 4, "Know the Business: Think and Act Strategically," in *What Type of Leader Are You?* (McGraw-Hill, 2007).

Be patient.

You probably drive yourself very hard, but you need to take time to relax, read, or do something that is calming, such as stretching or walking. This will not only give you more patience with yourself, it can actually prevent illness. Then, work on being patient with other people. Every time you become frustrated and want to confront someone for not living up to his or her commitments, ask yourself: *What might I not understand about this person and his/her perspective about this situation?*

Finally, learn to be patient with organizations. Organizations and systems are very much like people: some pressure may contribute to movement, but too much pressure creates resistance to change. If you want to use humor in learning to become more patient, remember this: *You don't change very easily either, so why should the organization?*

For more insights and information about strategy, please refer to the following: Chapter 4, "Know the Business: Think and Act Strategically," in *What Type of Leader Are You?* (McGraw-Hill, 2007).

DECISION-MAKING DEVELOPMENT STRETCHES

We all make decisions on a daily basis, but we rarely think about the process by which we make them. The wisest decisions are made utilizing our heads (rational analysis and planning), our hearts (to examine values, feelings, and impact on people), and our guts (for taking action), with all three used in an integrated way. In addition, when you are making decisions at work, you need to consider three other factors: the organizational culture, the decision-making authority structure within the organization, and the context of the decision itself.

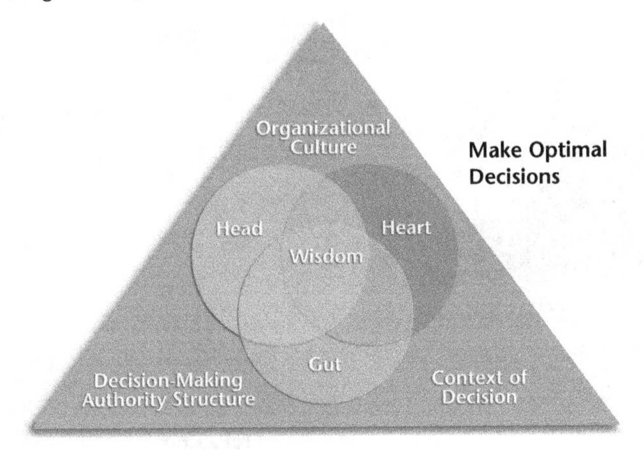

The following chart shows you how to develop each of your Centers of Intelligence (Head, Heart, and Gut) to assist you in making wise decisions.

	Centers of Intelligence		
	Head Center	**Heart Center**	**Body (Gut) Center**
Activities for Eights That Develop Each Center	**Objective analysis** Question your assumptions; ask the opinions of others; take in and consider multiple viewpoints when making decisions. **Astute insight** Honor your insights, but ask yourself what insights you might be missing that could alter your decisions. **Productive planning** Maintain your ability to do big-picture planning, but make sure you also plan for the operational aspects of implementation.	**Empathy** Take the time to sense the feelings of others, even when you don't respect the individuals. **Authentic relating** Become more aware of presenting yourself as bold and confident; when you allow yourself to be more vulnerable, people will support you and your decisions more. **Compassion** Consider the impact of your decisions on everyone, but don't make decisions to avoid feeling guilty.	**Taking effective action** Don't rush into decisions; don't make overly complex decisions when a simple solution would work just as well. **Steadfastness** Be clear, but be careful not to become inflexible or unresponsive. **Gut-knowing** Trust your gut, but when your reaction seems too strong or quick, pause and re-examine your decision.

For more insights and information about decision making, please refer to the following: Chapter 7, "Make Optimal Decisions," in *What Type of Leader Are You?* (McGraw-Hill, 2007).

ORGANIZATIONAL CHANGE DEVELOPMENT STRETCHES

In contemporary organizations, change has become a way of life. Companies exist in increasingly complex environments, with more competition, fewer resources, less time to market, higher customer expectations, increased regulation, more technology, and greater uncertainty. Organizations need to be flexible, innovative, cost-conscious, and responsive if they want to succeed. As a result, employees at all levels need to be able to embrace change and to function flexibly and effectively within their teams when an unforeseen direction must be taken.

Take Charge of Change

Formulate and articulate your vision.

Don't assume that others know what you are thinking, or that they know what to do and why they should do it. Formulate your vision in sufficient detail so that all the essential ideas are clear, then share your vision widely and solicit reactions. You can test your vision in advance by writing it down, showing it to others, and gaining their reactions before you disseminate it to a wider audience. You can also express your vision verbally to a small focus group, solicit members' feedback, and make adjustments before you share the vision more broadly.

Learn the art of timing.

Remember that not everything has to happen immediately. It is important to pace a change initiative so that people have time to adjust to and integrate the changes. It is also essential to avoid trying to get so much done so quickly that everyone, including you, becomes exhausted. When this occurs, many benefits of the change may not be fully utilized. Finally, some changes will be more readily accepted if you wait for the best opportunity to introduce them. Be patient and observant so you can develop and act from an artful sense of optimal timing.

For more insights and information about organizational change, please refer to the following: Chapter 8, "Take Charge of Change," in *What Type of Leader Are You?* (McGraw-Hill, 2007).

Remember that small things can produce big results.
There are many instances when a big impact occurs from a small change. For example, one company was able to retain more of its high-ranking female employees by changing its customary meeting time from 8:00 a.m. to 9:00 a.m. A manufacturing organization saved ten million dollars in an impromptu meeting by having all the managers and key engineers meet for an hour to identify the manufacturing areas causing product defects. Pay attention to the small changes that produce large impacts.

For more insights and information about organizational change, please refer to the following: Chapter 8, "Take Charge of Change," in *What Type of Leader Are You?* (McGraw-Hill, 2007).

TRANSFORMATION DEVELOPMENT STRETCHES FOR EIGHTS

In order to move from *pursuing the truth, needing to keep situations under control, wanting to make important things happen, and trying to hide their vulnerability* to the understanding that *there is a universal truth that arises from being receptive to understanding everything in all its dimensions*, Eights can work toward these transformations:

Mental Transformation

Transform the mental pattern of **vengeance** (the process of rebalancing wrongs through thoughts related to anger, blame, and intimidation) *into the higher belief of* **truth** (the ability to seek and integrate multiple points of view in search of a higher or larger truth).

Mental Activity

When you find yourself thinking about wrongs that have been done and the injustice of situations, and begin blaming others or considering ways to stand up to or intimidate other people, remember one or more times when you were able to solicit and integrate points of view that were contrary to your own. Allow those times to come back into your thinking and relive what was occurring within you at those moments. Keep your attention on those times when your understanding of the truth was highly expanded.

Emotional Transformation

Transform the emotional habit of **lust** (the desire for excessiveness in a variety of forms — for example, work, food, or pleasure — as a way of avoiding and denying one's feelings and vulnerabilities) *into the higher awareness of* **innocence** (the childlike feeling of vulnerability and openness) so that the need to control situations and to protect yourself or others is no longer present).

Emotional Activity

When you become aware that you are pursuing an activity in a relentless or excessive way, remember one or more times in your life when you felt the pure, innocent openness of a child without needing to control the situation or protect either yourself or others. Remember the circumstances, how you felt, and what you experienced during those times. Keep replaying those innocent moments until you feel fully reconnected with the experiences.

For more insights and information about personal transformation, please refer to the following: Chapter 7, "Transforming Yourself," in *Bringing Out the Best in Yourself at Work* (McGraw-Hill, 2004).

ENNEAGRAM STYLE NINE

ENNEAGRAM NINES

The search for harmony and comfort and the avoidance of conflict

Relaxed, easy to relate to, and accepting, Nines perceive and honor multiple viewpoints and are usually excellent facilitators, drawing out the ideas of others so everyone gets heard. While they value harmony, seek comfortable ways of relating, and are often adept mediators of conflict between and among others, most Nines are extremely uncomfortable with conflict when it's directed toward them and even more uncomfortable when they feel angry with someone else. As a result, Nines keep themselves from doing anything that might generate conflict or create disharmony; they keep themselves from being aware that they are upset; don't express opinions or preferences that could cause discord or disagreements; and diffuse their attention by engaging in activities that comfort them, rather than focus them on their own desires or priorities. As examples, Nines may do some of the following: watch television for hours, flip television channels on a regular basis; cut the grass or work in the garden when they have projects at work or home they should be doing; go shopping, walk the dog, or even do the dishes in an overly thorough way rather than have a difficult conversation with someone or do work they don't feel like doing.

While Nines appear easygoing on the outside, many experience some degree of internal tension, and they are not always as non-judgmental as they appear. In addition, some Nines tend to satisfy their desire for comfort through the satisfaction of their physical needs — for example, eating, sleeping, and/or reading; some Nines submerge themselves in service of group needs by working extraordinary hours, which allows them to forget about their own desires; and other Nines find such comfort in fusing or blending almost completely with other people who are important to them that they lose a sense of themselves in the process.

The Nine's interpersonal style is agreeable, relatively unassertive, and non-invasive, and they are often able to talk with others about a variety of topics in an easy-going manner. For example, Nines often nod their heads in affirmation or say "Uh, huh," which doesn't mean they agree with the other person, just that they heard what was said. Affable and humorous, they express themselves indirectly rather than boldly or directly as a way to create and maintain positive relationships and reduce potential discord between themselves and others.

While we can all prefer rapport and ease to discord, for Nines, the search for harmony and comfort and the avoidance of conflict is their primary, persistent, and driving motivation.

DEVELOPMENT STRETCHES FOR NINES

INDIVIDUALS SEEKING PEACE, HARMONY, AND POSITIVE MUTUAL REGARD AND DISLIKING CONFLICT, TENSION, AND ILL WILL

CONTENTS

SELF-MASTERY DEVELOPMENT STRETCHES

Self-Mastery — the ability to understand, accept, and transform your thoughts, feelings, and behavior, with the understanding that each day will bring new challenges that are opportunities for growth — is the foundation of all personal and professional development. Self-mastery begins with self-awareness, then expands to include the elements shown in the following graphic:

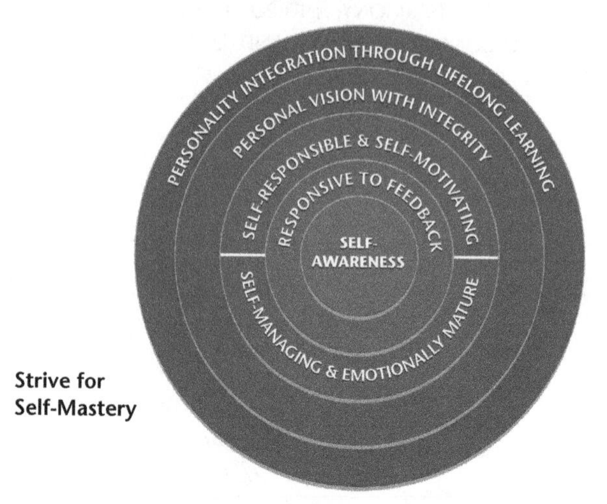

Strive for Self-Mastery

In this section on self-mastery, you will find the following:

- Three common issues for Nines related to self-mastery
- Three development stretches for working with the core issues of your Enneagram style, including one basic activity and one deeper activity for each stretch
- Three development stretches for working with your wings and arrow (stress-security) styles

Common Issues for Nines Related to Self-Mastery

Expressing your thoughts, needs, and preferences even when these oppose the wishes of others	Being active and assertive rather than acting de-energized and passive	Learning to embrace conflict and deal with it directly, with the understanding that resolving differences brings people together

For more insights and information about self-mastery, please refer to the following: Chapter 7, "Transforming Yourself," in *Bringing Out the Best in Yourself at Work* (McGraw-Hill, 2004) and Chapter 3, "Strive for Self-Mastery," in *What Type of Leader Are You?* (McGraw-Hill, 2007).

Development Stretches for Working with the Core Issues of Your Enneagram Style

Express your needs directly.

Basic Activity

Each day, express one need, preference, or desire to someone else. Suggest where to go for lunch, how to proceed with a project, or ask for a raise. Express these desires without someone first asking you what you want. Take the initiative.

Deeper Activity

Nines, of course, have needs like everyone else, and they often know what these needs are. At the same time, they can be reluctant to express their needs directly — for example, by stating *I would like to do this* or *I need some time to think about this* — because they tend to believe that their needs don't matter, or that expressing their needs will create conflict and disrupt the harmony they feel with other people. Learning to express your needs directly often starts with affirming that your own needs are as important as anyone else's. Ask yourself this question: *Do my needs really matter?* If your answer is no, then ask yourself, *Why do I feel that other people's needs matter, but not my own?* Write down your answer on a piece of paper and read it several times. Then, add any additional thoughts you may have regarding why you believe that your needs don't matter.

Next, divide the paper into two columns and write the answers to this question: *If I were to express my needs directly, what would I gain* [column 1] *and what would I lose* [column 2]? Analyze your responses. Is there sufficient benefit to you for expressing your needs directly compared to what you might lose? If your answer is no, it will be difficult for you to put forth the effort and take the risk to state your needs directly. In this case, you will need to follow the above activity once a week until the balance of gains versus losses tips in the positive direction.

Once you have affirmed to yourself that your needs do, indeed, matter and that you would benefit from stating them directly, practice expressing them daily. Verbalize one need per day for the first week, two needs per day the second week, and so forth. You can select either individuals you know or strangers — for example, you might say to a store cashier, "Please put that item in a bag with handles for carrying." Practice this daily activity until it feels completely comfortable and natural.

Set priorities, and keep them.

Basic Activity

Commit to completing two tasks or chores each day. Make sure you complete each task without any interruptions.

For more insights and information about self-mastery, please refer to the following: Chapter 7, "Transforming Yourself," in *Bringing Out the Best in Yourself at Work* (McGraw-Hill, 2004) and Chapter 3, "Strive for Self-Mastery," in *What Type of Leader Are You?* (McGraw-Hill, 2007).

Deeper Activity

Nines often have difficulty setting priorities and sticking with them. This leads to procrastination as the Nine begins one task, then another, and then both get put aside for an activity such as cleaning the desk or organizing the files. First, you have to be really honest about your tendency to shift priorities and put things off. You need to notice how and when you do this, then assess the consequences of this behavior. Your self-assessment should answer two questions. The first is this: *How do I really benefit from not setting or sticking with my priorities?* Be aware that an answer of *I don't benefit in any way* is not helpful, because there must be some benefit or the behavior would not be recurring. After you have answered that question honestly, ask yourself the second question: *What do I lose by not setting or sticking with my priorities?* If the costs of not setting and keeping priorities outweigh the benefits of doing so, then you are ready to change. Each day, make a priority list of key items to accomplish and rank order each item, with the most important item first and the least important last. Begin your tasks in order of their priority. Keep this list in front of you and check it hourly. If you stray from this list or reorder the priorities, get yourself back on track.

Take a position.

Basic Activity

Each morning, think about one opinion that you hold strongly; during the day, share that opinion with two people. Every day, select a new opinion or idea and discuss it with two new people. Continue this activity for two weeks and then reflect on it by asking yourself these questions: *Has it become easier to say what I really think? Are some topics easier to discuss than others? Are some people easier to share with?* After you've answered these questions, continue the activity for one month, each day selecting new topics and new individuals.

Deeper Activity

Can you dare to be provocative? Nines usually prefer to not take a stand or a strong position on issues for fear of creating conflict and disrupting positive relationships. Think about the issues that really matter to you, particularly those you generally keep to yourself. The issue can be something as significant as *I do not want to buy that house* or as simple as *I don't like the music that's on the radio.* Make a list of these issues, then add to the list daily. Once a day, take the risk of actually saying something about one of these issues to someone else. After you have become comfortable doing this, try communicating a position twice a day. Once this seems to be working well, increase the number of times you do this to five times per day. You are likely to find that rather than disrupting relationships, letting people know where you stand actually builds relationships.

For more insights and information about self-mastery, please refer to the following: Chapter 7, "Transforming Yourself," in *Bringing Out the Best in Yourself at Work* (McGraw-Hill, 2004) and Chapter 3, "Strive for Self-Mastery," in *What Type of Leader Are You?* (McGraw-Hill, 2007).

Development Stretches for Working with Your Wings and Arrow (Stress-Security) Styles

Wings are the Enneagram styles on either side of your core Enneagram style; arrow, or stress-security, styles are Enneagram styles shown with arrows pointing away or toward your core Enneagram style. Your wings and arrow styles don't change your core Enneagram style, but instead offer qualities that can broaden and enrich your patterns of thinking and feeling as well as enhance your behaviors. Your wings and arrow styles make you more complex and versatile because they provide more dimensions to your personality and serve as vehicles for self-development.

Integrate Your Eight Wing

Step into your personal power.

Personal power is a combination of qualities that include being fully present in given situations, the willingness to step in and influence others, and apparent self-confidence, among others. Eights typically understand the importance of power and influence and can usually leverage their behavior to have their presence felt and to affect different situations. In contrast, Nines tend to play more of a backseat role, listening to others and mediating between individuals and groups. Personal power starts with knowing what you are good at doing and believing that you have a right to influence other people. Start by making a list of all your strong positive attributes. When you have finished, ask five people who know you well what they would have you add to your list, then do so.

The next time you interact with others, do two things. First, keep your attention *completely focused* on yourself, the other person or persons, and the issues that are being discussed, all the while keeping the above composite list in mind. This will help you to feel more personally powerful. Nines have a tendency to diffuse their attention and energy, which reduces their sense of personal power. Once you are more comfortable with being completely focused, select an area of your life involving other people which you would like to have be different than it is. Practice stepping into your personal power by simultaneously keeping the ability to focus what you have learned and saying something to influence the other people involved.

For more insights and information about integrating your wings and/or arrow styles (stress-security points), please refer to the following: Chapter 1, "What Type Are You?" and the conclusion, "Stretch Your Leadership Paradigms," in *What Type of Leader Are You?* (McGraw-Hill, 2007).

Make friends with your anger.

Anger can be an ally as well as a source of energy. Most Eights seem to understand that anger is often a clue to distress and unease and that it also provides the impetus to action. The Nine's most common reaction to anger is to dull themselves to it. This is called "anger that went to sleep." When Nines do allow themselves to feel angry, they do not generally allow themselves to express it directly. More commonly, they tend to express their displeasure either through passive-aggressive behavior — for example, saying yes but meaning no — or other indirect means. Waking up to their own anger not only allows for more fluidity of feelings, but it also allows Nines to express themselves more clearly and to take immediate action. To help Nines really understand and befriend their anger, the following activities can be very useful:

1. Have a written dialogue with your anger. Ask your anger: *Anger, tell me about yourself — what you are like, why you function the way you do, and what you want from me.* Write down whatever comes to mind. Keep this dialogue going until the conversation feels finished. Continue this written dialogue over the next several weeks while you reach increasing clarity.
2. For two weeks, pay attention to your body's cues when you feel angry or upset in any way. Write these down and pay attention any time these physical sensations arise. This will help you understand more about your anger.
3. Ask five people whom know you well for feedback about your anger, asking these questions: *How do you perceive that I act when I am angry? How do you know when I'm angry? What advice would you give me about dealing with my anger?*

Take quick action.

Nines like to deliberate and think of various alternative perspectives, and they frequently begin a secondary activity rather than taking immediate action. Eights, by contrast, like to move things forward, so they take clear action and do so quickly. First, think about what you like to do as a secondary activity that distracts you from taking action and getting things done. For some Nines, it's working in the garden; for others it's a hobby, such as painting or carpentry; and for some its doing the dishes or watching television. Once you know what your preferred secondary activities are, you will be able to stop yourself when you begin one of them and ask yourself this question: *What task or work am I avoiding by doing this activity?* Then, make yourself return to what should be your priority, and take the action required to take that more important task to completion.

For more insights and information about integrating your wings and/or arrow styles (stress-security points), please refer to the following: Chapter 1, "What Type Are You?" and the conclusion, "Stretch Your Leadership Paradigms," in *What Type of Leader Are You?* (McGraw-Hill, 2007).

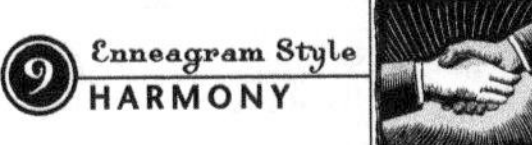

Integrate Your One Wing

Stay on top of your tasks.

Simply put, Nines tend to put tasks off, and Ones tend to get things done as quickly as possibly. Ones make to-do lists mentally or in writing and take pleasure in working through this list to completion. Nines can emulate this behavior by making to-do lists every day and checking off each item as it is completed. As a secondary suggestion, Nines can also emulate the One behavior of completing the smallest tasks first because they are easy to do and give immediate satisfaction.

Trust your gut.

Although both Nines and Ones are Body Center Enneagram styles, Ones trust and use their instinctual (gut) reactions, while Nines often don't pay enough attention to information from their guts. The reason Nines ignore their guts is that they feel uncomfortable being angry, believing that their assertion of anger would sever the harmony with others they value so highly. However, this has the secondary effect of disabling the Nine's access to their gut-knowing.

To become more aware of their gut reactions, Nines can ask themselves the following question on a regular basis: *What does my gut tell me about this?* Don't argue or censor your gut; simply allow the information to become available to you. Experiment once a day with expressing yourself and taking action based on this information from your gut. You are likely to find that the information is highly accurate and very helpful to you.

Express your reactions to people, ideas, and events.

Ones tend to have a lot of opinions, and they usually express quite a few of them. Nines also have opinions (and even judgments) but tend to express them far less readily. Here is an easy way to start learning to express your reactions. Every day, express one opinion about anything you choose to at least one new person. Make sure the opinions and the person with whom you talk change daily. After two weeks, discuss two different opinions with two different people. Continue during the third week with three opinions daily with three different people; in the fourth week, increase the number of both opinions and people to four. By that time, you will probably find that you have become more comfortable expressing your reactions.

Integrate Arrow Style Six (Stress Point)

Trust your insights.

Sixes can be quite insightful; Nines can emulate Sixes in this and reap benefits from accessing their own insights. First, Nines need to pay attention to the perceptions they actually have. Because these perceptions may not always be conscious, Nines can ask themselves this question: *What do I really think about this?* Once Nines have gained more clarity of perception, they can do a "perception check" with several other people. Perception checking can confirm the perception or help the Nine refine it. These refined and realistic perceptions are insights to be honored.

Create plans.

Sixes tend to create alternative plans in their minds, and this process of thinking through the multitude of issues involved in a situation as well as possible consequences can be useful to Nines. Nines may develop plans but not follow them, and some Nines may develop plans that are either too detailed or not detailed enough. To increase your planning skills, it can be helpful to use a format similar to the one described below:

1. Determine your goal or objective.
2. Develop a sequential plan for achieving this goal. Make sure you include all the steps until you goal is accomplished.
3. Conduct an assessment of this plan and include both what could go wrong with the plan and what factors could make it go well.
4. Revise your plan to take into account methods for minimizing what could go wrong and maximizing what could go well.
5. Show this plan to someone whom you regard as an organized person and solicit his or her feedback.
6. Revise your plans as needed.

Be courageous and assert yourself.

Most Sixes are aware of their fears and can summon the courage to face their fears and do what they feel is required. Nines, by contrast, are not so keenly aware of their fears, and when they do become more conscious of them, they are more likely to withdraw than to go forward and face them. Instead of backing away, Nines can use the following words to help them develop their courage: *Although I feel fearful, I have the courage to take action.* Use this idea to bolster your courage, letting yourself experience the exhilaration of taking action.

Integrate Arrow Style Three (Security Point)

Focus on results.

Threes and Nines both focus on results, but there are some specific ways in which Threes do this that can be helpful to Nines. First, Threes usually define goals for almost everything they do, whereas Nines may only select goals for certain activities.

For more insights and information about integrating your wings and/or arrow styles (stress-security points), please refer to the following: Chapter 1, "What Type Are You?" and the conclusion, "Stretch Your Leadership Paradigms," in *What Type of Leader Are You?* (McGraw-Hill, 2007).

Second, Threes continuously keep their goals in their mind and align their behavior to best achieve these goals; Nines, by contrast, may not keep their goals at the forefront of their thinking at all times, as other priorities emerge and recede or as the Nine becomes distracted by routine tasks. Nines can learn from Threes by using the following idea: for every task or project you have, develop a clear goal or goals. Write the goals on a piece of paper that you then attach to a highly visible place — for example, your computer or your mirror at home. Refer to these goals each time you do any activity related to the task or project, and ask yourself this question: *Will what I am about to do take me further toward this goal?*

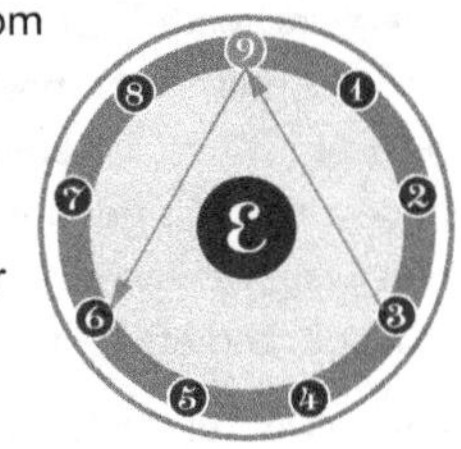

Develop verbal self-confidence.

Threes usually know how to appear confident even if they don't feel that way (although they often do). Nines tend to come across as more humble or even self-effacing at times. To develop more self-confidence that is also evident to others, the following suggestion can be helpful. First, Threes usually think through the key points they want to make ahead of time. Because they often have had so much practice doing this, they have developed the ability to think quickly on their feet. Nines can also do this through advance preparation. Every time you know you are going to converse with someone or give a presentation, jot down an outline of your three to five key points, using bullet marks and trying not to use complete sentences. Arrange your points in sequential order, then add an opening comment designed to get people's attention and a closing comment that provides a provocative summary. After this, add a few more bulleted points to support your key points. Then, practice what you plan to say in front of someone else or in front of the mirror. Make sure your posture is straight and that you breathe into your chest.

Be more directive.

Threes don't apologize for taking charge and organizing other people because they believe in their ideas and feel compelled to get results. Nines usually have more difficulty being directive. They don't like others directing them, and they don't want to behave in ways others might find offensive. However, Nines often have excellent ideas, and most people respect rather than take offense at another's providing clear and effective guidance. Because you probably have a good sense of what direction another person or a team should take, simply make the suggestion early in the conversation (Nines tend to wait until the end of the conversation). Practice making no apologies for your suggestion, such as explaining why the person doesn't have to do what you've suggested or explaining why your idea may not be the best course of action. Simply make the suggestion, doing so in as few words and possible, then wait until the other person responds.

For more insights and information about integrating your wings and/or arrow styles (stress-security points), please refer to the following: Chapter 1, "What Type Are You?" and the conclusion, "Stretch Your Leadership Paradigms," in *What Type of Leader Are You?* (McGraw-Hill, 2007).

NINES: Communication

COMMUNICATION DEVELOPMENT STRETCHES

When you communicate with someone, three kinds of unintentional distortions may be present: speaking style, body language, and blind spots. *Speaking style* refers to your overall pattern of speaking. *Body language* includes posture, facial expressions, hand gestures, body movements, energy levels, and hundreds of other nonverbal messages. *Blind spots* are elements of your communication containing information about you that is not apparent to you but is highly visible to other people. We all unknowingly convey information through an amalgam of our speaking style, body language, and other inferential data.

The receivers of the messages you send also distort what they hear through their *distorting filters*. These are unconscious concerns or assumptions, often based on the listener's Enneagram style, that alter how someone hears what others say.

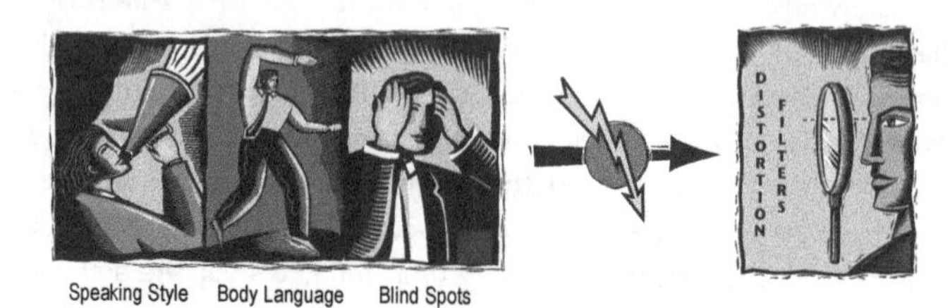

Speaking Style Body Language Blind Spots

Change one communication style behavior at a time.

It is most effective to work on changing one behavior at a time, preferably in the following sequence: speaking style, body language, blind spots, and listening distorting filters. It is easiest to change the behaviors of which we are most aware, and this sequence represents the most common order of awareness, from most to least aware.

Nines: Speaking style

- Give highly detailed information in a sequential manner
- Use soft, even-toned speaking voice
- Make an effort to be fair and present all perspectives
- May say yes but mean no
- Use agreeing words, such as *yes* and *uh-huh,* which mean "I hear what you're saying" and don't necessarily mean agreement

Nines: Body language

- Easygoing and relaxed
- Smile frequently
- Few displays of strong emotions, particularly negative feelings
- Face rather than body is animated

For more insights and information about communication, please refer to the following: Chapter 2, "Communicating Effectively," in *Bringing Out the Best in Yourself at Work* (McGraw-Hill, 2004) and Chapter 5, "Become an Excellent Communicator," in *What Type of Leader Are You?* (McGraw-Hill, 2007).

Nines: Blind spots

- Prolonged explanations can cause the listener to lose interest
- Presenting multiple viewpoints negatively affects their degree of influence and credibility because others don't know what is being proposed
- Often fail to make true wants or desires known to others

Nines: Distorting filters when listening to someone else

- Demands on them to change or do something
- Being criticized, ignored, or put down
- Someone having an opposing view to their own
- The possibility that anger from another person will be directed at them

Note: Some of the above characteristics may be positive, some negative, and some neutral or mixed. They are intended as an overview to allow you to select from among them.

Use e-mails to expand and adjust your language patterns.

- Review your e-mails before you send them for language and tone.
- Alter the use of overly affirming language.
- Use language that states a clear position and message.
- Do not use strident and overly formal language when you are upset and ready to express it.
- Express concerns thoroughly, using a respectful tone.
- Consider talking in person or via the phone instead of writing an e-mail when you are distressed.

For more insights and information about communication, please refer to the following: Chapter 2, "Communicating Effectively," in *Bringing Out the Best in Yourself at Work* (McGraw-Hill, 2004) and Chapter 5, "Become an Excellent Communicator," in *What Type of Leader Are You?* (McGraw-Hill, 2007).

FEEDBACK DEVELOPMENT STRETCHES

Honest, positive, and constructive *feedback* — direct, objective, simple, and respectful observations that one person makes about another's behavior — improves both relationships and on-the-job performance. When you offer feedback, the Feedback Formula, combined with the insights of the Enneagram, helps you tailor your delivery. When someone gives you feedback, the more receptive you are to hearing what is being said, the more likely it is that you will be able to discern what is useful and utilize what has been suggested.

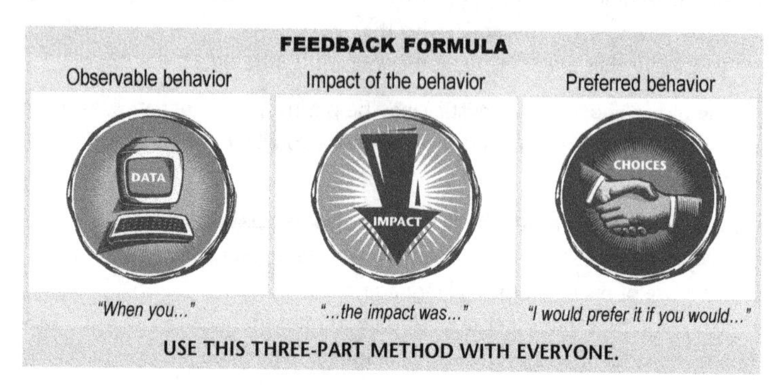

How Nines Can Enhance Their Ability to Deliver Feedback Effectively

When you offer feedback to someone, you want to be prepared and also to encourage the feedback recipient to be as receptive as possible. Remember that how and when you deliver feedback is just as important as what you actually say.

Use the three components of the **Feedback Formula** together with the following suggestions to plan and deliver the feedback.

- Keep creating rapport and maintain your kindness, but also deliver a clear message.
- Retain your capacity to understand a situation from many viewpoints, but stay focused on your main point.
- Think of other issues that may be related, and save them for further discussion; try to keep your feedback focused on one issue at a time.
- Remember that while taking the time to create harmony and comfort is helpful, the feedback recipient may want to deal with the issues more quickly and directly.

For more insights and information about feedback, please refer to the following: Chapter 3, "Giving Constructive Feedback," in *Bringing Out the Best in Yourself at Work* (McGraw-Hill, 2004) and Chapter 5, "Become an Excellent Communicator," in *What Type of Leader Are You?* (McGraw-Hill, 2007).

How Nines Can Be More Receptive When They Receive Feedback

- When someone gives you negative feedback, it may elicit in you a concern that the person is angry with you, that your relationship is in jeopardy, or that you are going to feel bad. Because of this, you may not fully listen to the message. Try to be open and ask clarifying questions as often as you desire.
- It is probably important to you that you have ample opportunity to respond to what the feedback giver is saying, whether the feedback is positive or negative. If the other person doesn't provide as much dialogue as you would like, make sure you mention this, saying "I'd like to respond as we go along so I can more fully understand what you are saying."
- Remember that very few people are comfortable giving feedback, and that the feedback giver may be just as concerned about the relationship as you are. Relationships often deepen from an honest conversation in which both parties are genuine and forthcoming.

For more insights and information about feedback, please refer to the following: Chapter 3, "Giving Constructive Feedback," in *Bringing Out the Best in Yourself at Work* (McGraw-Hill, 2004) and Chapter 5, "Become an Excellent Communicator," in *What Type of Leader Are You?* (McGraw-Hill, 2007).

CONFLICT DEVELOPMENT STRETCHES

Relationships both at work and at home often involve some degree of conflict, which may be caused by a variety of factors and usually follows the pinch-crunch cycle below:

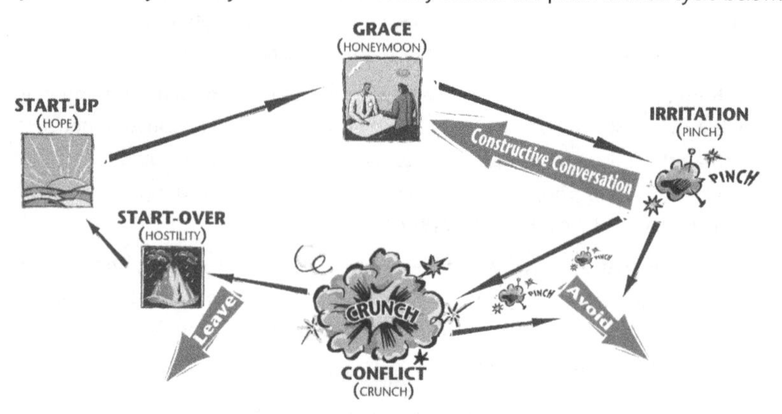

Whatever the root cause of the conflict, the Enneagram styles of the key parties involved will always be a factor in the conflict dynamics and resolution. The Enneagram enables each individual involved to make conflict resolution a constructive rather than destructive experience. The more people know themselves, understand their own responsibilities in the conflict interaction, engage in constructive self-management, and know how best to approach others through knowledge of the Enneagram, the greater the chances of a swift and effective outcome.

There are specific pinches (anger triggers) for each Enneagram style — that is, certain situations that will invariably ignite anger in a person of one style, yet may not affect someone of a different style. For Nines, these pinches include:

Disruption of peace and harmony · Being told what to do · Feeling ignored · Rudeness in others · Overt hostility from others · Feeling taken advantage of · Being confronted directly · Not feeling supported

For more insights and information about conflict, please refer to the following: Chapter 4, "Managing Conflict," in *Bringing Out the Best in Yourself at Work* (McGraw-Hill, 2004) and Chapter 5, "Become an Excellent Communicator," in *What Type of Leader Are You?* (McGraw-Hill, 2007).

Development Stretches for Transforming Anger into an Opportunity for Growth

Share your likely pinches (anger triggers) with others at the beginning of your working relationship.

Spending the time to build rapport at the beginning of a working relationship is something that many Nines do quite easily, even without prompting. They do, however, tend to do this is a more casual way — for example, by stopping at someone's office and schmoozing, or by going to lunch with the other person and talking either about work or about things unrelated to the work environment.

Talking about pinches, however, requires a bit of structure and focus. Offering an open-ended invitation to the new colleague works well for Nines — for example, "Could we take a few minutes to talk about what each of us would like from the other to make working together productive and harmonious? It could help us keep things running smoothly all along the way." To communicate their pinches, Nines can say, "I like to be included in decisions and conversations about work, and I like to include others as well" rather than "I don't like to be ignored." Instead of saying "I don't like being told what to do," Nines can say, "When someone wants me to do something, I highly prefer that the person make a genuine request rather than a demand or a veiled expectation. In fact, it helps when I have input and influence over how and when something gets accomplished."

As a caveat, Nines need to make sure that they actually initiate the conversation about pinches. They may intend to do so, but if the conversation feels comfortable and the topic is interesting, the time may slip away before the pinch conversation can occur. Nines may also unintentionally avoid the conversation about pinches because of their general aversion to conflict. It can be helpful for a Nine to remember that the discussion of pinches is *not* the same as conflict; in fact, the conversation can prevent conflict from arising.

Say something as soon as you are aware of feeling pinched or upset.

This can be difficult for Nines, for three reasons. First, as noted earlier, Nines who feel pinched may not even be aware that they are experiencing displeasure. However, when they start paying closer attention to themselves and their reactions, Nines become more aware of feeling agitated and angry. They do, however, need to take a serious look at what is truly causing the pinch and not direct their displeasure toward a secondary source.

Second, when Nines are aware of feeling pinched, they may not say anything for fear of creating a conflict. It can be helpful to reassure yourself that discussing pinches as soon as they occur usually decreases conflict, increases rapport, and builds trust with coworkers because of the self-disclosure that is involved.

For more insights and information about conflict, please refer to the following: Chapter 4, "Managing Conflict," in *Bringing Out the Best in Yourself at Work* (McGraw-Hill, 2004) and Chapter 5, "Become an Excellent Communicator," in *What Type of Leader Are You?* (McGraw-Hill, 2007).

Finally, as noted earlier, Nines may fully intend to say something to the other person but may procrastinate about initiating the conversation. The time may never seem right, or other pressing work issues may draw the Nine's attention. Thus, Nines must make a firm commitment to raising the issue soon after a pinch has occurred; they need to realize that while doing so may feel a little awkward, it will be far less so than the conversation that would take place if the pinches have been allowed to accumulate without discussion.

When you start to behave in ways that indicate you are feeling pinched or distressed, do something physical if you can, such as working out or taking a walk.

Physical activity works just as well for Nines when they feel pinched as it does for individuals of the other eight Enneagram styles. However, Nines need to make sure that they do not use walks or other forms of exercise as a way of avoiding conflict. Being in nature and engaging in physical activity often soothes Nines to such a degree that they may "space out" or forget that anything was troubling them. When they begin to shift their focus away from themselves and toward the activity in which they are involved, they need to bring their attention back to themselves. The following structured practice can assist Nines in refocusing on themselves. At ten-minute intervals during the physical activity, ask yourself these two questions: *Am I still paying attention to the issue that caused me the pinch? What am I thinking and feeling about it right now?*

When you have a negative reaction and feel a pinch, ask yourself: *What does my reaction to this situation or to the other person's behavior say about me as a Nine and about the areas in which I can develop? How can working on my pinches and crunches help me to bring out the best in myself?*

This question may be difficult for some Nines, because it requires them to really pay attention to themselves. Enneagram Style Nine is known as the "self-forgetting" style, which means that Nines tend not to pay attention to what they think, feel, need, or should be doing. In this sense, Nines neglect themselves. While individuals of the other eight styles also engage in self-forgetting and self-neglect, it is not usually to the same extent as it is with Nines. For Nines to focus on themselves to the degree required to answer the above question can be a challenge, but it can also be a highly transforming experience for them.

Conflict avoidance is central to the Nine's personality structure. When Nines focus on how they deal with conflict, they often find that they feel taken advantage of or ignored in large part because they have difficulty expressing their true feelings, standing up for themselves, and stating what they truly believe. Nines often discover that their way of dealing with potential conflict is to acquiesce and then become passive-aggressive, saying or implying yes when they mean no.

For more insights and information about conflict, please refer to the following: Chapter 4, "Managing Conflict," in *Bringing Out the Best in Yourself at Work* (McGraw-Hill, 2004) and Chapter 5, "Become an Excellent Communicator," in *What Type of Leader Are You?* (McGraw-Hill, 2007).

TEAM DEVELOPMENT STRETCHES

There is a difference between a group and a team. A *group* is a collection of individuals who have something in common; a *team* is a specific type of group, one composed of members who share one or more *goals* that can be reached only when there is an optimal level of *interdependence* between and among team members.

Team members also have *roles* — predictable patterns of behavior – within the team that are often related to their Enneagram styles. *Task roles* involve behaviors directed toward the work itself; *relationship roles* involve behaviors focused on feelings, relationships, and team processes, such as decision making and conflict resolution.

In addition, teams have unique yet predictable dynamics as they go through the four sequential stages of team development: *forming, storming, norming,* and *performing.* At each stage, there are questions the team must resolve before moving to the next stage.

TEAM STAGE	QUESTIONS
FORMING	*Who are we, where are we going, and are we all going there together?*
STORMING	*Can we disagree with one another in a constructive and productive way?*
NORMING	*How should we best organize ourselves and work together?*
PERFORMING	*How can we keep performing at a high level and not burn out?*

Nines: Development Stretches for Team Members and Team Leaders

Team Goals

Although you may prefer team goals that are extremely *concrete and meaningful* and are *developed by consensus,* other team members may need goals that are more lofty and visionary, and some goals need to be developed by the leader without consensus. Allow yourself to also work from the bigger picture when you create team goals, and to support the idea that not all goals need to be developed through a consensual group process.

Team Interdependence

Although you may prefer to work in *teams with interdependence for specific tasks* in a stable, harmonizing team environment, remind yourself that some teams need to work interdependently beyond specific tasks to be effective — for example, overall strategy, planning, and project coordination — and that teams need to have conflicts and differences brought to the surface and resolved so they can work at even higher levels of performance. Work to support the type of interdependence the team needs, and work to develop the capacity to be effective in teams even where there is ongoing disagreement and disharmony.

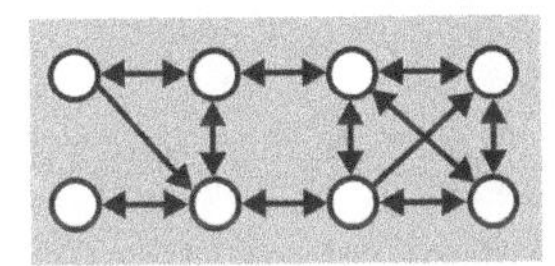

For more insights and information about teams, please refer to the following: Chapter 5, "Creating High-Performing Teams," in *Bringing Out the Best in Yourself at Work* (McGraw-Hill, 2004) and Chapter 6, "Lead High-Performing Teams," in *What Type of Leader Are You?* (McGraw-Hill, 2007).

Team Roles

Your typical task-related team role is likely to involve *giving information* within the team by providing others with information related to the task, such as information about what, how, why, when, and who. Your likely relationship-related team role may be *harmonizing team interactions* and *facilitating the positive resolution of conflict* by helping people get along, feel comfortable, connect with others, and achieve consensus, as well as by drawing out the feelings and perspectives of others in relation to conflict and facilitating its constructive resolution. Stretch yourself to go beyond these typical roles and adopt the following additional team task and relationship roles:

Task Roles

New task role

Evaluating information, reacting to and evaluating ideas and information presented by others

New relationship role

Challenging by confronting, questioning, and asking direct questions or making direct statements

Relationship Roles

Team Dynamics

During the four stages of team development — *forming, storming, norming,* and *performing* — experiment with expanding your repertoire of behavior in the following ways:

FORMING	STORMING	NORMING	PERFORMING
Work hard to maintain your focus, and be patient even when the process of forming seems unproductive or takes longer than you like.	Allow yourself to stay in the middle of team conflict, even when your facilitative attempts do not seem to be working, and encourage others to do the same.	Maintain your strength in helping the team to work by consensus, and be open to ideas that may seem restrictive to you but are in the team's best interests.	Maintain your ability to enjoy yourself and be careful to not exhaust yourself.

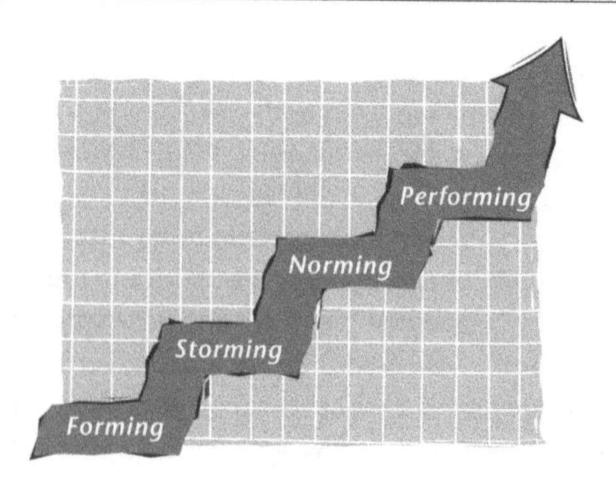

For more insights and information about teams, please refer to the following: Chapter 5, "Creating High-Performing Teams," in *Bringing Out the Best in Yourself at Work* (McGraw-Hill, 2004) and Chapter 6, "Lead High-Performing Teams," in *What Type of Leader Are You?* (McGraw-Hill, 2007).

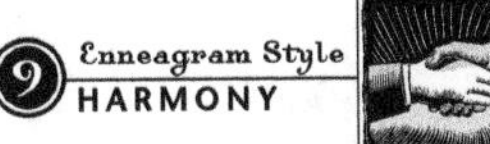

Additional Team Development Stretches for Nine Team Leaders

Learn to leverage team structure as well as process.

It is a challenge to determine whether changing the team's structure — for example, organizational chart, design of jobs, roles, and task force structure — or redesigning the team processes is the best approach to dealing with issues and creating higher team performance. Depending on the circumstances, either might work, or one might be better. Every time you are about to change a team process, ask yourself this question: *Before I support changing the team process, what structural changes could we make instead?* If you have no answer, solicit ideas from others, then experiment with structural changes until you become as comfortable with these as you are with process changes.

Practice being clear.

Although being very clear and explicit with others about what you think and what you want from them will feel strange at first, you are likely to end up feeling exhilarated by it once you start. When you are communicating with others, ask yourself: *What do I really think? What do I really want them to do?* Then tell them — kindly, nicely, but firmly.

Don't dig into the details.

Team members may look to you for guidance, feedback, support, and resources; they want you to remove obstacles from their path but not to dig deeply into the details. Although you may enjoy details, your team needs you to operate at a higher level so that you will have time to deal with the more important issues and the work will flow from your desk more easily.

For more insights and information about teams, please refer to the following: Chapter 5, "Creating High-Performing Teams," in *Bringing Out the Best in Yourself at Work* (McGraw-Hill, 2004) and Chapter 6, "Lead High-Performing Teams," in *What Type of Leader Are You?* (McGraw-Hill, 2007).

LEADERSHIP DEVELOPMENT STRETCHES

The intense challenges of leadership are complex, demanding, unpredictable, exciting, and rewarding, and they require the ability to manage oneself and to interact effectively with hundreds of others in both stressful and exhilarating circumstances. For these reasons, leaders must spend time in honest self-reflection. Individuals who become extraordinary leaders grow in both evolutionary and revolutionary ways as they push themselves to meet challenges even they cannot predict in advance.

Excellent leadership comes in many forms, and no Enneagram style has a monopoly on greatness. However, your Enneagram style shows both your strengths as a leader and the areas that would most likely create obstacles to your success.

Enneagram Style Nine leaders usually display this special gift: *inclusion and consensus*. However, their greatest strength can also become their greatest weakness: in their efforts to foster collaboration, provide clear structure, and stay on top of operational details, Nine leaders can create organizations that avoid conflict, do not respond quickly enough, and have insufficient work delegation.

Development Stretches to Enhance Your Leadership

Express yourself directly.

Instead of first finding out what others are thinking, express your own thoughts and feelings and let others react to you.

Emphasize what is most important.

Instead of talking in paragraphs and using abundant detail, practice communicating with others by highlighting the key points you want to make, as if you are a making a PowerPoint presentation.

Move things off your desk.

Make sure you are not an organizational bottleneck by delegating more, moving administrative items quickly from your desk, and spending a specified amount of dedicated time each day for paperwork.

For more insights and information about leadership, please refer to the following: Chapter 6, "Leveraging Your Leadership," in *Bringing Out the Best in Yourself at Work* (McGraw-Hill, 2004) and the book, *What Type of Leader Are You?* (McGraw-Hill, 2007).

RESULTS ORIENTATION DEVELOPMENT STRETCHES

It is important to build credibility with customers by delivering sustained, high-quality results, continually driving for results, and reaching your potential. When you do this, you make gains in productivity, push the envelope of new product development, and support the organization as a leader in its field.

Keep the work moving, especially off your desk.

While you may have a desire to do your work thoroughly and in a time frame that is comfortable for you, this can create strains, stresses, and bottlenecks for other people. This is especially true when projects are large or complex and when people are depending on you for a response before they can do their own work. It is especially important that you keep the work flowing at a more rapid pace than you might set for yourself alone.

Focus on the big picture.

Day-to-day operations are important, but when you are in a key role, it is more important that you keep your eye on the big picture. Delegate more to others, and when you do, be specific about what you want others to do. Don't be hesitant to direct their activities; this is part of being a leader.

Assert yourself more.

The people who work for and with you really want to know where you stand, even if they disagree with you. If someone has an opinion contrary to yours, having a dialogue about this can bring you and the other person into an even closer work relationship. Don't keep your thoughts and insights to yourself. Make a commitment to share more about what you truly think *early in the discussion* and to ask others directly for what you want and need from them.

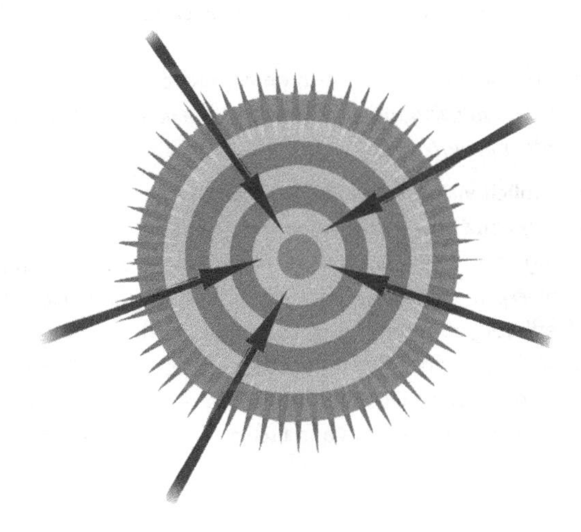

For more insights and information about results orientation, please refer to the following: Chapter 2, "Drive for Results," in *What Type of Leader Are You?* (McGraw-Hill, 2007).

STRATEGY DEVELOPMENT STRETCHES

Leaders and individual contributors must understand the actual business of their organizations and be able to think and act strategically in both big and small ways if their teams and organizations are to reach the highest levels of performance, effectiveness, and efficiency.

"Knowing the business" and "thinking and acting strategically" go hand in hand. Unless you know the business, you have no context for thinking and acting strategically. When you have this information, you need to be able to use it in a strategic way, working from a compelling and common vision, a customer-focused mission, a smart strategy, and effective goals and tactics aligned with that strategy.

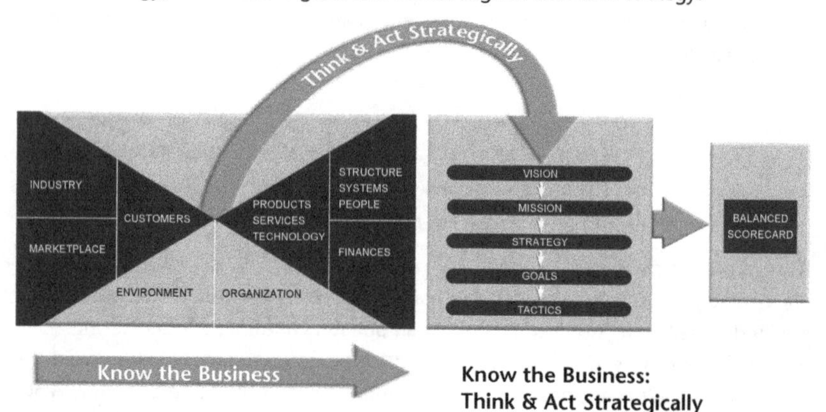

Know the Business: Think & Act Strategically

Be strategic.

Although you may be comfortable with the details, when these are in another person's area of responsibility, you have to force yourself to let that person handle them.

As soon as you are engaged in too much detail, say to yourself: *I'm getting too involved in minutiae. I'm being too tactical when I should be strategic. What should I really be paying attention to?*

Work from an explicit vision, mission, and strategy.

If you are a leader, write down your vision, mission, and strategy on one page. Practice describing them to at least three other people, then ask each person this question: *Was my explanation viable, compelling, evocative, and brief?* Make revisions based on the feedback you receive, then communicate the revised vision, mission, and strategy to three other people and ask them for feedback. Repeat this process until you receive only positive feedback. Finally, communicate the vision, mission, and strategy, together with the goals and tactics, to the people who work for you.

For more insights and information about strategy, please refer to the following: Chapter 4, "Know the Business: Think and Act Strategically," in *What Type of Leader Are You?* (McGraw-Hill, 2007).

If you are not a team leader, you still need to work from a vision, mission, and strategy. Write down the vision, mission, and strategy for your work unit. Ask yourself this question for every task you undertake: *How is my work related to the team's strategy, mission, and vision?* If you can't find the answer, review this work with your boss to determine whether you really need to be doing it.

Set organizational priorities and keep them.
Make a list of the three to five areas that will be the most important to address in the next six months. Make four copies of this list, then put these copies in places where you will see them and read them daily. Each time you are about to spend more than half an hour on a task, ask yourself: *Does this task fit with my organizational priority list?* If the answer is no, decide whether this task really needs to be done and, if so, determine who else could complete it.

For more insights and information about strategy, please refer to the following: Chapter 4, "Know the Business: Think and Act Strategically," in *What Type of Leader Are You?* (McGraw-Hill, 2007).

DECISION-MAKING DEVELOPMENT STRETCHES

We all make decisions on a daily basis, but we rarely think about the process by which we make them. The wisest decisions are made utilizing our heads (rational analysis and planning), our hearts (to examine values, feelings, and impact on people), and our guts (for taking action), with all three used in an integrated way. In addition, when you are making decisions at work, you need to consider three other factors: the organizational culture, the decision-making authority structure within the organization, and the context of the decision itself.

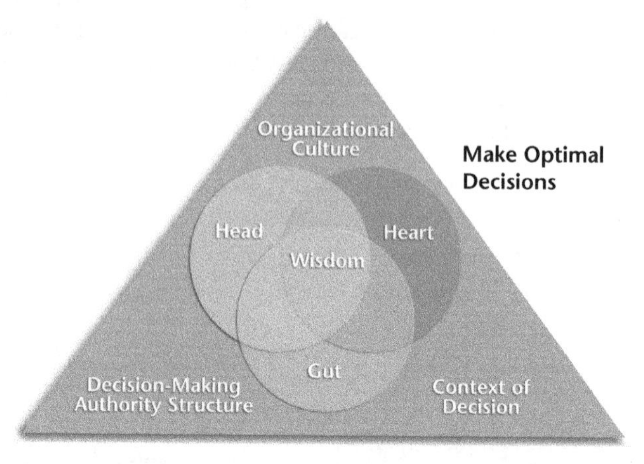

The following chart shows you how to develop each of your Centers of Intelligence (Head, Heart, and Gut) to assist you in making wise decisions.

	Centers of Intelligence		
	Head Center	**Heart Center**	**Body (Gut) Center**
Activities for Nines That Develop Each Center	**Objective analysis** Remember that you can collect too much data and then overanalyze a situation; this creates confusion about which information is the most relevant. **Astute insight** Honor your insights related to decisions you are making and be willing to verbalize them. **Productive planning** Keep to your deadline dates by planning your time schedule carefully and then following through.	**Empathy** Make sure to maintain your empathy, even with people you perceive as negative and complaining. **Authentic relating** Share how you really feel about different aspects of a decision and the decision-making process early in the discussion. **Compassion** Maintain an attitude of kindness even toward people who stridently disagree with your decisions.	**Taking effective action** Figure out why you procrastinate; err on the side of taking action too quickly rather than too slowly. **Steadfastness** Without being stubborn, hold firm on decisions that you believe are best, even in the face of opposition and conflict. **Gut-knowing** Every time you make a decision, consult your gut for additional information.

For more insights and information about decision making, please refer to the following: Chapter 7, "Make Optimal Decisions," in *What Type of Leader Are You?* (McGraw-Hill, 2007).

ORGANIZATIONAL CHANGE DEVELOPMENT STRETCHES

In contemporary organizations, change has become a way of life. Companies exist in increasingly complex environments, with more competition, fewer resources, less time to market, higher customer expectations, increased regulation, more technology, and greater uncertainty. Organizations need to be flexible, innovative, cost-conscious, and responsive if they want to succeed. As a result, employees at all levels need to be able to embrace change and to function flexibly and effectively within their teams when an unforeseen direction must be taken.

Take Charge of Change

Learn to express your thoughts, needs, and feelings to other people.

The more you practice expressing yourself to others, the more comfortable you will feel in doing this. It will also improve your rapport with others, because they will know more about who you really are. Expressing your thoughts and feelings may feel awkward at first, but if you practice it with people you know well and let them know this behavior is new for you, they are likely to be far more receptive than you might expect. During change initiatives, it is particularly important that you have a strong voice in what occurs and that others can benefit from your influence.

For more insights and information about organizational change, please refer to the following: Chapter 8, "Take Charge of Change," in *What Type of Leader Are You?* (McGraw-Hill, 2007).

Let your anger emerge in its earlier stages.

Change efforts usually elicit strong emotions in people affected by the change, and feelings of widespread anger are not unusual. It is particularly important during times of change that people express their deeper emotions. Although feeling angry is quite normal, Nines do not usually allow themselves to bring their angry feelings to the surface for fear of upsetting themselves and others and creating discord. However, unexpressed anger does not usually go away. It lies beneath the surface, where it festers until it finally explodes. When you learn to read the early signs that you are upset — for example, a certain sensation in your stomach or a particular recycling of thoughts in you mind — and acknowledge to yourself and others that something is wrong, you will be able to discuss your anger in a less emotionally charged and more reasoned way.

Be direct when you enlist the help of other people.

During times of change, there is usually twice as much work and more interdependence among coworkers to accomplish both new and old tasks. You really can count on many people to help you if you ask for assistance directly. Not everyone will respond affirmatively, but many people will be delighted to support you because you support them. Ask for help directly and delegate work. If you ask indirectly — for example, by saying that you are fatigued or by asking someone how to do something — others may not understand that you are actually asking them to do something concrete for you.

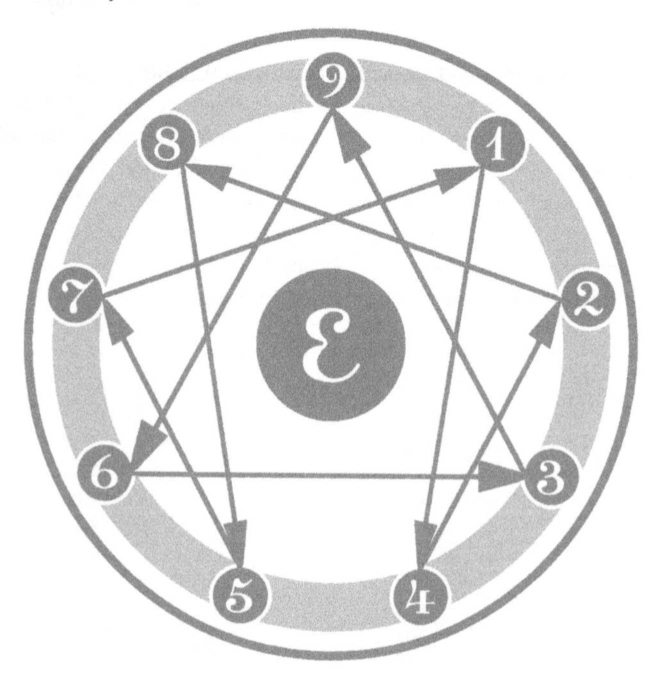

For more insights and information about organizational change, please refer to the following: Chapter 8, "Take Charge of Change," in *What Type of Leader Are You?* (McGraw-Hill, 2007).

TRANSFORMATION DEVELOPMENT STRETCHES

In order to move from *seeking peace, harmony, and positive mutual regard and disliking conflict, tension, and ill will* to the understanding that *underneath conflict and ill-will, unconditional regard and respect connects everyone and everything separate from anything they try to do,* Nines can work toward these transformations:

Mental Transformation

Transform the mental pattern of **indolence** (the process of mentally diffusing your attention so that you forget what is important to you and also refrain from stating your opinions and positions, thereby minimizing your conflicts with other people) *into the higher belief of* **love** (the belief that there is an underlying universal harmony in the world based on unconditional regard and appreciation for one another).

Mental Activity

When your focus becomes diffused, you begin forgetting your priorities, or you engage in any other behavior that helps you to avoid conflict, remember one or more times when you were able to sustain your attention and also recognize that there was an underlying harmony between people based on their deep regard and/or affection for each other. Allow those times to come back into your thinking and relive what was occurring within you at those moments. Sustain your focus, remembering these incidents for several minutes.

Emotional Transformation

Transform the emotional habit of **laziness** (lethargy in paying attention to your own feelings and needs, thus disabling you from taking the action you most desire) *into the higher awareness of* **right action** (the state of feeling fully present to yourself and others so that you know exactly what action you must take).

Emotional Activity

When you become aware that you are not paying attention to yourself and your deeper feelings and needs, remember one or more times in your life when you felt totally present and aware of both yourself and others and thus knew instinctively what you must do. Remember the circumstances, how you felt, and what you experienced during those times. Keep replaying those fully aware moments until you feel fully reconnected with the experiences.

For more insights and information about personal transformation, please refer to the following: Chapter 7, "Transforming Yourself," in *Bringing Out the Best in Yourself at Work* (McGraw-Hill, 2004).

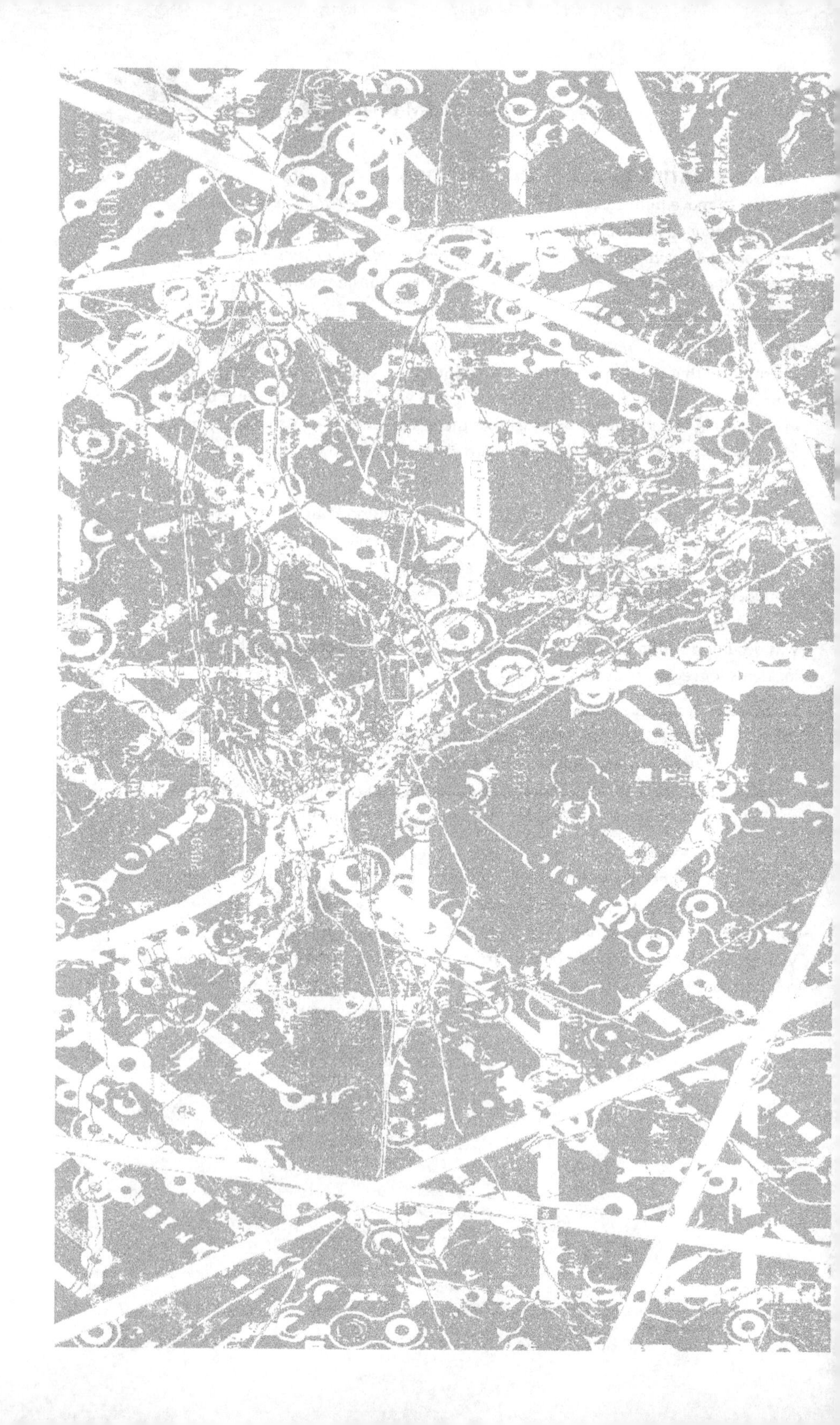

ALL ENNEAGRAM STYLES
9
1
2
3
4
5
6
7
8
ℰ

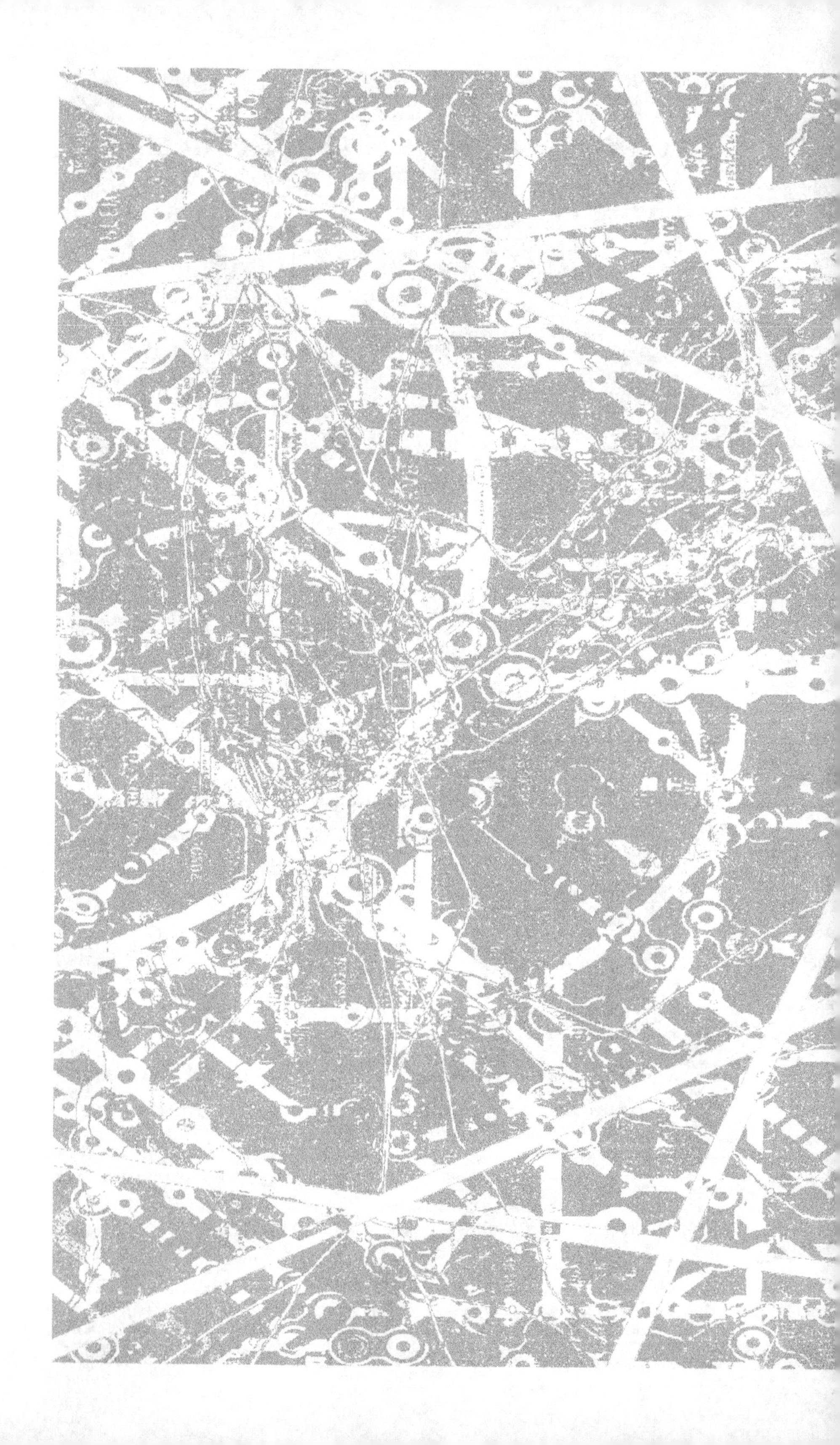

DEVELOPMENT STRETCHES FOR EVERYONE

INDIVIDUALS WHO HAVE A STRONG COMMITMENT TO THEIR OWN GROWTH AND WHO TAKE RESPONSIBILITY FOR THEIR SELF-DEVELOPMENT

CONTENTS

DEVELOPMENT STRETCHES FOR EVERYONE

SELF-MASTERY DEVELOPMENT STRETCHES

Self-Mastery — the ability to understand, accept, and transform your thoughts, feelings, and behavior, with the understanding that each day will bring new challenges that are opportunities for growth — is the foundation of all personal and professional development. Self-mastery begins with self-awareness, then expands to include the elements shown in the following graphic:

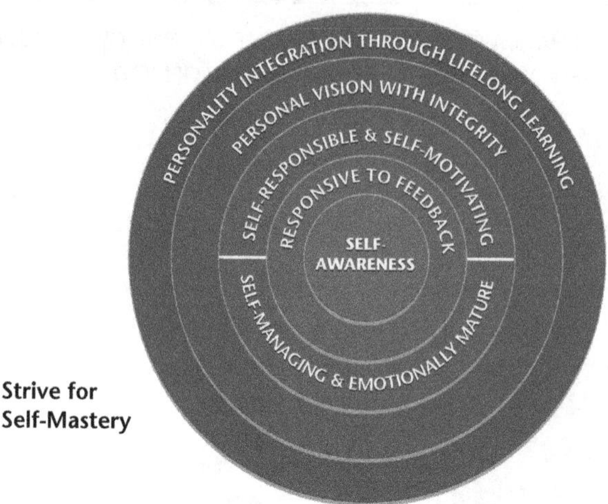

Strive for Self-Mastery

In this section on self-mastery, you will find the following:

- Three common issues related to self-mastery for everyone
- A chart showing the three levels of self-mastery and how individuals behave at each stage
- Three development stretches for everyone

Common Development Issues for Everyone

Becoming more aware of your own patterns of thinking, feeling, and behaving, thus having a realistic sense of yourself and accepting who you are	Taking responsibility for yourself and being able to differentiate between your responsibility and that of other people	Maintaining your commitment to lifelong learning, not simply pursuing growth and development when you are under duress

The Levels of Self-Mastery

The following chart shows the three levels of self-mastery[1] — low, moderate, and extreme — and describes how individuals behave at each stage with respect to the Competency Components of Strive for Self-Mastery. For the purpose of greater clarity, the six Competency Components are subdivided into the following categories: Self-Awareness, Responsiveness to Feedback, Self-Responsibility, Self-Motivation, Self-Management, Emotional Maturity, Personal Vision, Integrity, Personality Integration, and Lifelong Learning Commitment.

[1] The Enneagram authors who created and developed the Levels of Development, which can be applied to the issue of self-mastery in leadership, are Don Richard Riso and Russ Hudson in their books, *Personality Types* and *The Wisdom of the Enneagram*. The following material has its genesis in their work, which I am grateful to have their permission to use.

DEVELOPMENT STRETCHES FOR EVERYONE

	LOW <<<<<<< DEGREE OF SELF-MASTERY >>>>>>> EXTREME		
	LOW SELF-MASTERY	**MODERATE SELF-MASTERY**	**EXTREME SELF-MASTERY**
SELF-MASTERY COMPONENT General Behavior	Exhibits reactive, unproductive behavior most of the time; demonstrates minimal personality integration	May be aware of own inner experience, but responds out of habit more often than not; demonstrates some degree of personality integration	Is highly aware of own inner experience and able to respond out of choice in productive and highly flexible ways; demonstrates a high degree of personality integration
SELF-AWARENESS Self-awareness involves the capacity to be self-observing (being conscious of one's own thoughts, feelings, and behaviors while these are occurring)	Is unaware of own thoughts, feelings, and behaviors and/or is dishonest about true motivations; not self-observing	Can be self-aware, although does not routinely put a high priority on this; has more difficulty being self-aware under duress; is intermittently self-observing	Routinely accesses and is honest about own thoughts, feelings, and behaviors; has a realistic self-image; is able to be self-observing most of the time
RESPONSIVENESS TO FEEDBACK	Defends against, denies, and ignores feedback and/or blames others when criticized	Sometimes responds effectively to feedback, but can also under- or overrespond	Welcomes feedback and uses it constructively; can distinguish between accurate feedback and biased opinion
SELF-RESPONSIBILITY	Has distorted perceptions of own motivations; sees others as causing his or her behavior; projects own thoughts and feelings onto others	Can act self-responsibly; under duress, has difficulty differentiating own responsibility from that of others	Takes full responsibility for own actions
SELF-MOTIVATION	Is either motivated or unmotivated by negative factors such as internal fears or external threats	Is partially self-motivated; often expects others to be the motivating force	Is highly self-motivated and self-determining
SELF-MANAGEMENT	Is either overcontrolled or out of control; behavior is highly reactive	Sometimes makes conscious choices, but more often acts as if on automatic pilot	Highly self-managing rather than reactive or acting out of habit; is in control without being controlled or controlling; makes conscious and constructive choices
EMOTIONAL MATURITY	Perceives self as victim	Fluctuates between personal reactivity and the ability to have perspective on self, others, and events	Is mature in almost all situations; can rise above personal responses to understand multiple factors and perspectives affecting the situation
PERSONAL VISION	Has no personal vision or has a negative vision	Has an unarticulated or oversimplified personal vision	Has a clear, positive personal vision
INTEGRITY	Engages in behaviors and actions inconsistent with values, or has destructive values	Has generally positive values, but behavior is not always consistent with values	Has positive values and "walks the talk"
PERSONALITY INTEGRATION	Behavior reflects a low level of accurate self-knowledge as well as incongruity among thoughts, feelings, and behaviors	Behavior reflects intermittent self-knowledge and/or an overemphasis on thoughts, feelings, or actions; behavior not always congruent with feelings or stated intentions	Behavior demonstrates a high degree of self-knowledge and is congruent and integrated with thoughts and feelings
LIFELONG LEARNING COMMITMENT	Has no commitment to self-development or lifelong learning	Has a moderate to low commitment to self-development; engages in self-development when under duress	Has a high commitment to ongoing self-development, demonstrated through continuous action

DEVELOPMENT STRETCHES FOR EVERYONE

Development Stretches

Keep a journal.

Keep a daily journal of your personal reactions to events and of your progress on self-mastery. Once a week, review your journal entries to look for patterns of responses and progress, and note these in the journal.

Observe yourself.

Observe yourself daily in both your work and personal interactions and practice your self-mastery skills. The more you practice and refine both your skills related to self-development and your interpersonal skills, the better you will become at self-mastery.

Read.

Read *Emotional Intelligence* by Daniel Goleman (New York: Bantam Books, 2005).

For more insights and information about self-mastery, please refer to the following: Chapter 7, "Transforming Yourself," in *Bringing Out the Best in Yourself at Work* (McGraw-Hill, 2004) and Chapter 3, "Strive for Self-Mastery," in *What Type of Leader Are You?* (McGraw-Hill, 2007).

COMMUNICATION DEVELOPMENT STRETCHES

When you communicate with someone, three kinds of unintentional distortions may be present: speaking style, body language, and blind spots. *Speaking style* refers to your overall pattern of speaking. *Body language* includes posture, facial expressions, hand gestures, body movements, energy levels, and hundreds of other nonverbal messages. *Blind spots* are elements of your communication containing information about you that is not apparent to you but is highly visible to other people. We all unknowingly convey information through an amalgam of our speaking style, body language, and other inferential data.

The receivers of the messages you send also distort what they hear through their *distorting filters*. These are unconscious concerns or assumptions, often based on the listener's Enneagram style, that alter how someone hears what others say.

Speaking Style Body Language Blind Spots

Change one communication style behavior at a time.

It is most effective to work on changing one behavior at a time, preferably in the following sequence: speaking style, body language, blind spots, and listening distorting filters. It is easiest to change the behaviors of which we are most aware, and this sequence represents the most common order of awareness, from most to least aware.

Increase your awareness.

1. Increase your knowledge of the ways in which you distort both giving and receiving messages. For one week, spend 15 minutes at the end of each day thinking about the communications you have had with other people that day. Answer these questions: *How effective were my communications with others? How do I know this? Is there anything I would like to change?* Write down your answers so you can remember them.
2. After following step 1 for one week, look over your notes and try to identify the patterns in your communications.
3. For the next week, simply observe yourself behaving in the ways you identified in step 2.
4. At the end of the week for step 3, select *one* behavior you want to change. Then, for the next week, observe all the times you exhibit this behavior. If you can, try to notice yourself doing the behavior when you are right in the middle of doing it.

For more insights and information about communication, please refer to the following: Chapter 2, "Communicating Effectively," in *Bringing Out the Best in Yourself at Work* (McGraw-Hill, 2004) and Chapter 5, "Become an Excellent Communicator," in *What Type of Leader Are You?* (McGraw-Hill, 2007).

5. Finally, you are ready to change your behavior. For one week, *change this one behavior.* You can either change it right when you are about to do it, or you can change your behavior when you catch yourself in the middle of it. Either way is effective.
6. Continue the process from step 4, selecting a new behavior to change; repeat the process as needed, working through one behavioral change at a time.

Solicit feedback.
Ask others, including coworkers, for feedback on your communication style; select people who know you well and whom you respect.

Audiotape or videotape yourself.
Audiotape your side of a telephone communication with someone else; review it several times, and ask other people to listen and give you their impressions. Videotape yourself during a meeting or when giving a speech, and review the tape multiple times to observe your behavior.

Listen actively.
Use active listening to decrease your receiving distortions; paraphrase both the content and feelings you hear from the other person so he or she can give you a reality check on the accuracy of your listening skills.

Use a coach.
Use an experienced coach, and ask the coach for feedback.

For more insights and information about communication, please refer to the following: Chapter 2, "Communicating Effectively," in *Bringing Out the Best in Yourself at Work* (McGraw-Hill, 2004) and Chapter 5, "Become an Excellent Communicator," in *What Type of Leader Are You?* (McGraw-Hill, 2007).

Use e-mails to expand and adjust your language patterns.

Review your e-mails before you send them for language and tone.

Include a salutation, such as "Dear David" or "Hi Janet."

This personalizes the e-mail and makes the recipient more responsive.

Use an appropriate ending, such as "Looking forward to your response" or "Regards."

This helps e-mail recipients not to speculate about what you are thinking or about what they should do next.

Include your name at the end of the e-mail.

This personalizes the e-mail and makes it easier for recipients to reference later if they save it to a desktop file.

Use CAPITAL letters sparingly; for emphasis, use bold font or underlining.

Remember that you may not mean to shout the words you capitalize, but many people read capitalization this way.

Use complete sentences whenever possible.

This simply makes your statements clearer to the recipient.

E-mail should not be used for all your communications.

Sensitive conversations are usually best done in person or at least by telephone. Remember that any e-mail you send can be forwarded to hundreds of people.

Reread your e-mail before you send it.

Rereading helps you to be more conscious of your communication style, and you are likely to catch words, tone, or statements that don't reflect what you really want to say.

Read.

Read *Crucial Conversations: Tools for Talking When Stakes Are High,* by Kerry Patterson et al. (New York: McGraw-Hill, 2002).

For more insights and information about self-mastery, please refer to the following: Chapter 7, "Transforming Yourself," in *Bringing Out the Best in Yourself at Work* (McGraw-Hill, 2004) and Chapter 3, "Strive for Self-Mastery," in *What Type of Leader Are You?* (McGraw-Hill, 2007).

DEVELOPMENT STRETCHES FOR EVERYONE

FEEDBACK DEVELOPMENT STRETCHES

Honest, positive, and constructive *feedback* — direct, objective, simple, and respectful observations that one person makes about another's behavior — improves both relationships and on-the-job performance. When you offer feedback, the Feedback Formula, combined with the insights of the Enneagram, helps you tailor your delivery. When someone gives you feedback, the more receptive you are to hearing what is being said, the more likely it is that you will be able to discern what is useful and utilize what has been suggested.

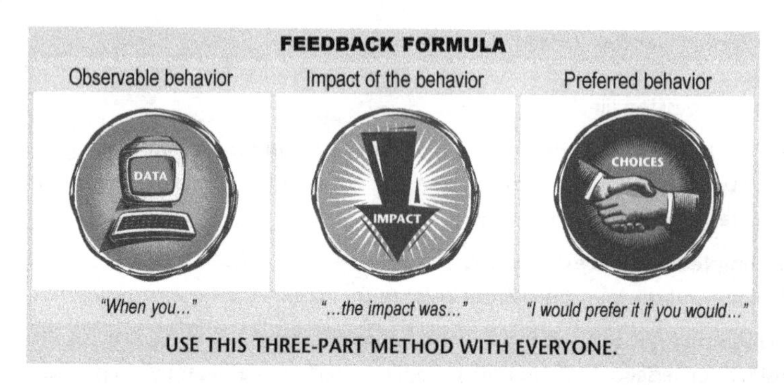

How to Enhance Your Ability to Deliver Feedback Effectively

When you offer feedback to someone, you want to be prepared and also to encourage the feedback recipient to be as receptive as possible. Remember that how and when you deliver feedback is just as important as what you actually say.

Use the three components of the **Feedback Formula** together with the following suggestions to plan and deliver the feedback.

- Think about what you want to say before saying it.
- Give feedback on areas the person can change.
- Make sure your intent is to help, not to hurt or to force change.
- Pay attention to your nonverbal communication.
- Give feedback in private.
- Be clear and respectful simultaneously.
- Be sure the other person is in an emotional state in which he or she can hear you.
- Give positive as well as negative feedback.
- Resist the temptation to interpret the other person's behavior.
- Make sure the conversation is a two-way dialogue.
- Role-play the meeting with someone else first, for practice and for obtaining suggestions.

Remember: No one changes another person; people change themselves.

For more insights and information about feedback, please refer to the following: Chapter 3, "Giving Constructive Feedback," in *Bringing Out the Best in Yourself at Work* (McGraw-Hill, 2004) and Chapter 5, "Become an Excellent Communicator," in *What Type of Leader Are You?* (McGraw-Hill, 2007).

How to Be More Receptive When You Receive Feedback

- Think of feedback as a gift that you may either keep or return. This will help you to discern whether the information is accurate and helpful. Remember that even if the feedback giver didn't wrap the package very well, its contents may still be useful.
- Be equally receptive to positive and negative feedback. Although it may surprise you, many people are more uncomfortable receiving positive feedback than negative feedback.
- When you receive feedback, feel free to ask clarifying questions. However, if you begin to explain yourself in some detail, stop. This is the time to listen fully to what the other person is saying. The best time for a more prolonged two-way conversation is after the feedback giver has given the full feedback.

For more insights and information about feedback, please refer to the following: Chapter 3, "Giving Constructive Feedback," in *Bringing Out the Best in Yourself at Work* (McGraw-Hill, 2004) and Chapter 5, "Become an Excellent Communicator," in *What Type of Leader Are You?* (McGraw-Hill, 2007).

DEVELOPMENT STRETCHES FOR EVERYONE

CONFLICT DEVELOPMENT STRETCHES

Relationships both at work and at home often involve some degree of conflict, which may be caused by a variety of factors and usually follows the pinch-crunch cycle below:

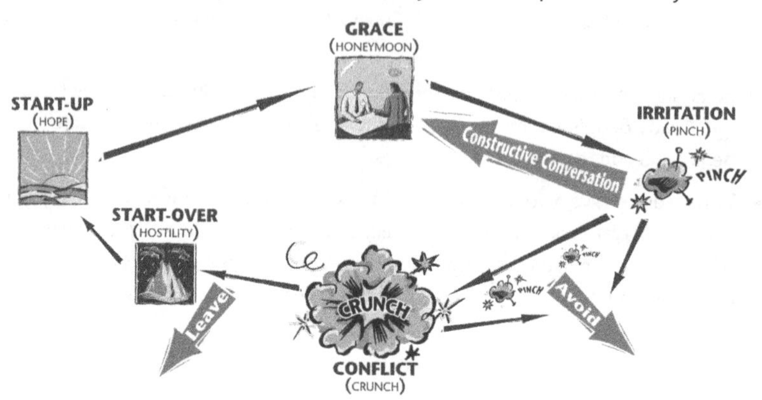

Whatever the root cause of the conflict, the Enneagram styles of the key parties involved will always be a factor in the conflict dynamics and resolution. The Enneagram enables each individual involved to make conflict resolution a constructive rather than destructive experience. The more people know themselves, understand their own responsibilities in the conflict interaction, engage in constructive self-management, and know how best to approach others through knowledge of the Enneagram, the greater the chances of a swift and effective outcome.

Development Stretches

Share your likely pinches (anger triggers) with others at the beginning of your working relationship.

Early on in a working relationship, engage the other person or persons in a conversation about your newly formed working relationship, including both your and their working styles. During the working styles discussion, both of you can highlight the types of behaviors in others that tend to pinch you.

Say something as soon as you are aware of feeling pinched or upset.

Sharing a pinch as soon as it is felt creates the opportunity for a reasoned conversation with less emotional intensity than occurs after pinches begin to accumulate. The Feedback Formula on page 262 provides a structure for giving feedback about what caused the pinch, the impact of the pinch, and the preferred behavior.

For more insights and information about conflict, please refer to the following: Chapter 4, "Managing Conflict," in *Bringing Out the Best in Yourself at Work* (McGraw-Hill, 2004) and Chapter 5, "Become an Excellent Communicator," in *What Type of Leader Are You?* (McGraw-Hill, 2007).

When you start to behave in ways that indicate you are feeling pinched or distressed, do something physical if you can, such as working out or taking a walk.
When we begin to feel angry, we typically become physically tense, and our muscles tighten automatically. Simultaneously, our mental processing and emotional reactivity become heightened. Engaging in a physical activity interrupts this cycle, and we often perceive what has occurred in a new and constructive manner.

When you have a negative reaction and feel a pinch, ask yourself: *What does my reaction to this situation or to the other person's behavior say about me as this Enneagram Style and about the areas in which I can develop? How can working on my pinches and crunches help me to bring out the best in myself?*
This is undoubtedly the most constructive and useful way to understand and work with your pinches and crunches. All it takes is a frame of mind in which you say the following to yourself: *I just had a strong negative reaction to this event. What can this teach me about myself? How can I use this experience to experiment with a very different reaction, including my mental interpretation of events, my particular emotional responses, and the way in which I am now behaving?*

Read.
Read *Crucial Confrontations: Broken Promises, Violated Expectations, and Bad Behavior*, by Kerry Patterson et al. (New York: McGraw-Hill, 2004).

For more insights and information about conflict, please refer to the following: Chapter 4, "Managing Conflict," in *Bringing Out the Best in Yourself at Work* (McGraw-Hill, 2004) and Chapter 5, "Become an Excellent Communicator," in *What Type of Leader Are You?* (McGraw-Hill, 2007).

DEVELOPMENT STRETCHES FOR EVERYONE

TEAM DEVELOPMENT STRETCHES

There is a difference between a group and a team. A *group* is a collection of individuals who have something in common; a *team* is a specific type of group, one composed of members who share one or more *goals* that can be reached only when there is an optimal level of *interdependence* between and among team members.

Team members also have *roles* — predictable patterns of behavior – within the team that are often related to their Enneagram styles. *Task roles* involve behaviors directed toward the work itself; *relationship roles* involve behaviors focused on feelings, relationships, and team processes, such as decision making and conflict resolution.

In addition, teams have unique yet predictable dynamics as they go through the four sequential stages of team development: *forming, storming, norming,* and *performing.* At each stage, there are questions the team must resolve before moving to the next stage.

TEAM STAGE	QUESTIONS
FORMING	*Who are we, where are we going, and are we all going there together?*
STORMING	*Can we disagree with one another in a constructive and productive way?*
NORMING	*How should we best organize ourselves and work together?*
PERFORMING	*How can we keep performing at a high level and not burn out?*

Development Stretches for Team Members and Team Leaders

Suggestions for Team Members

- Make suggestions either to the team leader or to the whole team regarding the importance of team goals and interdependence.
- In order to help the team articulate its goals, you can say, for example, "It would be helpful to me if we spent some time discussing our team goals to make sure we're all on the same page."
- If the team does not have a common understanding of the team's interdependence, you can suggest the following: "Can we spend some time examining the ways in which we depend on each other's work, so that we can make sure we're giving each other the necessary information or work products?"
- Suggest to the team leader that he or she recommend to the team that they experiment with new task and relationship roles.

For more insights and information about teams, please refer to the following: Chapter 5, "Creating High-Performing Teams," in *Bringing Out the Best in Yourself at Work* (McGraw-Hill, 2004) and Chapter 6, "Lead High-Performing Teams," in *What Type of Leader Are You?* (McGraw-Hill, 2007).

DEVELOPMENT STRETCHES FOR EVERYONE

Make the following suggestions to help the team progress through the first three stages of team development:

FORMING	STORMING	NORMING
Suggest that the team members get to know one another. For example: "It might be helpful for us to spend some time getting to know our individual backgrounds so that we can better understand how to use one another as resources." If the team has an unclear direction, you could say, "Can we examine what our team's purpose or charter is supposed to be so that we'll be sure to move in a common direction?"	Encourage the team members to share their honest feelings and opinions by suggesting, "I think it would be a good idea to discuss this issue in more detail, because it isn't clear whether everyone agrees with our recent decision."	Make suggestions about the ways in which the team can work even better together. An example of this is the following: "If we were to meet twice a month instead of once a month, we could stay more up to date on the latest organizational changes. What do the rest of you think?"

Suggestions for Team Leaders

In addition to taking all of the actions suggested above for individual team members, as a team leader you can leverage your leadership role in the following ways:

- Make certain that your team has clear goals and that team members have a realistic understanding of their interdependence.
- Design your team and your team meetings so that the team forms, storms, and norms effectively.
- Educate the team members about teams, so that all members are prepared to behave constructively on the team.
- Have team members examine their typical team roles and suggest that they experiment with new roles for at least one team meeting.
- Teach the members about the stages of team development; use the framework of team development stages to analyze the connections between individual behavior and team performance.

Read.

Read *The Wisdom of Teams: Creating the High-Performance Organization,* by Jon R. Katzenbach and Douglas K. Smith (New York: HarperCollins Essentials, 2003).

For more insights and information about teams, please refer to the following: Chapter 5, "Creating High-Performing Teams," in *Bringing Out the Best in Yourself at Work* (McGraw-Hill, 2004) and Chapter 6, "Lead High-Performing Teams," in *What Type of Leader Are You?* (McGraw-Hill, 2007).

DEVELOPMENT STRETCHES FOR EVERYONE

LEADERSHIP DEVELOPMENT STRETCHES

The intense challenges of leadership are complex, demanding, unpredictable, exciting, and rewarding, and they require the ability to manage oneself and to interact effectively with hundreds of others in both stressful and exhilarating circumstances. For these reasons, leaders must spend time in honest self-reflection. Individuals who become extraordinary leaders grow in both evolutionary and revolutionary ways as they push themselves to meet challenges even they cannot predict in advance.

Appreciate and use your leadership gifts.

Learning to appreciate what comes naturally to you can be a challenge. Every leader must have followers, and these gifts are what attract people to you. Know who you are and appreciate what you bring to leadership.

Expand your leadership paradigm.

Your leadership paradigm or worldview determines what you think is important, which in turn influences how you behave. Paradigms are not necessarily good or bad; they are useful, yet they also limit behavior. Expand your leadership paradigm, and you will expand your leadership repertoire.

Leverage your leadership strengths, but do so in moderation.

Strengths, used to excess, invariably become weaknesses. Know your strengths and use them, but not to an extreme. Using your strengths in moderation will also encourage you to expand your skills into new areas and to rely on the strengths of others in new and productive ways.

Take your leadership derailers seriously.

Derailers can take even the best leaders off-track. It is best to know what these areas are and to work on them as a preventive measure *before* they cause any serious difficulties.

Solicit feedback.

Discuss your strengths and potential derailers with people at work who know you well, and ask them for honest feedback on how these compare with your leadership behavior.

Work with a coach.

You might find it useful to work with an experienced coach who can help you work to accomplish your development goals.

Read.

Read *The Leadership Challenge,* by James M. Kouzes and Barry Z. Posner (San Francisco: Jossey-Bass Publishers, 2003).

For more insights and information about leadership, please refer to the following: Chapter 6, "Leveraging Your Leadership," in *Bringing Out the Best in Yourself at Work* (McGraw-Hill, 2004) and the book, *What Type of Leader Are You?* (McGraw-Hill, 2007).

RESULTS ORIENTATION DEVELOPMENT STRETCHES

It is important to build credibility with customers by delivering sustained, high-quality results, continually driving for results, and reaching your potential. When you do this, you make gains in productivity, push the envelope of new product development, and support the organization as a leader in its field.

Lead (or co-lead) a complex team or project.

For example, manage one of the following projects: the integration of a system, process, or procedure across two teams or business units; a construction, renovation, or major move to new office space; or a high-priority project whose resources are in high demand. Use a mentor, peer, or co-leader with excellent project management skills to review your plan and process at the beginning, at key milestones, and on completion.

Use a coach.

Use the services of a mentor or coach with demonstrated expertise in Drive for Results to help you create a specific development plan and provide you with ongoing feedback and advice.

Read.

Read *Execution: The Discipline of Getting Things Done,* by Larry Bossidy and Ram Charan (New York: Crown Business, 2002).

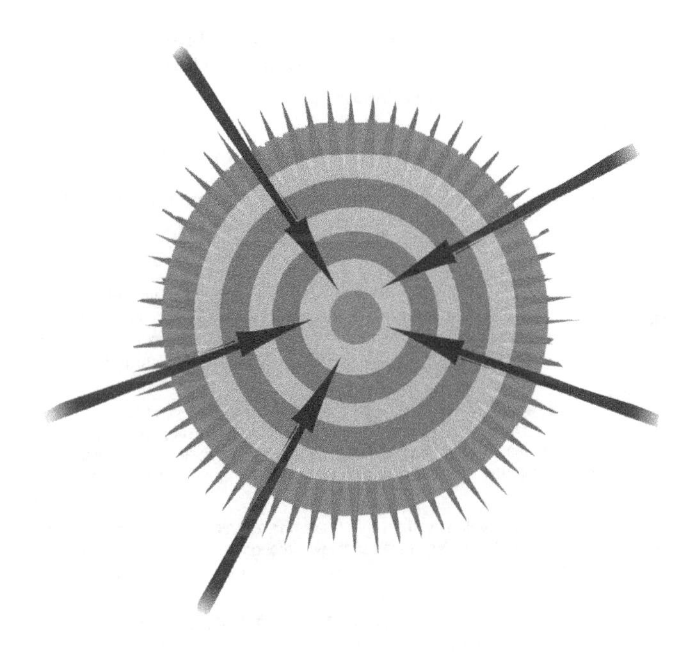

For more insights and information about results orientation, please refer to the following: Chapter 2, "Drive for Results," in *What Type of Leader Are You?* (McGraw-Hill, 2007).

DEVELOPMENT STRETCHES FOR EVERYONE

STRATEGY DEVELOPMENT STRETCHES

Leaders and individual contributors must understand the actual business of their organizations and be able to think and act strategically in both big and small ways if their teams and organizations are to reach the highest levels of performance, effectiveness, and efficiency.

"Knowing the business" and "thinking and acting strategically" go hand in hand. Unless you know the business, you have no context for thinking and acting strategically. When you have this information, you need to be able to use it in a strategic way, working from a compelling and common vision, a customer-focused mission, a smart strategy, and effective goals and tactics aligned with that strategy.

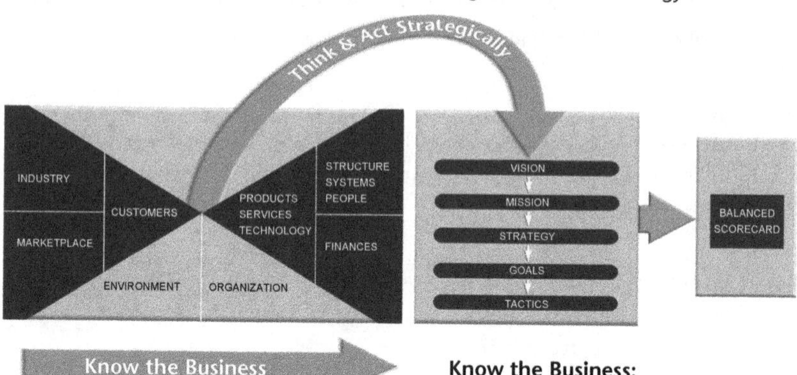

Know the Business: Think & Act Strategically

The five strategic elements are defined below:

Strategic Element	Definition
VISION	**A shared, compelling, and enduring picture or understanding of the preferred future** The vision endures for a number of years (3 to 5 or longer) and is the first strategic element to be developed.
MISSION	**The concrete business you are in; the value you add to your customers that enables you to achieve your vision** The mission supports the vision and represents your specific contribution to the vision; it remains steady, changing only if the environment changes dramatically.
STRATEGY	**The approaches you will take in order to accomplish your mission and vision; strategy determines resource allocations and other critical decisions** Strategies contain an action orientation but are *not* specific activities; they are changed only if altering tactics and/or goals proves ineffective or the environment changes significantly.
GOALS	**Measurable outcomes that represent key milestones for the strategies** There are usually 3 to 5 goals per strategy, although some goals can be leveraged and used for more than one strategy; goals are changed only if alternative tactics prove ineffective.
TACTICS	**Specific actions for accomplishing each goal** There are usually 3 to 5 tactics per goal, although some tactics can be leveraged and used for more than one goal; tactics can be readily changed if they are not achieving the goals, strategy, and mission.

For more insights and information about strategy, please refer to the following: Chapter 4, "Know the Business: Think and Act Strategically," in *What Type of Leader Are You?* (McGraw-Hill, 2007).

Development Stretches

Create a Balanced Scorecard.

Develop a two-page document for your area of responsibility. On the first page, use words and/or graphics to outline the key elements in your environment. For example, identify the following: key trends in the industry and marketplace; current and future customers and their most critical needs; the organization's key products, services, and technologies; a brief description of the organization's structure, systems, and people; and, finally, information about the financial situation.

On the second page, identify your area's vision, mission (including for whom you provide work and your value-added proposition), strategy, goals, and tactics. At the bottom of this page, add a statement that reflects your Balanced Scorecard for the organization, business unit, or team. The scorecard would include the following factors: financial indicators of success; intellectual and other intangible assets; high quality goods and services that are important to valued customers; a motivated and capable workforce that is able to meet current and future business needs; and a satisfied and loyal customer base.

Finally, have someone whom you consider skilled in Know the Business and Think and Act Strategically provide you with feedback; make adjustments as needed. Then share the document with your boss, the people who work for you, and peers with whom you are interdependent. Solicit the feedback of each of these people, then make changes as desired.

Understand the strategies of other leaders.

Read biographies or watch DVDs that reveal the thought processes and actions of leaders who mobilized people and resources to make significant changes in their organizations (for example, Mahatma Gandhi, Nelson Mandela, Franklin D. Roosevelt, Rudy Giuliani, and Oprah Winfrey). Write down what you believe were his or her vision, mission, strategy, goals, and tactics.

Read.

Read *Strategy Maps: Converting Intangible Assets into Tangible Outcomes,* by Robert S. Kaplan and David P. Norton (Boston: Harvard Business School Press, 2004).

For more insights and information about strategy, please refer to the following: Chapter 4, "Know the Business: Think and Act Strategically," in *What Type of Leader Are You?* (McGraw-Hill, 2007).

DEVELOPMENT STRETCHES FOR EVERYONE

DECISION-MAKING DEVELOPMENT STRETCHES

We all make decisions on a daily basis, but we rarely think about the process by which we make them. The wisest decisions are made utilizing our heads (rational analysis and planning), our hearts (to examine values, feelings, and impact on people), and our guts (for taking action), with all three used in an integrated way. In addition, when you are making decisions at work, you need to consider three other factors: the organizational culture, the decision-making authority structure within the organization, and the context of the decision itself.

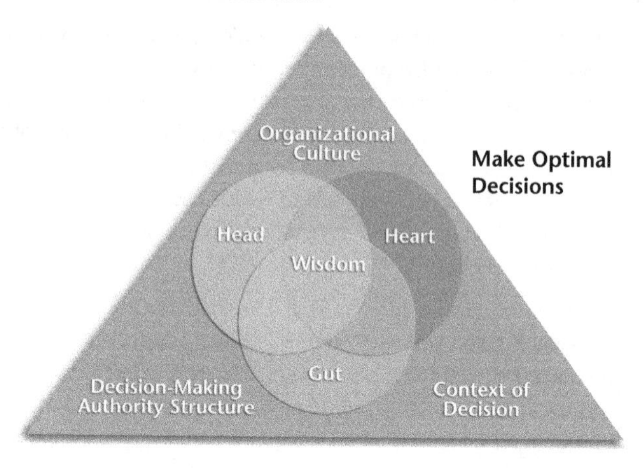

The following chart shows you how the Three Centers of Intelligence (Head, Heart, and Body) are optimally used when making wise decisions.

Productive Uses of the Three Centers of Intelligence		
Head Center	**Heart Center**	**Body (Gut) Center**
Objective analysis Understanding data without bias **Astute insight** Understanding the meaning and implications of data **Productive planning** Structuring sets of activities effectively	**Empathy** Identifying with and understanding another person's feelings **Authentic relating** Relating without pretense **Compassion** Heartfelt kindness toward another person	**Taking effective action** Taking well-chosen and timely action **Steadfastness** Being firm and resolute **Gut-knowing** Having a clear and trustworthy instinctive response

For more insights and information about decision making, please refer to the following: Chapter 7, "Make Optimal Decisions," in *What Type of Leader Are You?* (McGraw-Hill, 2007).

Development Stretches

Assess your past use of the Centers of Intelligence.

Think of three personal and/or work-related decisions you have made in the past year. Write each one down on a separate piece of paper. Underneath each decision, make three columns and label them *Head, Heart,* and *Body (Gut)*. For each decision, write down how you used that Center to make that particular decision. Next, review all three decisions and look for patterns related to how you used your head, heart, and gut. Finally, assess how you could use each Center better to make optimal decisions.

Integrate your Head, Heart, and Body Centers.

The next time you need to make a decision and have already collected the relevant information, ask yourself: *What does my head tell me to do? What does my heart say? What does my gut tell me?* If you have the same responses to each question, you likely have an optimal decision, as long as you have also factored in the organizational culture, organizational decision-making authority structure, and the context of the decision. If you have different answers to two or more of the questions, ask yourself why. Your answer to this question will give you excellent guidance regarding what to do next.

Read.

Read *Winning Decisions: Getting It Right the First Time,* by J. Edward Russo et al. (New York: Currency, 2002).

For more insights and information about decision making, please refer to the following: Chapter 7, "Make Optimal Decisions," in *What Type of Leader Are You?* (McGraw-Hill, 2007).

DEVELOPMENT STRETCHES FOR EVERYONE

ORGANIZATIONAL CHANGE DEVELOPMENT STRETCHES

In contemporary organizations, change has become a way of life. Companies exist in increasingly complex environments, with more competition, fewer resources, less time to market, higher customer expectations, increased regulation, more technology, and greater uncertainty. Organizations need to be flexible, innovative, cost-conscious, and responsive if they want to succeed. As a result, employees at all levels need to be able to embrace change and to function flexibly and effectively within their teams when an unforeseen direction must be taken.

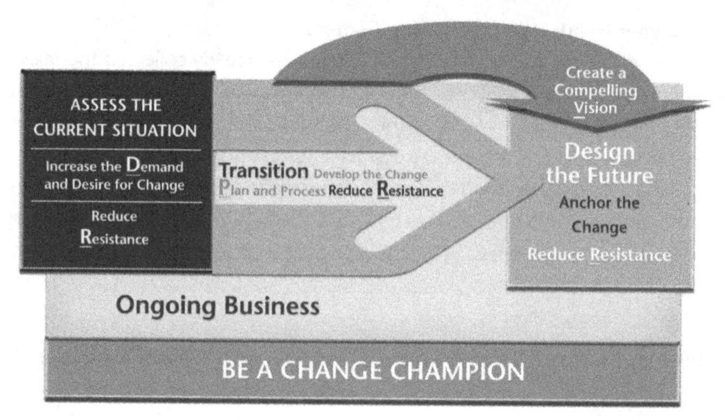

Take Charge of Change

Become a change champion.

Assess the extent to which you are regarded as a champion of change in your organization by asking the following question of your boss, your peers (select three peers if you can), and three subordinates: *On a five-point scale, with 1 being low and 5 being high, to what extent do you perceive me as a champion of change?* Write down all of the answers you receive. After each person has answered the above question, ask two follow-up questions: *What factors caused you to give that answer? What would you recommend I do more of and less of to become even more of a change champion?* Analyze all the responses to determine what you can do to increase your capability as a champion of change.

For more insights and information about organizational change, please refer to the following: Chapter 8, "Take Charge of Change," in *What Type of Leader Are You?* (McGraw-Hill, 2007).

Use the Change Strategy Formula.
At the top of separate sheets of paper, write down the organizational changes you have been involved with over the last five years. Underneath each change heading, write down the Change Strategy Formula $\mathbf{D} \times \mathbf{V} \times \mathbf{P} > \mathbf{R} = \mathbf{C}$, where

- **D** = Demand, dissatisfaction, and desire for change
- **V** = Vision or model for the change
- **P** = Plan and process for the change
- **R** = Resistance to the change
- **C** = Results of the change

Do an assessment of each change effort, assigning numbers 0-5 (0 = low; 5 = high) to the first four elements of the formula. Multiply your assigned numbers for $\mathbf{D} \times \mathbf{V} \times \mathbf{P}$ to assess whether or not the product of these numbers is greater than **R.** Review each part of the equation to gain insight into why the change effort was successful and/or how it could have been more effective.

Read.
Read *The Fifth Discipline Fieldbook: Strategies and Tools for Building a Learning Organization,* by Peter M. Senge et al. (New York: Currency, 1994).

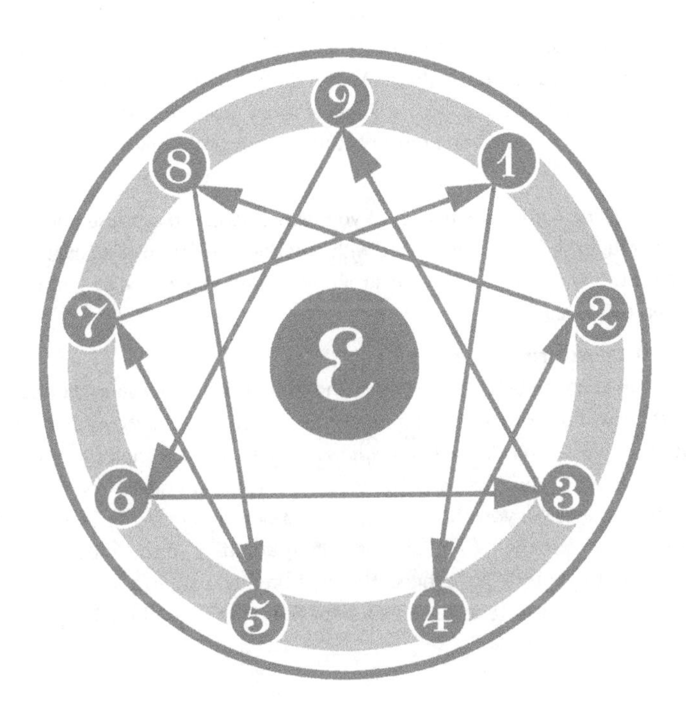

For more insights and information about organizational change, please refer to the following: Chapter 8, "Take Charge of Change," in *What Type of Leader Are You?* (McGraw-Hill, 2007).

DEVELOPMENT STRETCHES FOR EVERYONE

TRANSFORMATION DEVELOPMENT STRETCHES

In order to move from functioning in *habitual and reactive patterns of thinking, feeling, and behaving* to functioning with *increasing self-awareness, self-mastery, and choice,* you can work toward these transformations:

Mental Transformations

At least once per day, spend five minutes sitting still and observing your thoughts and patterns of thinking without judging them, contemplating their meaning, or overly identifying with them. Simply watch your thoughts appear in your mind; do not focus on them. Allow them to emerge, float through your mind, and then disappear. You can even imagine windshield wipers wiping them away.

Taking this time to observe your thoughts without being attached to them will allow you to be more objective about your thought patterns, as well as to disengage from them at will when you are involved in day-to-day activities. This gives you the choice of whether to continue thinking the same thoughts, to discard them, or to substitute different ways of thinking.

Emotional Transformations

When you experience strong feelings, whether the emotions are negative or positive, allow yourself to fully experience them throughout your body. Once you have done this, allow yourself to imagine more space around these feelings by visualizing or sensing additional space around them. As you do this, the feelings will shift into something different. When this occurs, imagine more space around them. Continue allowing more and more space around these feelings until they have entirely transformed.

This activity will be particularly helpful to you with emotions that cause duress, but it is also helpful to shift your experience with emotions that are pleasurable. When you practice this way of responding to strong emotions, you will be able to transform them when they occur.

Behavioral Transformations

When you are about to behave in habitual and reactive ways, tell yourself: *I have a choice right now. I can choose to act in my habitual way, or I can choose something different. What else could I choose to do right now?* Then, make a choice. If you choose to react according to your customary patterns, take full responsibility for this choice and its consequences. If you choose to react in a new and different way, take full responsibility for your choice, and also pay closer attention to the impact of your behavior on both yourself and others. The next time you are in a similar situation, you can choose either to repeat the new behavior, if you found it effective, or to select another alternative.

For more insights and information about personal transformation, please refer to the following: Chapter 7, "Transforming Yourself," in *Bringing Out the Best in Yourself at Work* (McGraw-Hill, 2004).

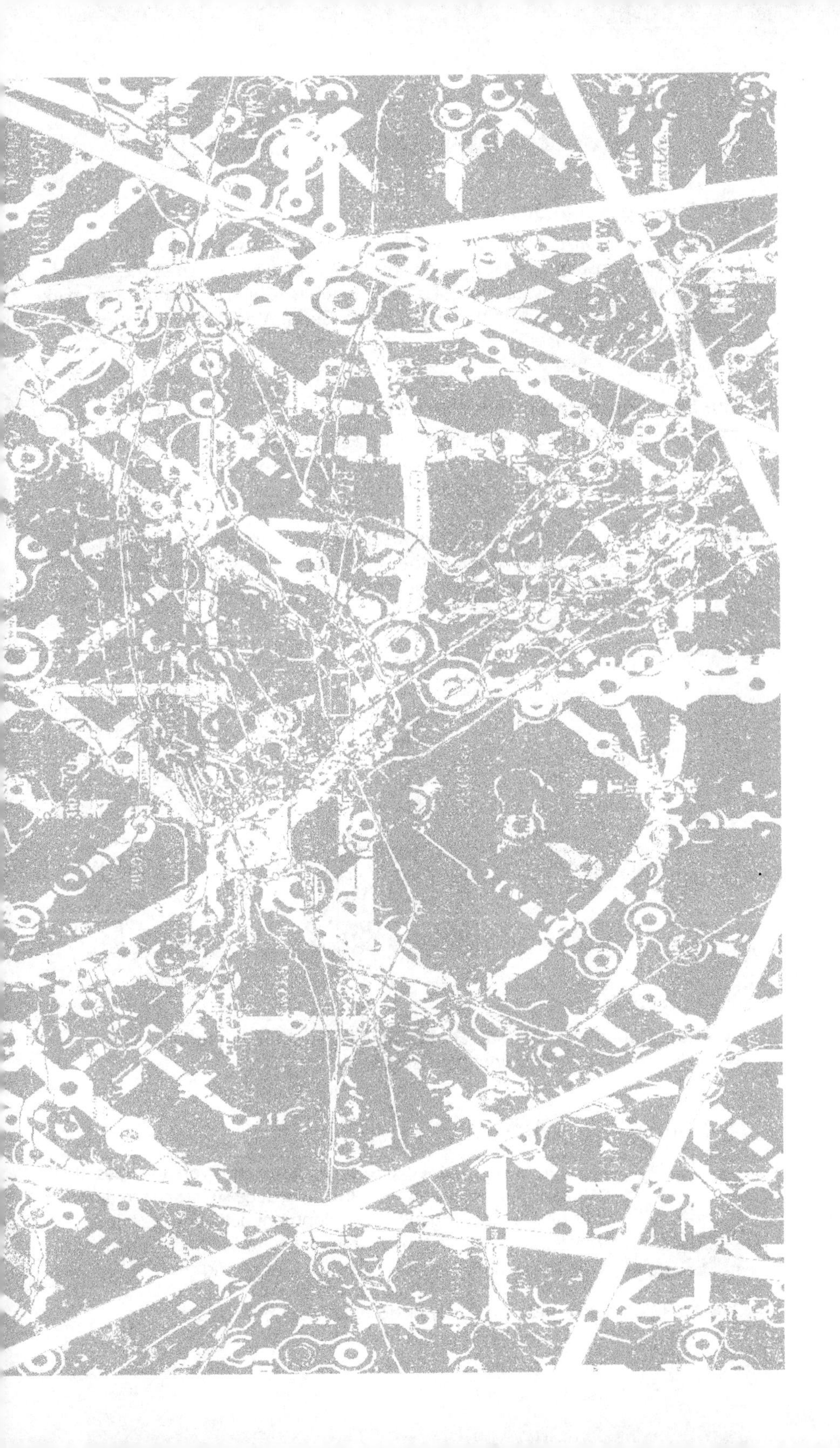

MORE ENNEAGRAM RESOURCES

The Enneagram in Business Network

A network of seasoned, savvy, and best-in-class professionals across the globe
You can find consulting, training, and coaching professionals across the US and in countries such as Australia, Brazil, Czech Republic, China, Colombia, Denmark, Finland, France, Germany, Iran, Ireland, Korea, South Africa, and Thailand at *TheEnneagramInBusiness.com.*

The Enneagram in Business Website

TheEnneagraminBusiness.com, a robust Enneagram-business website includes resources and information about Enneagram typing, how the Enneagram is being used in different countries, industry and business applications, and more

The EnneagramInBusiness eLearning Portal, a subscription-based eLearning portal to learn in-depth information about the Enneagram and its business applications; go to *TheEnneagramInBusiness.com*; individual and group rates available

Books

Training Tools

Over 25 full-color training tools are available for your use in organizations. Available online at *TheEnneagramInBusiness.com*

Enneagram iPhone App

This animated, interactive App for home and work includes typing and how to prevent conflict; reduce stress; coach; interact with others; and engage in development activities specific to your type. There are type videos, a way to test your Enneagram knowledge in real-world situations, theory, and more.

Only $2.99 on the iTunes App Store, or go to *EnneagramApp.com*

ABOUT THE AUTHOR

Ginger Lapid-Bogda, Ph.D.

A consultant, trainer, and coach with over 35 years of experience, Ginger works with Fortune 500 companies, nonprofits, and service organizations and is a member of NTL and the ODN. Some of her clients include Apple Computer, Clorox, Disney, Federal Reserve Bank, Genentech/Roche, Hewlett Packard, Whirlpool, and numerous law firms and non-profit organizations.

Ginger has become a world-class leader in using the Enneagram in business and organizations. She has written three seminal Enneagram-business books that have been translated into more than ten languages; has certified over 600 consultants, trainers, and coaches worldwide to use the Enneagram in their professional work; provides state-of-the-art Enneagram-business training materials; and conducts Train-the-Trainer programs on her books *Bringing Out the Best in Yourself at Work* and *What Type of Leader Are You?* In addition, Ginger offers ICF accredited "Coaching with the Enneagram" certificate programs around the world based on *Bringing Out the Best in Everyone You Coach*.

An award-winning speaker and author, as well as an expert consultant and facilitator, Ginger works with the Enneagram in businesses across the globe, offering local and global services to companies ready to respond to the challenges of the 21st century.

Ginger@TheEnneagramInBusiness.com | 310.829.3309

CPSIA information can be obtained
at www.ICGtesting.com
Printed in the USA
BVHW072254040720
582971BV00004B/355

9 780615 342504